*Gay Novels of Britain,
Ireland and the
Commonwealth,
1881–1981*

Gay Novels of Britain, Ireland and the Commonwealth, 1881–1981

A Reader's Guide

DREWEY WAYNE GUNN

McFarland & Company, Inc., Publishers
Jefferson, North Carolina

LIBRARY OF CONGRESS CATALOGUING-IN-PUBLICATION DATA

Gunn, Drewey Wayne, 1939–
Gay Novels of Britain, Ireland and the Commonwealth,
1881–1981 : a reader's guide / Drewey Wayne Gunn.
  p.   cm.
Includes bibliographical references and index.

ISBN 978-0-7864-9724-9 (softcover : acid free paper) ∞
ISBN 978-1-4766-1841-8 (ebook)

1. English fiction—History and criticism.   2. Gays in literature.
3. Homosexuality and literature.   4. Gays' writings, English—History
and criticism.   5. Gays' writings, English—Ireland—History and criticism.
6. Gays' writings, Commonwealth (English)—Ireland—History and criticism.
I. Title.
PR830.G34G86 2014   823.009'352664—dc23   2014035635

BRITISH LIBRARY CATALOGUING DATA ARE AVAILABLE

© 2014 Drewey Wayne Gunn. All rights reserved

*No part of this book may be reproduced or transmitted in any form
or by any means, electronic or mechanical, including photocopying
or recording, or by any information storage and retrieval system,
without permission in writing from the publisher.*

On the cover: Man in vintage suit
(© 2014 Andrejs Pidjass/iStock/Thinkstock)

Printed in the United States of America

*McFarland & Company, Inc., Publishers
Box 611, Jefferson, North Carolina 28640
www.mcfarlandpub.com*

CONTENTS

Authors, by Entry
vii

Introduction
1

The Novels
5

Postscript: Novels After 1981
185

General Bibliography
187

Index
191

Authors, by Entry

1. *Sins of the Cities* author
2. Walter Pater; A. C. Benson (as Christopher Carr); Hall Caine
3. Oscar Wilde
4. Howard Overing Sturgis
5. *Teleny* authors
6. Robert Hichens
7. A. W. Clarke; H. A. Vachell
8. Samuel Butler; Edward Perry Warren (as A. L. R.)
9. *Memoirs of a Voluptuary* author
10. Forrest Reid
11. E. M. Forster; Lytton Strachey
12. D. H. Lawrence
13. Rose Macaulay
14. Gerald Hamilton (as Patrick Weston)
15. Joseph Conrad
16. John Gambril Nicholson
17. E. F. Benson
18. Alec Waugh
19. Rose Allatini (as A. T. Fitzroy); John Buchan
20. Ronald Firbank
21. Ernest Raymond
22. Beverley Nichols
23. Compton Mackenzie; T. H. White (as James Aston); Norman Douglas
24. Kenneth Macpherson; Bryher
25. Rosamond Lehmann; Radclyffe Hall; Mary Butts
26. Sylvia Townsend Warner; Wyndham Lewis; Virginia Woolf; James Hanley; Frederick Rolfe
27. Ernest Milton
28. Evelyn Waugh
29. Keith Winter
30. William Plomer
31. Christopher Isherwood
32. Fortune Press novelists: Terence Greenidge; Richard Rumbold; Reginald Underwood; Michael Scarlott (Stanley T. Fisher); Aubrey Fowkes
33. Cyril Connolly
34. Noel Langley; Noël Coward
35. Seaforth Mackenzie
36. John Lehmann
37. Frank Sargeson
38. W. Somerset Maugham
39. Tom Hopkinson
40. Ernest Frost
41. Nancy Mitford; Villiers David; Pamela Hansford Johnson
42. Norah Lofts; Helen A. Mahler; Margaret Campbell Barnes; Alfred Duggan
43. Walter Baxter
44. Michael Meyer; Graham Greene
45. Desmond Stewart
46. Douglas Sanderson
47. Colin MacInnes; Hal Porter
48. G. F. Green
49. Robert Liddell; Lawrence Durrell
50. Angus Wilson
51. Rodney Garland (Adam de Hegedus)
52. Mary Renault.
53. Jocelyn Brooke
54. Francis King
55. Edith de Born; Gillian Tindall
56. Audrey Erskine Lindop
57. John Taylor
58. James Mitchell; John Cantwell; Michael Hastings; Colin Wilson
59. Kenneth Martin
60. C. H. B. Kitchin
61. Martyn Goff
62. Angus Heriot; Michael Nelson
63. Lennox Cook

64. Iris Murdoch
65. James Courage
66. Paul Buckland
67. David Caute
68. Simon Raven
69. John Rae
70. Hugh Ross Williamson
71. Arthur Calder Marshall (as William Drummond)
72. Gillian Freeman (as Eliot George)
73. Julian Mitchell
74. John Broderick.
75. Stuart Lauder (David Leslie)
76. Michael Power.
77. David Storey
78. Colin Spencer
79. Nicholas Monsarrat; Anthony Firth; Peter Leslie
80. Montague Haltrecht; Richard Chopping
81. Maurice Leitch
82. G. M. Glaskin (as Neville Jackson)
83. John McIntosh
84. Wole Soyinka
85. Desmond Cory
86. John Pollock
87. Rodney Garland (Peter de Polnay)
88. George Moor; Royston Ellis
89. Leonard Cohen; Scott Symons
90. Robin Maugham
91. Michael Campbell
92. Christopher Dilke
93. Angus Stewart
94. Maurice Capitanchik; Andrew McCall; Richard Green; Peter Kortner
95. Charles Dyer
96. Marc Deschamps; Jonathan Lynn
97. Michael Porcsa
98. Rupert Croft-Cooke
99. C. J. Bradbury Robinson
100. L. P. Hartley
101. Paul Bailey
102. T. C. Worsley
103. Susan Hill
104. Reginald Hill; William McIlvanney
105. V. S. Naipaul
106. Leo Madigan
107. Hunter Davies
108. Laurence Collinson; Mark Harris (Carl Ruhen); Robert Adamson and Bruce Hanford
109. Yulisa Amadu Maddy
110. Aubrey Menen
111. John Batchelor
112. Clive Murphy
113. Eleanor Spence; Barrie Hughes
114. John Bruce; Thomas Keneally
115. David Watmough
116. Eve Zaremba
117. Roderick Grant
118. David Rees
119. Patrick White
120. Frank Moorhouse
121. Anthony Burgess
122. Michael Schmidt
123. Julian Barnes (as Dan Kavanagh)
124. Roger Raftery; Lance Peters
125. Edward Phillips

Introduction

The title of the book sums up its scope and its goal: to provide a map, across 101 years, of longer fiction in which homosexual or bisexual males play important roles: gay novels and novellas written in English by authors associated with the British Isles and seven Commonwealth nations, regardless of the writer's gender or sexuality. While this map does not chart entirely virgin territory, it blazes a trail across a landscape that has been, generally, "a bit off the map," to borrow the title of a short story by Angus Wilson. In contrast to the attention paid to gay American fiction, nothing comparable has been accorded gay British or Commonwealth fiction. There have been studies of gay aspects of eighteenth and nineteenth century fiction, and a few critical works have edged towards the present, but scholars have tended to stick to the well known in their choices of texts to examine. This guide includes both canonical works and lesser known novels that deserve attention.

This survey begins with a book published in 1881. To be sure, there are homosexuals in Tobias Smollett's *The Adventures of Roderick Random*, 1748; John Cleland's *Memoirs of a Woman of Pleasure* (also known as *Fanny Hill*), 1749; and Charlotte Cibber Charke's *The History of Henry Dumont, Esq.*, 1756. They are, however, minor characters. (The relevant pages about their exploits are available in Mark Mitchell and David Leavitt's anthology *Pages Passed from Hand to Hand*. Additional passages from *Roderick Random* appear in Byrne Fone's *The Columbia Anthology of Gay Literature*.) One might also be tempted to ferret out closeted characters in gothic novels from Horace Walpole's *The Castle of Otranto*, 1765, through William Beckford's *Vathek*, 1816, and *The Episodes of Vathek*, 1912, to such later examples as Robert Louis Stevenson's *Strange Case of Dr. Jekyll and Mr. Hyde*, 1886; Bram Stoker's *Dracula*, 1897; and the anglicized Henry James's *The Turn of the Screw*, 1898.

One could also make a case for beginning with the narrative poem *Don Leon*, based on the life of Byron and published anonymously in 1866. And there are male couplings in the anonymous *The Romance of Lust*, 1873–76. So why begin with a piece of pornography, *The Sins of the Cities of the Plain, or The Recollections of a Mary-Ann*? For one thing, it is the first prose work I have found with an unabashedly homosexual protagonist, one who enjoys sex to the fullest (sometimes also with women) without guilt or any particular shame despite Victorian morals. Unlike *Don Leon* or the *Romance*, it has a decidedly modern tone. More: since we know that Oscar Wilde read the novel, it has links to both his sole novel and the anonymous *Teleny*, neither of which can be ignored. And it remains a fun, even an educational, read.

A newspaper article tragically determines the *terminus ad quem*. After the advent of AIDS the gay novel could never be the same. By this time also, a new generation of gay writers was making its mark: Neil Bartlett, Alan Hollinghurst, Adam Mars-Jones, Geoff Ryman, Colm Tóibín, Peter Wells. They joined such American writers as Christopher Bram, Michael Cunningham, Andrew Holleran, Armistead Maupin, and Edmund White to create fiction with a decidedly different feel from that of earlier works. The post-plague decades have been a time of intense political, social, and scholarly ferment in English-speaking countries in an effort to bring the formally marginalized more towards the center. The 1970s saw a shift in paradigms in much the same way that the 1890s witnessed the beginnings of a movement that even Wilde's trial could not derail, that in fact his incarceration kept alive: what we now call gay liberation.

This guide does not have the goal to be all-inclusive. The decision to include a book rested on whether the protagonist or at least a major character is a gay or bisexual male, even a pederast. Thus, with a few exceptions (for reasons given when they occur), you will not find works by writers, such as Martin Boyd, Denton Welch, or Bill Pearson, who display "a gay sensibility." Nor have I included writers, such as David Ireland, David Malouf, or Timothy Findley, whose early novels fall within the time frame but whose concerns are focused elsewhere than on sexual identity. Purely lesbian fiction is also omitted. Terry Goldie (*Pink Snow*, 2) has written, "Studies of homosexuality sometimes attempt to treat both lesbians and gay males as two parts of one whole. As the two primary identities of persons driven by same-sex desire they are obviously linked. Still, myriad aspects of culture show the extreme divisions between lesbians and gay males. [...] These differences are at times so extreme as to suggest different epistemologies."

In deciding whether to include a work, stories involving male bonding posed a peculiar problem. Is such friendship automatically homoerotic? Gregory Woods (*A History of Gay Literature*, 184) holds that "critics with an anti-homosexual agenda have made a point of separating love between men from sex between men. They call the former 'friendship' (or, at most, 'platonic love') and only the latter 'homosexuality.' Their aim is to appropriate all texts about male love for the institution of heterosexuality, and, at the same time, to diminish the literature of homosexuality by allowing it only to be about sex." Woods argues "that 'platonic' texts belong no less to gay literature than do our more explicitly homosexual texts." Such a position sounds sensible, but ultimately is not very helpful. For example, should James Joyce's *Ulysses* be admitted to the gay canon on the basis of the bond that develops between Stephen Dedalus and Leopold Bloom? Even the issue of sex is touched upon. Leaving the library, Buck Mulligan warns Stephen about Leopold: "He looked upon you to lust after you. [...] O, Kinch, thou art in peril. Get thee a breechpad"—this in a chapter in which the spirit of Wilde has already been invoked. Consider also the gender play in the Nighttown (or Circe) chapter and the sexual innuendoes in the Emaeus section. Yet *Ulysses* has hardly become a staple of the gay canon. Clearly, lines must be drawn somewhere by the critics' own sensibilities. Some genital stirring seems to me as good a delineation as any.

The schoolboy novel presents another problem. Here Woods argues (324): "Implicit in most such narratives, and explicit in some, is the idea that whatever homosexual behavior occurs in boarding-schools is not likely to extend into the later lives of their old boys." He cites Alec Waugh's *The Loom of Youth* as having "set both the parameters and the standard" for the genre. He sums up (326): "A boy may love boys in such a place without, once he leaves it, ever being tarnished by actually having to *be* homosexual." But Woods—though he discusses Roger Peyrefitte's *Amitiés particulières*—ignores examples in British literature in which one or both of the boys involved awaken to an awareness of their homosexuality. When Havelock Ellis decided to include a brief look at homosexual fiction in the 1926 edition of *Studies in the Psychology of Sex* (339–40), his three British examples were all schoolboy romances. These novels have flourished to such an extent, in fact, that, were they to be omitted from this guide, it would be considerably shorter.

Certain subgenres emerge as particularly receptive to gay stories. For most of this period the military was the other all-male institution, after the all-boys school, in which gays might hide in plain sight. Some novels in fact show how public schools bred military officers who fit easily into a homosocial setting. The Boer Wars and World War I in themselves had little impact on the development of gay novels. World War II was a different case. Not only do we have a number of novels with gay officers and enlisted men, but in a strange link of the all-boys school with the military, we have vicious schoolboys thinking they are defending their country in two novels. Until the collapse of colonialism, many gays also held peacetime military positions, as well as political and cultural appointments, in different parts of the empire—as is seen in a number of novels. The expatriate novel is another subgenre that often depicts gay characters. From the time of William Beckford and Lord Byron on, many gays escaped the possibilities of disgrace in England by exiling themselves to the Continent or to Northern Africa. Their fictional descendants followed suit. There are also a few novels about gay tourists in search of culture or sex. Racial, ethnic, and class differences often play an important role in both colonial and expatriate novels.

As Anthony Slide's bibliography *Gay and Lesbian Characters and Themes in Mystery Novels* documents, gays generally functioned as villains or victims for the greater stretch of the history of crime and spy novels. There has been speculation that the earliest gay villain appears in Charles Dickens's unfinished novel, *The Mystery of Edwin Drood*, 1870. Many feel that E. W. Hornung's A. J. Raffles, "gentleman thief," must be gay. Though Sherlock Holmes has repeatedly come under scrutiny, the first openly gay sleuth did not appear until 1953. But it is striking how many crime novels turn up in which gays play important roles. A few prison novels of interest also appear, but most of the incarcerated gays in them have been arrested for victimless crimes.

Science fiction was similarly slow to introduce gays into its pages. True, Mary Shelley's *Frankenstein*, 1818, has become fertile ground for all kinds of new readings, including several by queer theorists. Fantasy was more receptive to gay themes, beginning with Wilde's *The Picture of Dorian Gray*. There is nothing gay per se about Kenneth Grahame's *The Wind in the Willows*, 1908, but its depiction of an all-male world made a strong impression on Evelyn Waugh (who flirted with fantasy in both early and late novels). Then there is J. M. Barrie's *Peter and Wendy*, 1911, the novelization of his play. Two daring works from 1936, reflecting Freudian thought, took their heroes through a brief homosexual stage: Olaf Stapledon's science fiction novel *Odd John* and Frank Baker's fantasy *The Birds*. In 1937 Katharine Burdekin published *Swastika Night* under the pseudonym Murray Constantine. It depicts a homosexual dystopia seven hundred years in the future as a result of the conquering Nazis' misogyny. Then one jumps to the 1960s with Anthony Burgess's own dystopian satire, *The Wanting Seed*, and New Wave novelist Michael Moorcock's bisexual hero in his ongoing Cornelius Chronicles. Bisexual characters also appear in Arthur C. Clarke's *Rendezvous with Rama*, 1973, and *Imperial Earth*, 1975. None of these works, save Wilde's gothic tale, gives readers any insight into gay identity.

Historical novels remind readers that same-sex relationships are by no means a recent phenomenon. Various Greeks, Roman emperors, English kings, and earlier literary figures have been outed in their pages. As one might expect, any number of gay love stories show up, particularly after World War II. Other labels that one might use to define subgroups include *pornography*, *camp*, *satire*—all slippery terms. But many gay novels belong to no easily labeled subgroup, unless one lets adjectives such as *social* or *psychological* define a set.

Certain tropes reappear. Class plays an important part in British novels, not so much in Commonwealth works. Many novels throughout the period contain a defense of homosexuality couched in the phraseology of the time. As many find the character's homosexuality so natural that no explanation is needed. Some characters agonize about their sexuality, even killing themselves; even more enjoy its pleasures. Some are fairly closeted about their orientation; others are blatantly open. A strong strain of bisexuality runs throughout British letters.

The majority of these writers have a similar background. They attended public schools and then went on to Cambridge or Oxford, forming lasting friendships and sometimes sexual liaisons with each other. They later associated together in London and around the globe wherever English-speaking writers clustered. Minor feuds occasionally broke out, but generally they supported one another. And certainly they read, and reviewed, each other's work.

Though from the beginning a few adventurous writers brought out privately printed editions of their work, most writers relied on presses that were already established or were trying to establish themselves. And publishers, with good reason given obscenity laws in all English-speaking countries before the 1960s (and even afterwards), looked askance at the inclusion of gay titles in their catalogues. Thus, gay themes were generally muted or obscured in the early fiction. R. A. Caton founded Fortune Press in 1924. Although its publications were far from exclusively homosexual, the press was gay-friendly. In the late 1950s, early 1960s, American and British publishing houses became more venturous, seeming, for the first time, to become aware of the existence of a significant gay readership. The first gay presses were established in the United States, then later Canada. Not until 1979 was Gay Men's Press, or GMP, launched in England.

There follow those novels that have come to my attention as being important to the evolution of gay British and Commonwealth letters. To give some sense of development I have listed them in chronological order, though I sometimes muss up strict chronology by listing all of an individual author's work together in one entry and by sometimes grouping novels of a similar kind. Working with WorldCat, I have listed the first editions, plus any contemporaneous American editions. (In addition to title changes, there are sometimes textual differences between the two.) I sometimes had to use later reprints. I indicate which text I read with an asterisk (*). In quotations, all ellipses not in brackets are in the original. As for nomenclature, enough has been said about the correct use of the labels *gay, homosexual, queer*, etc. Forgive me if I beg off adding more to the debate.

I would like particularly to thank Rob McDonald and Stephen Delaney for bringing titles to my attention. As always, Aggie Gonzalez, the interlibrary loan officer at Texas A&M University–Kingsville, was indispensable.

THE NOVELS

1   Anonymous: *The Sins of the Cities of the Plain*, 1881.

The French bookseller Charles Hirsch recounted in his preface to the 1934 French edition of *Teleny* how, after he opened his bookstore, the Librairie Parisienne, in London in 1889, trusted customers such as Oscar Wilde and some of his friends would order books through him of a special kind designated as "Socratic," works that had been published clandestinely in England and on the Continent. They included a book whose title page for the first edition reads in full: *The Sins of the Cities of the Plain, or The Recollections of a Mary-Ann, with Short Essays on Sodomy and Tribadism in Two Volumes. London: Privately Printed, 1881*. There were later editions in one-volume formats. Its form is that of an episodic novel; its contents, the adventures of a London male prostitute. Though his sexual experiences are not exclusively homosexual, he seems to be the first gay protagonist of a long prose work in English.

In 1992 Masquerade Books included the book in its Badboy series; Olympia Press reprinted this text in 2006, naming Jack Saul as its author. A number of scholars cautioned that the text was corrupt, but the general reader was unlikely to encounter their warnings. Not until Valancourt Books brought out its edition in 2013 did it become obvious to the nonspecialist just how extensively the Badboy editors had rewritten the book. Not trusting the original to be exciting enough, they added gobs of extra stimulation at irregular intervals; more, they homosexualized all the women out of the novel. Thus one of the more bizarre comical scenes was lost: that wherein a dairymaid positions herself under a cow and becomes thoroughly aroused by having a farmboy push one of the cow's teats into her vagina and continue milking, while the hero first sucks off, then buggers him (22–25).

The novel opens with an account by one Mr. Cambon of the Cornwall Mansions about how he encountered one afternoon "last November" (presumably 1880) an "Adonis-like" youth, whose "tight-fitting" trousers showed that "he was favoured by nature by a very extraordinary development of the male appendages." Hoping to inspect "such a manly jewel" more closely, he invited the young man to his home (3–4). There he learned that his name is Jack Saul. After the two exhausted themselves sexually, Saul proving to be quite the expert at oral sex, Cambon asked him "how he had come to acquire such a decided taste for gamahuching, to do it so deliciously as he did." Declaring that it "would be too long a tale to go into now," Saul offered to write out "the whole history" in exchange for "at least twenty pounds" (7). The rest of the work, save for three appendices at the end, comprises that story.

Saul's sexual appetites are ravenous. He enjoys all varieties of sex, cross-dressing, and "birching." Though he prefers males, he does not lose an opportunity to bed an occasional woman. Along with the work's desire to arouse the reader sexually, it explores the ways sodomy is intricately woven into the very fabric of Victorian culture by presenting ample evidence of buggery among boys in boarding schools and remarking on how soldiers, particularly the

Royal Guards, supplement their meager incomes by prostitution. In addition, it introduces two characters whose only purpose in the novel is to dramatize the dangers of wealthy clients being blackmailed and robbed and to acknowledge the existence of child slavery. The novel also mentions, in passing, fisting (85) and the persistent rumors of what we would now call snuff orgies (74). The work is a trove of information about the London gay demimonde in the last quarter of the century.

Halfway through the novel, Saul asks, "You remember the Boulton and Park case? Well; I was present at the ball given at Haxell's Hotel in the Strand" (38). Now the line between fiction and nonfiction becomes slippery, leaving the reader to wonder if, after all, he is reading a memoir. In 1870 the real-life Ernest Boulton and William Frederick Park—who as cross-dressers used the names Fanny (Laura, in the novel) and Stella—were arrested and charged with "conspiring and inciting persons to commit an unnatural offence." Boulton's lover was Lord Arthur Clinton, who allegedly died of scarlet fever the day after receiving a subpoena for the trial but who almost certainly killed himself. Saul recounts how he spied on the two making love and goes on to describe his own trysts with Boulton. He also notes that he was a guest at a party given in honor of the Prince of Wales, during which much clandestine activity took place in the gardens (55–56). The notion that we may be reading an early form of a nonfiction novel is reinforced by the fact that a rent boy named John Saul was connected to the Dublin Castle scandal of 1884 and was also one of the principal witnesses in the trial following the Cleveland Street scandal of 1889. Since these occurred three and eight years respectively after the novel was published, the author could not be striving for a sense of verisimilitude by using an already established name.

No one seems to have attempted even a mini-biography of Saul, but comparing the novel to the historical sources available reveals correspondences and discrepancies. The age seems to be right; both Jack Saul and John Saul were born in the early 1850s. But John was apparently a native of Dublin, whereas Jack grew up the son of initially well-to-do farmers in Suffolk (11). He was sent to a public school in Colchester, but had to leave early when his father was accidentally killed, leaving the family less financially secure than they had thought. Jack is fairly well read, at least in salacious literature. He cites *Fanny Hill* (38) as well as materials published in the underground publication *The Pearl* (50). So present-day readers have the titillation of an arousing one-hand reading experience coupled with the teasing uncertainty whether they are reading fact, fiction, or something in between. Theo Aronson in writing his biography of Prince Albert Victor, *Prince Eddy and the Homosexual Underworld*, obviously accepted *Sins of the Cities* as truth. Morris Kaplan in *Sodom on the Thames*, regards it as fiction, something along the lines of E. L. Doctorow's *Ragtime*.

Not so well known is a book purporting to be its sequel. There is a record that the work first appeared in 1883. Hirsch printed a second edition in Paris in 1899. No copies of either edition are known to exist. The third edition came out in 1903; the sole known copy belongs to the British Library. Its title page reads in full: *Letters from Laura and Eveline, Giving an Account of Their Mock-Marriage, Wedding Trip, etc. Published as an Appendix to The Sins of the Cities. London: Privately Printed, 1903.* The novella has in common with *Sins* a number of names, but the characters do not completely correspond. The novella consists of two letters detailing two couples' "wedding" festivities and the subsequent "loss" of each "bride's" anal virginity. One sexual exploit follows another, designed solely to arouse the reader. In this way, it resembles an earlier, though much better written, work that has a number of homosexual scenes, beginning with the second volume, scattered among its many heterosexual encounters: *The Romance of Lust; or, Early Experiences*, published anonymously in four volumes, 1873–76, by William Simpson Potter (1804–1879).

In 1885 all the sexual acts between men described in these three novels were criminalized. For a number of years Parliament had been debating enacting a Criminal Law Amendment to the existing Offences against the Person Act of 1861 in order to better protect "women and girls." On August 6, just eight days before the legislature finally passed, Henry Labouchère, the Liberal representative for Northampton, introduced an addendum to Section 11 which would have far-reaching and pernicious consequences for the next eighty-two years. It reads: "Any male person who, in public or private, commits, or is party to the commission of, or procures the commission by any male person of, any act of gross indecency with another male person, shall be guilty of a misdemeanor, and being convicted thereof shall be liable at the discretion of the court to be imprisoned for any term not exceeding two years, with or without hard labour." Informally among lawyers it became known as the blackmailer's charter. Within ten years Wilde would become its most famous victim.

Letters from Laura and Eveline [...]. 1883 [no copies extant]. London: Privately printed, 1903. *Ed. Justin O'Hearn. Richmond, Va.: Valancourt, 2013.

The Romance of Lust [...]. 4 vols. London: Privately printed, 1873–76. *N.p.: Digireads, 2012.

The Sins of the Cities of the Plain, or The Recollections of a Mary-Ann [...]. London: Privately printed, 1881. *Ed. Wolfram Setz. Kansas City, Mo.: Valancourt, 2013.

2   Walter Pater: *Marius the Epicurean*, 1885. Christopher Carr (A. C. Benson): *Memoirs of Arthur Hamilton*, 1886. Hall Caine: *The Deemster*, 1887.

If enough readers approach a novel as gay fiction, does it then become such, ipso facto? Three novels from the 1880s, by three writers who we know, or have cause to suspect, had homosexual tendencies, raise the question. All three books show up regularly on lists of gay novels; editor Brian Reade includes excerpts from them in his anthology of gay Victorians, *Sexual Heretics*. Any sexuality in the three works, however, is (not surprisingly, given the temper of the times) muted, more homoerotic than homosexual.

There is no denying that Pater had a major influence on gay writers at the time. And there is no doubt that by temperament he was homosexual, whatever his actual physical experiences may have been. *Marius the Epicurean* is a romance masquerading as a historical novel set in second century Rome. It traces the philosophical and spiritual growth of its eponymous hero as he examines the conflicting ideas of the time, a period of flux much like the late Victorian period in Pater's eyes. In the course of his explorations Marius forms strong male bonds with Flavian and, after his death, with Cornelius. Are they enough to label *Marius* a gay novel? Reade (20) insists that "male friendships were among the most powerful emotions described [in the novel]; and not only were these dependent on physical attractiveness and therefore strictly erotic, but they were linked dramatically to religious crises." I am not convinced. Pater seems to me more interested in clarifying his philosophical position and diverting suspicions about his morals raised by his monumental *Studies in the History of the Renaissance*, 1873—particularly its controversial "Conclusion," which seemed to some to endorse an unhealthy hedonism—than in exploring the emotional ties between men.

Memoirs of Arthur Hamilton, originally published under the pseudonym Christopher Carr, is a novel in the guise of an autobiography. Carr, the "editor," has selected the telling moments from the life story of his friend. There is strong male bonding between Hamilton and Carr, who remain fast friends from their Cambridge days until Hamilton's death. Incidents also include Hamilton's adoption of a teenager, the son of an English nobleman he encounters in Teheran, but there is no indication that he has any sexual interest in the boy. Moreover, Hamilton expresses "agony, disgust, and rage," along with "repulsion," when he finds out that a friend at Cambridge "was not only yielding, but deliberately impure" (15). Is this a question, as some readers have insisted, of the closeted author's trying to have it both ways: to titillate those in the know but to throw off the scent for the uninitiated? Or is it, as Brian Masters (*The Life of E. F. Benson*, 77) argues, another sad example of how even in their youth "the Benson children were already crippled, self-denying, prudish?"

The Deemster recounts the conflicts between the two Mylrea brothers on the Isle of Man—one, a callous judge (the deemster); the other, a pious bishop—and their effects on their three children. Dan, the son of the bishop, is headstrong and careless like his uncle, the deemster. Ewan and his sister Mona, the children of the deemster, resemble the bishop. Dan falls in love with Mona. Undoubtedly Dan and Ewan also have deep feelings for each other: "Never were cousins more unlike or more fondly attached" (66). The two men are compared to Jonathan and David (one chapter is titled "Passing the Love of Women"), but it is unclear what clue the biblical story is meant to convey about the nature of their friendship. The two men are also compared to brothers Esau and Jacob. They might better have been compared to Cain and Abel, as one discovers a third of the way through the novel. The author himself at times seems confused about the exact nature of Ewan and Dan's relationship.

London-born Walter Horatio Pater (1839–1894) was educated at Oxford, with which he was associated the rest of his life, though not gaining the post he had hoped for. His disciples included Wilde and other important figures in the aesthetic movement. Arthur Christopher Benson (1862–1925) was one of three gay sons of the Reverend Edward Benson, Archbishop of Canterbury, but many doubt that he ever had a sexual experience. He became master of Magdalene College, Cambridge, but is perhaps best remembered for his song "Land of Hope and Glory," set to Edward Elgar's well known music. Henry Hall Caine (1853–1931) was born in Cheshire of a Manx father and became enamored of the Isle of Man when he visited relatives. Both men and women were attracted to his striking looks. He was friends with Bram Stoker (Caine is the Hommy Beg to whom Stoker dedicated *Dracula*) and served as secretary for Dante Gabriel Rossetti. He married and had two sons. One of them played the role of Dan in a 1917 film adaptation of the novel. Marion Zimmer Bradley in her bibliography cites his novel *The Bondsman*, 1890, as also of interest to gay readers.

Allen, Vivien. *Hall Caine: Portrait of a Victorian Romancer*. Sheffield, Eng.: Sheffield Academic, 1997.
[Benson, A. C.] *Memoirs of Arthur Hamilton, B.A. of Trinity College, Cambridge [...] by Christopher Carr*. London: Kegan Paul, Trench, 1886. New York: Holt, 1886. *Gloucester, Eng.: Dodo, n.d.
Caine, Hall. *The Deemster: A Romance*. London: Chatto & Windus, 1887. *New York: Appleton, 1896.
Donoghue, Denis. *Walter Pater: Lover of Strange Souls*. New York: Knopf, 1995.
Pater, Walter. *Marius the Epicurean: His Sensations and Ideas*. London & New York: Macmillan, 1885. *New York: Cosimo Classics, 2005.
Williams, David. *Genesis and Exodus: A Portrait of the Benson Family*. London: Hamilton, 1979.

3 Oscar Wilde: *The Picture of Dorian Gray*, 1890; *The Portrait of Mr W. H.*, 1921.

For gay readers, even for some straight readers, the figure of Wilde dominates the end of the Victorian era. His martyrdom, which initially seemed his disgrace, ensures him a permanent place in the history of the fight for gay rights, and his wit continues to sparkle. The wisdom concealed in his epigrams never ceases to startle. The number of film adaptations of *The Picture of Dorian Gray* testifies to its enduring power. A gothic novel, it describes how the face in the painting becomes more and more hideous as its subject commits sin after sin, while the man himself retains his phenomenon looks. It takes its place alongside two contemporary gothic novels involving a metamorphosis of good into evil: *Strange Case of Dr. Jekyll and Mr. Hyde*, 1886, by the Scotsman Robert Louis Stevenson, and *Dracula*, 1897, by fellow Irishman Bram Stoker—both of which reward gay readings.

Wilde's road to publishing *Dorian Gray* is a tale in itself. In spring 1881 Gilbert and Sullivan's satire of the aesthetic movement, *Patience*, opened in London, followed by its debut in New York City early in the fall. Although Wilde was not the primary target in Gilbert's creation of the poet Bunthorne, he quickly became assimilated in the public's mind with the figure, so much so that the producers decided as a gimmick to have Wilde give a series of lectures in each American city just as the operetta was scheduled to open there. He arrived in January 1882 and was greeted with much enthusiasm throughout his tour. In Philadelphia his host was J. M. Stoddart, who owned the American publishing rights for Gilbert and Sullivan's works. At Wilde's request, Stoddart obtained an invitation from Walt Whitman to visit the poet at his Camden home, just across the river. The two writers hit it off so well that Wilde returned for a quick visit in May. (The very name *Whitman* was by then already becoming a code term used by homosexuals to recognize each other, just as *Gide* would later on.)

Stoddart reentered Wilde's life in August 1889, when the publisher had dinner with him and Arthur Conan Doyle in London. Acting in his role as managing editor of *Lippincott's Magazine*, he commissioned the two men to contribute a story each to the publication. *The Sign of Four* appeared in February 1890 and *The Picture of Dorian Gray* in July. It was Wilde's only novel. The holograph copy of the manuscript is in the Morgan Library in New York. The typescript that was made from it and that served as the basis for the magazine text is part of the holdings of the Clark Memorial Library at the University of California, Los Angeles. This typescript was edited by Nicholas Frankel in 2011, giving us for the first time Wilde's novel as he originally envisioned it. The first printed version was censored by Stoddart and his associate, removing passages "that make clearer and more vivid the homoerotic nature of the painter Basil Hallward's feelings for Dorian Gray" (40), as well as "passages related to promiscuous or illicit heterosexuality" (47) and "anything that smacked generally of decadence" (48).

This is the version that a gay reader wants to read now. But throughout the period under consideration, the magazine version, though bowdlerized, was the closest a reader could get to Wilde's original intentions. The novel opens with the artist Basil Hallward finishing his portrait of Dorian Gray, a young socialite not yet of age. Basil is obviously in love with Dorian and fears that his canvas reveals too much of his romantic attachment to the youth. He confesses to him that "from the moment I met you [...] I quite admit that I adored you madly, extravagantly, absurdly" (232). The narrator says of his love for Dorian, in one of the bolder statements in the novel, "It was such love as Michael Angelo had known, and Montaigne, and Winckelmann, and Shakespeare himself" (236). His love blinds him to the fact, perceived at once by his friend Lord Henry Wotton, that Dorian is cold-hearted, narcissistic, and incapable of loving anyone save himself.

Dorian, however, is fascinated by Lord Henry, the consummate rake ready to lead him astray for his own personal pleasure. Though he is married, he has as little to do with his wife as possible and feels relief when she leaves him. Over a course of a dozen years the two men pal together, sharing a villa at Trouville, France, and a "little white walled-in house at Algiers" (251), both sites frequented by homosexuals. Of Dorian's other activities, we are given only hints: of nights spent "in the sordid room of the little ill-famed tavern near the Docks, which, under an assumed name, and in disguise, it was his habit to frequent" (243), and the report that "he had been seen brawling with foreign sailors in a low den in the distant parts of Whitechapel" (252). Basil questions, "Why is your friendship so fateful to young men?" He adds, "What about your country-house, and the life that is led there?" (258).

Early on, there is a brief, overcharged affair with a woman, the actress Sibyl Vane, but it is significant that Dorian proposes to her the evening she plays Rosalind / Ganymede and repudiates her the evening she is Juliet. (Her brother does not exist in this version.) Chapter 9, the introspective description of how Dorian was "poisoned by a book" (255), is particularly interesting from a gay viewpoint. It is filled with allusions to "the author of the 'Satyricon'" (243); "the favorites of James I," Edward II and Piers Gaveston, Henry II, Charles the Rash, Elagabalus (249); and Tiberius, Caligula, Domitian, Nero, and again Elagabalus (254).

Throughout the story, the reader is not permitted to forget the portrait and the fearful changes it records. The day that it is finished, Dorian gazes at it and avers, "If it was I who were to be always young, and the picture that were to grow old! For this—for this—I would give everything!" (191). And so it comes to be. The deeper Dorian falls into corruption, the more hideous his painted image becomes, while he retains his youthful beauty. He hides it away in the old schoolroom at the top of the house, where he continually inspects it, fascinated by the ruin it depicts. No one else is permitted to see it, until one fatal evening when Basil tries one last time to redeem Dorian. In a fit of anger, Dorian murders him and then blackmails one of his former boyfriends to dispose of the body. In this version, Dorian's decision to "murder" the portrait the same way he murders its painter swiftly follows, with the ironic results that make Wilde's ending even more memorable than those achieved by Stevenson and later Stoker.

This version was included in the 1988 Norton critical edition. The editor, Donald L. Lawler, records (viii) that in the United States the novel "was well received critically as a modern morality tale." He goes on to say, "Stoddart must have been stunned by its reception in England, however." It "produced such critical storms in the London press for months after its appearance" that the publishers "felt obliged to withdraw the remaining copies from the newsstands." Its timing was unlucky, coming so close on the heels of the Cleveland Street scandal. As a result, when Wilde began preparing the novel for separate book publication, "he removed further vestiges of the homoerotic innuendo" and he added six new chapters (III, V, XV–XVIII), "further developing the social criticism, introducing the revenge motif of James Vane, and placing greater emphasis upon Dorian's increasingly gothic consciousness. The formula worked so well that the revised version did not produce anything like the sensation of the serial text, [and] it did receive a far greater measure of critical acclaim." Ward, Lock published the novel in April 1891. This far less gay version remains the one that most readers know.

According to the Internet Movie Database, there have been over twenty-five film and television adaptations of the novel, the earliest a Danish short from 1910, with the first English version dating from 1917. The 1945 version perhaps retains the greatest critical acclaim; the 1970 version with Helmet Berger is the most scrumptious to view. The novel has also provided the basis for at least two pornographic films, Wash Westmoreland's being particularly ingenious. Two graphic novels, both 2008, have been based on Wilde's text. And Ivan Albright's painting, commissioned for the 1945 film version, now hangs at the Art Institute of Chicago.

Dorian Gray was not Wilde's first gay story. In July 1889 *Blackwood's Edinburgh Magazine* published "The Portrait of Mr W. H.," his inventive exploration of the mysterious youth to whom Shakespeare addressed the greater part of his sonnets. He saw the possibilities and expanded the three-part story into a five-part novella. It was announced for publication in 1893, with an illustration of the portrait by Charles Ricketts, but was delayed, possibly because of the rumors already swirling around Wilde. The manuscript and the illustration were returned, and both disappeared in the upheaval after Wilde's conviction when his belongings were auctioned. The manuscript, but not the portrait, showed up in the hands of New York publisher Mitchell Kennerly, who brought out a limited edition in 1921. The expanded version did not achieve mass distribution until a Metheun edition of 1958.

As fiction, the short story version is the better. For insight into Wilde, the expanded version, blending as it does fiction with inventive scholarship, is more interesting. The basic frame remains the same. George Erskine describes to an unnamed narrator his friend Cyril Graham's obsession with proving the identity of Mr. W. H., to whom Shakespeare dedicated his sonnets. Through close reading of the poems he becomes convinced that the dedicatee was a boy actor named Willie Hughes. When Erskine refuses to take his findings seriously, Graham commissions a fake portrait of the boy resting his hand on the dedicatory page of the printed sonnets as proof. By accident Erskine meets the forger, whereupon Graham kills himself in a bizarre gesture to prove how firmly he believes in his theory.

The narrator is converted and sets out to confirm Graham's theory. The basic story, as he reconstructs it, is that Shakespeare fell in love with the boy's artistry in playing the women's roles in his plays. Then Marlowe lured young Hughes away to play Gaveston. Upon Marlowe's death, Hughes returned to Shakespeare's company and was forgiven. The sonnets are his confession of his love.

As a result of the fervor of his quest, the narrator is enervated. He presents his outline to Erskine and then renounces it as utterly false. In another exchange of positions, now Erskine becomes the convert. However, he departs for the Continent, and two years pass before the narrator hears from him. Then arrives a letter from Cannes announcing that he has decided to kill himself in the same way Graham had to prove the strength of *his* conviction. The narrator hurriedly journeys to Cannes, but arrives too late to attend even the funeral. He meets Erskine's mother and his doctor. While the mother goes to search for the painting, which Erskine has bequeathed to him, he discovers from the doctor that the mother had known of his impending death for months: "'Knew it for months past!' I cried. 'But why didn't she stop him? Why didn't she have him watched? He must have been out of his mind.' The doctor stared at me. 'I don't know what you mean,' he said. 'Well,' I cried, 'if a mother knows that her son is going to commit suicide—' 'Suicide!' he answered, 'Poor Erskine did not commit suicide. He died of consumption'" (229). In the last line of the story, the narrator, who has hung the portrait in his library, muses that "sometimes, when I look at it, I think there is really a great deal to be said for the Willie Hughes theory of Shakespeare's Sonnets" (231).

Wilde's biographer Neil McKenna sums up (103): "*Mr W. H.* is a dazzling conjuring trick, telling three intertwined love stories simultaneously: the story of Shakespeare's love for Willie Hughes, the story of Erskine's love for Cyril Graham, and the story of the anonymous narrator's discovery of his love for young men." McKenna (106) also insists that there is "a strong element of autobiography" in the story, feeling that Wilde's relationship with Robert Ross particularly colored the story. At the same time, Wilde's reading of the sonnets is ingenious enough that the essay has been reprinted in collections of Shakespeare scholarship. The expanded version moves well beyond the realm of fiction to explore at some depth the phenomenon of boy actors in the Elizabethan theater (196–201). Wilde also adds a long digression about neo–Platonism, his final tribute to Walter Pater. During this part of his discourse the narrator pays particular tribute to Michelangelo's friendship with Tommaso Cavalieri and Montaigne's with Etienne de la Boëtie; he also mentions briefly Marsilio Ficino's attraction to Pico della Mirandola and Winckelmann's to a Roman youth (190–94). He ponders the role of the dark woman of the sonnets, and he adds further details to the perceived presence of Hughes in Shakespeare's poems, finding him also in "A Lover's Complain" and "Venus and Adonis."

Early in 1895 Wilde brought an ill-advised suit against the Marquess of Queensberry, the father of his lover Alfred Douglas, who had accused him in writing of being a "posing somdomite" [sic]. During the trial, in which the Marquess's general accusation, if not the specific one of sodomy, was confirmed, Wilde's writings were introduced as evidence against him. The short story version of "The Portrait of Mr W. H." was alluded to only once in the defense's cross-examination, but *The Picture of Dorian Gray*, especially the magazine version, came up repeatedly. The defense also tried to charge Wilde with guilt by association because of his relationship to an Oxford journal *The Chameleon*, which in December 1894 had published Douglas's gay poems "Two Loves" and "In Praise of Shame" and John Francis Bloxam's pederastic short story "The Priest and the Acolyte."

Oscar Fingal O'Flatherie Wills Wilde (1854–1900) was born in Dublin. Educated at Oxford, he came under Pater's influence. He married in 1884 and had two sons. (After Wilde's conviction, the three changed their last name to Holland.) In 1886 Wilde met Ross, who may have been his first male lover. In 1891 he was introduced to Douglas, who desired to meet the author of *The Picture of Dorian Gray*. Wilde died in Paris; his remains, along with Ross's, rest in Père Lachaìse in a tomb designed by Jacob Epstein.

Holland, Merlin, ed. *The Real Trial of Oscar Wilde: The First Uncensored Transcript of the Trial of Oscar Wilde vs. John Douglas (Marquess of Queensberry), 1895*. New York: Fourth Estate, 2003.

McKenna, Neil. *The Secret Life of Oscar Wilde*. New York: Basic, 2005.

Wilde, Oscar. *The Picture of Dorian Gray*. Lippincott's Monthly Magazine, July 1890. **The Picture of Dorian Gray: Authoritative Texts, Backgrounds, Reviews and Reactions, Criticism*. Ed. Donald L. Lawler. New York: Norton, 1988. 171–281.

———. *The Picture of Dorian Gray*. Revised. London & New York: Ward, Lock, 1891.

———. *The Picture of Dorian Gray: An Annotated, Uncensored Edition*. Ed. Nicholas Frankel. Cambridge, Mass.: Harvard University Press, 2011.

———. *The Portrait of Mr. W. H.* New York: Kinnerley, 1921. **The Decay of Lying and Other Essays*. London: Penguin, 2010. 151–231.

4   Anonymous (Howard Overing Sturgis): *Tim*, 1891.

Tim is an example of the sentimental novel whose ending is designed expressly to induce tears from its gentle readers. As a consequence, it becomes a subversive novel, for its plotline is the unrequited romance of a younger boy for another five years his elder. The title page carries the epigraph "Thy love to me was wonderful, passing the love of women" (2 Samuel 1:26). Those words ring out again midway through the novel and again at the end. An unidentified narrator recounts the story. At age eight, Tim Ebbesley falls in love at first sight with Carol Darley and never wavers in his affection until his death at age sixteen. Carol has no idea of the depths of the boy's feelings until too late, and there is no evidence that Tim ever connects his deep passion with sexuality.

Tim has grown up motherless (it is implied that she was Indian and abandoned her family for another man) and, for seven years, fatherless, while this parent has been trying to make money in India. When he returns, it is painfully evident that father and son have nothing in common. William Ebbesley tries to force Tim into the mold of what he conceives a son should be, and he resents the boy's friendship with the local squire's grandson. When Tim determines to achieve the academic standard that will admit him to Eton, just so he can join Carol there, the father is pleased, not understanding the real reason. The novel's title is often cited as *Tim: A Story of School Life* or *Tim: A Story of Eton*. Both subtitles are misleading. Though we see Tim's interactions with a number of boys, the school plays little role in the plot of the novel. Because of the hierarchy in public schools, Tim and Carol might as well be on separate campuses.

It is established early on that Tim's health is fragile. For one moment, he stands up to his father when the latter disparages the boys' friendship, but it strains him physically. Then, after he overhears Carol's ladyfriend complain that Carol spends too much time "running after that nasty little Ebbesley friend of his," he determines "that he would never repay all Carol's kindness by ruining his life for him" (96–97). To his father's joy, Tim resolves to cut their ties, but this fatal action completely undermines his nervous system. As the boy lies dying, the father relents. The final chapter is a race against time: will Carol arrive before Tim dies? The answer is obvious. The friends not only reconcile, but Carol finally understands the depths of Tim's love for him. Their renewed friendship is sealed with a kiss. All that is missing is the assurance that Carol's first son will be christened Timothy.

Howard Overing Sturgis (1855–1920) was born in London to wealthy American parents. He was educated at Eton and Cambridge. *Tim* was published anonymously, but Sturgis was identified as its author on the title page of his second novel. He and his lover, William Haynes-Smith, were an intimate part of Henry James's circle, though the relationship was strained by James's overly candid criticism of Sturgis's third novel, *Belchamber*, 1904. That novel has also been labeled a gay classic, but it would be more accurate to call it a queer classic, for it plays games with gender roles, just as its author did throughout his own life, without exploring sexuality. It was his final novel.

The authors of all the chapter epigraphs in *Tim* are named, save, significantly, the two penned by William Johnson Cory. He was fired from his position at Eton in 1872 after an "indiscreet" letter to one of his pupils was found by the boy's parents. Sturgis had Cory as a teacher. The two were members of an unorganized group of writers who have been labeled Uranians. The term comes from German pioneer sexologist and gay rights activist Karl Heinrich Ulrichs by way of British writer John Addington Symonds. Heinrich coined *urning* by association with the Greek goddess Aphrodite Urania in order to define male homosexuals. As described in Plato's *Symposium*, she was created from Uranus's testicles and thus was all male. Those in England who took up the term tended, in the main, to be pedophiles, and so *Uranian* has come to be associated in particular with works celebrating male youths. Edward Perry Warren published *A Defence of Uranian Love*, 1928–30, under the pen name Arthur Lyon Raile. The majority of the Uranians' literary output was poetry, but novels such as those by Sturgis, Forrest Reed, and John Gambril Nicholson also fit the mold, as does John Francis Bloxan's short story brought up during Wilde's trial.

[Sturgis, Howard Overing.] *Tim*. London: Macmillan, 1891. *New York: Mondial, 2009.

5 Anonymous (attributed to Oscar Wilde and others): *Teleny*, 1893.

Charles Hirsch records in the preface to the French edition of *Teleny* how one day towards the end of 1890 Wilde brought a carefully wrapped manuscript into his London bookstore and asked him to hold it until it was called for. Some days later, one of the youths that Hirsh had seen in Wilde's company received the package. Then, a few days later, he returned it and asked him to hold it until yet a third man picked it up. This occurred three times more. The last time the package was carelessly sealed, and Hirsh could not resist temptation. He found a manuscript whose title he misread as *Feleny*. The pages, according to him, were in different handwritings, with many interlineations, additions, and erasures.

Various guesses have been made as to the collaborators. One author at least, on the evidence of the novel, must have been heterosexual. This manuscript was published by Leonard Smithers in two volumes in 1893. Hirsch noticed many differences from the text he had read, including a change of setting from London to Paris (with bizarre results), the omission of a prologue, and the addition of a subtitle, *The Reverse of the Medal*. At least some of these were changes that Smithers introduced, as he acknowledged to Hirsh when the two met at the 1900 Paris Exposition.

Teleny is the tragic love story of a businessman, Camille Des Grieux, and a pianist, René Teleny, as recounted by Camille to an unnamed recorder. Chapter 1 describes the men's first meeting at a concert. The affinity between the two is so powerful that they share the same series of mental pictures as Teleny plays "a wild Hungarian rhapsody," climaxing in a vision of Antonius. Camille maintains an erection throughout their social encounter afterwards. Chapters 2 through 5 are mostly heterosexual in nature. In an improbable dream Camille has sex with Teleny in the form of a nonexistent sister. There follow two scatological episodes involving women, a trip to a brothel in company with schoolmates, and Teleny's sexual encounter with a countess. After a bout of jealousy when Camille sees Teleny kissing young Briancourt, a flamboyant dandy, he tries to seduce a chambermaid and fails. A coachman subsequently rapes her, and she kills herself.

With Chapter 6, the opening of the second volume, the romance builds between the two men. He hears that Teleny's playing has suffered as a result of Camille's distancing himself. But when next they encounter, Teleny is again with Briancourt. Camille follows the two and becomes aware of other men out cruising the streets and the public conveniences. Demoralized, he decides to drown himself in the Seine, but is stopped by Teleny's sudden appearance. Camille yields and enjoys the delirious happiness of "the lonely male finding at last a mate" (112). The two play out all sorts of sexual variations, described in such pornographic detail that the language is still capable of arousing a reader. In Chapter 7 Camille wants to declare their love to everyone, only to be frightened when Briancourt threatens blackmail. But Teleny reveals that Briancourt has long been in love with Camille and actually wants the three of them to "form a kind of trinity of love and bliss" (139).

When next the lovers encounter Briancourt they accept his invitation to attend an orgy at his home. Again, various sexual acts are described in explicit detail, ending with a horrifying scene in which one man has a bottle forced up his rectum, wherein it breaks. Chapter 8, the conclusion to the novel, goes all over the place. Teleny accumulates debts. Camille thinks long and hard about the nature of homosexuality and society's attitude. After another intense encounter, Teleny mysteriously disappears. By accident Camille discovers him making love to Camille's mother. He again decides to kill himself but is saved by his "doppelgänger" (183). Teleny stabs himself and dies. At the end, Camille promises the narrator a sequel recounting what happens to Briancourt and to his mother.

Teleny was not reprinted until 1958, when the first of a series of defective editions appeared. In 1984 Gay Sunshine Press brought out the first scholarly edition. It, however, used the French edition as its guide in an attempt to reconstruct the original manuscript. It awaited GMP in 1986 to reprint the original English edition (with obvious errors corrected). The novel is a mess. Clearly no one of the several collaborators attempted to bring some sort of overall coherence to the final manuscript, or if one did, he failed. Yet the results have a curious appeal. The artist Jon Macy succumbed to it, and the resulting graphic novel, *Teleny and Camille*, 2010, demonstrates the impact *Teleny* had on him not only for its celebration of sexuality but also as evidence of a political and social statement that retains validity.

Leonard Charles Smithers (1861–1907) was born in Sheffield. He worked as a lawyer and a London bookseller, championing the Decadents even after Wilde's trial. Forming a partnership with Sheffield publisher Harry Sidney Nichols in 1885, he began clandestinely publishing pornography. He went bankrupt and died of alcoholism and drug abuse. Alfred Douglas took the responsibility to mark his grave.

Homosexuality, *heterosexuality*, and *bisexuality* (in its present sense) all entered the English lexicon in 1892 via Charles G. Chaddock's translation of the German psychiatrist Richard von Kraft-Ebing's *Psychopathia Sexualis*. Throughout Victorian pornography, whenever same-sex acts between men enter the story, bisexuality is the norm. Two minor works that appeared shortly before *Teleny*, neither of any literary worth, illustrate the point well. *Laura Middleton: Her Brother and Her Lover*, 1890, the better written of the two, concerns the sexual exploits of Frank. He enjoys sex equally with the older Laura and her younger brother, also named Frank (including a three-way between them), as well as with maidservants and Laura's fiancé. With the men he lustily plays both top and bottom roles. Never does he feel any sense of shame; forget Douglas's 1894 poem "In Praise of Shame." Nor does Frank of *The Power of Mesmerism*, 1891, in his romps with his father, a groom, a friend, and the vicar. Influenced to some extent by the works of de Sade, to which the author alludes (29), this often off-putting novella includes incest, bestiality (58), flagellation, and even infliction of wounds during orgasm (103). Both works go much further than *Teleny* to invert conventional Victorian morality.

Laura Middleton: Her Brother and Her Lover. Brussels: Privately printed, 1890. **The Power of Mesmerism and Laura Middleton: [...] Two Novels from the Victorian Underground*. New York: Grove, 1969. 105–218.

The Power of Mesmerism: A Highly Erotic Narrative of Voluptuous Facts and Fancies. Moscow: Printed for the Nihilists, 1891. **The Power of Mesmerism and Laura Middleton* (see above). 1–104.

Teleny, or The Reverse of the Medal: A Physiological Romance of To-day. London: Cosmopoli, 1893. *Intro. John MacRae. London: GMP, 1996.

6 Anonymous (Robert Hichens): *The Green Carnation*, 1894.

During the winter 1893–94 Alfred Douglas was in Egypt, much of the time with Wilde's friend Reggie Turner. There they met Hichens and Fred Benson. In their company Douglas felt at ease to reveal his passion for Wilde, and Turner undoubtedly contributed his share of stories. Unbeknownst to them, Hichens was keeping notes. In September 1894 *The Green Carnation* was published. Its anonymous author, after much speculation, including the rumor that it was by Wilde himself, was finally revealed on the title page of the fourth printing, 1895, just before it was removed from sale in the wake of Wilde's trial. No mention was made of the work during the trial, but some felt that its publication contributed to Wilde's downfall. From the beginning, it was obvious that the two principal characters, Esmé Amarinth and Lord Reggie Hastings, were caricatures of Wilde and Douglas.

The novel is a satire of Victorian culture in general, of the aesthetic movement in particular. What negligible plot there is concerns the widowed Lady Locke's growing attraction to Reggie while they are both guests at a country house. Its pages are peppered with witty aphorisms in the style of Wilde (who is mentioned by name), providing an interesting exercise in distinguishing the difference between the real thing and its imitation. Reggie says of Wilde, "Poor Oscar! He is terribly truthful. He reminds me so much of George Washington" (67). The title comes from the artificially colored flower that Esmé's followers, including Reggie, all wear on their evening coat (just as Wilde's admirers did for the premiere of *Lady Windermere's Fan* in 1892). While still in London, Lady Locke observes them at a production of *Faust* and comments that "all the men who wore them looked the same. They had the same walk, or rather waggle, the same coyly conscious expression, the same wavy motion of the head" (17). Esmé "calls it the arsenic flower of an exquisite life" (21).

The closeted Hichens attacks gays rather viciously, nowhere more so than when Lady Locke overhears Reggie's symbolic attempt to seduce her nine-year-old son. He asks the lad, "Do you love this carnation, Tommy, as I love it?" He then explains, "It has the supreme merit of being perfectly unnatural. To be unnatural is often to be great. To be natural is generally to be stupid. To-morrow I will give you a carnation, Tommy" (151). When Reggie proposes marriage, she rejects him specifically because of his attachment to Esmé and his "cult of the green carnation" (207); unspoken is her awareness that she needs to protect her child. Reggie's ego is bruised, his hopes of gaining her fortune are dashed, but his allegiance to Esmé remains firm. The two men depart together for London. Esmé has the final word. He asks Reggie, "When did you decide to be refused? Only last night. You managed it exquisitely. I think that I am glad. I do not want you to alter, and the refining influence of a really good woman is as corrosive as an acid." Now he tells Reggie, he can continue to maintain his "marvelous scarlet life" (209–10).

Robert Smythe Hichens (1864–1950) was born in Kent. He was educated at the Royal College of Music and for a time served as a music critic. Wilde, who met Hichens a number of times in 1894, professed to be amused by the work and took a crack at it in the four-act version of *The Importance of Being Earnest* (Lady Bracknell says, "This treatise, *The Green Carnation*, as I see it is called, seems to be a book about the culture of exotics.") Now mostly forgotten, his novels at the time were hugely successful as movies, in particular *The Garden of Allah*, 1904. In 1917 he met married Swiss immigrant John Knittel (1891–1970) and fell in love. In 1921 the three, along with the beginnings of Knittel's family, settled in Switzerland. Knittel himself became a novelist, writing in English. They were friends with Somerset Maugham, among others. Hichens died in Zurich. There have been two stage adaptations of the novel.

[Hichens, Robert.] *The Green Carnation*. London: Heinemann, 1894. New York: Appleton, 1895. *Ed. Stanley Weintraub. Lincoln: Univ. of Nebraska Press, 1970.

7 A. W. Clarke: *Jaspar Tristram*, 1899. H. A. Vachell: *The Hill*, 1905.

Following the lead of *Tim*, other authors began to admit romantic attachments among boys into their stories of public school life.

Clarke's and Vachell's were not only among the earliest, but they also used similar plot structures: one boy is pulled between two very different types of schoolmates, to the point where the story verges upon allegory with a dark and a fair angel vying for his affection. Both were presumably based on the authors' own experiences. Edward Ashley Walrond Clarke (1860–1931) was at Radley 1876–79. Horace Annesley Vachell (1861–1955) attended Harrow, 1876–78, and later Sandhurst. This was Clarke's only novel. He followed a career in the Foreign Office, ending as Consul-General to Zanzibar, 1909–13, where he died. He married in 1908 and was widowed less than a year later. A native of Kent, Vachell was a prolific writer, largely forgotten today. For a time he lived in Southern California, where his wife died as a result of the birth of their second child. He himself died near Bath.

In a letter postmarked November 2, 1899, Wilde wrote to a Radley schoolboy who had initiated a correspondence with him: "Have you read *Jasper* [sic] *Tristram*? published by *Heinemann*. It is about Radley obviously: there are two boys in it, one of them like you to look at, the other like you to listen to. Our age is full of mirrors and masks: if you have not read the book, order it. The early part—half Hellenic—is charming." The title character, albeit very human in his self-absorption, is not a terribly sympathetic figure. At times he doubts that his high estimation of himself is valid, but in general he has a grandiose vision of his worth, constantly comparing himself favorably with Napoleon, various heroes of Shakespeare, and other persons of valor. He is intelligent, quick to learn from books, but blind to much of life. How much his personality may have been shaped by his having been orphaned at an early age and thence placed as a ward of Chancery to grow up in a Rectory under the unloving care of the minister and his family is left unexplored.

At Scarisbrick school Tristram becomes fixated on a headboy, Orr (the only name he is ever given). Asserting his authority over the initially defiant Tristram, Orr canes him and otherwise misuses him. In a classical psychological reaction, the abused becomes enamored of the abuser—"He would gladly have suffered a hundred times more to have gained the approval of one who was so tall and strong and had such stern imperious ways" (14–15)—and thus jealous of the attention he pays another boy. This is L. C. Southwood, nicknamed Elsie or Els, later to become Lord Tremlett. Once Orr finishes his schooling and leaves, Els makes overtures of friendship to Tristram, and the latter shifts his affections onto the younger boy: "how absolutely he was his!" (63). But at Bridwell (i.e., Radley), Els distances himself from Tristram, then breaks with him altogether when Orr reappears. Tristram alternately takes refuge in pride or grovels, trying to regain the younger boy's affections: "He even tried to excite his jealousy by taking up with young Clavering, but dropped him again when he saw that Els was not even aware of what he was about" (94). Tristram abases himself to the point of sending Els a note begging to restore their friendship, to receive back an envelope with his torn-up note inside. He finds himself alone, with no special friend, but he remains incapable of mastering his infatuation.

With no reason given for his change of heart, Els suddenly lets it be known at the end of term that he would like to patch up their quarrel. He invites Tristram for an extended visit to his family home. There, in another classical psychological turn, Tristram transfers his feelings for the brother onto the sister. Underscoring the homoerotics of the plot, he notes how Nita "was quite as much boy as girl. And as one of Elsie's greatest charms had been that he had something in his dress and manner and looks and limbs of the delicacy and grace of a girl; so now he took delight in finding in her a delicious flavor of the roughness of a boy" (207). So much difference in their ages exists, however, that nothing can come of the transferred passion for the time being. Later, when the main characters reassemble in France, Orr continues to be his rival for Els's affections and now for Nita's as well. The reader has to question the intensity of Tristram's feelings for Nita, however, since he never declares his affection and never writes her when he returns to England. They meet up again when the family arrives in London, and Tristram proceeds to make an ass of himself for the umpteenth time. Els marries, Orr becomes engaged to Nita, and she dies for no apparent reason save to end the novel with a lugubrious funeral (which, curiously enough, Orr does not attend).

Vachell's pair of novels about John Verney use the same triangular dynamics. *The Hill: A Romance of Friendship* records the struggle between the hero, nicknamed Jonathan, and Reginald Scaife, nicknamed The Demon, to gain the friendship of Henry Desmond, nicknamed Caesar. The story recounts the usual games and studies, quiet pleasures and escapades, with an added threat: the call of the Anglo-Boer War. Desmond heeds that call and is killed. Distressed, Verney spills his heart to his housemaster, revealing the strength of his feelings for Desmond and his hatred of Scaife: "The romance of this friendship stirred him profoundly; the romance of the struggle for good and evil; a struggle of which the issues remained still in doubt; a romance which Death had cruelly left unfinished—this had poignant significance for the house-master" (230). *John Verney*, 1911, continues the story, but now the Verney–Scaife rivalry is over the hand of Desmond's sister Sheila, as well as political battles for Parliament.

Clarke, A. W. *Jaspar Tristram: A Story*. London: Heinemann, 1899. *N. p.: Nabu, n. d.
Vachell, H. A. *The Hill: A Romance of Friendship*. London: Murray, 1905. New York: Dodd, Mead, 1906. **The Hill: An English Public School Story*. Los Angeles: Viewforth, 2011.
───. *John Verney*. London: Murray, 1911. New York: Hodder & Stoughton, 1911. **John Verney: The Honourable Gentleman*. Los Angeles: Viewforth, 2011.

8   Samuel Butler: *The Way of All Flesh*, 1903. A. L. R. (Edward Perry Warren): *A Tale of Pausanian Love*, 1927.

The Way of All Flesh is another novel that pops up constantly on gay lists for no compelling reason. Narrated by Edward Overton, it follows the fortunes of young Ernest Pontifex as he seeks to make his way in the world. One obvious homosexual crosses his path. Chapters 51–59 (out of eighty-five) introduce Pryer, a curate with whom Ernest serves in London during a period in which he is pulled towards a religious life. Pryer keeps returning to "the wretched lack of definition concerning the limits of vice and virtue, and the way in which half the vices wanted regulating rather than prohibiting. [...] He dwelt also on the advantages of complete unreserve, and hinted that there were mysteries into which Ernest had not yet been initiated, but which would enlighten him when he got to know them" (361). However, Pryer succeeds only in taking Ernest's money, not his virginity. In fact, Ernest is sentenced to prison for raping a girl; he marries (not realizing that he has entered a bigamous relationship) and fathers two children. But the work ends with Ernest and Edward, the perpetual bachelor, as the closest of friends, to the exclusion of almost all others. Their relationship has often been read as homoerotic, of course.

Finished by 1884, the novel was published posthumously. Parts are autobiographical, with the major difference being that the author, though discreet, was more obviously homosexual. Samuel Butler (1835–1902) was born in Nottingham. After attending Cambridge, he emigrated in 1860 to New Zealand to try his hand as a sheep farmer; there he came under the unhappy influence of Charles Paine Pauli (d. 1892), who badly misused him for financial gain. Upon their return to England in 1864, other men became important to Butler emotionally, in particular Henry Festing Jones (1851–1928) and Hans Faesch, whose departure for Singapore in 1895 occasioned Butler's poem "In Memoriam H. R. F." Butler sent the poem out to various magazines for consideration, but withdrew it in a panic because of the Wilde trials.

The short novel *A Tale of Pausanian Love* by "A. L. R." was also written in the 1880s, but it was not published until almost the end of the writer's life, and then in such a limited edition that it probably had little impact on other writers. The initials stood for Arthur Lyon

Raile, who published *A Defence of Uranian Love*, 1928–30. But Raile itself is a pseudonym concealing the American-born art collector Edward Perry Warren (1860–1928). At the time of publication he had been living for some forty years in England, first as a student at Oxford, later in his country home, the Lewes House in Sussex. Among the gems in his collection were the famous Warren Cup, now in the British Museum, and Lucas Cranach's *Adam and Eve*, now in the Courtauld Institute of Art. He was friends with Robbie Ross and others of the Wilde circle and in 1920 had Siegfried Sassoon as a guest at his American home. Warren's lover was another Oxford student, John Marshall (1862–1928). The main characters, in the novel, Claud Sinclair and Alfred Byngham, are loosely based on the two men and their life.

The novel was written largely in Naples in 1887. Copies are extremely rare and expensive when available. Martin Green in his history of the Warrens provides a useful synopsis. The title comes from a character in Plato's *Symposium*. Pausanias distinguishes two kinds of love, an earthy one linked to Aphrodite Pandemus, in which a man feels physical passion for either women or boys, and a heavenly kind linked to Aphrodite Uranian, found only between males and innocent of lewdness. The novel thus boldly announces by its title that it is about male–male love, and indeed Sinclair and Byngham are lovers at Oxford. It becomes evident, however, that Byngham is also in love with the handsome Ralph Belthorpe and that even Sinclair is smitten by Belthorpe's beauty and wishes to sketch him. After Byngham magnanimously gives up Belthorpe, Sinclair proves his equal generosity by conniving to get the two back together, in the same bed in fact. But eventually Belthorpe yields to social pressure and marries. Byngham returns to Sinclair's arms, to the latter's happiness.

Butler, Samuel. *The Way of All Flesh*. London: Richards, 1903. New York: Dutton, 1910. *New York: Modern Library, 1950.
Green, Martin. *The Mount Vernon Street Warrens: A Boston Story, 1860–1910*. New York: Scribner's, 1989 (online).
Raby, Peter. *Samuel Butler: A Biography*. Iowa City: University of Iowa Press, 1991.
Sox, David. *Bachelors of Art: Edward Perry Warren & the Lewes House Brotherhood*. London: Fourth Estate, 1991.
[Warren, Edward Perry.] *A Tale of Pausanian Love* by A. L. R. London: Cayme, 1927. *The Collected Works and Commissioned Biography of Edward Perry Warren*. 2 vols. Ed. Michael Matthew Kaylor. Brno, Czech Rep.: Masaryk University Press, 2013. [not seen]

9 Anonymous: *The Memoirs of a Voluptuary*, 1905.

In 1971 Grove Press published a facsimile edition of a rare pornographic novel whose title page reads: *The Secret Life of An English Boarding-School—The Memoirs of a Voluptuary*. The first part, however (as the font size indicates), is to be treated as a surtitle. There were 150 copies "issued to subscribers only," published in three volumes, the place and date of publication given as New Orleans, 1905. The first chapter of each volume has the heading "Youthful Days," as a kind of subtitle. The novel was reissued in 1908 in two volumes, the publisher and place given this time as James Kennedy, London.

The actual publisher was probably Charles Carrington, and the place was Paris for both editions. Born Paul Harry Ferdinando (1867–1921) Carrington grew up in a London slum. He married and had two children; he had a third son with his mistress. In the early 1890s he moved to Paris and opened a bookshop. He published his first book in 1896. Wilde saw him there in August 1898 and reported to Leonard Smithers that he "looked twisted and hysterical." In 1907 France deported Carrington to Brussels for selling obscene literature. He continued publishing, including an edition of *The Picture of Dorian Gray*. In 1912 he returned to Paris. By 1920 he was blind from syphilis and was committed to a mental hospital in Ivry-sur-Seine, south of Paris, where he died. The website *The Erotica Bibliophile* contains much information about him and a checklist of his publications.

No one seems to have identified or even speculated about the author of *The Memoirs*. He obviously knew Paris well. His one description of a Devonshire landscape (95) is so sentimentalized, what with babbling brooks and bright-colored moths and butterflies, that one suspects he was not at home in the English countryside. The writing is lively, but the novel's only purpose is to stimulate the reader with descriptions of nonstop sex; there is the barest sense of milieu, little character development, and no social insights, although it does offer an interesting attack against circumcision (121). In language that seems almost contemporary, it covers the gamut of sexual expression—straight, bi, gay, and pederast—as it charts its hero's progression into ever more unorthodox forms of seminal release. For certain, the novel serves as an antithesis, even an antidote, to the usual schoolboy literature. We hear not a word about cricket, corporal punishment, or lessons; and the only schoolmaster is one who lusts after a student. The only areas of the school that we see, in fact, are the bedroom and the bathing area.

The story is narrated by thirteen-year-old Charles Powerscourt. He shares a chamber with sixteen-year-old Bob Rutherford. Bob initiates Charlie's first sexual experience and teaches him a number of physiological lessons that he has hitherto been ignorant of. These lessons expand when he meets his other two roommates: Bob's cousin Jimmy, the Duke of Surrey, and Gaston de Beaupré, nicknamed Blackie. Between bouts of sexual play, Blackie entertains the three with detailed stories of his heterosexual encounters in Paris and his experience, while disguised as a girl, of witnessing a lesbian orgy. On a visit to Blackie's home in Paris, Charlie has his first sexual experience with a woman and gets to witness a similar Bacchanalian orgy. The final stage in his sexual education comes with a visit to Jimmy's uncle, Lord Henry Wilmot, a twenty-nine-year-old pederast. Under his tutelage, with the eager assistance of two African adults, two Japanese boys, and an English lad whom Harry has taken in, Charlie is taken further into the pleasures of voluptuous excess. Lord Henry offers what could be considered the novel's message: "all boarding-schools and colleges are very much alike, and always have been. There is ever the chance for enjoyment, if one looks for it" (202).

The Memoirs of a Voluptuary. New Orleans [Paris]: Privately printed, 1905. Facsimile. New York: Grove, 1971. *Ware, Eng.: Wordsworth, 1996.

10 Forrest Reid: *The Garden God*, 1905; *Uncle Stephen*, 1931.

The Garden God: A Tale of Two Boys seems to be another schoolboy novel (or novella), but it actually belongs more to the world of the pastoral, a magical kind of fairyland. Before he goes off to boarding school, at a more advanced age than usual, Graham Iddesleigh has lived simultaneously in his father's house and a dreamscape, a garden in which he has glimpses of an "imaginary playmate who had made his life beautiful; the messenger of Eros; the fair boy who had come to him from his strange garden, his meadow of asphodel" (12–13). Now at school, he meets his dream in the flesh: Harold Brocklehurst. Graham longs to touch that flesh and permits himself a kiss when Harold is asleep. Seeking validation for his intense feeling, he turns to books: "And it seemed to Graham that nowhere, save only in a few poems, and in one or two passages of Plato, he could find the expression of a sentiment even approximating to that he felt for his friend" (39). He mentions Shakespeare's sonnets and specifies Plato's *Phaedrus*. In a brilliant reversal of heterosexual strategy to capture homoerotic poetry by reversing the pronouns, young Graham annexes two poems by Rossetti.

According to the convention established by Sturgis, the novel must end, of course, in the death of one of the boys. Harold sacrifices his life in order to save Graham's by diverting a runaway horse and its cart just as it is about to strike the boy. As he mourns, Graham comes to a new understanding of another of Plato's dialogues: "In the *Phaedo* he had found many arguments for the immortality of the soul, but more lately he had realised, in his own life, the only one perhaps that actually counted—and this no argument at all; but merely a very simple human desire, a desire to look again upon the face of his friend, the face of him who was buried in the grave" (68).

Michael Matthew Kaylor's notes to his edition of the novel disclose much that would be unknown to most modern readers. For example, he points out (87) that Reid's citation of Matthew 5:8—"Blessed are the pure in heart, for they shall see God" (46)—"contained, for the Uranians, an imbedded pederastic suggestiveness, with the word 'pure' playfully constituting *puer* (Latin for 'boy')." Kaylor also shows how much the novel was under the influence of Pater, both *Marius the Epicurean* and *The Renaissance*. Reid dedicated *The Garden God* to Henry James, whose homoerotic novellas *The Pupil* and *The Turn of the Screw* influenced its development. Still nervous in the wake of the Wilde trials, James was not pleased and cut off all further communication. This chilliness is ironic since James remained the best of friends with Sturgis.

Reid continued to intertwine the homoerotic and the fantastic in later novels. *Uncle Stephen* is the one most often cited. Orphaned, fifteen-year-old Tom Barber runs away from his stepmother's to find his uncle, Stephen Collet, a mysterious figure with the reputation of being a magician. The first two-thirds of the novel seem conventional enough, with Tom torn emotionally between love for three males: his uncle; the housekeeper's ne'er-do-well son, James Deverell; and a mysterious boy who lives in an abandoned lodge on the estate, Philip Coombe. Each loves him in return. Then, abruptly, the reader learns that Philip is actually a manifestation of Uncle Stephen, even though in personality the two seem little alike.

Eric Garber and Lyn Paleo (*Uranian Worlds*, 175) have an entry on *Demophon: A Traveller's Tale*, 1927, a fantasy based on Greek mythology. In a biographical note (176) they write: "Reid invariably chose young boys as the protagonists in his novels, and intense male-male (often boy-boy) friendships are a predominant theme throughout his work." The note mentions two more works containing "homoemotional characters and situations": *Pirates of the Spring*, 1919, and *Denis Bracknel*, 1947. They also note that Reid's translation of *Poems from the Greek Anthology*, 1943, is "primarily of gay male interest." Forrest Reid (1875–1947) spent his entire life, save for his years at Cambridge, in or near Belfast, Northern Ireland. In addition to his novels, he wrote critical studies of other writers. All his life he idealized youthful males, but Wendy Moffat records in her biography of E. M. Forster (117) that the union of two men in *Maurice* left Reid as nervous as Reid's dedication to James had left the earlier novelist.

Reid, Forrest. *The Garden God: A Tale of Two Boys*. London: Nutt, 1905. *Ed. Michael Matthew Kaylor. Kansas City, Mo.: Valancourt, 2007.
_____. *Uncle Stephen*. London: Faber & Faber, 1931.
*Tom Barber [...]. New York: Pantheon, 1955. 337–572.

11 E. M. Forster: *The Longest Journey*, 1907; *Maurice*, 1971. Lytton Strachey: *Ermyntrude and Esmeralda*, 1969.

The Longest Journey follows the life of Rickie Elliot from his Cambridge years into his disastrous marriage to Agnes Pembroke (on the rebound from the accidental death of her fiancé), their visit to his dead mother's sister-in-law and their encounter with the unconventional Stephen Wonham, who Rickie learns is his half-brother; thence though years of misery as a master at the public school where his brother-in-law serves, all mixed up with a muddle created by Agnes's avarice and her attempt to have Stephen disinherited; and on finally to Rickie's accidental death saving Stephen from an oncoming train. The reader is reminded often that Rickie suffers from a congenital lameness, but so weak is his character that never is he compared to Byron. Throughout the novel, the reader senses another story struggling to get out, but one always being deflected by the author (who, after all, was writing in 1906): one about homosexual desire.

A key to this reading is Stewart Ansell, Rickie's best friend at Cambridge. He physically pops up at crucial moments in the plot, and his influence permeates it from beginning to end. Is he gay? And what is the relationship between him and Rickie? In one teasing scene, Stewart and Ansell are lying in a pasture, absorbing the sun; Rickie has "plaited two garlands of buttercups and cow-parsley, and

Ansell's lean Jewish face was framed in one of them" (78). They are discussing philosophy (Stewart's specialty) and various abstractions, which leads Rickie to musing: "Nature has no use for us; she has cut her stuff differently. Dutiful sons, loving husbands, responsible fathers—these are what she wants, and if we are friends it must be in our spare time. Abram and Sarai were sorrowful, yet their seed became as sand of the sea, and distracts the politics of Europe at this moment. But a few verses of poetry is all that survives of David and Jonathan." Then he recalls Shakespeare's sonnets: "he wished there was a society, a kind of friendship office, where the marriage of true minds could be registered" (80–91). Evoking a stereotype, one of their friends comments that he has always found Rickie to be "a little effeminate" (101).

Rickie's own marriage from the start is based on false premises. Gerald Dawes bullied Rickie at public school, but Rickie can't escape the pull of the "young man who had the figure of a Greek athlete" (43). After he suddenly dies during an athletic contest, Rickie proposes to Agnes. She is aware of "something abnormal" in his willingness to take Gerald's place, all the while insisting that her dead fiancé was her "greatest thing" (94). Stewart is totally "cut up" by the engagement (101) and tries to avert the marriage, correctly foreseeing catastrophe. Rickie remains dense. When it becomes apparent just how disastrous the marriage is, Stewart pays a visit. We are told of his feelings for Rickie: "Love remained. But in high matters he was practical. He knew that it would be useless to reveal it" (261). But when Stephen unexpectedly shows up also, Stewart prepares to battle Agnes—and Rickie too. He reveals that Stephen is not his father's illegitimate son (as Rickie has thought) but his sacred mother's. After Rickie's death Stewart transfers his allegiances to Stephen.

The novel opens with a philosophical discussion about what part human perception plays in the reality of things—whether "the cow" is there or not. Forster's four other antemortem novels, in particular the two connected to Italy, have all received gay readings.

Where Angels Fear to Tread, 1905, is a satire on English culture in which the morally rigid Herriton family decides to rescue a child their widowed daughter-in-law had in Italy by her second marriage, even though they have not the slightest right to the infant. Claude J. Summers (*The Gay & Lesbian Literary Heritage*, 281) claims that the son's, Philip Herriton, "real sexual attraction is not the intellectual response he develops for his Sawston neighbor Caroline Abbott but the physical passion he feels for Gino Carelli, the good-looking, young Italian who functions in the novel as a kind of Pan figure, a symbol of natural sexuality and freedom from social restraints." True, when Caroline declares that she loves Gino, Philip responds, "I love him too!" (a line not quoted by Summers), but for me the cow is not there. Philip seems just a weak young man who causes the entire tragedy (the infant is killed) by allowing the female members of his family to manipulate him to gain their own hypocritical ends.

It's much easier to find the cow in *A Room with a View*, 1908 (dedicated to Hugh Owen Meredith, upon whom the author had a crush during his Cambridge years). Lucy Honeychurch is engaged to Cecil Vyse, a young dandy who will obviously bring her grief. On a tour of Italy with her cousin (who seems to be lesbian), she meets George Emerson, the man she should marry. Of the Reverend Arthur Beebe, their minister back home, we are told that he is, "from rather profound reasons, somewhat chilly in his attitude towards the other sex" (50). So his remark has weight when he says, "Mr. Vyse is an ideal bachelor," and then adds, "like me—better detached" (130). When Emerson decides to fight for Lucy's hand, he says to her, "You cannot live with Vyse. He's only for an acquaintance. He is for society and cultivated talk. He should know no one intimately, least of all a woman" (254). Lucy picks up the phrase and throws it at Vyse ("you're the sort who can't know anyone intimately"). It hits home: "A horrified look came into his eyes" (264).

Readers have to work harder to find "the cow" in *Howards End*, 1910, less hard to discern possibilities between Dr. Aziz and Cyril Fielding in *A Passage to India*, 1924 (dedicated to Syed Ross Masood, who likewise cast a spell over Foster). But no question exists about *Maurice*. From beginning to end, it is a gay novel. It is a romance that cuts across the rigid British class system and ends happily for almost everyone involved. Perhaps even more than before in Forster's world, it shows characters trying to behave decently in unprecedented situations. The forward-looking, unrepentant Alec Scudder is one of the great creations of British literature. There was not a chance that the book could be openly published until almost the end of Forster's life, when the British legal system loosened up somewhat, with the result that it became, in gay circles, one of the most famous *unpublished* books of all time. Not surprisingly, when it was finally published posthumously in 1971 many critics, including some gay critics, seemed loath to say the obvious: that the novel is one of the great achievements of the century.

Maurice Hall is, in some ways, a stronger, more manly version of Rickie. The only boy of three siblings, he follows the accepted path of his class: prep school, public school, Cambridge. At the university he encounters Risley, a flamboyant aesthete, and feels in some obscure way that Risley "might help him" (34). Going to his chambers, instead Maurice finds Clive Durham, who is seeking out Tchaikovsky's Sixth Symphony, the Pathétique. As a result of their encounter, for Maurice "his heart had lit never to be quenched again, and one thing in him at last was real" (40). But his understanding does not lead to automatic acceptance of himself, and he remains tied up by the prejudices of his time. When Durham, after introducing Maurice to Plato's *Symposium*, declares his love (58), Maurice priggishly recoils. It takes him three days to recover and admit that he has lied: "He would not—and this was the test—pretend to care about women when the only sex that attracted him was his own. He loved men and always had loved them. He longed to embrace them and mingle his being with theirs." The authorial voice sums up: "After this crisis Maurice became a man" (62–63). He, in turn, declares his love to Clive (65).

Clive, however, is not the mate for Maurice. More introspective and thereby more troubled about their outlaw status, he works himself into a nervous breakdown, in Greece of all places, and emerges from it—against his own wishes, he says—as a heterosexual. While Maurice has entered his dead father's profession of stockbroker, Clive accepts his as a minor country squire who will marry, stand for public office, and act his part to the end. Maurice tries to rekindle the emotion, still convinced that "Two men can defy the world" (135). The note of the greenwood theme—the haven for outlaws, including his own sort—that has already sounded in the novel becomes stronger. Thwarted, momentarily lust takes the place of love, frightening him. He visits the family doctor for help. He also, at a concert, has another faithful encounter with Risley, who reveals to him the story behind the Pathétique Symphony.

On a visit to the newlywed's home, Maurice meets Alec Scudder: badly educated, working class, a common laborer. Also, honest and unafraid. Forster (though admittedly working in the security of non-publication) goes further than D. H. Lawrence could ever summon up nerve. Maurice himself has an attack of nerves, however, and desperately tries a course of hypnotism. It does not prevent his standing numbly at the guestroom window in Clive's house, calling out into the night, "Come!" And to his stupefaction and joy, Alec climbs a ladder left behind by workmen and enters his room and his bed (192). The way ahead remains troubled; Alec's entry has left behind a symbolic "flake of mud" (199). It takes all of Alec's stubbornness and Maurice's basic decency to effect a union, and even then it is touch and go. The great moment occurs in the British Museum. Convinced that Scudder is trying to blackmail him, Maurice schedules a meeting in this most public place. There he encounters one of his prep school teachers, who totally mixes him up with another boy: "To his own name Maurice would have responded, but he now had the inclination to lie; he was tired of their endless inaccuracy, he had suffered too much from it. He replied, 'No, my name's Scudder.' The correction flew out as the first that occurred to him. It lay ripe to be used, and as he uttered it he knew why" (223).

One wonders just what would have happened had Forster and a publisher dared to bring out the novel when it was finished. Forster was very aware, as he revealed in a terminal note to the novel written in 1960, that, "If it ended unhappily, with a lad dangling from a noose or with a suicide pact, all would be well [...]. But the lovers get away unpunished and consequently recommend crime" (250). He goes on to voice his pessimism that no liberalization of the homophobic laws will ever occur: "police prosecutions will continue and Clive on the bench will continue to sentence Alec in the dock. Maurice may get off" (255). But in the novel he expressed optimism about what two lovers against the world might accomplish: "His journey was nearly over. He was bound for his new home. He had brought out the man in Alec, and now it was Alec's turn to bring out the hero in him. He knew what the call was, and what his answer must be. They must live outside class, without relations or money; they must work and stick to each other till death. But England belonged to them. That, besides companionship, was their reward. Her air and sky were theirs, not the timorous millions' who own stuffy little boxes, but never their own souls" (238-39).

Forster dated the genesis of *Maurice* from a visit he paid the sexual liberation pioneer Edward Carpenter and his lover, George Merrill, in 1913. During the course of the visit Merrill touched Forster just above his buttocks, a gesture Forster recorded as normal for Merrill. But in this case the touch "seemed to go straight through the small of my back into my ideas, without involving my thoughts" (249). He returned home with the scheme for *Maurice* already full flown in his mind. He finished the novel the next year, aware also that he was correcting the record he had left muddled in *The Longest Journey*. Select friends were granted the privilege of reading the manuscript, so it executed an influence on gay letters even in its unpublished state. As a result of their comments and Forster's own evolving thought, revisions were made in 1920, 1932, and 1959. Christopher Isherwood was one of those trusted to read the manuscript. Later he was granted American rights to publish the book. He and John Lehmann brought the final typescripts into order and secured Forster's place in the pantheon of gay writers.

The year after *Maurice* was published, eight gay short stories that Forster had written between 1922 and 1958 were collected in a volume, *The Life to Come and Other Stories*. In them Forster examines the sheer maliciousness of heterosexual power. As he pointed out in that terminal note, "what the public really loathes in homosexuality is not the thing itself but having to think about it" (255). There have been screen adaptations of all his novels save *The Longest Journey*, two television adaptations of the short story "The Obelisk," and various telecasts of Benjamin Britten's opera *Billy Budd*, for which he wrote the libretto.

Born in London, Edward Morgan Forster (1879-1970) was educated at Tunbridge and Cambridge, where he was one of the Apostles. He was loosely associated with the Bloomsbury group. (The character Risley in *Maurice* is based on Lytton Strachey.) Although he associated with gays from the time he was at Cambridge and had strong emotional relationships with Meredith (the model for Clive) and Masood, whom he helped prepare for his entry into Oxford, his first sexual encounter was with a British soldier in Egypt in 1916, *after* he had finished *Maurice*. Forster subsequently fell in love with a tram conductor, Mohammed el Adl. There followed a string of affairs. Then, in 1930 he met Bob Buckingham (1904-1975). They remained lovers even after Buckingham's marriage, and Forster died in the their home. Even so, Forster continued to have encounters; Wendy Moffat (274) records that he spent a June evening in 1947 in the company of the dancer José Martinez having casual sex in New York's Central Park; Forster would then have been sixty-eight.

Strachey's *Ermyntrude and Esmeralda*,

more a long short story than a true novella, is another work that came out posthumously. Written in early 1914 in epistolary form, it did not appear in print until 1969, when it was first published in *Playboy* magazine and then reprinted as a book. It is a soufflé, an amusing read that appeals to the smutty adolescent in one. Two sheltered teenage girls are trying to make sense of sex. Having no education on the matter, they resort to calling their genitals "pussies" and those of men "bow-wows"; when they are aroused, their genitals "pout." Esmeralda accidentally discovers that her brother Godfrey is having sex with his Oxford tutor, Mr. Mapleton (35–37). Esmeralda replies in her next letter, "I suppose, as you say, two bow-wows can't have babies, but I can't see why on earth they shouldn't pout at one another. The great question is—how do they pout?" (38). Godfrey's father unfortunately catches them together in Godfrey's bed; he threatens Mr. Mapleton with exposure unless he decamp England at once and prepares to send Godfrey to Germany.

Shortly afterwards the middle-aged pastor who is visiting Esmeralda's home is waxing sentimentally about love. She seizes the moment to ask why her father then was so angry with Godfrey: "if it was not wrong to be in love, why shouldn't he be?" When he recoils, calling the men's love "a profanation," she brings up the Greeks, whom she has heard Godfrey speak of. And then, remembering something her brother had said about school romances, she asks "whether he hadn't very likely felt the same as Godfrey when he was at school himself" and then blurts out, "Oh, Dr. Barlett, I believe you were in love with Papa!" (52–53). Michael Holroyd in his introduction to the book writes (11): "By using nursery terms for the genitals, he makes all the more ludicrous society's standard reaction of horror to sex and to sexual deviation. Implicit throughout the lightly-written satire is a scathing criticism of the taboos under which [Strachey] himself suffered and the repressive procedures that governed the upbringing of adolescents."

Also born in London, Giles Lytton Strachey (1880–1932) too was one of the Apostles at Cambridge and became one of the central figures in the Bloomsbury group. *Eminent Victorians*, 1918, allowed him to become financially independent and ultimately to buy a home in Wiltshire. He fell in love with the painter Duncan Grant, the publisher Roger Senhouse, and perhaps the economist John Maynard Keynes, among others. His strangest relationship was with the painter Dora Carrington, with whom he lived from 1917 until his death, a great part of the time as part of a *ménage à trois* with her husband; she killed herself upon Strachey's death. He died of cancer.

Forster, E. M. *The Longest Journey*. London: Arnold, 1907. *Edinburgh: Blackwood, 1907. New York: Knopf, 1922.
———. *Maurice*. London: Arnold, 1971. *New York: Norton, 1971.
———. *A Room with a View.** London: Arnold, 1908. New York: Putnam's, 1911.
Holroyd, Michael. *Lytton Strachey: The New Biography*. 1995. New York: Norton, 2005.
Moffat, Wendy. *A Great Unrecorded History: A New Life of E. M. Forster*. New York: Farrar, Straus, & Giroux, 2010.
Strachey, Lytton. *Ermyntrude and Esmeralda*. Intro. Michael Holroyd. London: Blond, 1969. *New York: Stein & Day, 1969.

12 D. H. Lawrence: *The White Peacock*, 1911; *Women in Love*, 1920.

On the surface, *The White Peacock*, is the story of the relationship between two Nottinghamshire families, the Beardsalls and the Saxtons. Structurally, it is a tragic romance about narrator Cyril Beardsall's unfulfilled love for George Saxton. In part, the romance is impossible because of the times. All the other characters seem aware of George's physical attraction for Cyril, and at least one insists on calling him Sybil (24). But neither Wilde nor Edward Carpenter seems to have influenced this corner of England. In greater part, the romance is impossible because it is one-sided: George does not seem to feel for Cyril what Cyril does for him. We can never be sure, though, since we never enter George's mind, and it is worth noting that he either is or wants to be in love with Cyril's sister, a classical transference. Cyril tries the same strategy, trying to will himself to be in love with George's sister, but the affair never comes off, and she gives up and marries another. At novel's end, Cyril is very much a middle-aged bachelor living all alone.

Cyril's acknowledgment of his feelings for George comes out by stages across the novel. At first it's just the physical: of George cutting wheat, Cyril says, "There was something exceedingly attractive in the rhythmic body" (47). Later comes the emotional: "I loved him when he looked up at me [from his reading], and as he lingered on his quiet 'Hullo!' His eyes were beautifully eloquent—as eloquent as a kiss" (87). The climax of their relationship, at least for Cyril, arrives in a chapter titled "A Poem of Friendship." In the first part of the chapter he stumbles over a nest holding two larks and thinks, "In my heart of hearts, I longed for someone to nestle against, someone who would come between me and the coldness and the wetness" (220). In the second part, Cyril and George skinny-dip like teenagers in the nearby pond. When they emerge to dry off, "laughing, he took hold of me and began to rub me briskly, as if I were a child, or rather, a woman he loved and did not fear. I left myself quite limply in his hands, and, to get a better grip of me, he put his arms round me and pressed me against him, and the sweetness of the touch of our naked bodies one against the other was superb. It satisfied in some measure the vague, indecipherable yearning of my soul; and it was the same with him [...] and our love was perfect for a moment, more perfect than any love I have known since, either for man or woman" (222–23). The memory of the larks and the pond will abide with Cyril, but the Jonathan-David idyll will not endure. George marries and becomes an innkeeper. At novel's end he is a drunkard.

There has long been speculation about the exact nature of Lawrence's sexuality. In a December 2, 1913, letter, he wrote: "I should like to know why nearly every man that approaches greatness tends to homosexuality, whether he admits it or not." His biographer John Worthen concluded (172–73), "It had taken him a long time before he was prepared to admit that his need of men *did* have a component of physical attraction. But attraction was not the same as desire. He never seems to have wanted to have sex with a man. If anything, the opposite: he actively wanted *not* to." He lists various men with whom Lawrence had tried to form the kind of friendship he needed: Alan Chambers (the model for George Saxton), George Neville, Arthur McLeod, David Garnett, John Middleton Murray (a model for Gerald Crich), William H. Hocking, Maurice Magnus. Of these only Garnett and Magnus were gay.

Worthen also records (161–62) how Lawrence recoiled from Maynard Keynes, the Bloomsbury economist, who he felt was a predator on vulnerable males—something Worthen claims Lawrence felt he was capable of himself. His short story "The Prussian Officer" (originally titled "Honour and Arms"), 1914, Lawrence's most overtly homosexual story, depicts the destruction such a homosexual predator could wreak. Captain Hauptmann becomes obsessed with his orderly, the completely heterosexual young Schöner, and makes his life unbearable. What makes the story more terrifying is that not only is he unable to control his emotions, he is incapable of even admitting that they exist. In a desperate attempt to free himself, the orderly kills the captain, but by then his life has become so disoriented that he ends up dying himself.

Ken Russell's 1969 film of *Women in Love*, based on a screenplay by the gay American writer Larry Kramer, certainly left no doubt in gay viewers' minds that the author must have had a strong homosexual component. The nude wrestling scene, taken directly from the book, between actors Alan Bates and Oliver Reed in front of a blazing fireplace sears itself on the mind. The novel was Lawrence's fifth, a sequel to *The Rainbow*, 1915. Like it, it ran into charges of obscenity that delayed its publication and even then brought fresh charges against the author. The novel is about the Brangwen sisters, Ursula and Gudrun, and their relationship to two men, Rupert Birkin, a school inspector, and Gerald Crich, heir to a local mining operation, as well as the two men's attraction to each other. It is also about will versus blood consciousness, the mechanical versus the natural, a desire for balance and integrity between individuals, the death of old religions and the need for new, love, death, and the role of sex. The four main characters are often seen naked, as if stripping themselves of the inessential. Lawrence's critique of current psychological thought sharpens in this novel, and he proposes alternative approaches to understanding body and mind.

The first time we see the two men together, we are told that there is a "strange enmity" between them, of "either hate or love, or both" and that they "burned with each other, inwardly." At this point, "They had not the faintest belief in deep relationship between man and man, and their disbelief prevented any development of their powerful but suppressed friendliness" (33–34). But Birkin begins to comprehend that it is not enough to love only a woman, that he needs to "love a man purely and fully" and that, in fact, "he had been loving Gerald all along, and all along denying it." Referring to the custom of German knights "to swear a Blutbrüderschaft," he proposes to Gerald "to swear to love each other, you and I, implicitly and perfectly" (206–07). This is a step to the famous wrestling scene, during which the two "seemed to drive their white flesh deeper and deeper against each other, as if they would break into a oneness" (270). Yet Gerald proves incapable of following Birkin's lead: "Surely there can never be anything as strong between man and man as sex love is between man and woman. Nature doesn't provide the basis." Birkin daringly counters, "Well, of course, I think she does. And I don't think we shall ever be happy till we establish ourselves on this basis. You've [...] got to admit the unadmitted love of man for man. It makes for a greater freedom for everybody, a greater power of individuality both in men and women" (352). While Birkin is associated with plants and growth, Gerald is "arctic," "a smiling wolf" (14), governed by "a dual consciousness" (53). The chill closes in upon Gerald, dooming him and leaving Birkin unfulfilled.

In spring 1963 *Texas Quarterly* published the original opening chapter of *Women in Love*, which Lawrence had discarded, knowing no publisher would print it. It has been reprinted in a number of gay anthologies and is included in the Penguin edition that follows the Cambridge text of the novel. Birkin's and Gerald's basic character is slightly different, and here the two nervously realize almost on first meeting that "they loved each other, that each would die for the other" (500). Birkin is more forthright in recognizing that "although he was always drawn to women, feeling more at home with a woman than with a man, yet it was for men that he felt the hot, flushing, roused attraction which a man is supposed to feel for the other sex." He further acknowledges that "the male physique had a fascination for him, and for the female physique he felt only a fondness, a sort of sacred love, as for a sister. In the street, it was the men who roused him by their flesh and their manly, vigorous movement" (511–12).

Lawrence was making no special plea for homosexuality per se, but some of his arguments were in advance of current psychological positions. He asks, "How can a man *create* his own feelings? He cannot. It is only in his power to suppress them, to bind them in the chain of the will. And what is suppression but a mere negation of life, and of living" (512). He concludes, "He wanted to cast out these desires, he wanted not to know them. Yet a man can no more slay a living desire in him, than he can prevent his body from feeling heat and cold. He can put himself into bondage, to prevent the fulfillment of the desire, that is all. But the desire is there, as the travelling of the blood itself is there, until it is fulfilled or until the body is dead" (514). This so-called prologue does not really change one's conception of the novel, but it does emphasize its importance to gay literature.

Intense relationships between males, quasi-homoerotic, exist in subsequent novels: *Aaron's Rod*, 1922 (Aaron Sisson and Rawdon Lilly); *Kangaroo*, 1923 (Richard Lovat Somers and Benjamin Cooley); *The Plumed Serpent*, 1926 (Don Cipriano and Don Ramon). Two stereotypical homosexuals (Franz Dekker and Angus Guess) appear in *Aaron's Rod*. Other characters in the novel are based on homosexuals he befriended—Norman Douglas, Reggie Turner, and Maurice Magnus—just as Witter Bynner and Willard "Spud" Johnson served as models for characters in *The Plumed Serpent*; but their sexuality plays no part in the stories. It has been suggested that Duncan Grant served as a model for a character in *Lady Chatterley's Lover*, 1928, while Edith Sitwell was convinced that her brother Osbert was a source for the depiction of Lord Chatterley. Much has been made of Lawrence's friendship with the Cornwall farmer William Hocking, some asserting that their relationship was even physical. Certainly the name that Lawrence gave to Hocking's fictional counterpart in "The Nightmare" chapter of *Kangaroo*—John Thomas Buryan—is suggestive, but within the novel there is no indication of anything particularly erotic about the friendship between the two men.

David Herbert Lawrence (1885–1930) was born in Eastwood, Nottinghamshire, the son of a coal miner. He spent nine years as a teacher while he was trying to make his way as a writer. In 1912 he met Frieda Weekley, the wife of one of the teachers at Nottingham University College, and they eloped to the Continent. Through David Garnett he met Lady Ottoline Morrell and thus Forster and Bertrand Russell. Gradually his circle of literary friends expanded. The war scarred Lawrence's psyche. After it was over, he began wandering the globe, searching for a place he could find peace. His pilgrimage took him to Italy, Ceylon, Australia, the United States, and Mexico. He died in Vence, France, and his ashes were interred in the cement altar of a chapel on his New Mexican ranch. All the while censorship problems continued to plague him. The Cambridge Lawrence Edition project was launched in order to restore his original texts; they have been largely reprinted by Penguin Books. These are the editions a gay booklover wants to read.

Lawrence was developing his thoughts on sex during the period in which English sexologists were building on the work of such German pioneers as Richard von Krafft-Ebing, who published *Psychopathia Sexualis* in 1886; Magnus Hirschfeld, who began his campaign with the pamphlet *Sappho und Sokrates*, 1896; and Sigmund Freud, whose *Drei Abhandlungen zur Sexualtheorie* came out in 1905. The year that Lawrence was born, Richard Burton published his theory of the "Sotadic Zone" as part of the terminal essay to his translation of *The Arabian Nights*. John Addington Symonds published *A Problem of Modern Ethics* in 1891. Edward Carpenter published *Homogenic Love* in 1894, followed by *The Intermediate Sex* in 1908. The French-born Marc-André Raffalovich published *Uranisme et unisexualité* in 1896. And Havelock Ellis, with Symonds's assistance, brought out the first of several editions of *Sexual Inversion* in 1897. Lawrence's recognition of the importance of the body, including the genitals, balances the traditional emphasis on the mind.

Lawrence, D. H. *The White Peacock*. London: Heinemann, 1911. New York: Duffield, 1911. *London: Penguin, 1995 (Cambridge text).
———. *Women in Love*. New York: Privately printed [Thomas Seltzer], 1920. London: Secker, 1921. *London: Penguin, 2007 (Cambridge text).
Worthen, John. *D. H. Lawrence: The Life of an Outsider*. New York: Counterpoint, 2005.

13 R. Macaulay: *The Lee Shore*, 1912.

Peter Margerison is an unusual hero. His stepbrother, Denis Urquhard, sums him up: "I don't mean that Peter means any harm; but [...] he's weak" (226). As a result, he reels from one failure to another. The remarkable thing is: Peter is happy. Denis is obviously his great love. They were reared apart but came to know each other at Cambridge. The author is discreet, in accord with the times, but early on we are told that "Peter, in brief, was a lover of his kind, and the music life played to him was of a varied and complex nature. But, looking back, it was easy to see how there had been, running through all the variations, a dominant motive in the piece." At that point, "the dominant motive came in and stood by the fire"—Denis (30–31). The note is struck repeatedly across the novel. Peter thinks, "Well, hadn't he long since given to Denis, to use as he would, all the self he had?" (154). The woman Peter marries because of a thoughtless promises says, "You care for him awfully, Peter [...]; more than for anyone in the world, don't you?" (197). Denis's wife tells him, "Peter cares for you [...]; and you can't compare carings, but the way he cares for you is the most wonderful of all, I believe" (227). Poor Peter, like so many gay men, however, has fallen in love with a total heterosexual. As he tries to reach the comforts of the lee shore, one stage is for him to recognize: "I don't want Denis's affection" (304).

The plot is not, however, merely a lovesick longing for the unattainable. Because of his weakness, Peter tries to help his even weaker and basically dishonest half-brother, Hilary Margerison. They are both art appraisers. Because of his moral code, Peter has to speak out against Hilary's shoddy business practices, with the results that he loses the respect of Denis's uncle, Lord Evelyn Urquhart, and the whole Margerison family (Hilary is married, with three boys) sinks deeper into poverty. Peter's own misguided marriage does bring him a joy, and then a comfort when his wife abandons him for another man: a son, Thomas. Peter also has a deep, brotherly relationship with Lucy Hope, who becomes Denis's wife, and only her awareness of Peter's feelings for Denis prevents them from thinking they could have a relationship.

Peter's fixation blinds him to two other men who have strong feelings for him. He meets Stephen Rodney at Cambridge, where he is an Apostle (35), a member of the secret society that preached aestheticism and practiced homosexuality with remarkable freedom. We are told later, however, that he is "a celibate" (195), though that term is immediately coupled with heterosexual matrimony. Certainly, he takes a great interest in Peter, saves him from running off with Lucy, and leaves the reader wondering. The other is the older Lord Evelyn, who seeks Peter out after his final failure and begs him to come live with him. Finally he speaks directly to Peter: "My good boy, haven't you ever guessed, all these years, that I rather like your company?" (302). Then, when Peter turns him down, he tries to pass it off: "I loved your mother; my brother's wife. Did you ever guess that?—guess why I liked you a good deal?" (305). Perhaps he is telling the truth. But it sounds a bit too pat.

Then there is Livio Ceresole. When Peter, Thomas, and Francesco, the dog they have acquired, become Italian vagabonds, they fall into his company. One might assume it is simply the convenience of two men down on their luck pooling their resources, save that the author carefully notes that Lucio has "the petulant, half sensuous, spoilt-boy beauty of a young Antinuous" (288), the reference by now a code word as surely the author knew. *The Lee Shore* really is an audacious novel, and one that can yet captivate the reader. If it does not exactly have a happy ending, at least no one (save Thomas's mother) dies. And the final sentence is fairly upbeat: "Peter, with a mind at ease and Francesco grinning at his heels, sauntered down the warm, dusty road to find Thomas and have lunch" (308).

Emilie Rose Macaulay (1881–1958) was born in Rugby, Warwickshire. She attended Oxford. Her father was Rupert Brooke's tutor, and the poet served as the model for characters in two of her novels (*The Secret River*, 1909, and *Views and Vagabonds*, 1912). She worked for the government during World War I. For some twenty years she was in a relationship with the Irish writer Gerald O'Donovan, an ex–Catholic priest, married and with children. She published thirty-five books, winning the James Tait Black Memorial Prize with her final novel.

Macaulay, R. *The Lee Shore*. London: Hodder & Stoughton, 1912. *New York: Doran, 1912.

14 Patrick Weston (Gerald Hamilton): *Desert Dreamers*, 1914.

The Mediterranean in general, not just Italy, functioned as a safe zone in the eyes of gay Englishmen. They escaped there in order to free themselves of their cultural bindings, to come out of the closet, and to seek love or at least pleasure. Twenty-two-year-old Julian Thelluson leaves London for Algiers. There the rigid moral code he has simply accepted without thinking is shaken. Under the influence of Robert Hichens's novel *The Garden of Allah*, he decides to push deeper into the desert. Biskra, his destination, is an oasis town some 250 miles southeast of Algiers. It is one of the settings for André Gide's *L'Immoraliste*, 1902, and also the place where he, Wilde, and Douglas joined up for a while. If it did not exactly have a reputation as a gay mecca, clearly it was seen as the site for exotic romance and easy virtue. When Julian announces his decision to go there, Maisnon, a French doctor whom he has met, tries to dissuade him, telling him that the town is "dangerous for one of your neurotic passionate temperament" (20).

Indeed, his first evening there he sees the seventeen-year-old Tayeb ben Mahmud and falls in love: "He realized that a strange chord of sympathy existed between the young Arab and himself. He delighted in the lad's society, and he felt, he knew, subconsciously, that his affection was ardently reciprocated. Yet this seemed incredible" (41). Nothing in his Victorian upbringing has prepared him for his tumultuous feelings. With the scent of mimosa filling his nostrils, the two come together in the open: "With a cry of resignation to fate, with a cry of joy or rather of sorrow ended, he drew Tayeb to him; and, as there is a God in heaven, those two souls became united in that one sacred moment" (53). The next chapter has as its epigraph the concluding lines of Douglas's poem "Two Loves."

Their Edenic happiness is threatened by Joseph Hoxton, a London barrister who is a friend of Julian's mother. He catches the two of them kissing in the Jardin de Landon. Seeing himself through Hoxton's eyes—"Worthy fellows still wrangled as to whether a prison or a lunatic asylum was the better place for people with such tendencies" (59)—Julian asks Tayeb whether God condemns their love. Tayeb answers that each person's heart must judge right and wrong. He asserts that he never does what he knows is wrong (61). But Hoxton's disapprobation acts as a subtle poison. Tayeb falls ill with a fever. In terror, Julian writes the French doctor, begging him to come to his succor. Just as Dr. Maisnon seems to be succeeding, Hoxton, who has disappeared in the interim, returns—"a sad expression on his hypocritical face, the very embodiment of British respectability" (72)—with Julian's mother in tow. The doctor, however, knows about Hoxton's own peccancies in Algiers, with the result that Hoxton suddenly finds that his business urgently demands he depart for London at once. The novella ends sadly, but not tragically. Tayeb dies. But Julian has embraced his sexuality, and his mother accepts her son as he is. The good doctor has the last line: "'I am glad,' said the doctor, simply" (84).

Mark Mitchell and David Leavitt reprint four chapters in *Pages Passed from Hand to Hand*. I can discover nothing about the novella's origins or original publication. Gerald Frank Hamilton Souter (1890–1970) was born in Shanghai. He was dismissed from Rugby after being caught in bed with another boy. His political sympathies for Germany and Ireland brought him under government scrutiny, and his sexuality landed him in trouble with the law. Throughout his life he was involved in any number of shady schemes, even as he moved in powerful cultural, religious, and royal circles. He is remembered today for having been the model for the title character in Christopher Isherwood's *Mr Norris Changes Trains*. He died in London of a heart attack.

Cullen, Tom. *The Man Who Was Norris: The Life of Gerald Hamilton*. Ed. Phil Baker. Sawtry, Eng.: Dedalus, 2014.

[Hamilton, Gerald.] *Desert Dreamers: A Romance of Friendship* by Patrick Weston. London: At the Sign of the Tiger Lily, 1914. *Intro. Christopher Isherwood. Washington, D.C.: Guild, 1966.

15 Joseph Conrad: *Victory*, 1915.

Male bonding and a certain misogyny seem endemic to Conrad's world. Think of the often anthologized stories *Heart of Darkness*, 1899, and "The Secret Sharer," 1910. It is not surprising that scholars have sought to out various characters. Richard J. Ruppel has devoted a monograph to *Homosexuality in the Life and Work of Joseph Conrad*. He applies a gay reading to seven novels. He explores *The Nigger of the "Narcissus,"* 1898, as an example of male intimacy on board ship. He examines Jim's erotic appeal to Marlow, the narrator, and other men in *Lord Jim*, 1900. He argues that male desire between John Kemp and Carlos Riego is doubly triangulated via the bodies of the two women they supposedly love in *Romance*, 1903 (a novel Conrad wrote in collaboration with Ford Madox Hueffer, later Ford). He postulates that the narrator of *Under Western Eyes*, 1911, is a closeted homosexual. *Chance*, 1913, becomes for him "an extended study of gender and gender conflict." And he makes a case for an erotic attraction between the captain and the cook in *The Shadow Line*, 1917. With *Victory* his gay reading seems now to be the generally accepted one.

The novel is set on two fictional islands in the Java Sea. Before it opens, its hero, Axel Heyst, helped a "cornered man" (154) named Morrison and became his trading partner. Facing failure, Morrison returned to England to try to raise capital and died there. A villainous local hotelkeeper, Wilhelm Schomberg, spreads lies that Heyst killed Morrison. His enmity becomes a blind rage when Heyst rescues a member of an all-woman orchestra from his unwanted advances and takes her back to his island. When three equally villainous soldiers of fortune—Mr. Jones, his "secretary" Martin Ricardo, and their animal-like servant, Pedro—show up at the hotel, the cunning Schomberg convinces them that Heyst has an enormous cache of money just there for the taking. The three set out to steal it. The novel ends with five people dead, only an islander of Chinese descent surviving to tell what has happened. Bloated and tedious, the novel, nevertheless, was a popular success; it has been the basis for a play, an opera, and at least fourteen film adaptations. Its contribution to gay letters is less clear.

Still, a sense that Mr. Jones is homosexual has become so accepted that Peter Lancelot Mallios felt able to casually drop a sentence into his introduction to a Modern Library edition of *Victory* without defending it or explaining it: "Jones's 'queer' orientation offers up interesting insights on how the specter of homosexuality informs and polices Heyst's heterosexual dysfunctionality" (whatever that means). The clues that have led to this conclusion are many. Jones's physical appearance (81) and his choice of attire have something of the feminine about them. We are informed that he was thrown out of "his proper social sphere because he had refused to conform to certain usual conventions" (250), that he has been "hounded out from society by a lot of highly moral souls" (298). We hear about "a ragged, bare-legged boy that he picked up in the street" (118). The emotions that he feels for Martin Ricardo, his "companion—er—secretary" (186) are not exactly those of an ordinary employer-employee bond. Jones has a morbid hatred of women (never mind that misogyny does not exactly equate to homosexuality). When he discovers that Ricardo has betrayed him with a woman, he kills both of them before drowning himself.

Most readers find it harder to think that Heyst might also be homosexual. They accept that there was a deep friendship with Morrison, but their argument would be that it was, at most, homosocial in nature. That is clearly not the way Schomberg views the relationship. More important, Jones immediately feels some kind of kinship with Heyst and stresses their similarities. At one point, he observes, "It's obvious that we belong to the same—social sphere." Note that dash, marking some kind of ambiguous pause. He continues, "Something has driven you out—the originality of your ideas, perhaps. Or your tastes" (296). Later, Jones also mentions Morrison. Early in the novel Conrad stresses Heyst's indifference to women; a character says of his life, "nothing could have been more detached from feminine associations" (48). True, he has sex with the woman he has rescued (168), but the context may be telling: it occurs as a climax to her revelation that people believed he killed Morrison. Finally, one should try to decipher exactly what Conrad means by "gentleman," a term applied to both Jones and Heyst. Conrad's biographer Jeffrey Meyers (291) is one of the few to call Heyst a "repressed" homosexual.

The novella *Heart of Darkness*, the story of Marlow's epic journey up the Congo in search of the ivory hunter, Kurtz, tantalizes more when one realizes that the Russian who worships Kurtz was probably based on the Irish patriot Roger Casement. Whether Conrad knew of his homosexual activities in Africa, however, remains unknown. A short story, "Il Conde," 1908, makes sense only when it is read as a gay mugging. The count enters a poorly lit public Neapolitan park, clearly cruising. There, a young man asks him for a light, but when the count searches for matches, the youth pulls a knife on him. The youth is a student, a member of a powerful family that can make trouble for the count, so he flees Italy. The character was based on a Polish homosexual whom Conrad met on Capri, Count Zygmunt Szembek.

Józef Teodor Konrad Nalecz Korzeniowski (1857–1924) was born in Russian-occupied Poland. In 1874 he left for Marseilles to enlist in the French merchant service. After running into difficulties with Russian authorities and attempting suicide, he departed for England, where he joined the merchant marine and became a British citizen in 1886. There followed numerous voyages around the world and up the Congo. They provided the raw materials for his tales, the first of which was published in 1895 under his Anglicized name. He married and had two sons, but his biographer Jeffrey Meyers observes (225), "Many of Conrad's friends were homosexuals—his French translator Vicomte Robert d'Humières, the young novelists Stephen Reynolds and Hugh Walpole, Casement, André Gide and Norman Douglas—and the last three were recklessly indiscreet." Meyers notes though that Conrad dropped both Casement and Douglas when they ran afoul of the law. Conrad died in Kent near Canterbury.

Conrad, Joseph. *Victory: An Island Tale*. Garden City, N.Y.: Doubleday, Page, 1915. London: Methuen, 1915. *Intro. Peter Lancelot Mallios. New York: Modern Library, 2003.
Meyers, Jeffrey. *Joseph Conrad: A Biography*. New York: Scribner's, 1991.
Ruppel, Richard J. *Homosexuality in the Life and Work of Joseph Conrad: Love Between the Lines*. London: Routledge, 2008.

16 John Gambril Nicholson: *The Romance of a Choir-Boy*, 1916.

According to the dates at the end of the novel, Nicholson wrote it between 1896 and 1905. It was privately printed in 1916 and not reprinted until 2013. Andrew May's edition omits long discussions of hymns and minute descriptions of cricket matches, but he assures the reader (12) that "nothing having to do with the central relationship between Philip and Teddy has been omitted or abridged." That relationship, which begins when Philip Luard is twenty-one and Edward Faircloth is twelve, is chaste, but there is no denying that the attraction is physical at base. When Philip first takes notice of Teddy and photographs him—taking snapshots that he regards "long and wistfully while preparing for bed" (67)—the boy is completely naked, having just emerged from swimming in a stream. Two years later, we are told, that "the grey trousers fitted [Teddy] well, and Philip liked watching him from behind" (229). More than with Sturgis's and Reid's fiction, the novel serves as a perfect example of Uranian ideals.

There is a class difference between the two. Philip belongs to the village gentry; Teddy to the laboring class. Discovering that he has a remarkable singing voice, Philip determines to take him into his care and find him a place with a choir school. "Thirsty already for love, he had dreamed of a deep inexhaustible well of which he might drink daily. The illusion had seized him three or four times already since he had gone up to Oxford [...]. In some instances the approach had been impossible, and in the one exception to this experience he had proved that it was distance which lent the view its enchantment [...]. The illusion had faded; the promising appearance had given place to a most disappointing and undesirable reality, and the effect of the episode on Philip's life was revealed by a series of about fifty erotic sonnets." After meeting Teddy, however, he feels that "the companion for whom he had been waiting, the someone to love without whom his individuality was only a semi-circle" (65–66), has appeared. He self-tattoos *EF*, the initials of his "sweetheart's name," on his arm (182).

Teddy becomes a student in London. Philip is a curate living in the same Clergy House as his Oxford friend Gerrard. His other good friend is a church organist, Lorey. While various incidents occur along the way, the greater portion of the novel is given over to a discussion of the nature of love. For Lorey, love expresses itself in "absolute and complete union with the beloved one; mental, moral, and physical"; it is "breaking down every possible barrier—withholding nothing" (132). When he learns that Teddy will be staying overnight with Philip, sharing the same bed, but sleeping in pajamas rather than a nightshirt, Lorey says, "I'd as soon sleep with an iron-clad" (176). For Gerrard, for whom religious yearning is paramount, "Love was abstract, spiritual, unearthly [...]. To degrade Love into a physical experience was unpardonable" (128–29). When Philip persists in acting like a lovesick swain—"a spoilt child," as he acknowledges at one point (209)—Gerrard cautions him, "You must recognize a boy's limitations" (189).

After making a mental catalog of his belongings, including a volume of his own poetry and eighteen portrait photographs of adolescent boys, Philip impulsively tells Teddy all that he has been wrestling with: "He outlined love; as it was from Gerrard's standpoint, as it was from Lorey's. Without mentioning names he made himself quite well understood by Teddy; he said 'some men' and he said 'some boys' when he illustrated his points." He goes on to assure the boy that "he knew what was the right way, that he was resolved to take it; and he appealed to Teddy, who had helped him in all his difficulties hiterto, to help him henceforth in this matter" (238). Teddy seems to take in all he has been told and discloses a secret of his own, which the reader is left to guess. At novel's end Philip and Teddy reassure Gerrard that, when they share a bed, they will be like two safety-matches in the box, not like squibs (243).

The novel is clearly autobiographical. John Gambril Francis Nicholson (1866–1931) was born in Essex. Frederick Rolfe was one of his early teachers; the two had a rocky friendship in later years. After attending Oxford, he became a schoolteacher. One of the Uranian poets, he published four collections of verse. In 1914 Nicholson was one of the founders of the British Society for the Study of Sex Psychology. He was also an amateur photographer. An 1892 photograph taken of him with the young Alec Melling has been reproduced several times.

Nicholson, John Gambril. *The Romance of a Choir-Boy*. London: Privately printed, 1916. *Ed. Andrew May. Portsmouth, Eng.: Callum James, 2013.

17 E. F. Benson: *David Blaize*, 1916; *David of King's*, 1924; *The Inheritor*, 1930; *Ravens' Brood*, 1934.

Dejan Kuzmanovic (in George Haggerty's *Gay Histories and Cultures*, 112–13) writes that Benson's "public school and university novels [...] radiate with ubiquitous but suppressed homoeroticism. Sexual urge is represented in these novels, however, as a 'bestial' temptation that must be resisted if the friendship between men is to survive. Homoerotic feeling is also strong in *Raven's* [sic] *Brood* [...], a remarkable novel in Benson's opus both for choosing its heroes among farm workers and for its heavy atmosphere of barely controlled sexuality. It also contains the only one among Benson's numerous characters who comes close to being openly homosexual." Presumably Professor Kuzmanovic in this last comment is referring to Mr. Willis, a painter and summer lodger in the Pentreath house on the coast of Cornwall. He is described as effeminate, "a pretty capering thing with a pink silk vest, and pink silk pants, wrapping himself in a lovely blue dressing-gown" (175), when seen for the first time, preparing for a bath. Thenceforth, he is called "girlie," though the point is made several times that he is really sexless. When he throws himself on nineteen-year-old Dennis Pentreath, in "greed for the contact of his rough vigour," Dennis looks upon him with amusement rather than affront. Willis "was queer enough, but he was kind, and it was a pity to see his loneliness and his eagerness to talk to any of them" (184–85).

But Professor Kuzmanovic could also be referring to Dennis's best friend, Willie Polhaven. (Notice the similarity of names: Willis, Willie.) The two youths share an easy camaraderie (even though their friendship began with a fight), swim naked together, and are unafraid to display their affection for one another. But whereas Dennis begins to feel "the natural call of sex" (51) and to become interested in the house servant, Nell, Willie admits to feeling no attraction to the opposite sex: "I reckon it's a kink in me, and not like to come out," he says, and then recalls hearing the story of David and Jonathan read aloud in church. To Dennis's approval, he says, "That made me think of us" (196). Nor does Willie threaten Nell; after she realizes that she is pregnant, she begs Dennis, when the time comes (with apparently unconscious wordplay), to "get hold of your Willie, to take your mind off me. Lord, how you two fellers love each other: it's fine to think on" (218). Once the child is born, Willie becomes a kind of surrogate nurse. The curse on this family, in fact, is rampant patriarchy and unloving heterosexuality. The grandfather is a hypocritical fire-and-brimstone-spouting drunkard. He accidentally causes the death of his second wife (who uses witchcraft to try to seduce him into impregnating her even at her age). He letches after his widowed daughter-in-law. He physically abuses Dennis until he becomes old enough to defend himself; he tries to swindle him out of part of his inheritance; and he plots to murder him. His machinations lead to the final holocaust. A curious combination of Victorian prudery and contemporary frankness, however, creates a less than satisfying novel.

The slightly earlier *The Inheritor* is even gayer. It recounts a love story that fails because of a family curse. At Cambridge, a twenty-five-year-old don, Maurice Crofts, and a twenty-year-old student, Steven Gervase, fall in love. The author could hardly be more explicit. After Steven quotes a line from Whitman, "Maurice felt a sudden thrill of comprehension. Something secret within him knew what Steven meant" (48). In an ascending triad of emotional responses, the author takes us from one student who finds "rapture" with a girl, to a second who has known "passionate friendship," and culminates with "Steven, who had gone farther afield and into less trodden places, [...] on the scent of something rarer than they, of something that prowled, and was *perdu*, and Steven was certainly signaling to [Maurice] out of that dark of things" (58). True, Benson being Benson, their romance must take them into a "region [that] lay outside sex altogether" (78). But the fact that they must fight the physical discloses how aware of the body both are.

Steven invites Maurice to his ancestral home in Cornwall. There he encounters Stephen's cousin Tim, Steven's twin in appearance but the embodiment of Pan in manners. More is said of the family curse, the idea that the first child in a marriage will be some sort of monster, a curse that the Adonis-like Steven seems to have escaped. Now he allows Tim to exert some sort of magical hold over his mind and spirit, to Maurice's disgust. After he stumbles onto a Bacchanalian revel in which Steven gets the younger boy dangerously drunk, Maurice pulls back into himself. The "love" that was giving shape to their existence dissolves (211), and Stephen is forced to acknowledge that he has not escaped the curse after all (227). He marries, and, when the child arrives, "the silence was broken by the noise, not of a crying child, but of something bleating" (304). The bestial here, rather than being a manifestation of a temptation that must be resisted, seems to represent Stephen's failure of nerve to accept the love that Maurice offers, a type of sin against the body by his entering a heterosexual relationship.

Two much earlier school stories have especially attracted gay readers. The title character in *David Blaize* looks up to Frank Maddox, three years older than he and one of the stars at the public school they attend. Clearly the older boy is attracted to David and entertains carnal thoughts about him when he catches David naked in his bath, enough so that it provokes a "sense of choking discomfort" in the younger boy (146). Maddox is mortified by his own impulse: "All these weeks that intense friendship which was spring up between himself and David had been splendidly growing, and till now his influence over him had been exerted entirely for David's good. He had constantly shielded him [...] from all that could sully him, he had checked any hint of foul talk in David's presence, for, of all his loveable qualities, there was none so nobly potent to the elder boy than David's white innocence, his utter want of curiosity about all that was filthy. It didn't exist for him, but the danger of it (though, thank God, it had passed) he knew that he himself had brought near to him.... Then he got up and looked at himself in the mirror above his mantelpiece, hating himself. 'You damned beast,' he said. 'You deserve to be shot' (148–49). He apologizes to David and promises, "It shan't happen again" (151). From there on Maddox protects the boy.

Benson's biographer, Brian Masters, records (214) the irony that at the time "a few of the fans claimed *David Blaize* as their own for reasons [Benson] would genuinely abhor, and he would not have been pleased to learn that the novel is still on the list of homosexual book clubs. Clearly, it does not belong there, for it contains nothing overtly erotic and, indeed, bases its theme upon the purifying power of goodness. Yet the undercurrent is so strong that men who found it awkward to admit their emotional needs felt liberated by the novel, and in complicity with its author." In *David of King's* their nonsexual Jonathan and David friendship is picked up again at Cambridge (though David now professes to like girls). The novel is by moments downright campy, not least in its portrait of Alfred Gepp, modeled on Oscar Browning. A Cambridge Apostle, a pupil of William Johnson Cory, he was dismissed from Eton for a homosexual scandal but again found a niche at Cambridge, where he was instrumental in reforming the teaching of future educators. His recent death perhaps prompted the sequel.

Edward Frederic Benson (1867–1940) was the son of Edward Benson, an educator and ecclesiastic, the Archbishop of Canterbury, 1883–95. Educated at Marlborough and Cambridge, he spent some time in Greece and Egypt before dedicating himself full time to writing. After World War I he lived in Henry James's former home in Rye and regularly holidayed in Capri. Benson's mother was lesbian, and both his surviving brothers—A. C. Benson (*q.v.*) and Robert Hugh Benson (1871–1914)—were homosexual. Benson's friends were mostly gay, but Masters says of him (252): "He was wary of sex, distrusted it, feared it, and probably in the end avoided it."

Benson, E. F. *David Blaize*. London: Hodder & Stoughton, 1916. New York: Doran, 1916. *Intro. Peter Burton. London: Hogarth, 1989.
_____. *David of King's*. London: Hodder & Stoughton, 1924. *David Blaize of Kings*. New York: Doran, 1924. *Original title. Intro. Peter Burton. Brighton, Eng.: Millivres, 1991.
_____. *The Inheritor*. London: Hutchinson, 1930. Garden City, N.Y.: Doubleday, Doran, 1930. *Intro. Peter Burton. Brighton, Eng.: Millivres, 1992.
_____. *Ravens' Brood*. London: Barker, 1934. *Garden City, N.Y.: Doubleday, Doran, 1934.
Masters, Brian. *The Life of E. F. Benson*. London: Chatto & Windus, 1991.

18 Alec Waugh: *The Loom of Youth*, 1917.

In his preface to a new edition in 1955, the author claims "no book before *The Loom of Youth* had accepted as part of the fabric of School life the inevitable emotional consequences of a monastic herding together for eight months of the year of thirteen year old children and eighteen year old adolescents" (xiii). Benjamin Watson (*English Schoolboy Stories*, 154) adds, "The book contained the first public representation of homosexual acts between schoolboys, as opposed to the ardent, but chastely romantic friendships of earlier fiction." Following the lead of Arnold Lunn's *The Harrovians*, 1913—an iconoclastic novel which, according to Watson (100), Lunn wrote "to refute Horace Annesley Vachell's romantic picture of Harrow in *The Hill*" and which the protagonist of *Loom*, Gordon Caruthers, reads with appreciation (161–62)—Waugh's novel certainly provides an antidote to the sentimentality of such popular school novels as Thomas Hughes's venerated *Tom Brown's Schooldays*, 1857. Waugh's schoolboys take a jaundiced view of sports. They waste time playing practical jokes. Caning seems to be the prescribed punishment for infractions of rules. Rather than study, the boys rely on cribs. And the school masters are almost all second-rate. But, as Waugh notes, "The modern reader will find nothing here to shock or startle him" (xiii).

The reader may, in fact, miss any hint of sexual, or even emotional, liaisons. Waugh recounts a telling anecdote: "Several years ago a friend was reading the book in my company. 'When do I reach the scene?' he asked. I looked over his shoulder. 'You've passed it, ten pages back,' I told him" (xiii). A boy gets "bunked" because the headmaster finds out "all about" him and another boy (52–53). Gordon spurns an older boy's invitation "to meet him out for a walk" (37), but gradually "Gordon began to look on things which he once objected to as quite natural and ordinary." When Tester, the boy with whom he shares a study, asks him to clear out for a bit because another boy is dropping in ("You quite understand, don't you?"), he obligingly disappears (100). Then one day "Gordon asked Tester, rather shyly, if he would leave him alone a little. 'I've often cleared out for you, you know'" (101). Later he announces to Tester out of the blue, "I've broken it off with Jackson" (152). Still later he feels an attraction for a boy named Morcombe, and one gets a faint glimpse of their friendship in a chapter titled "Romance" (298–302). As Waugh said, it's all pretty tame stuff.

Alexander Raban Waugh (1898–1981) was the son of the writer and publisher Arthur Waugh, to whom he dedicated the novel. Like his father, Alec was educated at Sherborne, the model for the fictional school. A heterosexual, ironically he was expelled for homosexual activities. Written over a three-month period in 1916, when he was seventeen years old, the novel was published while he was serving in France and became a best seller, in great part because the reactions of parents and public school administrators created a scandal that his publisher used to advantage. The school became so infuriated by the controversy that it refused Alec's brother Evelyn a place there. For a long while, *Loom* provided a code for reviewers to indicate homosexual content in schoolboy stories without having to spell it out. Thus, the anonymous reviewer for the *Sydney Morning Herald* wrote of Lionel Birch's *Pyramid* (October 16, 1931, online): "Implications which appeared in Mr. Alec Waugh's 'Loom of Youth' also characterise this story, and Mr. Birch may be said to discuss the romantic and sentimental side of his hero's nature with tact and fairness."

Waugh, Alec. *The Loom of Youth*. London: Richards, 1917. New York: Doran, 1920. *Intro., author (1955). London: Bloomsbury Reader, 2012.

19   A. T. Fitzroy (Rose Allatini): *Despised and Rejected*, 1918. John Buchan: *Mr Steadfast*, 1919.

Would the importance of *Despised and Rejected* have been recognized from the beginning had the novel been prosecuted for obscenity, for its defense of homosexuality, instead of (as it was) for violation of the Defence of the Realm Act on the grounds that its pacifist tenets could hurt recruitment of military personnel? Appearing less than six months before the end of World War I, the publisher was found guilty and ordered to destroy all remaining copies of the novel. Nevertheless, it is a major document for the troubled road to gay liberation in Great Britain. Cultural historian H. G. Cocks (*Nameless Offences*, 196) sums up: "Her novel shows that the unspeakable quality of homosexual desire, when combined with the spiritual and evolutionary idiom which developed in the culture of British socialism [...] had clearly fostered a durable tradition which associated comradeship, homosexuality and higher consciousness."

A great part of the novel is taken up with the maneuvers of a rather mixed bohemian group—many of them Irish, many of them connected with various aesthetic pursuits—in support of conscientious objectors. The novel also supports feminist aims. But it presents an unabashed argument that homosexuality is actually normal. In essence, the author took the tenets of early crusaders such as Edward Carpenter (whose collection of poetry, *Towards Democracy*, 1883–1905, is mentioned in the novel in passing) and put them into the mouths of her characters. The critics were right: in this wise she was indeed subversive.

One has a wealth of passages to choose from as an example. Here is one from the very end of the novel, the passage that provides its title: "perhaps these men who stand mid-way between the extremes of the two sexes are the advance-guard of a more enlightened civilisation. They're despised and rejected of their fellow-men to-day. What they suffer in a world not yet ready to admit their right to existence, their right to love, no normal person can realise; but I believe that the time is not so far distant when we shall recognise in the best of our intermediate types the leaders and masters of the race. [...] From them a new humanity is being evolved" (348–49).

Some of its assumptions seem outdated now, but were common until recently. The cliché of the doting mother and the stern father appears. The idea that a lesbian has "a certain amount of the masculine element" in her, while the gay has "the feminine element" in him (220), is accepted: "what had nature been about, in giving him the soul of a woman in the body of a man?" (107). Several times an analogy is made between homosexuals and people who are physically crippled, arguing (as was done through the 1960s) that both should be treated with similar compassion. At the same time, through her characters, the author maintains that one's sexuality is not a matter of choice, and she has them argue that the true perversion is "to try and force ourselves to love differently" (250). The damages caused by the closet (though it has no label yet) are clearly delineated. The author anticipates the Kinsey scale (250). She notes the subtle way what we now call gaydar works (217), and she depicts, perhaps for the first time in a non-pornographic novel, the excitement and fears a person experiences in cruising the streets of London (185).

Dennis Blackwood is the eldest of four children. It is significant that he is a composer, since "musical" was one of the code words for homosexual at the time (think of *Teleny*). He has known that he is different since he was a boy and is able to recognize that difference in others (79–80). By the time he is fifteen he has accepted the fact but has been unable to act on it (221). Then, while on a walking tour in Cornwall, he meets Alan Rutherford, and the two fall instantly in love (not so improbable an event as some people think). But as before he is afraid of his own intense feelings and flees. War breaks out; Dennis files for exemption from the draft and begins to support the pacifist cause. Nearly two years later he encounters Alan again, another campaigner for pacifist principles. This time Dennis accepts his nature: "The senselessness of all his repression and self-denial stood revealed to him" (304). But now their happiness must be delayed while the two serve out brutal, inhumane prison sentences for their beliefs. The hard labor Dennis is sentenced to ruins his hands and thus his future as a pianist forever.

The novel is also of interest to lesbian readers. Between the first and the second encounter with Alan, Dennis tries to will himself into love with Antoninette de Courcy, whom he first meets at a hotel where his family has gone for the holidays. He recognizes in her "the same kink of abnormality" that he has in himself and thinks the two can "fight the loneliness better together" (215). But, "whereas he had always striven against these tendencies in himself, in herself she had never regarded them as abnormal" and they "had never caused her the slightest uneasiness" (217–18). Nevertheless, she is more thwarted than Alan in her pursuit of happiness. She earlier falls in love with another woman, but that flirtation comes to naught. By the end, however, she has become something of a fighter herself.

There were apparently links in the public mind at the time between pacificism, bohemianism, aestheticism, and homosexuality. The year after the war ended, Buchan published the third in his Richard Hannay series, *Mr Steadfast*. The hero is ordered to quit his military service for the moment to go undercover and make contact with a group of pacifists, one of whom is suspected of being a mastermind sending the Germans information of great usefulness to them in their war efforts. One of the first he encounters is Lancelot Wake, a young man with "hot" eyes and "rather more hair on his head than most of us" (315). Later Hannay encounters Wake in a manner that leads him to think he is a German agent, only to realize that he has gotten it wrong. Although Wake remains a committed pacifist, he does not ask for exemption and serves in a non-fighting position with the military. He pops up periodically thereafter, a constant thread through a complex and convoluted story in which he plays a minor but all-important role.

At one moment Wake bears his soul to Hannay: "My type of man is not meant for marriage, for women must be in the centre of life, and we must always be standing aside and looking on. It was a damnable thing to be born left-handed." He goes on to say that he has "ladylike nerves" and sums up: "I'm the kind of stuff poets are made of, but I haven't the poet's gift, so I stagger about the world left-handed and game-legged" (479–80). But it is Wake who guides Hannay on a seemingly impossible journey to save the woman with whom Hannay is in love. Hannay takes him onto his staff—"You're a stout fellow and I can't do without you" (544)—even though he knows that he will not violate his principles and fight. Wake is so efficient that another officer tells Hannay, "I wish to Heaven we had a few more conscientious objectors in this show" (550). Wake's final action is to get a crucial message to another commander in order to save the day. He is hit (symbolically?) in the groin and dies. At least Allatini saved her gay pacifists.

Rose Laure Allatini (1890–1980) was born in Vienna, the daughter of a Polish mother and an Italian father, but was reared in England. She was on the fringes of the Bloomsbury crowd. In 1921 she married music composer Cyril Scott and had two children. They separated in 1941, and Allatini thereafter shared a home in Rye with Melanie Mills. She wrote novels under the names R. Allatini, Lucian Wainwright, and Eunice Buckley, with just this one book as A. T. Fitzroy and another as Mrs. Cyril Scott. She was early interested in Jewish themes, then shifted to an interest in the occult.

A Scot, John Buchan, Baron Tweedsmuir (1857–1940), was born in Perth but grew up in Kirkcaldy. He attended the University of Glasgow and then studied at Oxford. He began simultaneously a diplomatic and a literary career. He served first as secretary to the British government's representative in South Africa. He enlisted in World War I and thereafter served in a number of important positions in Scotland. He was Governor General of Canada from 1935 until his death. Though he married and had four children, there has been speculation about his sexuality based on the evidence of the novels. For example, Robert Aldrich (*Colonialism and Homosexuality*, 137) notes, "Sexual ambivalence is evident in Buchan's most famous African novel, *Prester John*," 1910. One of the German villains in the second Hannay novel (*Greenmantle*, 1916) is described in terms that leave no doubt that he is homosexual.

Buchan, John. *Mr Steadfast*. London: Hodder & Stoughton, 1919. Boston: Houghton Mifflin, 1919. *The Complete Richard Hannay Stories*. Ware, Eng.: Wordsworth, 2010. 305–569.

Fitzroy, A. T. *Despised and Rejected*. London: Daniel, 1918. *Intro. Jonathan Cutbill. London: GMP, 1988.

20 Ronald Firbank: *Valmouth*, **1919;** *The Flower Beneath the Foot*, **1923;** *Concerning the Eccentricities of Cardinal Pirelli*, **1926.**

Though Firbank's fiction is generally included in any list of gay writing, in truth it is not so much gay as polymorphously perverse. Sexuality is slippery in his novels; innuendo is pervasive. The reader runs the dangers both of seeing too much in the author's casual comments and of missing a sly insinuation. Take, for example, an incident in the opening scene of *Concerning the Eccentricities of Cardinal Pirelli*. The cardinal has just baptized a puppy when the dog gets away and engages in an "incestuous" romp with his father, a police-dog also present. In the fracas, "Monsignor Silex started slightly, as, from the estrade beneath the dome, a choir-boy let fall a little white spit" (647). Much later, Madame Poco, who is being paid to spy on the cardinal's antics, is cleaning his chasuble, "worn last by his Eminence at the baptism of the blue-eyed police-pup of the Duquesa DunEden, which bore still the primrose trace of an innocent insult. […] Not everyone knew the dog was christened in *white menthe* ... 'Sticky stuff,' she brooded" (667). Is one being dirty-minded or attuned to Firbank's style to suspect the choirboy has ejaculated on the scene below? For, obviously, spit and menthe could be just that and the insult, the dog's urine. If ever an author needs an annotated edition, Firbank is one.

Cardinal Pirelli is routinely described as his gayest novel. Certainly the cardinal has a fine eye for male flesh, especially his acolytes. One of them is overheard saying that something "frightened me like Father did, when he kissed me in the dark" (656). Pirelli recalls with pleasure "the persistent officer who had the effrontery to attempt to molest him" when he was younger (651). He likes to go disguised, sometimes as a caballero, sometimes as a matron, into the streets. And the book is filled with innuendos that are indeed innuendos. When Madame Poco mentions that she thinks to take some ailing choirboys "some melons," the cardinal adds, "And, perhaps, a cucumber" (650). The novel is virtually plotless, taken up with the little affairs of the church (the setting is mostly in Spain), the one constant thread being the tension created by his increasingly erratic conduct. Before there can be any showdown between the pro- and the anti–Pirellian factions, however, the cardinal suffers a heart attack, brought on by overexertion while chasing a choirboy, and dies: "Dispossessed of everything but his fabulous mitre, the Primate was nude and elementary now as Adam himself" (697).

All of his works, though short in length, have a large cast of characters, generally christened with recherché names. Gays, bisexual males, and androgynous figures play only minor roles in earlier novels. Women, straight and lesbian, are the major figures. Their dialog is likewise filled with double entendres. Take this, for example, from *Valmouth*, a story about the caprices of women in an English spa town: "'I once peeped under a bishop's apron!' 'Oh...?' 'And what ever did you see?' [...] 'I saw ... the dear Bishop!'" (407). According to Partridge's *Dictionary of Slang*, 8th ed., the term was used for the penis dating from the late 19th century; surely Firbank heard it thus employed. His big topics, however, are society and religion, race and sexuality, in equal measure. To emphasize the sexuality is to follow only a thread of a densely woven fabric.

There does seem to be an evolution in Firbank's introduction of gay themes the further Wilde's trials recede in time. In *Vainglory*, 1915, we get just a glimpse of the musician Winsome Brookes (who is contemplating changing his name to Rose de Tivoli) and his roommate painter, Arthur (105–09). In *Valmouth* Captain Dick Thoroughfare—a man who "has a many-sided nature" (447)—dwells fondly on his life on sea and his relationship with "his middy-chum, Jack Whorwood, who was not much over fifteen, and the youngest hand on board. 'That little lad,' he had said, with a peculiar smile [...], 'upon a cruise, is, to me, what Patroclus was to Achilles, and even more'" (398). Jack, we find, "resembled singularly some girl masquerading as a boy for reasons of romance" (453), and later the author mentions he has "romantical curls" (465). Too, the town has suspicions about the role the painter Victor Vatt plays for his pupils. They grow "quite hot and red and religious-looking" while watching him at work (397). When Dick Thoroughfare's mother asks, "Those disciples of his [...], oh; are they all they seem?" the answer is, "Lady Lucy Saunter swears not!" (405).

In *The Flower beneath the Foot*, we watch the Honorable Eddy Monteith being bathed by his manservant: "Beneath the rhythmic sponge, perfumed with *Kiki*, he was St. Sebastian, and as the water became cloudier, and the crystals evaporated amid the steam, he was Teresa ... and he would have been, most likely, the Blessed Virgin herself but that the bath grew gradually colder" (536). Like others of Firbank's characters Eddy enjoys flagellation and regrets that the early death of his friend Robbie Renard has deprived him of that lad's discipline (537). On an archeological dig in the ruins of Sodom and Gomorrah, he meets his own demise: "the shock received by meeting a jackal while composing a sonnet had been too much for him" (581). We are also introduced to Count Cabinet, who lives on the island of St. Helena, attended by "his 'useful' secretary and amanuensis, Peter Passer." When we first see them, the count has just landed "a distinguished mauvish fish with vivid scarlet spots." Pondering on "the subtle variety there is in Nature," he thinks about "its trials and persecutions, its hours of superior difficulty ... and the Count with a stoic smile recalled his own" (565). It is a quintessential Firbankian moment.

Arthur Annesley Ronald Firbank (1886–1926) was born in London. He attended Cambridge but did not take a degree. A convert to Catholicism, he was openly gay. He was also an alcoholic. He traveled widely around the Mediterranean and died in Rome. Firbank described himself in his novel *Sorrow in Sunlight*, 1924, as "a dingy lilac blossom of rarity untold" (631). He was influenced by Wilde (who is the model for a character in his play *The Princess Zoubaroff*, 1920, while Firbank's novel *The Artificial Princess*, 1934, is a retelling of Wilde's play *Salomé*), and in turn he influenced such writers as Aldous Huxley, Evelyn Waugh, and Angus Wilson. Sandy Wilson turned *Valmouth* into a musical comedy in 1958, importing Cardinal Pirelli to play a part.

Benkovitz, Miriam J. *Ronald Firbank: A Biography*. New York: Knopf, 1969.
Firbank, Ronald. *Concerning the Eccentricities of Cardinal Pirelli*. London: Richards, 1926. **The Complete Ronald Firbank*. Intro. Anthony Powell. London: Duckworth, 1961. 645–98.
———. *The Flower Beneath the Foot: Being a Record of the Early Life of St. Laura de Nazianzi and the Times in Which She Lived*. London: Richards, 1923; New York: Brentano's, 1924. **The Complete Ronald Firbank* (see above). 499–592.
———. *Valmouth: A Romantic Novel*. London: Richards, 1919. **The Complete Ronald Firbank* (see above). 387–477.

21 Ernest Raymond: *Tell England*, 1922.

Even more than in Vachell's novel, the all-male world of the public school is yoked here to that of the military. The first part is set in the tranquil days before World War I; the second part takes place during the deadly Gallipoli campaign. The two principal characters are Rupert Ray, the narrator, and Edgar Gray Doe—"twins," since they share the same birthday and age. They are compared both to David and Jonathan (23) and to Orestes and Pylades (107). Ray acknowledges the enormous impact Cicero's *De Amicitia* has had on his emotions. Doe is girlish in appearance and behavior, and Rupert muses "that this feeling of love at first sight for the girl Doe, who never existed, I count as one of the strongest forces that helped to create my later affection for the real Edgar Gray Doe" (38). Doe has crushes on various males. Of a schoolmaster he says, after being punished, "I simply loved being whacked by him" (37). The more sinister and slightly older schoolmate Freedham holds that "there must be no sensation—a law, or no law—which he has not experienced," to which Doe replies, "There are not many things we haven't done together" (117). But he returns to Ray as his great friend.

The two boys go off to war together. Both, as we know from the beginning, will be killed (Ray's manuscript comes to us through the offices of the army chaplain). While waiting orders, Ray says, "we began to believe that vicious things, which in our boyhood had been very secret sins, were universally committed and bragged about," while Doe sententiously professes that "human nature is human nature, and you can't alter it. I don't think any man is, or can be, what they call 'pure.'" Ray further records, "And, after all this, it was an easy step, lightly taken to the things of night. We set out for the strange streets" (173–74). In the course of the novel we get some unconscious but delicious double entendres: Ray says of Doe, "my affection for him began at once to throb into activity" (113), and he later writes, "a certain abnormality in the conversation had stimulated me" (117). In the first volume of his autobiography, *The Story of My Days*, 1968, the author mused, "Another thing that is a cause of wonder to me as I re-read the book is the indubitable but wholly unconscious homosexuality in it."

Ernest Raymond (1888–1974) was born in Argentieres, France, the illegitimate son of an army officer. He grew up in the home of his mother's abusive sister; his own, unacknowledged mother and her family lived nearby. He obtained a theological degree from Durham University and was ordained a priest in the Church of England in 1914, serving as a chaplain during World War I. He was married twice and had three children. The novel was the basis for two movies.

Raymond, Ernest. *Tell England: A Study in a Generation.* *London: Cassell, 1922. New York: Doran, 1922.

22   Beverley Nichols: *Crazy Pavements,* 1927.

It is regretful that Nichols felt unable to write the story he wanted to tell. Bryan Connon, his biographer, recalls (127) that in a 1982 interview Nichols discussed the problems he faced muting any hints of actual sex between the main character, Brian Elme, and his best friend, Walter Moore, and disguising the fact that the chief woman character, Lady Julia, was actually based on a predatory queen. Still, Brian and Walter's emotional dependence on each other is obvious. In his introduction to a new edition of the book, David Deutsch writes (viii): "Nichols champions, then, for perhaps the first time in British literary history, a fairly physical, if not overtly sexual, homoeroticism between two men with modest incomes as a successful ideal."

Twenty-year-old Brian writes the gossip column for *The Lady's Mail.* That is to say, he makes up stories about rich and titled people, generally those who are off for foreign places or otherwise engaged and thus unlikely to chance onto his fictions. An attractive young man, with "quite exceptional charm," he receives "absurd hero-worship" from Walter, a young ex-naval officer, from the time the two "had casually come across each other" (13–14). Their actual living arrangements are left vague, even confusing. The important matter is: they are extremely happy together. But their idyllic world falls apart as a result of an item Brian concocts about one Lady Julia. Instead of being amused, she threatens his job unless he publicly apologizes (which would mean he would still lose his job). In an attempt to avert disaster, his editor suggests that he make an appointment with the lady and apologize in person. The result is that she decides to cultivate the naïve youth and introduce him into the society of the Bright Young People. Because of his looks and his innocence, he becomes the season's item. All the attention turns Brian's head. When he refuses to listen to Walter concerning the truth about his new friends and strikes out, Walter can take no more and disappears (126).

As one would expect, any number of homosexuals appear in Julia's company. The two most prominent are Lord William Motley and Maurice Cheyne. Maurice we are told left Eton under a cloud. At a climatic moment, he accuses Brian: "You think I'm a freak, effeminate, something that ought to have been strangled at birth." But he has the courage to accept, "I can't help how I'm made" (175). Lord William came of age during the Gay Nineties, but he confesses, "I was not of them. I ignored them. If I had found green carnations growing in Hyde Park, I should have suspected them to be lettuces. Besides, I have no use for an age in which one could gain a bad reputation merely by wearing a flower" (53). Many of his remarks seem modeled on Wilde's. But for all his apparent superficiality, he is capable of penetrating the various faces that the fashionable people put on. In a secret room filled with masks, caricatures he has created that reveal the truth behind the facade, his latest creation shows "a face of extraordinary charm, but the face of a fool, [...] a face curiously like that of the hero of our story" (69).

The revulsion that Brian feels when Lord William's own mask slides awry to reveal his inner corruption precipitates a final confrontation between him and Lady Julia. When he refuses to go along with a scheme she concocts for him, without hesitation she dismisses him: "What *are* you? [...] A pretty boy. Not quite so pretty as he was, but still pretty enough. And rather spoilt. [...] Well, let me tell you that you're merely rather a vulgar second-rate reporter. That and nothing more. [...] Well, you've had a long run for your money. You can disappear. And the sooner you disappear the better" (209–10). Just as quickly as Brian has been taken up, he is dropped. His first reaction is to seek revenge by creating items for his gossip column that are truthful, but as a sign of his growth, he recognizes the futility. He goes searching through the pubs for Walter, and the two men return home.

John Beverley Nichols (1898–1983) was born in Bristol. He attended Marlborough and Oxford. Beginning as a journalist, he wrote all kinds of books and plays but is remembered primarily for his works about gardening. From 1932 until his death he lived with the actor Cyril Butcher (1909–1987). Nichols was convinced that Waugh cribbed a great part of *Vile Bodies*, 1930, from *Crazy Pavements*.

Connon, Bryan. *Beverley Nichols: A Life*. 1991. Portland, Ore.: Timber, 2000.

Nichols, Beverley. *Crazy Pavements*. London: Cape, 1927. *Intro. David Deutsch. Kansas City, Mo.: Valancourt, 2013.

23 Compton Mackenzie: *Vestal Fire*, 1927; *Thin Ice*, 1956. James Aston (T. H. White), *They Winter Abroad*, 1932. Note on Norman Douglas: *South Wind*, 1917.

Between the time of Wilde's trials in 1895 and the great depression, the island of Capri witnessed a steady stream of homosexuals, some just passing through, others seeking longer term residence. They included, in rough chronological order, Somerset Maugham, Fred Benson, John Ellingham Brooks (who later married the American artist Romaine Goddard, though both were homosexual), Robert Ross, Alfred Douglas, Wilde himself, the German munitions maker Friedrich Alfred Krupp, Norman Douglas, the French poet Baron Jacques d'Adelswärd-Fersen, Mackenzie, Reggie Turner, and Kenneth Macpherson, as well as Conrad and Lawrence. And of course there were gay Italians, many of note. James Money has written a comprehensive history of life on the island, homosexual and heterosexual, expatriate and native: *Capri: Island of Pleasure*.

George Norman Douglas (1868–1952) was the first to see the fictional possibilities. His *South Wind* became a prototype for expatriate novels. Recreating the island as Nepenthe, he follows the story of an Anglican bishop paying a visit on his female cousin who resides there. The bishop meets various natives, compatriots, and other visitors. Despite having a riot and ending with a murder, there is more talk than there is action. Robert Aldrich (*The Seduction of the Mediterranean*, 131–32) notes, "Sexual tension and ambiguity suffuse the novel." His catalog of its homosexual components cannot be bettered: "Douglas writes straight-forwardly of the heterosexual interests of the expatriates but is more coy in reference to homosexuality. One young Briton, Denis Phipps, 'an absurdly good-looking youth,' is the object of desire for several men and the object of curiosity to many. As one says to him, 'You're a queer fellow, Phipps. Don't you ever look at women?' [...] As Denis serves drinks to a group of men, 'the priest smiled at the sight. Light-hearted allusions to Ganymede rose to his lips, but were repressed.' Phipps openly flirts with the visiting bishop, a local aristocrat, Count Caloveglia, and others; in one scene, he disports himself in the sun in 'a voluptuous pose.'" However, none of the earliest gay bibliographies considered *South Wind* gay enough to include it on their lists.

Mackenzie's *roman à clef* is a different matter. The novel gives a thinly disguised account of real people and events on the island of "Sirene." In an appendix to his book, Money identifies the real-life person behind the pseudonyms. It is amazing that Mackenzie was not sued. Dedicated to Brooks (who was a model for the character Ernest Eames in Douglas's novel), *Vestal Fire* is relatively open, at least for the times, about the homosexuality of many of its characters, male and female. When the American Nigel Dawson first appears, his proclivities are left vague: merely that "several people had hinted at the most extraordinary things" (24). But a bit later, a woman gushes, "Such a dear boy! One of those. But what does it matter? Why shouldn't he be?" (47). Still later a male objects that "he is an effeminate and corrupt young decadent" (96). From the beginning, however, the reader is left no doubts about the new Anglican chaplain, the Reverend Cyril Acott. One of the women plans to impress him "by gushing over the beauties of *The Pilgrim's Process* [...] but diving his tastes within ten minutes she had transformed *The Pilgrim's Progress* into *The Picture of Dorian Gray* so swiftly that before the visit was over Mr. Acott was confiding to her what difficulty he had to make his altar-boys see life steadily and see it whole" (87). A self-righteous woman complains: "Imagine that little whippersnapper of an Acott having the jolly impudence to make that unhealthy young Dawson his churchwarden. An American too! And then he's a friend of that filthy Duncan Maxwell [based on Douglas]. I'm told that the orgies in the Villa Partenope last Winter were unspeakable. Unspeakable, my dear! Are we living in the time of Tiberius, or are we living in the time of Edward VII?" Further revelations about Acott link him to "Oxford decadence" (98–99).

The novel centers on a French expatriate, Count Robert Marsac-Lagerström (obviously, d'Adelswärd-Fersen). No sooner does he arrive with his "secretary," Signor Carlo di Fiore (Nino Cesarini), than he secures allies in the persons of two lesbians, Miss Virginia Pepworth and Miss Maimie Norton, or the Pepworth-Nortons. As a result, "Marsac's triumph in Sirene was immediate and conspicuous. People were so much fascinated by the unusual combination of wealth, youth, rank, and good looks that they received the volumes of his poems that he dealt round like a hand at bridge with more respect than they would have accorded to first folios of Shakespeare" (54). Then rumors reach Sirene that Marsac was "mixed up in a rather unsavoury mess in Paris" with minors that led to his being sentenced to a year's imprisonment. (In one of several comic moments in the novel, the churchwarden thinks he has corrupted miners: "Good lord, what a degenerate brute! Not coalminers surely?" [157].) Public opinion with regard to Marsac divides into two opposed factions. By now a hopeless opium addict, the count hardly helps his case with his flamboyant disregard for others' tastes and feelings. Seeking revenge, he publishes a novel *La Statue Mutilée* that leaves "hardly a person or a profession, a nationality or an individual on Sirene that did not find something to insult him" (247). The community bands together to demand he be banned from Italy. Four years pass before he and Carlo are permitted to return. World War I provides further disruptions, Carlo being called to serve in the military. Even the novel seems to wind down. Marsac's suicide comes as a relief.

In talking about Marsac's novel, the author of *Vestal Fire* drops a tantalizing comment: "It is remarkable how nearly always fatal prose is to the pretentiously styled Uranian temperament, which time after time shirks honest self-revelation in such a medium, but continually seeks by an endogenous understanding of women, an almost uterine intelligence, to atone for its inability to create men. One day a novelist with that temperament will have the courage to write about himself as he is, not as he would be were he actually Jane or Gladys or Aunt Maria. And that will be a novel worth reading, not an obstetrical feat" (246). In 1959 the French author Roger Peyrefitte published his fictionalized biography of Adelswärd-Fersen, *L'Exile de Capri* (translated into English in 1961). It is a more satisfying work. Douglas plays a prominent role; Mackenzie gets only a sentence in the epilogue.

The satiric novel *They Winter Abroad* provides something of a coda. When the English tourists take an excursion to Capri from the mainland, they stop by a bookstore: "There were books in every European language; but chiefly there were books by Compton Mackenzie, Norman Douglas [...]" (271). The professor in their group, recalling stories about Tiberius and Adelswärd-Fersen, says, "a regular brand of Capri literature has developed, and the legend has grown to such an extent that it has assumed flesh and blood. Real homosexuals visit the island incognito, hoping to meet their kind. Fiction has given birth to fact" (255). Already on the boat over, the thirty-three-year-old Mr. McInvert has "come to a decision. For about the second time in his life he was going to try it, to risk it, whatever the consequences" (247). After the professor's little speech, "Mr McInvert's mind returned to the workers in the ravine. When he got back he would definitely chance it. It was no good going on living like this. And, besides, his love might be returned" (256). He has become smitten with a construction worker at his hotel in Positano, one who is as "beautiful as Adonis" and who plays "a set of reeds, the authentic Pan-pipe" (45). But when he returns from Capri, the workers are not there, having been given the day off for a fiesta. With no explanation, the lonely Englishman climbs over the railing and plunges to the rocks below. Learning that there is a document wherein the dead man has written "the story of his life, a protest against authority, a vehement petition of right" (239), the professor hastens to destroy it before the police arrive and thus avert any further scandal. To be honest, however, the story begs for comparison with Forster's two Italian novels more than it does with Mackenzie's.

The Aston pseudonym conceals T. H. White, the author of *The Once and Future King*, 1938–58. According to his biographer, Sylvia Townsend Warner, an earlier homosexual novel was shelved when the scandal erupted around Radclyffe Hall's *The Well of Loneliness*, then retrieved and rewritten as a heterosexual romance, *First Lesson*, 1932, also published under the Aston name. Terence Hanbury White (1906–1964) was born in Bombay to unhappily married English parents. Sent to his grandparents' home in England, he attended Cheltenham and Cambridge. After teaching for a number of years, he turned to writing, including science fiction and then his retelling of the Arthurian legends. White lived in neutral Ireland during World War II. After the war, he settled on Alderney Island in the English Channel. Warner transcribes diary entries, 1957–60, that record his hopeless love for a boy named Zed. White died aboard a ship at Piraeus, Greece, while returning home from a lecture tour.

Nearly thirty years later, Mackenzie published his second gay novel, *Thin Ice*, also something of a *roman à clef*, about a British politician. According to historian Patrick Higgins (*Heterosexual Dictatorship*, 98), it came about because of a comment made two years earlier at the first meeting of the Wolfenden Committee. The problem of blackmail that the Labouchère amendment of 1885 created was discussed. Mackenzie overheard one barrister who "estimated that three-quarters of all suicides were blackmailed homosexuals," and this provided the germ for the novel. Mackenzie includes the comment in *Thin Ice* (177) but ascribes it to the year 1939. In possibly another anachronism, a character in 1929 says, "Nowadays [...] the jury would take the word of any policeman before that of any politician" (127–28). Higgins goes on about the novel (98), "The main character was mainly based on his friend Lord [George] Lloyd (who had died in 1941) but had elements of Tom Driberg and Chips [Henry] Channon as well." Driberg, in his memoirs (*Ruling Passions*, 146) recognized himself "clearly" in the novel.

George "GeeGee" Gaymer, the straight (and sometimes dense) narrator of *Thin Ice* says that his account "is not a biography of my friend Henry Fortescue but merely an account of my own relationship with him" (138). It covers the years 1896 to 1941, from the time they first met at Oxford until Henry's death in a blitz attack on London. Henry serves as a member of Parliament until his party loses power; when he is killed, he is serving as Director of the Eastern Bureau because of his expertise in the Middle East. Throughout he is defiantly sexual: "I realized that for me discretion was impossible. It had to be complete self-denial, or complete surrender. And walking about for ever on thin ice does not appeal to me" (57). GeeGee records his relationships with Edward Carstairs, a career diplomat; Guy Liscombe, Henry's young secretary until he falls in love with Edward; rent boys, one of whom tries to blackmail him and brutally attacks him with a blackjack; and a series of casual pickups, one of which leads to his arrest.

The novel betrays a confused attitude towards homosexuality. Anecdotes about the sexual demimonde are all fairly negative, including the ones put in Henry's mouth. Gays are presented as misogynists (55), to the point of putting down effeminate gays (104), fair weather friends when it comes to sex (121), and always promiscuous. At the same time GeeGee, records his horror that men "who earned a livelihood from the sale of themselves" should possess "the evil power the law placed in the hands of such creatures" to blackmail their clients Hard on the heels of that comment, he says, "I began to study the phenomenon of homosexuality and was amazed to discover that so far from being the sign of a decadent society it was conspicuously prevalent in England during the first quarter of the eighteenth century when the national vigour was at its height" (176). Henry brings up the unfairness to both the wives and any children when gays feel forced by society to marry (123). And he comments wryly on the fact "that in this respectable century of ours we still set the Second Eclogue of Virgil to be learnt as repetition by twelve-year-olds" (125).

Edward Montague Compton Mackenzie (1883-1972) was born in England but self-identified as a Scot. Educated at Oxford, he became a widely popular novelist. One finds conflicting statements about his sexuality. His biographer, Andro Linklater, claims that he was straight (although possibly having engaged in the usual public school affairs), but enjoyed the company of gays. Shirley Hazzard in her memoir of Graham Greene on Capri asserts he was bisexual. *Vestal Fire* was followed by a lesbian "sequel," *Extraordinary Women*, 1928, dedicated to Douglas. Widowed, Mackenzie married twice more. He died in Edinburgh.

Aston, James. *They Winter Abroad.* *London: Chatto & Windus, 1932. New York: Viking, 1932.
Douglas, Norman. *South Wind*. London: Secker, 1917. *New York: Modern Library, 1924.
Holloway, Mark. *Norman Douglas: A Biography*. London: Secker & Warburg, 1976.
Linklater, Andro. *Compton Mackenzie: A Life*. London: Chatto & Windus, 1987.
Mackenzie, Compton. *Thin Ice.* *London: Chatto & Windus, 1956. New York: Putnam's, 1957.
———. *Vestal Fire*. London: Cassell, 1927. *New York: Doran, 1927.
Money, James. *Capri: Island of Pleasure*. 1986. London: Faber, 2012.
Peyrefitte, Alan. *The Exile of Capri*. Trans. Edward Hyams. 1961. *New York: Fleet, 1965.
Warner, Sylvia Townsend. *T. H. White: A Biography*. 1967. New York: Viking, 1968.

24 Kenneth Macpherson: *Gaunt Island*, 1927; *Rome 12 Noon*, 1964. Bryher: *The Player's Boy*, 1953.

The intricate web of relationships that husband and wife established with other artists may be more important to gay literature than their actual writing. Bryher (1894-1983), the older of the two, was born Annie Winifred Ellman in Margate, the illegitimate daughter of one of the wealthiest men in England; she legally changed her name. In 1918 she began a longtime alliance with the American poet Hilda Doolittle (H.D.). On a trip to the United States, the two met the closeted American writer and later Paris publisher Robert McAlmon; he and Bryher entered into a marriage of convenience in 1921. On their return to Europe, Bryher established a home in Switzerland, but the McAlmons were frequently in Paris, where they became part of the expatriate scene. In 1926 Kenneth Macpherson (1902-1971) entered the scene. He was bisexual. His early years remain obscure, but in London in 1924 he met Frances Gregg, an American writer and H.D.'s former lover; she introduced the two in 1926, and Macpherson fell in love with H.D. But it was Bryher whom he married in 1927, upon her divorce from McAlmon. They adopted H.D.'s young daughter and set up a *ménage à trois* with H.D. in Switzerland. The three formed the Pool Group, a filmmaking and publishing enterprise. The group brought out the important film magazine *Close Up*, 1927-33. Under its auspices, in 1930 Macpherson created the avant-garde film *Borderline*, his only feature length movie, with H.D. and the singer Paul Robeson. His father, the Scottish painter John Macpherson, did the lighting.

Pool also published Macpherson's first two novels. *Gaunt Island* was based on his own family. It is so elliptical and its language often so precious that it is difficult to follow the story. It recounts a fateful summer in the lives of the Mannering family, the inhabitants of Quhele. Sons Robin and Geoffrey are in love with each other. Robin tries to explain his emotions to his parents. He begins, "This morning at lunch I spoke of a book where the love of two men was the motif, and to me it was extremely beautiful." He then asks, "Is there any reason why—say why I should not love Geoffrey if I want to? Is there any logical reason why it should be open to censure? Has anyone any possible right to judge it or forbid it?" The father responds: "Two words spat weakly, like dazzled moths; singed and burnt out." When Robin looks at him unbelieving what he has heard, he says, "There you have it in plain language. Do you like it?" (78–79). What the two words are, we are given no clue. And this is typical of the entire novel.

The implications of incest are never discussed, but Robin's and Geoffrey's love is given no chance anyway. The wife of the local Justice of the Peace, Agnes Scott, desires to seduce Robin. Already declared insane, Elmo Gauvain, a new arrival to the Little House, a short way from them, also poses a threat. The two women (based on Frances Gregg and Brigit Patmore) destroy him. Robin contrasts the world's attitude towards homosexuality and heterosexual transgressions: "Geoffrey, the Michael-Angelo David was ugly, and he was ugly for holding out hands. Aggie Scott, was approved and chosen. She met their standards" (86). Robin's death prepares Geoffrey for the next stage in his existence, a freedom he has not known before (199).

A copy of Macpherson's second novel, *Poolreflection*, 1927, has eluded me. Barbara Guest, H.D.'s biographer (who compares it to her *Hedylus* in the passages here omitted), describes it (185) as "a struggle between a woman and the father of her son for the love of the son. The son returns to the father, although warned by the mother [...] that his father desires not only his soul [...] but his body as well."

In 1935 Macpherson began a twelve year association with New York City, where Peggy Guggenheim became his patron and lover, but his true sexual interest was the African-American men whom he was meeting. Bryher remained in Switzerland, helping people escape Nazi persecution before she was forced to flee herself. She and H.D. spent the war in London. Upon Macpherson's return to Europe in 1947, he and Bryher divorced, and she bought a home for him and his lover, the Welsh photographer Islay Lyons (1922–1993) on Capri, with the request that they take in the ailing Norman Douglas.

During the 1950s Bryher wrote a number of historical novels. One, *The Player's Boy*, set in the period 1605–26, follows a boy actor, James Sand, who does not succeed in the profession. It consistently appears on lists of gay novels. That seems a stretch, even more so by comparing it to truly gay novels being published at the same time. Renée Curry (*Gay & Lesbian Literature,* edited by Sharon Malinowski, 57) sums up the plot thus: "In this novel, the author depicts her primary male character, Sands, as inept in his male role by situating him in [...] homoerotic relationships [...]. Sands must ultimately decide whether he wants to spend his life with his good friend Martin as a sailor or remain on the stage as a mediocre player; in the end, his fear of the relationship renders him unable to accompany the sailor. Over the remainder of the plot, Sands becomes involved with another man who betrays him and participates in an ill-fated love triangle. It is only when he finally prepares to die that Sands realizes he should have gone to sea with Martin." Curry's facts are accurate, but it is not the synopsis that I would have made.

After Douglas's death in 1952, his will making Macpherson his principal beneficiary, he moved to Rome, the setting for his third novel, *Rome 12 Noon*. Conventional in manner, the novel's plot is set in motion by an accident involving three people. Adriana, the widowed daughter of a count and mother of a teenage son, steps into the traffic without looking. She is stuck by Peppino, who has just completed his military service and bought a new Vespa. Paolo Falconieri is the policeman on duty. Adriana is only shaken up, but their lives are now fatefully intertwined. The major portion of the novel follows what happens to her, including her marriage to Paolo, her fights with her domineering father, and her worries over her son and his future. Taken by Peppino's courtesy after the accident, she is instrumental in getting him a job as chauffeur for her father and his mistress. His new position brings the family to the attention of Carlu Cossu. Before Peppino's army service, he and Carlu were sexual buddies; Peppino is on the way to see him when he strikes Adriana.

A flamboyant gay who peroxides his hair and uses makeup (12), a "creature both monstrous and beautiful," his hand usually "lovingly round his groin" (122), Carlu restakes his claim on Peppino, addressing him with terms of insincere endearment: "Funny the way I can't live without you, and you such a half-wit. Why do I think of you? Not because of your brilliance, your hopeless, passionate love for me, or even your gorgeous girth [...] I'm human, honey, getting envious of all those others, tired of waiting loveless and lonely" (244). Unfortunately for Peppino, Carlu retains the mentality of a petty criminal. He sees Peppino as the means to robbing the family he works for. Aldo Arnini, Adriana's butler, turns out to be a third gay character. He and Peppino become lovers. But they are powerless to stop Carlu. Disguised in drag, Carlu and an accomplice truss up poor Aldo and reconnoiter her apartment. Outraged, Peppino, agrees to Paolo's scheme to trap Carlu. But he then makes the fatal mistake of telling his sister too much. The last words Peppino hears are, "Baby doll [...], I really hate to do this to that sweet warm flesh; it's just because I love you so" (290).

In 1965 Macpherson moved to Tuscany to work on Elisabeth Moor's memoirs. She served as physician on Capri, including attending to Douglas. The book was published posthumously in 1975 with an introduction by Graham Greene. Macpherson died in Cetona, willing everything, including his Douglas inheritance, to Lyons. Bryher died at her home in Vevey, Switzerland.

Byrher. *The Player's Boy*. New York: Pantheon, 1953. London: Collins, 1957. *Intro. Patrick Gregory. Ashfield, Mass.: Paris, 2006.
Guest, Barbara. *Herself Defined: The Poet H.D. and Her World*. Garden City, N.Y.: Doubleday, 1984.
Macpherson, Kenneth. *Gaunt Island*. Territet, Switzerland: Pool, 1927.
———. *Rome 12 Noon*. London: Collins & Harvill, 1964. *New York: Coward–McCann, 1964.
Rooney, Padraig. "The Hominterm: The Photographic World of Islay Lyons (1922–1993)." Basel Blog, 10 Mar. 2013 (online).

25 Rosamond Lehmann: *Dusty Answer*, 1927. Radclyffe Hall: *The Well of Loneliness*, 1928. Mary Butts: *Armed with Madness*, 1928; *Death of Felicity Taverner*, 1932.

This set of novels with a strong woman protagonist for whom a gay male plays a role of importance is probably of more interest to lesbian readers than to gay ones.

Lehmann's first novel created something of a scandal when it was published. The heroine, Judith Earle, falls in love with a fellow student, Jennifer Baird, at Cambridge, but then Jennifer is lured away by the more worldly Geraldine Manners. At the same time Judith is increasingly captivated by Roddy Fyfe, whom she has known since they were children. Just as she remains unaware of the threat posed by Geraldine until too late, she does not recognize that her rival for Roddy's affections is the obviously gay Tony Barron. He is stereotypical both in appearance ("sensitive face," "sensuous lips," "a slight lisp," and "thin unmasculine hands,—queer hands") and in manner: "She heard him call Roddy 'my dear,' and once 'darling'; and had a passing shock" (95–96). Julian Fyfe tells her, "I gather from his conversation he is *quite* the thing at Cambridge—in certain circles" (100). Even after she knows that the two men have moved into an intimate relationship, she still thinks she can win, until she sees them through a window together. When Roddy symbolically "slipped with his companion towards the edge of the pane; and vanished," she finally accepts that "Tony would have him all to himself now" (300–01).

Hall's polemical lesbian novel calling for tolerance, along with its subsequent obscenity trials in both England and New York, remains one of the most notorious publications of the 20th century. The struggle of its heroine Stephen Gordon, an author, to accept her sexuality is aided at three significant points by a popular, closeted playwright: Jonathan Brockett (modeled on Noël Coward). Curiously, he is also identified in part by his hands: they "were as white and soft as a woman's" (226). Jonathan is honest about the shortcoming of Stephen's last book. He encourages her to move to the freer society that she would find in Paris, And after she settles in with an ambulance driver she meets during the war, he urges her to mingle more in the Parisian lesbian salons. Among their company she meets a number of other gay men, including a designer, Adolphe Blanc, a man "of all men, the most normal abnormal" (351). The novel is chaste and actually paints a dismal picture of the homosexual demimonde. It seems incredible that it was brought to trial. Not only that, but in the courtroom farce created by a bigoted judge, it lost. The American publisher was determined that that would not be the case in the U.S.; when it went to trial in New York, it was acquitted of obscenity charges. However, it was then subjected to a 1934 film adaptation by Richard Kahn—known by two different titles, *The Third Sex* or *Children of Loneliness*—that countered everything Hall had tried to achieve.

Set on the Cornwall coast, Butts's two *Taverner* novels are pretty simple stories rendered grandiose and opaque by allusions to Arthurian legends. The author was heavily influenced by Jessie Weston's study *From Ritual to Romance*, 1920. Drusilla (Scylla) Taverner is the central character. In the first novel she is circled by men vying for her favors, though the sexuality of several of them is ambiguous. An ancient cup is found in a well, and the myth of the Grail is invoked. Her brother Felix is gay. At the end, having flown momentarily to Paris, Felix returns with a White Russian, Boris Polteratsky (who first appears in Butts's epistolary novella, *Imaginary Letters*, 1928). Boris plays a definitive role in the second novel, a struggle over an inheritance with many references to the Sacred Wood. Readers of a certain temperament will be enchanted by her novels; others will be exasperated.

Rosamond Nina Lehmann (1901–1990) grew up in a literary family (her gay brother, John Lehmann, became an important publisher) and was associated with the Bloomsbury group. Although her novel is to some degree autobiographical, she was twice married and the mother of two children. Marguerite Radclyffe-Hall (1880–1943) grew up a lonely child. She was educated at King's College, London. She had relations with a number of different women, the sculptor Una Troubridge being her longest-lasting and most stable partner. During the 1930s they settled in Rye, where Fred Benson then lived. Though it is undoubtedly heresy to say so, the life of Mary Francis Butts (1890–1937) is far more interesting than her novels. She grew up in a home filled with original art by William Blake. She had a run-in with Aleister Crowley. She was friends with Jean Cocteau, who illustrated *Imaginary Letters*. She was a lesbian who married twice, the second time to the gay painter Gabriel Atkin (Sigfried Sassoon's first lover). Her brother Tony Butts was William Plomer's companion.

More Women than Men by Ivy Compton-Burnett (1884–1969) might appear to belong also to this group of novels, but the gay couple in it, Jonathan Swift and Felix Bacon, seem both of a different order and of less importance. Told almost entirely in artificial dialog, Firbank without the sparkle, the novel is strangely cold-blooded, a bit off-putting.

Butts, Mary. *Armed with Madness*. London: Wishart, 1928. New York: Boni, 1928. **The Taverner Novels*. Intro. Paul West & Barbara Wagstaff. Kingston, N.Y.: McPherson, 1992. 1–162.
———. *Death of Felicity Taverner*. London: Wishart, 1932. **The Taverner Novels* (see above). 163–365.
———. *Imaginary Letters*. Paris: Titus, 1928. *Intro. Robin Blaser. Vancouver: Talonbooks, 1979.
Compton-Burnett, I. *More Women than Men*. London: Heinemann, 1933.
Hall, Radclyffe. *The Well of Loneliness*. London: Cape, 1928. New York: Covici & Friede, 1928. *New York: Anchor, 1990.
Lehmann, Rosamond. *Dusty Answer*. London: Chatto & Windus, 1927. *Intro. Jonathan Coe. London: Virago, 2000.

26 Sylvia Townsend Warner: *Mr Fortune's Maggot*, 1927. Wyndham Lewis:

The Apes of God, 1930. Virginia Woolf: *The Waves*, 1931. James Hanley: *Boy*, 1931. Frederick Rolfe: *The Desire and Pursuit of the Whole*, 1934.

Five novels show up regularly on lists of gay fiction, but their contribution to an understanding of gay identity is minimal. True, Warner's South Pacific fantasy may be considered a sexless love story between the middle-aged Reverend Timothy Fortune and the teenager Lueli (whom he rechristens Theodore), his only convert after three years spent on the island of Fanua. (Actually he is not a convert; he has merely hidden his idol away out of sight.) But neither of them could self-identify his sexuality. For action, there is an earthquake and a math lesson, and that is about it. The novel is one of those that either garner loyal fans or bewilder readers who have no idea what the fuss is about. French television has broadcast an adaptation of it.

Lewis's 625-page long satire against Bloomsbury and, in particular, against the Sitwells follows the homosexual Horace Zagreus's education of Dan Boleyn (generally seen as modeled on Stephen Spender) in the ways of modernism (apedom). Another character, Matthew Plunkett, is based on Lytton Strachey. Lewis's choice of his characters' sexuality, however, seems dictated by the author's spleen (one could justly accuse him of homophobia) rather than by any desire to make a valid exploration of the links between sexuality and culture. The novel's avant garde style will appeal to certain tastes only.

As Gregory Woods (*History of Gay Literature*, 202–03) says in his brief but penetrating analysis of Woolf's *The Waves*, the character Neville never emerges from his unrequited passion for Percival "long enough even to label himself homosexual." One of the six interlocutors in the novel (also based on Strachey), he searches for love with a series of men after Percival's untimely death in India, but his emotions are so cloaked in the author's poetic prose as to render the portrait of him as a gay man of little import. There is even less self-awareness in Woolf's depictions of Septimus Warren Smith in *Mrs. Dalloway*, 1925, and William Dodge in *Between the Acts*, 1941.

In Hanley's *Boy* all the male sex is coercive, beginning with a masturbation scene among the teenage dock workers (Chapter 4) and culminating with the physical assaults the steward and the cook make upon the title character, Arthur Fearon. He stows aboard a ship in an attempt to escape his brutalizing environment at home. It is futile: "All men sailing at sea seemed to be obsessed with boys" (111), whom they call "brownies," and he is raped. The naïve teenager's end comes at the hands of the captain, a "mercy killing" after the boy supposedly catches syphilis in his only heterosexual encounter. However, earlier we have been informed that "the steward is laid up with a dose" (81). The novel gained notoriety by being banned for obscenity, but the author has always had a coterie of loyal fans.

All of Rolfe's works have garnered the claim that they are, at the very least, homoerotic, including his most famous, *Hadrian the Seventh*, 1904. This posthumous novel takes its title from Plato's *Symposium* (though I wonder if a pun is also involved). Its hero, Nicholas Crabbe, rescues a boyish-looking sixteen-year-old girl, Ermenegilda or Zilda, in the aftermath of the Messina earthquake of 1908. He returns with her to Venice, but in order to avoid scandal he disguises her as the boy Zildo, and third-person pronouns become slippery as a result. To make it all seem even more akin to boy actors playing girls disguised as boys in Elizabethan drama, the character is probably based on the real life Zildo Vianello, a gondolier with whom Rolfe was sexually involved. Since in the novel the girl is a girl, however, a claim that it is gay fiction seems strained, though it certainly belongs to any study of queer literature.

The most interesting work by the five authors, from a gay viewpoint, is, in fact, a queer short story by Hanley, published as a chapbook. *A Passion before Death* is a bizarre tale, surreal in its setting and action. Carter, a World War I veteran who lost a leg in battle, has murdered the man who raped his wife on their wedding night. Found guilty and condemned to hang the following morning, one of the two wardens guarding him asks if there is anything he wants. His reply is simple: "I want my wife." Carter propositions one of the guards. Then, "naked save for shirt and boots and socks" (125), he flings himself on the chaplain and tries to tear off his trousers. One of the replacement guards, aptly named Hope, embraces the condemned man, whereupon Carter successfully opens his pants. Now totally aroused, Carter throws himself onto the cell door and attempts copulation with the keyhole. Finally, Hope, though he has never done anything similar before, strips naked and, "murmuring, 'There! There!' like a mother suckling her child, [...] yielded himself" (143). The story is bizarre—and unforgettable.

Sylvia Townsend Warner (1893–1978) was born at Harrow, where her father was a housemaster. For seventeen years she was in a relationship with editor Percy Buck; then she fell in love and moved in with poet Valentine (Molly) Ackland. She was T. H. White's biographer. Percy Wyndham Lewis (1882–1957) was born on his father's yacht off the coast of Nova Scotia. He attended the Slade School of Art in London and later developed a style of painting labeled Vorticism. By 1951 he was completely blind, the result of a tumor. Though he lived in Canada and the United States for a while, he returned to London, where he died. Adeline Virginia Stephens (1882–1941) was born in London. Educated at home and King's College London, she married Leonard Woolf in 1912. Founders of the Hogart Press, they were at the center of the Bloomsbury group. She was also in love with Vita Sackville-West, for whom she wrote the gender-bending *Orlando*, 1928. Suffering from acute depression, she drowned herself near her Sussex home.

James Hanley (1897–1985) was born in Liverpool of Irish parents. He went to sea at age seventeen and then served with Canadian forces in World War I. He was living in Wales when he met his wife, with whom he had a son. They continued to live in Wales or in London for the rest of his life. Much has been written of Frederick William Rolfe (1860–1913), including A. J. A. Symons's famous *Quest for Corvo*. He was born in London, served as a teacher, converted to Roman Catholicism, and enrolled to become a priest but was dismissed. For a time he engaged in a passionate but sexless relationship with Hugh Benson, one of the three Benson brothers. Rolfe died penniless in Venice. His affairs with various gondoliers are detailed in *The Venice Letters*, 1974.

Hanley, James. *Boy*. London: Boriswood, 1931. New York: Knopf, 1932. Paris: Obelisk, 1935. *Intro. Anthony Burgess, Liam Hanley, & Chris Gostick. London: OneWorld Classics, 2010.

———. *A Passion Before Death*. London: [C. J. Greenwood], 1930. New York: Black Hawk, 1935. **The Last Voyage and Other Stories*. London: Harvill, 1997. 109–43.

Lewis, Wyndham. *The Apes of God*. London: Arthur, 1930. New York: McBride, 1932. *Intro. Paul Edwards. Santa Rosa, Calif.: Black Sparrow, 1981.

Rolfe, Frederick. *The Desire and Pursuit of the Whole*. London: Cassall, 1934. *Ed. Andrew Eburne. 1993. New York: Braziller, 1994.

Warner, Sylvia Townsend. *Mr Fortune's Maggot*. London: Chatto & Windus, 1927. New York: Viking, 1927. **Mr. Fortune*. Intro. Adam Mars-Jones. New York: New York Review, 2001. 1–152.

Weeks, Donald. *Corvo: Saint or Madman?* London: M. Joseph, 1971. *New York: McGraw-Hill, 1971.

Woolf, Virginia. *The Waves*. *London: Hogarth, 1931. New York: Harcourt, 1931.

27   Ernest Milton: *To Kiss the Crocodile*, 1928.

Launched unprepared into London society, Roy Ffolliott undertakes a Candide-like peregrination around the globe that ends with his premature death in Tré-Chemins, France. His flight from London is the direct result of his naïve presence at a gay house party in the country. In his usual passive way, he has accepted an unwanted invitation from Vernon Moore, a decadent youth smitten with Roy's beauty; once there he seems incapable of understanding the sensual undercurrents of the all-male gathering. Edgar Loring picks up on his discomfort and apologizes to him: "That you should get your first impression of—of the point of view—from—from this sort of thing. It's—it's this sort of people who make life impossible for the rest of us." Loring clearly wishes for a more idealized relationship. He asks Roy, "Have you read [Carpenter's] *Ioläus* or *Toward Democracy* or Walt Whitman's *Leaves of Grass*?" He continues, "I suppose you'll wonder, feeling as I do—that I come to a place like this at all. It's because I have to. Life is so difficult. People, conventions, won't let you live your life. It takes tremendous character and reserve to be true to your outlook, to live your own life, and yet keep your place in the world, in your calling, if you have one; in—in society" (149).

Shortly afterwards, Loring attacks Moore for trying to corrupt Roy. And then for no apparent reason Loring rushes out of the room and kills himself. While the rest of the party prudently make themselves scarce, Roy is cradling Loring's broken body when the police arrive. As a consequence, his name and a hint of the kind of party it was is made public by the London tabloids. Roy is cut by former friends, and his priest summons him home, saying his mother has taken to her bed. Still haunted by Loring's death, for the first time Roy asks himself, "What did he want out of life?" The answer comes immediately: "*To stretch himself!*" (185). And so he offers to replace a teenager who has been pressed into service aboard ship and begins a voyage that will circumnavigate the globe. In the Hawaiian Islands he experiences a deep friendship with a native, Lilo, but virgin to his core, he runs from a shipmate who pressures him to visit prostitutes. He searches for self-abnegation through opium and through wine. He kisses the crocodile: "And the reptile tore him to pieces.... Then he was recreated" (270). On his deathbed, he sees that that has been the pattern of his life. He now understands Loring as well as a woman who had stalked a London actor friend: "They were misfits. He belonged to their number" (331). Loring discerned the fact; at the fatal party, he says to Roy, "We—we have so much in common" (149).

Ernest Gianello Milton (1890–1974) was born in San Francisco. A stage and later film actor, he came to London in 1914. He was associated with the Old Vic from 1920 through 1952. He played the role of the sexually ambiguous Rupert Cadell in Patrick Hamilton's *Rope*, 1929, in both London and New York. In 1926, the same year he married the novelist Naomi Royde-Smith, he became a naturalized British subject. Milton wrote three plays, one on Christopher Marlowe being published in 1924. This was his only novel. He died in London.

Milton, Ernest. *To Kiss the Crocodile*. London: Duckworth, 1928. *New York: Harper, 1928.

28 Evelyn Waugh: *Decline and Fall*, 1928; *Vile Bodies*, 1930; *Put Out More Flags*, 1942; *Brideshead Revisited*, 1945; *Unconditional Surrender*, 1961.

Arthur Evelyn St. John Waugh (1903–1966) would normally have followed his father and his brother Alex in going to Sherburne, but after the scandal surrounding Alex's novel, that was not an option. Instead, he attended Lansing, where his classmates included Tom Driberg. He experienced a few schoolboy crushes, but in general Waugh was still sexually innocent. That would change at Oxford. Waugh's biographer Humphrey Carpenter quotes Alan Pryce-Jones (81) as saying that in those days "it was *chic* to be queer." Waugh was chic. Driberg in his autobiography (55) remembers a scene at the Hypocrites Club, where Waugh's friends gathered, with "Evelyn and another rolled on a sofa with [...] their 'tongues licking each other's tonsils.'" He fell in with a group that included Harold Acton, Alfred Duggan, Terrence Greenidge, L. P. Harley, Brian Howard, Anthony Powell, and John Betjeman, whose teddy bear, which he carried with him everywhere, would be memorialized in *Brideshead Revisited*.

Waugh fell heavily for his classmate Richard Pares, but they were incompatible since Pares was serious about scholarship and little interested in drinking. Waugh blamed Cyril Connolly, however, for breaking them up. Hugh Lygon may have been another boyfriend, but Waugh next fell in love with Alastair Graham. This friendship endured even after his first marriage. Indeed, Carpenter (182) thinks it may have contributed to its breakup. After having the marriage annulled, Waugh entered a second one and seems to have opted entirely for heterosexuality—though it is worth noting that generally marriage does not fare well in his fiction and that he betrays a continuing fascination with homosexuality. In the 1950s during a mental breakdown brought on by bromide poisoning—an ordeal that formed the basis of his novel *The Ordeal of Gilbert Pinfold*, 1957—he heard voices that accused him, among other things, of being homosexual. It was an identification he was anxious to refute, even as he brought it up. In his fiction before *Brideshead Revisited*, homosexuality is always portrayed satirically, to the point that it is not easy to label any one of them a gay novel.

In *Decline and Fall*, his first novel, his curiously passive but straight hero, Paul Pennyfeather, has a cheerful pederast as a colleague at the prep school where he teaches: Captain Edgar Grimes, "one of the blind alleys off the main road of procreation" (134), any one of whose confessions "would have glowed with outstanding shamelessness from the appendix to a treatise in sexual psychology" (49). When the headmaster can no longer close his eyes to his conduct, Grimes momentarily staves off disaster by proposing to his daughter (conveniently forgetting to mention that he had years before married an Irish woman in a drunken stupor, though the marriage was never consummated). Grimes can last only so long, however, before he finds it expedient to fake a suicide and disappear, only to show up intermittently across the rest of the novel. A number of fluttery gay men have minor roles in the second part. Waugh's biographer Selina Hastings (172–74) identifies the real-life figures on whom they have been modeled, including Cecil Beaton as David Lennox. They are all regarded with amused detachment. The novel was filmed as *Decline and Fall ... of a Birdwatcher*.

Miles Malpractice, who has a cameo role in *Decline and Fall*, becomes a more important character in *Vile Bodies*. One of the *Bright Young Things* (the name given to the film adaptation), Miles is part of the irresponsible set to which the on-and-off fiancée of the equally passive hero, Adam Fenwick-Symes, belongs. Through a series of turns he becomes Mr. Chatterbox, a columnist who invents gossip much like the hero of Nichols's *Crazy Pavements*. Miles takes up with a dirt-track racer ("the things that go on" [134]). This relationship leads to one of the longer and funniest set pieces in the novel: a race that goes horribly awry. The last we hear of Miles he has "had to leave country" (294); the reason is left up to the reader to guess. An effeminate Italian waiter at a hotel also pops up intermittently in something of a running gag. And several lesbians make guest appearances. The novel's black humor is handled more assuredly than in *Decline and Fall*, but the blatant racism and snobbish attitudes mar the pleasures it offers. It was also adapted for the stage and television.

A gay character finally becomes a major figure in *Put Out More Flags*: Ambrose Silk—"A pansy. An old queen. A habit of dress, a tone of voice, an elegant, humorous deportment that had been admired and imitated, a swift, epicene felicity of wit, the art of dazzling and confusing those he despised—these had been his, and now they were the current exchange of comedians" (46). The figure was based so blatantly on Brian Howard that he regarded it as "an absolutely vicious attack." The novel is set in the early days of World War II; Ambrose feels in limbo, not knowing what has happened to Hans, his German lover (the real life Anton Altmann, one of Isherwood's and Klaus Mann's friends), at the hands of the Nazis. Ambrose does his best to survive in wartime London, joining the Ministry of Information with the assignment to create a magazine, but Basil Seal, Waugh's villainous hero, sabotages his every move, finally forcing him into exile, in disguise, in western Ireland. There is also a running attack throughout the novel on what, at the time, was perceived as Auden's and Isherwood's cowardly defection to the United States, but there is no hint of a sexual relationship per se between Parsnip and Pimpernell. Altogether, it's a nasty satire.

None of these portraits prepares one for the nonjudgmental quality and sense of nostalgia found in *Brideshead Revisited*. One difference strikes the reader immediately; here we have a first-person narrator: Charles Ryder. Billeted at Brideshead during World War II, he recalls his relationship with the young Sebastian Flyte, who lived there twenty years before. The two meet as students at Oxford. Sebastian stands out from the other students; not only does his teddy-bear go with him everywhere, but he is also "entrancing, with the epicene beauty which in extreme youth sings aloud for love" (26). It takes some time before they fall in love, and even then the nature of their love is vague, also how physical it becomes. Sebastian's father warns Charles that "Sebastian is in love with his own childhood. That will make him very unhappy. His teddy-bear, his nanny ... and he is nineteen years old" (91). Charles fails him at a crucial moment: "I had no love for Sebastian that morning; he needed it, but I had none to give" (127). Sebastian becomes a hopeless alcoholic. He drinks his way across Europe before ending up in Morocco with Kurt, a German suffering from secondary syphilis and a self-inflicted wound that stubbornly refuses to heal. As Sebastian's mother lies dying, Charles is sent to bring him back. Sebastian makes it clear that his return depends on Kurt: "You know, Charles [...], it's rather a pleasant change when all your life you've had people looking after you, to have someone to look after yourself. Only of course it has to be someone pretty hopeless to need looking after by *me*" (195–96). The last we hear of Sebastian he has been given shelter by a religious order outside Tunis, Kurt having been seized by the Germans and sent to a concentration camp, where he hangs himself.

Meanwhile, Charles marries, but he clearly cares nothing for his wife or his children. An old attraction to Sebastian's sister Julia, who could pass as his twin, revives, even though she is now married also. When the two accidently meet on a ship, Julia asks Charles why he married. He answers, "Loneliness, missing Sebastian." And when Julia more states than asks, "You loved him, didn't you?" he answers, "Oh yes. He was the forerunner" (232). Charles and Julia begin an adulterous affair. Later, Charles says, "I had not forgotten Sebastian. He was with me daily in Julia; or rather it was Julia I had known in him, in those distant Arcadian days" (274). But their affair comes to naught. When World War II arrives, Charles finds himself "homeless, childless, middle-aged, loveless" (314). He is as lost in his way as Sebastian was in his.

Across much of the novel, another Oxford friend—Anthony Blanche, "the 'aesthete' *par excellence*, a byword of iniquity" (27)—periodically turns up. During his Oxford years Anthony's friends are a virtual who's who of gay Europe: "he dined with Proust and Gide and was on closer terms with Cocteau and Diaghilev; Firbank sent him his novels with fervent inscriptions; he had aroused three irreconcilable feuds in Capri; by his own account he had practised black art in Cefalù [with Aleister Crowley?] and had been cured of drug-taking in California and of an Oedipus complex in Vienna" (40). He has his own formidable way of handling university bullies by flouting his sexuality (42). When he leaves the university—he settles in Munich, where he "has formed an attachment to a policeman" (93)—his absence creates a vacuum: "all his friends, among whom he had always been a stranger, needed him now" (95). The last we see of him is in a gay bar, where he has taken an uneasy Charles, in the company of a youth, Tom (244). Though Waugh attempts an upbeat ending, the novel closes on a minor key. The entire novel was extensively revised in 1960. It became the basis for a very successful television miniseries, as well as a later film.

Waugh had a strange military career during World War II, serving with the Royal Marines but getting leaves of absence in order to work on *Brideshead Revisited*. His war years ultimately produced the *Sword of Honour* trilogy, the story of Guy Crouchback's tour of duty in the infantry. Sir Ralph Brompton is introduced in the third volume, *Unconditional Surrender* (retitled *The End of the Battle* in the United States). A crypto-communist, he first appears, "a tall, grey civilian dandy" (25), in the studio of three RAF sergeants who make scale models of military targets. He courts the youngest one, whom he calls "Susie." We find out that he has earlier taken an interest in Major Ludovic (who appears in the second volume, *Officers and Gentlemen*, 1955, as a corporal-major and is directly responsible for the murders of a number of men). Under Brompton, Ludovic served as "'valet' at the embassy, as 'secretary' when they travelled on leave" (32). Now Major Ludovic turns into a writer and gains acclaim for his collection of *Pensées*, the title playing deliberately on *pansies* (35). Lieutenant Padfield is a third disturbing gay figure in the novel. He is a seemingly "ubiquitous" American with "no apparent military function" (20–21). Though he is often seen in the company of women, one who knows him says, "I don't think the Loot likes women" (112). He later becomes Ludovic's successful American book agent (318).

From Edgar Grimes through Lieutenant Padfield, not a one of Waugh's gay characters is an attractive human. The flamboyant Anthony Blanche and, to a lesser extent, Ambrose Silk—the two based on an amalgam of Brian Howard and Harold Acton—probably come off the best, not least for each's genuine concern for a German lover. In general, the author, like Saki before him, appeals more to our inner-adolescent than to our mature self. Carpenter points out (157–61) the importance of both Lewis Carroll's *Alice* books and Kenneth Grahame's *The Wind in the Willows* to the creation of his world. Yet its fascination cannot be denied.

Carpenter, Humphrey. *The Brideshead Generation: Evelyn Waugh and His Friends*. 1989. Boston: Houghton Mifflin, 1990.

Hastings, Selina. *Evelyn Waugh: A Biography*. Boston: Houghton Mifflin, 1994.

Waugh, Evelyn. *Brideshead Revisited: The Sacred and Profane Memories of Captain Charles Ryder*. London: Chapman & Hall, 1945. Boston: Little, Brown, 1945.

———. Same. Revised. London: Chapman & Hall, 1960. *Intro. Frank Kermode. New York: Everyman's Library, 1993.

———. *Decline and Fall*. London: Chapman & Hall, 1928. *New York: Farrar & Rinehart, 1929 (online).

———. *Put Out More Flags*. London: Chapman & Hall, 1942. Boston: Little, Brown, 1942. *New York: Back Bay, 2002.

———. *Unconditional Surrender*. London: Chapman & Hall, 1961. *The End of the Battle*. Boston: Little, Brown, 1962.

———. *Vile Bodies*. London: Chapman & Hall, 1930. *Boston: Little Brown, 1930.

29 Keith Winter: *Other Man's Saucer*, 1930.

From the beginning, Shaw Latimer is set apart by the color of his hair: "It was green. And light green at that" (7). But the color symbolizes only his sexual orientation, not the curious psychological kink that he develops. Here we have an unusual portrait of a gay youth who loses his sense of empathy. The problem begins with a set of losses he suffers while still a schoolboy. Shaw's first romantic attachment comes at age sixteen when he falls under the spell of Marcus Gerald, a prefect. In lines worthy of Alex Waugh, Winter writes: "On the assumption that friendship between boys of different ages is unnatural, not to say wicked, the public school recognizing regretfully the inevitability of such friendships decrees that they shall at least be conducted in decent secrecy. The authority which has driven boys underground like so many rabbits is then surprised to find them behaving like rabbits. So with Shaw and Marcus Gerald" (68). But all changes literally overnight, to Shaw's bewilderment. When next they meet in Gerald's study, the older boy attacks the younger viciously—to what extent the reader never fully knows; Shaw confides to his sister only that he has told her "everything that can be told" (89). As a result, the boy becomes convinced of "the essential beastliness of his fellow beings [...] and the criminal carelessness of God" (91). A second devastating blow to his psyche comes when Mac, Shaw's idealized younger brother, is struck and killed by a car. From then on, a shell surrounds his heart.

Shaw's magnetism in no way diminishes when he leaves for Oxford, but he becomes cruel, the kind of careless person who flicks his cigarette ash in another person's saucer (138): "It never occurred to Shaw that he was being selfish beyond belief. He had come to believe in all sincerity that this form of friendship was the only possible form for him—a friendship in which everything was taken and nothing given, or at least nothing that mattered" (151). Amidst the fervent homosexuality which surrounds him as the university, he becomes infatuated with Tony Gay and proceeds to use him as a play toy. When Tony falls in love with a female student, Shaw feels compelled to take her from Tony, even though he does not want her. A second infatuation is with Orm Lind. These two are evenly matched. When Shaw convinces himself that he is in love with a childhood friend and wants to marry her, Orm coolly takes her for himself and then drops her. In a final explosion of violence (there have been others across the novel), Shaw tries to drown Orm, but Orm defeats his purpose and ends by saving Shaw. The novel ends on a quiet note with a hint of possible redemption for the protagonist: "Above the mountain-behind-the-house the sun was rising. Full and red it was, like a Jaffa orange" (308).

John Keith Winter (1906–1983) was born in North Wales. He attended Oxford and worked briefly as a schoolmaster. He became a playwright and script writer for Hollywood—most notably *Above Suspicion*, 1943, and *The Red Shoes* (additional dialogue), 1948—and for television. In the early 1930s he and Noël Coward were briefly lovers. The playwright served as the model for the character Andrew Jordan in Winter's third novel, *Impassioned Pygmies*, 1936. He also attracted the attention of Somerset Maugham, who invited him and the Waugh brothers to visit him at his French villa. Evelyn was snide in his comments at the time, but was forced to meet with Winter in Hollywood when he was assigned to turn *Brideshead Revisited* into a script. (Nothing came of the project.) He died in an Actors Fund home in Englewood, New Jersey.

Winter, J. Keith. *Other Man's Saucer*. London: Heinemann, 1930. *Garden City, N.Y.: Doubleday, Doran, 1930.

30 William Plomer: *Sado*, 1931, *The Invaders*, 1934.

Plomer's biographer, Peter F. Alexander, calls the author (xvi) "an important artist who found himself ham-strung by an inability to accept, and to use in his work, a vital part of his own being—his sexuality. Plomer was a homosexual, and he found that fact almost intolerably painful, never losing his desire to escape from it. The consequences of his homosexuality were slow to come home to him, but they had a major and near disastrous effect on his work." In his novels we sense the story that Plomer wants to tell but feels he must obfuscate.

Take his second novel, *Sado*. The main character is a young European painter, Vincent Lucas. Almost on a whim, he ends up in Japan. There he meets an English woman, Iris Komatsu, married to a Japanese engineer. She falls in love with him and becomes frustrated and angry that he is oblivious to her. Instead, he gives all his attention to Masaji Sado, an aimless young man he meets on the street and invites to share his home, envisioning him as guide and as a model for a painting. For the emotional triangle to be fully effective, the two men should become lovers. Perhaps they do. Clearly something momentous happens between them—in a white space between two sections of a chapter (175). Thereafter, things go wrong between them: "In mortal affairs climax is the beginning of an end" (187). Lucas prepares to return to England. Sado accuses him: "you do not really regard me as a friend, you do not really respect and love me as you say" (237). Iris all but accuses Lucas of being homosexual. But all we know for sure is that "his own amiable vanity had blinded him" to the "susceptibilities" of both people. The style is exquisite; the story leaves one as frustrated as Iris.

The closest that Plomer came to writing a gay novel was his next, *The Invaders*. Set in London, it has three characters—Nigel Edge, Tony Hart, and Chick Steel—who are either gay, bisexual, or gay for pay. Tony, a newcomer to London from Lancashire, literally picks up Nigel when he falls entering the Marble Arch tube station. Nigel, the main character, lives with his uncle and his cousin Frances. He suffers from "profound loneliness"—"a symptom of what might be regarded as the twist in his nature—the nature of a sensitive boy made to suffer by his schooldays and obliged to go straight from school to the War, and cut off until maturity from the society of women" (39). Consciously standing against class distinctions, he strikes up a friendship with Tony. Though Tony has a strong sense of self-worth, it would appear that he is willing to engage his body not only in legal labor but probably illegally to secure money: "Encounters with strangers were an essential part of Tony's life" (17), and Marble Arch is a cruising ground. Nigel gets Frances to hire Tony to clean windows in their house; while on the job he becomes attracted by the new Midlands maid that Frances has hired.

Chick is the maid's brother. He is a new army recruit who has already learned the "process for getting acquainted with susceptible civilians for purposes of gain" (140–41), and he has met a fellow trooper "who, if taunted with being a 'nancy,' would say 'Of course I am' and then knock the speaker down for his impertinence" in a way that "would have graced the Theban Band" (143–44). Shortly after Nigel meets him, after years of living with his uncle he decides to move into his own flat. The only photograph he displays there is one of Chick (149). They spend much time together, the implications being that they are "lovers" (160), and Chick accepts money from Nigel. Unfortunately for him, Chick is leading a double life. He has fallen for one of his sister's friends and spends the money to entertain her. His deception leads Nigel to despair, even thoughts of suicide, and he ends the relationship. On holiday in the French Riviera, he is seen dancing with a working man in a Nice *boîte* (274). Back in London, he easily deflects a comical attempt at blackmail instigated by Tony's brother (292–97).

Telling the story thus, my leaving out other events that propel the plot, makes the novel sound much gayer than it is. Alexander reports (194) that "Plomer's publishers actually encouraged him to be more open [...], Rupert Hart-Davis writing that the one criticism he had of the manuscript was that Plomer had been vague about the scope of Nigel's relationship with Chick: 'You don't say, and hardly even infer, whether they went to bed together or not.' But Plomer declined to expand the passage" (194). The title of the novel, by the way, seems at odds with Nigel's equalitarian stance; the London invaders are the lower-class characters from the Midlands, who arrive, play their part, and then leave. At the end only Tony remains. He and Nigel have the last scene together, but what their relationship now is, or will be, remains ambiguous.

Plomer did write one short story that fits into any anthology of gay stories: "Local Color," 1933. Two English undergraduates are passing the long vacation in Greece. Various indications that they are gay are dropped (their dress, their reading Proust's *Sodome et Gomorrhe*), but nothing explicit is recorded. A letter of introduction to a native woman brings them an invitation to lunch. As a special treat, a glimpse of local color, she invites them to try an outdoor restaurant off the beaten track, but she gets more color than she anticipated. Four workmen are also dining there. After dancing a tango together, they openly kiss and then disappear behind some nearby rocks, all the while under the watchful eyes of a goat tied to one of the veranda posts. One wishes that Pomer had had the same courage in writing his novels.

William Charles Franklyn Plomer (1903–1973) was born in South Africa. Save for a period spent in England during World War I, he lived there until 1926. That year he left for Japan, where one of his students, the model for Sado, became his lover. Settling in England in 1929, he began a long-time relationship with Anthony Butts (1900–1944), to whom he dedicated *Sado*. The two of them spent time in Greece; there Plomer fell in love with a Greek sailor, to be robbed and dumped by him for a richer man, leaving him only a venereal disease. Back in England he took up with a trooper in the Royal Horse Guards, presumably the model for Chick, but continued to be promiscuous. As part of the Bloomsbury clique, Plomer networked with all the prominent members of the English literary set, in particular its gay writers. A year after being arrested for solicitation in 1943, a charge that was mysteriously dropped, Plomer met Charles

Erdmann and spent the rest of his life with him. In 1952 Plomer published his fourth and last novel, *Museum Pieces*. The somewhat fey Toby d'Arrey is based on Butts, but Plomer sidesteps gayness by having his narrator be a woman, so as to convert the story into a heterosexual one. He was also a librettist for Benjamin Britten. Plomer died in his and Erdmann's home near Brighton.

Alexander, Peter F. *William Plomer: A Biography*. Oxford: Oxford University Press, 1989.

Plomer, William. *The Invaders*. London: Cape, 1934.

———. *Sado*. London: Hogarth, 1931. *London: Chatto & Windus, 1951.

31 Christopher Isherwood: *The Memorial*, 1932; *Mr Norris Changes Trains*, 1935; *Goodbye to Berlin*, 1939.

The life and the writing of Christopher William Bradshaw Isherwood (1904–1986) are so intertwined that it is irresistible to interpolate readings into the texts that may not literally be there. This becomes all the easier to do once the author starts using a narrator who has his own name, William Bradshaw in *Mr Norris Changes Trains* and Christopher Isherwood in *Goodbye to Berlin*. Born in Cheshire, he was educated at Repton and Cambridge. He made his first trip to Germany in 1929 and returned the following year to live. Always attracted to younger men, he began a relationship with the teenage Walter Wolff; in 1932 he met another teenager, Heinz Neddermeyer, with whom he lived until politics intervened. Good friends early on with the poets W. H. Auden (they had attended the same prep school) and Stephen Spender and later a friend or associate with virtually a who's who of gay literary figures, Isherwood left behind a corpus that is an integral part of the foundation on which contemporary gay fiction has built. It divides naturally into two parts: the earlier works, in which the main character is closeted but is drawn to the sexual freedom found in pre–Nazi Germany, and the American works, which all have a more or less out, but displaced Englishman as a central figure.

Isherwood's first extended portrait of a gay man appears in his second novel, *The Memorial: Portrait of a Family*. Told out of chronological order, it introduces Edward Blake in 1928 as he prepares to kill himself in his hotel room in Berlin. He botches his suicide (though the attempt leaves a scar on his forehead, which he later explains away as the result of a motor crash). We shift to 1920 in England, where Edward joins the widow of his great friend Richard Vernon and Richard's sister, Mary Scriven, for the dedication of a war memorial. The third part takes us to Cambridge in 1925, where Eric Vernon and Maurice Scriven are students. Richard's son is studious; his nephew is a playboy who uses Edward to get him out of scrapes. Eric warns Edward to leave Maurice alone (220), but admits to himself that he is jealous of their relationship (227). In the last section, Edward appears in society as the escort of a painter who is convinced she can "cure" him (269), though she is aware that he is having a series of unsatisfactory encounters with various young men. After they part, Edward falls deeper into despair and tries to kill himself. But the last we see of him he is in his room in Berlin with a young German. Eric is the autobiographical character, but it is Edward who makes the same discovery his creator had: as he memorably says in his memoirs (*Christopher and His Kind*, 10), "To Christopher, Berlin meant Boys."

In *Mr Norris Changes Trains*—until recently published in the United States as *The Last of Mr. Norris*—much homosexual tension roils just under the surface, but only Baron Kuno von Pregnitz is openly identified as "a fairy" (200). He entertains a coterie of young males at his country estate (46–47) and recounts his adolescents-centered fantasies (126–27). But the reader has to imagine why William would be invited to join him in his revels and what, if anything happens on a journey they take together to Switzerland. The baron is caught up the shady machinations of Arthur Norris, with William acting as only a mildly reluctant accomplice. Blackmailed for indiscreet letters sent to one of his lovers and needing money, the baron is willing to sell state secrets. Caught, he tries to take the honorable way out, but makes a botch of it, leaving the "hospital to finish him off" (200). Meanwhile, Mr. Norris continues his devious set of transformations.

Goodbye to Berlin, arguably Isherwood's most famous novel, is a kind of sequel. It is a composite novel comprised of six short stories. Covering the years 1930–33, *Goodbye* records the impressions that various people left on its protagonist. The one openly gay character is Peter Wilkinson, an Englishman. We meet him when Chris retreats to Rugen Island in the Baltic Sea in order to write. Peter is there with his lover, the Berlin teenager Otto Nowak (based on Wolff), who is not so much gay, or even bisexual, as a sexual opportunist. There is no direct indication that Chris himself is gay, though he obviously forms some kind of a threesome with the other two and nowhere does he show any real sexual interest in women. Late in the novel an American tourist outside a gay and lesbian bar demands to know if he is queer, and he answers, "Yes [...] very queer indeed" (396). But given the ironic tone he has used throughout, the heterosexual reader presumably is not expected to take the declaration seriously. Of course, it is impossible nowadays for a reader not to view *Goodbye* through the lens of the musical film *Cabaret*, 1972, and *Christopher and His Kind*. So we *know* he is gay.

The novel covers the last years of the Weimar Republic and the rise of the Nazi Party to power. The other principal characters are his landlady, Fraulein Schroeder; Sally Bowles, an amoral singer of limited talent but enormous ambition; Otto's family, who knows his sex trade and welcomes what money he brings in; Natalia Landauer, the daughter of the Jewish owner of a large department store; her cousin, Bernhard Landauer, the manager of the Berlin outlet; and the slightly mysterious and sexually ambiguous Fritz Wendel, who also appears in *Mr Norris* and who continues to escort Chris to various dives. All the characters, male and female, have one thing in common: they are or will become victims of a crumbling economic structure, Nazi brutality, and their own illusions (or, perhaps one should say, delusions). Their portraits are vivid, and the work as a whole is frightening.

The "Sally Bowles" chapter (which was originally published as a chapbook, 1937) in particular took on a life of its own. John van Druten saw the possibility of dramatizing it. *I Am a Camera* opened at the Empire Theater in New York in November 1951. In *Christopher and His Kind* (53), Isherwood recorded with some amusement the subsequent history of his hero as a result of the play: "The leading male character in the play is called Christopher Isherwood. In dealing with his sex life or, rather, the lack of it, John used a scene from the novel [that] may be taken to suggest that Sally knows instinctively that Christopher is homosexual—or it may not. [...] In the film of *I am a Camera*, Christopher gets drunk and tries to rape Sally. She resists him. After this, they are just good friends. In the musical play *Cabaret*, the male lead is called Clifford Bradshaw. He is an altogether heterosexual American; he has an affair with Sally and fathers her child. In the film of *Cabaret*, the male lead is called Brian Roberts. He is a bisexual Englishman; he has an affair with Sally and, later, with one of Sally's lovers, a German baron."

The novel served symbolically as Isherwood's goodbye to Britain. Just before it was published, he and Auden made their well publicized defection to the United States. The English literary establishment, facing certain war with Germany, was outraged by what it perceived as the writers' treachery. They were ridiculed by Waugh in *Put Out More Flags* as the cowardly Parsnip and Pimpernell. Even in the United States their sexuality became the object of E. E. Cummings's homophobic scorn ("flotsam and jetsam"). Leaving Auden in New York, Isherwood moved to Los Angeles to work in the movie industry. There he fell under the influence of Gerald Heard, a convert to Vedanta. In 1945 appeared the inconsequential comedy *Prater Violet*, about Chris's role in London working on a romantic film set in Vienna to be directed by an Austrian filmmaker; it reprised many of the Berlin themes. Isherwood's biographer Peter Parker states (417) that by 1944 the novelist had adopted American orthographic conventions. In 1946 he became a U.S. citizen. In 1953 he began his relationship with Don Bachardy (1934–). Though he continued to mine his European past, the rest of Isherwood's literary career belongs to American rather than British letters. Emmanuel S. Nelson unquestioningly included him in *Contemporary Gay American Novelists*, the only one of its fifty-seven writers who was not native-born.

Isherwood seems detached from the gays in his European novels, incapable of pondering their relationship with the straight world. This disconnect disappears in the first of his four American novels. *The World in the Evening*, 1954, is the weakest, but it marks new stages in the development of the author's gay awareness. His bisexual narrator encounters a gay couple, one of whom is militant. Acknowledging the anti-sodomy laws in all forty-eight states, he self-identifies as "a professional criminal." His lover says of him, "He'd like for us to march down the street with a banner, singing 'We're queer because we're queer because we're queer because we're queer'" (112). The novel is also historically important for its definition of the difference between High and Low Camp (110–11). Isherwood returns to using a character named Christopher in *Down There on a Visit*, 1962. Four novellas, each with a different setting, make up the composite novel, in many ways the saddest of Isherwood's fiction. The section of greatest interest to gay readers is the second, "Ambrose," set on a Grecian island where a gay Englishman has set up his wholly masculine kingdom to escape the harassment and persecution that gays are subjected to.

Neither of these works prepares the reader for Isherwood's masterpiece, *A Single Man*, 1964. The account of the last day in the life of a fifty-eight-year-old California teacher, it follows George (no last name given) as he goes about his usual activities, carrying with him memories of his happiness with his dead lover, killed in a car accident. It is unclear why Isherwood felt compelled to kill off George too, especially since he had criticized "the Tragic Homosexual myth" at the time Gore Vidal, to whom *A Single Man* is dedicated, published *The City and the Pillar*. Perhaps he wanted to create a kind of *carpe diem* warning to readers. In 2009 Tom Ford's film adaptation premiered, bringing new attention to the novel. Isherwood's final novel was *A Meeting by the River*, 1967. This story of the reconciliation of two English brothers—the one, a businessman with wife and children in London and a male lover in Los Angeles; the other, a convert to Hinduism about to enter a monastery on the banks of the Ganges River—ended his career in fiction on a downbeat.

Thereafter, Isherwood turned entirely to religious studies and autobiography. In 1971 he was instrumental in getting *Maurice* published. During the last decades of his life he became a celebrity, indeed something of a cult figure, for younger gays and became more outspoken politically than had been his wont before. He died in Santa Monica, California. The publication of his 1939–83 diaries in three volumes, 1996–2012, uncensored save for necessary cuts to avoid slander, and of *Lost Years: A Memoir 1945–1951*, 2000, brought renewed attention to the writer.

Gordon, Mel. *Voluptuous Panic: The Erotic World of Weimar Berlin*, 2d ed. Los Angeles: Feral House, 2006.
Isherwood, Christopher. *Christopher and His Kind*. 1976. London: Eyre Methuen, 1977.
———. *Down There on a Visit*. New York: Simon & Schuster, 1962. London: Methuen, 1962. *Minneapolis: University of Minnesota Press, 1999.
———. *Goodbye to Berlin*. London: Hogarth, 1939. New York: Random House, 1939. *The Berlin Stories*. Intro., author & Armistead Maupin. New York: New Directions, 2008. 205–410.
———. *A Meeting by the River*. New York: Simon & Schuster, 1967. London: Methuen, 1967. *Minneapolis: University of Minnesota Press, 1999.
———. *The Memorial: Portrait of a Family*. London: Hogarth, 1932. Norfolk, Conn.: New Directions, 1946. *New York: Farrar, Straus & Giroux, 1988.
———. *Mr Norris Changes Trains*. London: Hogarth, 1935. *The Last of Mr. Norris*. New York: Morrow, 1935. *The Berlin Stories* (see above). 1–203.
———. *A Single Man*. *New York: Simon & Schuster, 1964. London: Methuen, 1964.
———. *The World in the Evening*. New York: Random House, 1954. London: Methuen, 1954. *Minneapolis: University of Minnesota Press, 1999.
Parker, Peter. *Isherwood: A Life Revealed*. New York: Random House, 2004.

32 Fortune Press novels—Terence Greenidge: *The Magnificent*, 1933. Richard Rumbold: *Little Victims*, 1933. Reginald Underwood: *Bachelor's Hall*, 1934, *Flame of Freedom*, 1936, *This Sorry Scheme*, 1960. Michael Scarlott (Stanley T. Fisher): *Ambassador of Loss*, 1955. Aubrey Fowkes: *The Star Brooch*, 1969; *A Youth of Fourteen*, 1969.

It is easy to get the impression that Fortune Press was a gay press. Ian Young in "Some Notes on Gay Publishing" (*The Male Homosexual in Literature*, 291) writes: "The most active of the English gay publishers was the Fortune Press." The website *Brighton Ourstory* says, "Until the Gay Men's Press was established in the 1970s, the closest thing to a gay publishing house in Britain was the Fortune Press." Gregory Woods (*A History of Gay Literature*, 10) writes that "in England from the 1930s onwards the Fortune Press—run by Reginald Ashley Caton from 1924 to 1971—put out novels about male homosexuality for opportunistic commercial reasons." And the Arbery Books website says of the press: "A small, but important, minority of [its] books had explicit or implicit gay characters [...] or covered subjects such as public school life or corporal punishment, which were of interest to many gay men." Timothy d'Arch Smith in his book *R. A. Caton and the Fortune Press* (16) merely notes that Caton (1897–1971) was interested in "amatory unorthodoxy." The truth is that gay novels were only a part, and not even a major part, of the press's publications. Probably the best descriptor of Fortune Press would be that it was "gay friendly."

His daring was enough to bring the wrath of the legal system down on him. In 1934 he was tried for obscene libel, found guilty, and ordered to destroy the offending books or, in some cases, to remove offensive illustrations. The books in question were *Don Leon*, Terence Greenidge's first two novels, one by Erik Warman, Alfred R. Allison's translations of Pierre de Brantôme and J. K. Huysmans, Shane Leslie's translations of Pierre Louÿs and Straton, two translations by Montague Summers, and translations of *The Perfumed Garden* and *The Satyricon*, plus illustrations for Plato's *Symposium* and Beresford Patrick Egan's *De Sade*. D'Arch Smith discovered, upon Caton's death, that he had simply warehoused many of the condemned works instead of destroying them. Caton, by the way, appears as a character in several novels by Kingsley Amis.

D'Arch Smith includes a complete list of all the titles that Caton published, but without annotations save for the books' genres. Since copies of these works are difficult to come by—the ones in libraries are often in their rare books collections and thus available only on site; titles rarely show up on booksellers' lists and are expensive when they do come onto the market—it is not easy to gain a sure sense of which works are relevant to this guide. Some works that seemed promising turned out to be false leads. For example, *Boy Sailors*, 1936, by Gundry Grenville-Hearne appears on some lists of gay novels. True, its hero has a kind of adolescent crush on the ship's cook, but nothing comes of it. Since Richard Blake Brown (1902–1968) was gay, his five Fortune novels seemed promising, but the one I obtained—*A Broth of a Boy*, 1933—turned out to be only campy. *True Yokefellow*, 1937, a historical novel set in the times of the Roman Servile Wars by Humphrey Lancaster (1888–1973), has more right to be included here. Its hero, offered as a hostage to a Roman commander, is straight, but his best friend, another hostage, is gay. However, his role is not that important. I have not seen Lancaster's *Barbarian Boy: The Story of a Young Slave in Ancient Rome*, 1940, set during the reign of Nero. Woods seems to have the best grasp of which titles a gay reader should consider. He lists "classics" that the press published—*Symposium*, *Strato's Boyish Muse*, *Satyricon*, and *Don Leon*—and "contemporary novels on homosexual themes"—*The Magnificent*, *Little Victims*, *Bachelor's Hall*, *Flame of Freedom*, and the twelve "Boy" diaries (though they are more homosocial rather than homosexual). The only important title I found that he missed is *Ambassador of Loss*. All these novels are set before the end of World War II; several in fact are historical novels.

One of the many remarkable aspects of *The Magnificent: A Story without a Moral* is its forthright acceptance of homosexuality without ever resorting to the use of such pejorative terms as *pansy, queer,* or even *invert*. The novel is set in the London film world of 1925–26, many of whose members are socialists supporting the coal miners' strike. It is narrated by Michael Trevor, a Oxford graduate who aspires to become an actor. While on the set of his first picture, he falls in love with the juvenile lead, Derek Alderstone—"the magnificent." Derek is very much on the make, ready to do whatever it takes to get ahead in the profession, Hollywood being his ultimate goal. He is willing to use equally a gay man, the director and song writer Mark Leslie, and the tempestuous female star of the movie, Ramona (no other name). He also becomes the boyfriend of the divorced Katherine Hartman. Complicating matters, Michael falls in love with her too: "The homosexual thoughts and emotions of years fell from me with a crash" (209). The novel ends with a marriage, a job, a Hollywood contract, and the promise of a bright future for all the principals, save perhaps the strikers. I suspect that the novel is a *roman à clef* whose real-life counterparts would be fairly obvious to anyone familiar with the British film industry in the last days of the silents.

A heterosexual scene is the closest one comes to an actual sexual description in the novel. But along the way, one encounters many wry comments about the treatment of gays. Mark says to Michael, "Isn't it a nuisance homosexuality being illegal in England and people all prejudiced against it? One's love ought to flow broad and calm just like a river. But instead, it's dashed against rocks and whirled over ravines, and sometimes even has to gurgle along underground. Good straight stuff gets filthily twisted. Don't you think so?" (128–29). A little later, on the same occasion, he adds, "Isn't existence difficult for us poor homosexuals? We can't help being what we are. We've got the laws of England against us, and all the prejudices which those laws set on foot. We've got a very limited number of people among whom to hunt, and the field is still more limited by the curious way in which some homosexualists suddenly become normal, without any warning" (137). A guardsman tries to blackmail him (176), a scene that will be played out in later novels by other authors. The novel has true historical significance and deserves reprinting.

Terence Lucy Greenidge (1902–1970) was born in England of a Barbadian father. His parents dying while he was young, he was reared by his godfather. He attended Rugby and Oxford, where he was a founding member of the Hypocrites Club, a gay hangout to which he introduced Waugh. His book *Degenerate Oxford?* had a *succès de scandale*. It was followed by *The Magnificent*. His other Fortune Press novels, none of which I have seen, were *Brass and Paint: A Patriotic Story*, 1934; *Tinpot Country: A Story of England in the Dark Ages*, 1937; *Philip and the Dictator*, 1938; and *Girls and Stations*, 1948. He also published *Four Plays for Pacifists* in 1955. He was a minor actor, but had a long career with the Royal Shakespeare Theater.

Little Victims badly needed an editor. Plot, characterization, point of view, and themes are all over the place. It becomes an attack on the family, public schools, the Catholic Church, Oxford aesthetes, and even its main character, the ironically named Christopher Harmsworth. The author cannot make up his mind whether homosexuality is a perverted condition deliberately incubated in the public schools (31, 139) or a natural state of humans (262–63). We follow Christopher from his dysfunctional family to prep school, where he is first introduced to sex and, as a result, takes for granted that "homosexuality was the most prevalent and natural of sex manifestations" (59). The author editorializes that "a lot of awful twaddle on the subject has been perpetrated by Mr. Alec Waugh and other young writers" (60). At Oxford, Christopher alternates between being an insufferable prig and a rather likeable young man. He observes about gays there: "He was of their tribe, divided by a barrier from the rest of the world. And when you met somebody, instinctively you wondered whether he was of your tribe, and if you liked him you hoped he was" (101). He falls in and out of love and has various sexual adventures, apparently always playing a passive role (240).

A character named Henry Armitage beds him and tries to educate him about the true nature of love, arguing that it is "only a more polite word for prostitution" since all relationships are really "a process of contracts" in which both parties benefit from an exchange (193). On a holiday in Spain he meets a young woman and wills himself into love with her, thinking that thus he will finally be able to talk openly about his sex life "with pride and boastfulness" (240). Her father opposes the marriage, having heard that insanity runs in his mother's family. And indeed he is called back home to his mother's deathbed, her having been committed, and shortly thereafter, as we have known from the opening pages, he kills himself. Much of the novel seems to be a *roman à clef*, but many of its most interesting moments come from literary discussions, in particular an assessment of D. H. Lawrence (161).

Richard William John Nugent Rumbold (1913–1961) was born in Ireland to an English father and a Norman-Irish mother. The father was a bully; the mother committed suicide. He attended school in England, France, and Germany and trained as a naval cadet before attending Oxford. He married an American, who was tolerant of his homosexuality. Though he was tubercular, he became a pilot with the RAF during World War II. He published a disguised autobiography, *My Father's Son*, 1947, under the pseudonym Richard Lumford. He was treated for schizophrenia in Switzerland and died in Spain as a result of falling out of a window. Extracts from his diaries, *A Message in Code*, 1964, were edited posthumously by his second cousin William Plomer.

Bachelor's Hall may be the best known of all the gay novels that Fortune Press published. Dedicated to Edward Carpenter, it apparently sold fairly well, for a second edition was called for within a year, with a new preface defending the contents of the novel. It presents the portrait of an emotional failure. Adrian Byfield from childhood feels different from everyone else in the rural English village where his war-widowed mother runs a bakery. He is thus delighted when he discovers that he is actually a bastard, his mother having married Tom Byfield to conceal her state. He is not so ready to accept that he is homosexual, though he knows he longs for "a companion, an *alter ego*, an end to aloneness." And he recoils at the thought of any physical relationship with another person: "If only this dream-friendship could materialize into an actual human bond, with no possibility of that insidious influence of physical desire, how marvelously satisfying earthly life might be" (91). He is the last youth that Ronald Whitlock should fall in love with.

They are thrown together when Adrian becomes organist for a church whose curate is Ron's tutor. Though much the younger of the two, Ron knows much more about his body than Adrian does. He has read on the subject, and the previous curate, Charlie Jefferson, was gay. From him Ron has learned about Shakespeare's sonnets and Whitman's poetry (which scares Adrian); Ron has also learned to consider Plato (whose "austere Platonic conceptions particularly appealed to Adrian" [128]) and Jesus Christ in a different light: "Whenever Christ expressed His personal love, it was always to a man" (121). But when Ron, acting on Jefferson's advice, begs for more, and when later Jefferson himself intercedes, Adrian is incapable of responding like a mature adult: "The test that Jefferson—secretly-wise Jefferson—had prophesied had come and passed, resulting in failure beyond all telling" (294).

Flame of Freedom is rare and, when found, expensive. Arbery Books has provided a chapter by chapter synopsis on its website. Julian Ferrers comes to London from the Midlands. There he finds himself torn between Olive Denwent, who sometimes works as a prostitute, and Donald Mackness, an author. He moves in with the latter, but still feels an attraction to Olive. An encounter with a sailor, Jacob, adds further complications. After many vacillations, Julian determines to marry Olive but cannot go through with the ceremony. When he discovers Don has left the country in pursuit of Jacob, he decides to follow. There is also a subplot involving a lesbian in an unhappy relationship who kills herself. The three following Underwood novels—*An Old Maid's Child*, 1935; *The House of Pleasant Bread*, 1941; and *Secret Fear*, 1943—I have not seen, nor have I found anything substantial about them.

This Sorry Scheme is a salacious portrait of strains that tear at a small English town during the 1930s and 1940s, generated by gossipy women, stern men, and an underlying rivalry between Anglicans and Methodists. Late in the story one of the gossips swirls up rumors about the curate, the Reverend Nicholas Selwyn. We are told that it has been no secret, not even to the police, that many a young man who has failed to score at the Saturday night dance ambles over to "Selwyn's cottage, apparently sure of a welcome in spite of the hour." But after Miss Levinger, "in the guise of avenging angel," lodges a formal complaint, they are forced to act (230–31). Selwyn refuses to act ashamed, and at his trial he argues that he "was neither mentally nor physically degenerate. He was just an ordinary, healthy invert. He was just as he had been made, with no more choice in the matter than anybody else and like everybody else was under compulsion to obey his own [...] personally natural instincts."

In fact, he goes on, introducing a new argument, "He was of a type which, properly appreciated, could have its own peculiar and very considerable value to the community, if only the community could be made to see it" (262). The verdict is obvious: "Selwyn would have to go to prison for three years, during which he would be under obligation to receive psychiatric treatment" (265). One of the townswomen, in recounting the trial, picks up Selwyn's argument to become the author's spokesperson; she discusses at some length the religious, moral, and psychological implications. But homosexuality is only one of several issues addressed in the course of the novel, the appearance of a bastard child clearly created as a result of miscegenation receiving equal attention. Clearly Underwood was asking for sympathy for the marginalized.

Details about the life of Reginald Underwood (dates unknown) remain singularly illusive despite his having written an autobiography. Its title, *Hidden Lights*, 1937, seems appropriate, since one finishes it feeling that very little has been revealed. We do learn that he grew up in a small town in the countryside but frequently visited an aunt in London. We also learn that he was an accomplished musician, that he worked as a tailor, and that a meeting with Edward Carpenter left a great impression on him. But I am not sure that Reginald Underwood is even his real name.

In 1937 Fortune Press began what would ultimately be a twelve-volume series, ostensibly a diary written by "A Boy" (the only indication of authorship given on the title pages). In his bibliography (*English Schoolboy Stories*, 52) Benjamin Watson writes: "They cover the years 1909–1920, following the diarist, who identifies himself in the texts as Aubrey Fowkes, from age eight to nineteen. He goes first to a suburban London day school called The Down, then to a prep school called Hazelbank, and finally to Portlow, a mediocre public school in the Midlands." I have read only the first, the relatively sexless *Fourteen*. Watson's summaries (53–55) indicate some romantic and sexual maneuvering going on later among the schoolboys. In *Fifteen*, 1938, Aubrey struggles to resist masturbating and, when tempted with sexual activities, refrains. In *Sixteen*, 1939, "several boys from other houses are expelled over a sex scandal. Aubrey diverts himself from these troubles by taking a protective and affectionate interest in Watkinson, an attractive new boy." In *Twelve*, 1950, "Aubrey feels ambivalent about his best friend, Dalyziel, an effeminate boy who tends to attract inconvenient attention from bullies." An online source (Intermale Gay Bookstore) says of *Nineteen*, 1952, "The youth's life at his boarding school is brightened by the arrival of a new student, with whom he forms a 'profound bond.'" Finally, Watson notes (56), "Though chronologically the first book in the Aubrey Fowkes series, *Eight to Nine* [1952] was one of the last to be published. The obsessive and graphic descriptions of excretion, flagellation, and sexual play seem to show the author growing bolder as the series nears its end."

Another school story, *Ushering Interlude*, 1936, was published under the name Esmond Quinterley. It is told from a teacher's prospective, that of Clive Elgen at a West Sussex prep school. Two other novels with young males as heroes also appeared under the Quinterley name. I have been unable to discover anything about *Ismay Somer*, 1937, beyond a blurb indicating it is a novel about the postwar conversion of the title character to a new faith. *Climbingboy: The Last Day in the Life of a Chummy in the Year 1750*, 1939, describes the activities of young Rob, a London chimneysweeper, on the day he suffocates in a flue.

Behind both the Fowkes and the Quinterley pseudonyms stands Richard Vere Cripps (1901–1976). Despite his long and productive connection with the press, there seems to be little information available about him. He was born in London. Before he began his association with Fortune Press, he published a play, *Nero and Sporus*, 1924. An Elysium Press catalog notes that its author "was very familiar with both scholastic and literary interpretations of Nero and of the role homosexuals have played throughout history. In the introduction, he argues that Nero has been unfairly maligned throughout history, starting with Suetonius and abetted by legions of Christian bigots. Although ostensibly an interpretation of the relationship between Nero and Sporus, it is also a hymn to sexual freedom and love." During World War II Cripps served in the special duties branch of the RAF; he published a memoir, *My Airman Days*, 1948, as Quinterley. An online note says that he lived for a time in Cornwall, caring for his ailing mother.

The six novels that I have read, of the twenty-three that he published with Fortune Press, along with what information I have garnered about the ones that I have not seen, indicate that few are truly gay. I suspect the press's gay-friendly reputation and the scarcity of the novels, so that they are more known about than actually read, have misled listmakers. All his works do depict youths under the age of twenty in an all-male environment; hence all present the possibility of a homoerotic reading. But they would appeal more to connoisseurs of flagellation literature than to readers interested in the construct of a gay identity. Three novels about the lives of young criminals, all under the Fowkes name (though they seem more appropriate to the Quinterley pseudonym)—*More Butterfly Days*, 1958; *Waif Triumphant*, 1958; and *"King John": Young Hero of Transportation Days*, 1969—for example, have young heroes who operate within a homosocial milieu, but none of them is gay.

Cripps also introduced a second set of novels under the Fowkes name with the very real school setting of Repton Hall. According to the Intermale Gay Bookstore website, *Butterfly Days*, 1957, is "famous for its description of flagellation practices in English boarding schools, and the suppressed sexual longings of older boys for younger." Of *The Blue Marble*, 1965, the site writes: "Herbert is nine at the outset of the book, and over the next few years is much adored by classmates and teachers at his new boarding school, Repton. Jealousies and the affection of a 'special friend' both complicate and inspire his life. A false accusation causes a drama. He is brutally punished, but vindicated at the end." *New Face at Repton Hall*, 1967, and *A Youth of Fourteen*, both subtitled *From the Private Papers of Francis Gresley*, are set in the early 1830s.

The second (which I have read) has a story within a story, showing William Shakespeare teaching there in 1578. One of his students is named Hews, a "little favourite whom he had dubbed Cupid" (83). (Obviously the author has read Wilde.) Will tells the boys stories about Ganymede and about the courting of Hyacinthus (86–87), and he later uses the same stories to defend his favoring Hews and another boy whom he calls Primrose after his headmaster warns him about what happened to Edward II and Richard II for "harbouring of creatures" (91). But nothing untoward happens with the boys, though the novel ends with Will planning "to cultivate other favourites in

Apollo's free and promiscuous fashion" (99). But once again corporal punishment is more interesting to the author than is sexual identity.

Though the novel opens and closes in Vienna, *The Star Brooch* takes place mostly at Repton Hall in the 1890s. It shows a new freedom, particularly in its opening and closing chapters. John Julian's father is a foreign correspondent covering central Europe for two English newspapers. After a talk with Francis Gresley, he decides to send John, who has reached the age of fourteen, to Repton. John, the novel's narrator, is already sexually precocious. He knows "the notorious Roman Baths, where the Ganymedes of the town resorted and where I had on one or two occasions actually been allowed to venture on my own and felt wiser for the experience" (10). In London, in transit to the school, he is cruised by "a gent," who wishes him luck "as soon as he had learnt that I was merely killing time there waiting to go off to school" (15). On the train he meets some of his future schoolmates. Shortly after his arrival a female visitor discovers she has lost a valuable brooch and makes a fuss. Though the pages are filled with details about school life (including flagellations, of course), this mystery now drives the plot of the novel. Having found that his father's allowance is not stretching far enough, John decides to pawn the locket that his dead mother used to wear and that he has brought with him for sentimental reasons. He is seen coming out of the pawn shop and thus becomes suspect of having stolen the brooch. Greatly upset, he writes a miserable letter to his father, with the results that the latter decides not to return John to school there when the term is up.

John experiences only one sexual adventure while at Repton, and that the last evening that he spends there. Finding he is "in the mood for adventure," he sneaks out to the outside toilets to find young Harlow there: "neither of us, it was perfectly plain, had come here to defecate." Soon, "after some first feeling he leant against me and actually kissed me. [...] And to me the most extraordinary part was that we were now hugging each other and going on wantonly like the warmest of lovers, I even kissing him back, yet we had scarcely exchanged two words before tonight. Indeed I felt, with the state he was in, that it would be a shame not to oblige him. So I did so, and I felt that he satisfied himself. I know well that I did so when he obliged me" (130–31). Back home, his father secures a stern German master to tutor him, but determines that his schooling should begin with a good caning for his conduct at the English school. Thinking about what is to come, the narrator "retired to our lavatory, a dark little hole that reeked strongly of all that goes with a lavatory [...] as I sat brooding not unpleasantly on my fundament, I took to playing with myself under the stimulus of these thoughts. Boyhood is half itch" (138).

The German master brings two pupils with him, Kurt and Hans, to aid in the caning. Requesting that he strip naked, "Kurt had, whether accidentally or not, touched me embarrassingly, and thus added to the delicate excitement of the moment for me" (140). The corporal punishment finished, the master departs, leaving the two boys behind. The German boys tend to his wounds. "They then both proceeded to paw with gusto my other parts of interest." But soon, "with nothing now to be considered but the speedy consummation of desire, Kurt proceeded to enjoy his Hans to the full, and next to give him complete relief, and neither of them appearing to mind me there in the very least." Indeed, "now it seemed to strike them almost simultaneously that it was only fair that I should enjoy a turn too, and on my declaring myself eager enough, and Hans not a bit backward in obliging, I seized the tempting chance" (142–44). There is nothing even remotely like these scenes in the other Fowkes novels I have read.

Ambassador of Loss is another schoolboy story, set in the academic year 1934–35. The title comes from Francis Thompson's poem "To Olivia." Its hero is Chris Stenning, a housemaster at a school in Dorset and the author's alter ego. An advocate of progressive education, he is finally driven beyond endurance by the calcified headmaster, who has just expelled two students, and retorts, "you are not really trying to keep the boys from immorality as such, but only from conventional immorality. And that's what is rotten in the whole Public School system of morals. You have no true standard to go by. Not Christ, but Cricket is your pattern." He continues, "It is conventionally immoral for two boys to love each other, so you beat them and expel them for it. So boys are trained to hate and made ashamed to love. Well, I'm through with it for ever!" (169).

There is a string of romances in the novel, none of them known to Stenning but none of which, in their basic innocence of discovery, would cause his disapproval. One of the boys, Peter Ryan, remembers back to his chance encounter at age twelve with sixteen-year-old Roland O'Neil, a fisherman who took him under his wing while on a summer holiday and through whom "love was revealed to him" (86). Peter thinks about his experience and extrapolates from it a number of pertinent observations (clearly speaking for the author in the process): "Sex to the public mind was 'smutty.' To talk of it was to talk smut. Why the hell? And suddenly Peter thought he knew why. The middle classes ruled the country and sent their sons to the Public Schools. They wrote the papers, formed the majorities in the House of Commons: the Public School voice controlled the B.B.C. And the Public School boy generally learnt about sex in 'bogs' or 'rears' and other dark places, furtively, guiltily, hating his initiation, generally loathing his initiator, only capable of mentioning its magic and mysteries in obscenities, under a defensive barrage of lewd laughter. [...] And the Churches, which would confine the purpose of marriage to procreation, and the avoiding of fornication, and count every child as 'born in sin,' did their little bit too to blaspheme against the real nature of sex, which was to be as vital for Love as nerve for impulse, as ether for the wave, as a poem for the emotion, to be for every living lonely creature the Divine Delight" (81–82).

Peter comes across his classmate John Deverill in the woods, where his love of botany has taken him. They pledge themselves with an exchange of blood to "three things: individual freedom, mutual assistance, joint secrecy" (121), but for the moment nothing further happens. Meanwhile, Michael Fairfax-Taylor, a perfect, confesses his love to John in a letter he posts on Easter day, and John responds frankly that he loves Peter (137–38). May-day John and Peter renew their pledge, and though there is physical contact, Peter says, "I insist that out love-making must not go too far," contrasting what they feel with what goes on at school "where only the Unnatural reigns, and where love is not distinguished from dirt" (155). But a jealous schoolmate has been keeping tabs on the two boys; his notebook is discovered by his father and turned over to the headmaster, with the results that, ironically, several lives may be spared the school's pernicious influence. Of all the Fortune Press novels after *The Magnificent*, *Ambassador of Loss* most merits recovery.

Arthur Stanley Theodore Fisher (1906–1989) stands behind the Michael Scarlott pseudonym. He was born in Uganda, the son of missionaries. He was educated at Oxford, where he was a member of the circle around Auden and Isherwood. He taught in India and then, upon being ordained a priest in the Church of England, became chaplain in various public schools. He married in 1936 and had two children. He wrote poetry and religious histories. This was his only novel. It was illustrated by his son-in-law, Barry Surie.

d'Arch Smith, Timothy. *R. A. Caton and the Fortune Press: A Memoir and a Hand-List*. North Pomfret, Vt.: Asphodel, 2004.
Fowkes, Aubrey. *The Star Brooch*. London: Fortune, 1969.
———. *A Youth of Fourteen: From the Private Papers of Francis Gresley*. London: Fortune, 1969.
Greenidge, Terence. *The Magnificent: A Story without a Moral*. London: Fortune, 1933.
Rumbold, Richard. *Little Victims*. London: Fortune, 1933.
Scarrott, Michael. *Ambassador of Loss*. London: Fortune, 1955.
Underwood, Reginald. *Bachelor's Hall*. London: Fortune, 1934. *2d ed. Intro, author. New York: Arno, 1975.

_____. *Flame of Freedom*. London: Fortune, 1936. [not seen]
_____. *This Sorry Scheme*. London: Fortune, 1960.

33   Cyril Connolly: *The Rock Pool*, 1936.

Edgar Naylor, a young Londoner on holiday, allows himself to be used by various hangers-on, the greater part of them lesbian, while visiting "Trou-sur-Mer" (i.e., Cagnes), France, under the pretense that he is making an anthropological study of the town. The consequence is his own rapid financial and physical deterioration. An artist who is trying to keep up with the ravishes that Naylor's irregular life is carving into his visage says, "It reminds me of the *Picture of Dorian Gray*, only it's the other way round; my portrait can't keep pace with all the changes" (79). As he seeks to bed one woman after another, his own sexuality comes into question. He is pursued by Jimmy, the boyfriend of a local bar owner, who insists Naylor is bisexual (34). And the woman he ends up living with in poverty sums him up: "I don't care if you do like women—you're queer—one part, if you can call it a part of you, is normal—but all the rest of you is queer. You're just a pansy that's gone wrong. You can't even be a proper pansy" (135).

Of Jimmy, Naylor thinks, "There was a great deal to be said for his type, the oldfashioned Taormina young men. They had their roots in the past, and were naturally social and cultured. The tradition of Oscar was still preserved. They were the heirs of the dandies and inherited his metallic wit" (37). As they talk literature, Naylor discovers that "Jimmy knew Gertrude Stein well, and Cocteau and Glenway Wescott, for he belonged to the charmingly dated Paris of the Select and the Bal Musette, and parties on the Ile Saint-Louis, having long been decoyed there from some ferocious small town by the *douceur de vivre*" (38). Jimmy ends up in a triangular relationship, pursued by a woman while he pursues the man who loves her. The novel remains amusing without being in the slightest profound. According to Peter Quennel, to whom the novel was dedicated, its characters were based on types Connolly had observed on the Côte d'Azur. Though it was clearly indebted to Douglas's *South Wind* and Mackenzie's *Vestal Fire* and *Extraordinary Women* for its form, it is in no way derivative.

When it was finished in the early 1930s, no English publisher would touch it, primarily because of its lesbian characters. In his dedication Connolly mentioned the obscenity trial that Hanley's *Boy* endured as also being a deterrent (xvii). It was brought out in Paris by the Obelisk Press, though owner Jack Kahane "declared that its Anglo-Saxon reticence positively disgraced his list" (vii). The novel was not published in England until 1947.

Connolly's short story, *Bond Strikes Camp* is also of interest to gay readers. Written with the complicity of Ian Fleming (who was a few years behind Connolly at Eton), the spoof was first published in *The London Magazine*, April 1963, then reprinted as a chapbook, and finally collected in *Previous Convictions*. M. requests that Bond assume gay drag in order to trap a top KGB operative. Disguised as Gerda Blond, Bond makes his way to the Kitchener Social Club (probably a sly dig at the gay British field marshal). Contact made, Gerda allows that her best friend and lover was Guy Burgess. Taken back to a hired flat, before anything sexual can happen, Bond accidentally dislodges M.'s fake mustache. M. confesses that his long harbored feelings for Bond have driven him to the deception. Bond coldly suggests that M. act like a gentleman, knowing that he will succeed M. upon his suicide. The story ends with Bond contemplating a return to the gay hideout.

Cyril Vernon Connolly (1903–1974) was born at Coventry, the son of an English army officer and an Anglo-Irish mother. His childhood was spent variously in England, Ireland, and South Africa. He was educated at Eton and Oxford. His biographer Jeremy Lewis recounts the strong passions he formed for a number of his schoolmates before he adopted a heterosexual lifestyle. Throughout Connolly's life, however, he remained fascinated by those who lived by a different sexual code. He established himself as a critic and an editor to be reckoned with. Along with Stephen

Spender and Peter Watson, he was one of the founders of *Horizon* magazine, 1940–49. Connolly was married three times.

Connolly, Cyril. *Bond Strikes Camp*. London: Shenval, 1963. *Previous Convictions*. New York: Harper & Row, 1963. 354–71.

———. *The Rock Pool*. Paris: Obelisk, 1936. London: Hamilton, 1947. Norfolk, Conn.: New Directions, 1948. *Intro. Peter Quennel. New York: Persea, 1981.

Lewis, Jeremy. *Cyril Connolly: A Life*. London: Cape, 1997.

34 Noel Langley: *There's a Porpoise Close Behind Us*, 1936. Noël Coward: *What Mad Pursuit?*, 1939; *Star Quality*, 1951; *Me and the Girls*, 1964.

Given the public perception of the ubiquity of gays in the entertainment industry, it is strange how few gay theater novels there actually are. *There's a Porpoise Close Behind Us* appears to be a first. Even so, gays here are secondary characters, center stage being taken by a young and decidedly heterosexual couple. Robin Gardner, the hero, is marked (so we told in the American edition), much like Waugh's early heroes, by "gauche simplicity and blundering gullibility" (305). He is terrified by gays; the first time a rentboy tries to pick him up, "he was horrified and shocked, and somehow mortally ashamed at being addressed by one of those" (36). The heroine, Diana Shand—the daughter of a famous actress who died giving birth to her—shows greater strength, without ever becoming one of Waugh's maneaters. She is not that dismayed by what she perceives, but she feels for Robin's discomfort. A third major player is a slightly older, also thoroughly heterosexual actor, Christopher Lovell, who ends up falling in love with Diana even as he recognizes the hopelessness of any suit he might pay her (and who, it is revealed in the last line of the novel, is its "author").

Most of the theater names dropped throughout the novel are those of closeted gays: Coward, Gielgud, Maugham, Novello. But overall gays are presented in a negative way. Christopher claims that "half the young men in the theatre slide into their jobs on their stomachs" (110), and he is not talking about groveling.

All the gay characters are, without exception, villainous, self-serving, hysterical, or stereotypical—or some combination thereof. "Vicious and filthy," Robin spits out (239). The chief villain is the actor Douglas Middleton. "He had, in spirit," we are told, "the length, breadth and depth of a playing-card (something in Spades with a warped pip) and about the same ability to feel pity, give affection or see himself for what he was" (132). As soon as he sees Robin, he determines to bed him. To this end "the Middleton" (as he is generally called) arranges to get Robin's first play produced. Diana instinctively foresees disaster, for she instantly recognizes Douglas's nature, though she feels she must keep silent so as not to jeopardize the project. Her sense of discretion doesn't help. When Douglas makes his move on Robin and is rebuffed (207–12), "It was the first time he had ever bungled the handling of his quarry, and his professional pride was touched" (218). From that point he sets out to destroy the production, using every theatrical trick at his disposal and finally resorting to hiring barrackers for opening night (by which time one of his rhetorical resignations has been accepted at face value).

Throughout, Garstin Bannock, Diana's cousin with whom she grew up but seldom saw (his being away at school), plays his own game. Garstin is bisexual. His motto is "Man, woman or dog, I throw it on a bed" (63, 226). As a schoolboy, he was Douglas's sexual toy; as an adult he willing pimps for him. When he meets up with Robin and Diana in London, he takes it upon himself, apparently for the pure mischief of it, to educate them. For their first lesson he takes them to a party thrown by Everard Carter, known to his friends as Flossie. Carter champions homosexuality, arguing that gays have "better senses of humour than *ordinary* people, *and* broader valuations," "more excitement, more artistic appreciation, deeper knowledge" (98–99). The two become more and more miserable before they are rescued by Christopher, and they leave, profoundly disturbed. Later, Garstin decides that he wants Diana, and when she repulses him, he attempts to rape her. Once again Christopher appears at the right moment (230). Garstin's warped soul cries out for revenge, and he writes a malicious letter to his parents, Diana's guardian. The father knows his son well enough to take the letter for what it is, but his response amplifies Garstin's maliciousness, causing him to unite with Douglas to bring the play down.

What neither Douglas nor Garstin anticipates is Robin's finally arousing himself from his usual lethargy and, in a grand and comical finale, physically attacking Douglas in the theater as his hired mob disrupts the play, thereby gaining unexpected publicity for himself and the play, leading to a Hollywood contract as a writer. American readers, however, missed out on this triumph. For some reason Langley revised his novel before publishing it in the United States as *So unlike the English*, 1937. Many of Christopher's authorial asides went, with no great loss, and one character was changed from a gauche Wisconsin to a gauche Yorkshire native, presumably not to insult American readers. But, most mysteriously, the entire final chapter and a half are cut. The play never opens within the pages of the American version. Douglas accepts that it will fail and that he will "never, never quiver in the arms of Robin Gardner, for all his months of determined pursuit." Robin and Diana lose their virginity together and "locked, barred and bolted doors against further onslaught from the Middleton and his ilk" (309). The novel became the basis for a film, *These Foolish Things*.

Noel Langley (1911–1980) was born in Durban, South Africa, and attended the University of Natal. He began his career as a playwright there but moved to London in 1934, where he also became involved with film. By 1937 he was in the United States. He was commissioned to write the screenplay for *The Wizard of Oz*, 1939. It is ironic that the man who wrote a line that has become part of gays' stock repartee—"Toto, I've a feeling we're not in Kansas anymore"—should have also created a hero who feels "disgust," a sense that he is "being dragged down into black, slimy water by something evil" (207, 211) when his lead actor makes a pass at him. Langley served as a lieutenant in the Canadian Navy during World War II. After the war he returned to England for a period, but continued his association with Hollywood. He became a U.S. citizen in 1961. Langley married twice and had five children by his first wife. He died in Desert Hot Springs, California.

Another man of the theater also named Noel—Noël Coward—wrote three short stories of novella length that are of real interest to gay readers. *What Mad Pursuit?* appeared in his first collection, *To Step Aside*. It is a comedy about a middle-aged English author, Evan Lorrimer, who, on a lecture tour in the United States, comes up against American hospitality with a vengeance. Invited to spend a quiet weekend at a country home on Long Island, he is instead subjected to a tour of one drunken party after another, somewhat similar to the party in Langley's novel. We are given little clue to Evan's sexuality, beyond the titillating information that he was "taken, at the age of fifteen, to the Musée Grevin by Marcel Proust" (55). Other houseguests include the fey actor Lester Gaige, a "Russian fairy who plays the piano" (65), and a belligerent (and at one time very naked) Hollywood actor, Don Lucas, as well as a couple of lesbians. The collection also contains the dark comedy "Nature Study," based according to Coward's biographer Philip Hoare (291) on Coward's perception of Maugham's marriage, while "The Wooden Madonna," is his takeoff on Maugham's *Ashenden* series, about an ex-antique dealer turned playwright (after his lover leaves him for another man) who, without realizing it, gets mixed up with spies in a Swiss resort.

The title story of his second collection, *Star Quality*, recounts the over-the-top fights that director Ray Malcolm has with star Lorraine Barrie to bring fledgling playwright Bryan Snow's work to London's West End. Ray's longtime partner, Tony Orford, proves to be essential in the task, providing some perspective and cohesion to a project that constantly threatens to slide out of control. Tony is actually among the most attractive gay characters to appear in British literature. As for Bryan, again the sexuality of the main character is left ambiguous; all we know is that the only personal item he has in his bed-sitting room is an enlarged snapshot of one Stuart Raikes "who had gone to Barbados after the War to grow bananas and wrote rather dull letters every month or so. Bryan missed him very much" (335). Of a totally different order is Coward's very moving *Me and the Girls*, which appears in his third collection, *Pretty Polly Barlow*. Here the narrator, George Banks, is openly, one might even say defiantly, gay. As he says, "I never was one to go off into a great production about being queer and work myself up into a state like some people I know. [...] You're born either hetero, bi or homo and whichever way it goes there you are stuck with it" (474). Dying in a Swiss clinic, he recalls highlights from his career and his former lovers. All three novellas became the bases for teleplays.

Noël Peirce Coward (1899–1973) was born just outside London. He remains one of the most successful British playwrights of the 20th century. Though he was always closeted, his longtime partner was actor Graham Payn (1918–2005). He also had affairs with writer Keith Winter, actors Louis Hayward and Alan Webb, his manager John Wilson, and composer Ned Rorem. He appears as a fictionalized character in novels by Winter and Radclyffe Hall. Though most of his plays, as well as his song lyrics, display a campy sensibility, only three are overtly gay: *Semi-Monde*, which was written in 1926 but not premiered until 1977 and only published in 1999; *Design for Living*, 1933, about a *ménage à trois*, which skims close to the relationship between the two men without ever going there; and *A Song at Twilight*, 1966, also based in part on Maugham.

Coward, Noël. *Me and the Girls*. *Pretty Polly Barlow and Other Stories*. London: Heinemann, 1964. *Pretty Polly and Other Stories*. New York: Doubleday, 1965. *The Collected Stories. New York: Dutton, 1983. 467–98.

———. *Star Quality*. London: Heinemann, 1951. *Star Quality: Six Stories*. Garden City, N.Y.: Doubleday, 1951. *The Collected Stories (see above). 310–68.

———. *What Mad Pursuit? To Step Aside: Seven Short Stories*. London: Heinemann, 1939. *To Step Aside: Seven Stories*. New York: Doubleday, Doran, 1939. *The Collected Stories (see above). 53–91.

Hoare, Philip. *Noël Coward: A Biography*. New York: Simon & Schuster, 1995.

Langley, Noel. *So Unlike the English*. New York: Morrow, 1937.

———. *There's a Porpoise Close Behind Us*. London: Barker, 1936. *London: Methuen, 1939.

35 Seaforth Mackenzie: *The Young Desire It*, 1937.

The novel is another school story, but one with significant differences. First and foremost, although the school is run along the same lines as the British model, it is located in Western Australia. Class differences do not play a role; perceptions of a boy's relative effeminacy or masculinity provide a dividing line. There is some sexual play. The novel's hero, Charles Fox, is stripped at least twice by the other boys, and the first time something vague happens: "A new and crueler devastation of pain gripped him from the loins upwards. He did not know what was being done to him" (20). He expresses a sense of indignation when he relates "how he had come stumbling upon a couple of lads closely communing in a hidden place," calling it "ridiculous" (247). But Charles is interested only in girls, and his relationship with a neighbor back home is described in lyrical terms. Though he feels close to Mawley, a fellow schoolmate, his overtures are a manly "claim of spiritual equality" (326).

The sole homosexual in the novel is a young master, Penworth, and he, not surprisingly, is English, a product of Oxford. Australians, despite the "couple of lads," are not like that. In fact, young Charles is so innocent he is not even aware that Penworth is trying to seduce him until Mawley more or less spells out what is going on. In the end the apparently salacious title is misleading. What the young desire, as a fabricated epigraph spells out, is a freedom of choice, though, as the epigraph continues, "they cannot use that freedom, but must be forced into the decision of choice by good or evil circumstances which while they can perceive them they cannot control" (8). Penworth, a dark, perplexing character, is the first undisguised gay male to enter Australian literature. Apparently he never gained any insight into his true nature while at Oxford. When he comes upon Charles, "white and naked" the second time that he is stripped, he recoils, "not understanding his sudden agitation," though he feels "some strange sensation of pleasure and shame course through him" (50). In his role as tutor, he takes every opportunity thereafter to touch the boy.

Coming upon him a second time naked, Charles's heading for the showers, he pulls the boy to him and holds him "hard against him" (122). Still later, he kisses the boy "clumsily and hard on the lips" (134). This time Charles understands "that something had been done which should not have been done, though he did not understand why there was argument against it," but that now "he had been made most conscious [...] of the vastness and danger of his ignorance" (135–36). As Penworth vacillates between irrational desire and acceptance that any relationship is impossible, he takes refuge in Plato's *Phaedrus*. But when Charles, steeled by Mawley, resists his overtures and makes it clear that he finally understands what he is resisting, Penworth reveals that he is more immature than Charles: "Your choice, my friend. There can be no other way; and I don't think I myself am exactly to blame for it" (280). Penworth resigns at the end of the school year, but he will remain in the country. At least, he does not commit suicide.

Kenneth Ivo Brownley Langwell Mackenzie (1913–1955) was born in South Perth, W.A. He attended Guildford Grammar School, the setting for this, his first novel. It won the Australian Literature Society Gold Medal. After briefly studying law, he moved to Sydney to work as a journalist. There he married and had two children. He published three more novels, all under the name Seaforth Mackenzie, and two volumes of poetry, under the name Kenneth Mackenzie. Having become an alcoholic, he was arrested for drunkenness, then released. A few hours later he was found drowned in Tallong Creek, near Gouldburn, N.S.W.

Mackenzie, Seaforth. *The Young Desire It*. London: Cape, 1937. *Intro. Douglas Stewart. North Ryde, N.S.W.: Angus & Robertson, 1963.

36   John Lehmann: *Evil Was Abroad*, 1938; *In the Purely Pagan Sense*, 1976.

Lehmann was a major figure in the publishing world through three decades at midcentury, but he published only two novels himself. *Evil Was Abroad* is set in 1933 as the Nazis consolidate power (hence the novel's poor choice of a title; the original short story out of which it grew was called, more appropriately, "The Boy Who Disappeared"). Peter Rains, an Oxford graduate, is in Vienna researching the life of an Austrian poet. In the company of Mihal, a Dalmatian medical student and former fellow roomer, he has a chance encounter in an automat with Rudi Slavanek, an impoverished, out-of-work nineteen-year-old shoemaker. Peter becomes entranced by the youth and begins to support him financially. Confined by "the genteel sexual translation forced on Lehmann"—as his biographer Adrian Wright phrases it (97)—the novel, despite Rudi's jealousy when he sees Peter in the company of two women (148–49), could be read, for the greater part, as an example of homosocial bonding. But in the last fifth the sexual breaks through. While Peter is on an extended stay in Prague, Rudi vanishes. Searching for him in vain, Peter stops in a café, where he glimpses former classmates. Their presence brings back memories of discussions in which, among other matters, they had held "that the great sin was to pretend that any relationship could be deep and strong without an undercurrent of simply physical attraction, entirely natural and inevitable" (195–96).

He runs into Mihal again and pleads for his help, admitting, "I didn't know how far it had gone until I'd lost him" (203). Mihal must be gay. Thinking it likely that Rudi would go to a gay bar seeking a pickup, he leads Peter into the Prater underworld (Chapter 14). Rudi does not show, but the two men encounter Paul, a youth who knows Rudi. Peter arranges to meet him to follow up a lead. As a result he learns that, though "Rudi didn't often get really worked up about a girl" (248), while Peter was in Prague he fell for Lisl, then accused her of giving him a venereal disease. Peter gives up his search. He muses, "How was it that he, Peter Rains, could feel intimate with some one for weeks, months, to find after all that he had not seen the real person?" (251). He blames himself for having been so self-absorbed, but he now realizes "that Rudi had left him a legacy": he has awakened in him a need to involve himself in social issues (255). Their relationship has also given him greater understanding of the poet he is studying. And his flirtatious manner with Paul suggests greater sexual awareness—though the author does not feel he can explore that possibility. Not yet. That will await his second novel.

In the Purely Pagan Sense reads so much like a memoir that one has a difficult time taking seriously the author's insistence that it is a work of fiction, and indeed, as his biographer makes clear, great swathes of it are thinly disguised accounts of the author's experiences. Yet there are enough differences between the life of its protagonist, Jack Marlowe, and Lehmann's own, that one cannot take it as the fourth volume of his autobiography. The book is, by design, essentially a catalog of sexual encounters, reminiscent at times of Renaud Camus's *Tricks*. It is structured chronologically from Marlowe's first sexual awakening in prep school, through his active pursuit of boys in London, Vienna, and across Europe, on to his diminished expectations in his fifties to ever find a lasting love. It is entertaining, at times sexually arousing, but it is ultimately not a very satisfactory read, hovering as it does between two genres.

Though Marlowe insists that he is seeking "illumination through sex" (75), the sex seldom leads to any particular insight. A number of observations about English homosexuality are scattered across the novel. Marlowe notes how British alliances move "vertically through society rather than horizontally," providing a gay man (a term he never uses, by the way) "far greater experience and understanding of his fellow men than the 'straight' young man" obtains (8). He holds that "Englishmen have a special bias towards bisexuality" (27). As war looms, Marlowe muses on the sexual appeal of English sailors and concludes that they are "symbols of freedom," although he admits that their uniforms are part of it (117). He appreciates "the pleasures and satisfactions to be found so easily in [the] military underworld" of the Guards and ponders briefly their traditional willingness to have sex with men, no matter their own sexual orientation (127, 250). There is relatively little in the novel about politics or the literary scene, and there is no real philosophy or code of conduct that shapes Marlowe's relentless pursuit of an orgasm.

Rudolph John Frederick Lehmann (1907–1987) was born in Buckinghamshire, brother to Rosamond Lehmann. He was educated at Eton and Cambridge. One of the most outstanding editors of his generation, he was a partner with the Woolfs of Hogarth Press and later founded his own publishing house. He was responsible for the *New Writing* series and later *London Magazine*. He also wrote poetry and literary biographies (Edith Sitwell, the Woolfs, Rupert Brooke) as well as three volumes of autobiography. In addition to numerous one-night stands, he had a number of lovers, the most enduring being the Russian ballet dancer Alexis Rassine (1919–1992). Lehmann died in London.

Lehmann, John. *Evil Was Abroad*. London: Cresset, 1938.
———. *In the Purely Pagan Sense*. London: Blond & Briggs, 1976. *Intro. Peter Burton. London: GMP, 1985.
Wright, Adrian. *John Lehmann: A Pagan Adventure*. London: Gerald Duckworth, 1998.

37 Frank Sargeson: *That Summer*, 1943–44; *A Game of Hide and Seek*, 1972.

That Summer employs a typically laconic and relatively uneducated narrator, the New Zealand voice that Sargeson is renowned for capturing in fiction. Upon arriving in the city, having quit his farm job because of a case of "itchy feet" (145), Bill becomes curiously passive. He is incapable of holding a grudge against a couple he meets at the beach when they rob him of all his money. When another lodger, Maggie, is beaten up by her sailor boyfriend on shore leave and accuses Bill of having been the culprit, he is only worried about not being able to take care of his tubercular roommate, Terry O'Connor. Ordered to stand trial, Bill makes no effort to defend himself, relying totally on Terry's promise (fulfilled) to get him off. Apart from a series of petty thefts to gain money, a short stint in a restaurant as a washer, and visits to the horse races, his only real burst of action occurs when he helps Terry escape the hospital to return to the lodging house to die. Nominally straight, Bill never carries through with any of the women he checks out. What he wants is a mate in the Anzac sense of the word.

That he finds in Terry. Though they momentarily share a bed and continue to room together, and though Bill feels jealous when Terry disappears for a while on some mysterious partnership with another fellow, there is no indication of any kind of sexual relationship between the two men. Bill rejects the advances of the cook, "a real old auntie," at the restaurant with indignation (177). But he is such an innocent that it takes an obscure outburst at a drunken party and a memory of feeling up a flat chest before he is able "to put two and two together" about Maggie: "it's not always so easy to make two and two add up right" (226). Finally he understands what threat Terry used against her to make her change her testimony. Interestingly enough, Maggie does not seem to be a true transsexual, for s/he declares, "I'm sick of wearing these glad rags round my legs" (225). Rather, it would appear that the boyfriend has forced him into disguise so as to circumvent the law and social disapproval.

The much gayer—in fact, downright campy—*A Game of Hide and Seek*, remains almost unknown. It is like the flip side of *That Summer*. Ivan, its nearly forty-year-old narrator, is well versed in literature, particularly gay literature (he admires Firbank above all), art, and home decor. He is quite campy, often elliptical in speech in a nudge-nudge wink-wink sort of way. He can keep a job no more than Bill and likewise is not above engaging in any number of dodgy practices (a particularly lucrative money-maker being the sale of contraband contraceptives). But, though discreet, he obviously enjoys fleshy pleasures. There is no doubt that he and a Samoan immigrant worker, Tua, a young bulldozer operator, are sexually lovers, though bound by no vows of monogamy. Ivan accepts Tua's "versatility" (181); he knows he is the father of a yet unborn child and a hustler on the side. Ivan also comes to realize that Tua is being used by two vicious Australians in a blackmail scheme. One of his clients, a barrister friend of Ivan's father, kills himself when the wife threatens to expose him. Ivan becomes concerned when he learns that his own father, who is his major financial support, may be another client. We leave the story, however, as uncertain of the true gender of the "slender young woman in slacks" whom Ivan sees join his father in his car as Ivan himself is (159).

By story's end, Tua plans to return to his island home. Facing the diminution of his father's financial support upon his upcoming retirement, Ivan (a name, by the way, that he has self-bequeathed upon himself on leaving home) agrees to his father's proposal to divide the family home into two so they can share the place yet maintain their privacy. Ivan proposes to Gaby, "the attractive besides attractively civilized young son" (226) of a doctor friend, to join him there: "He says he cannot contain his excitement over our new life together. His father does not disapprove of his decision to strike out on his own. But whether Gaby will ever be introduced to my father is another question" (232). The author employs a delightful strategy: having the narrator insist that what he is writing is fiction makes it sound all the more like nonfiction since Ivan's assertion is patently a lie designed to protect him should his papers fall into wrong hands. When the police come to question Tua, Ivan is not worried—first because he has already transferred the bulk of the story to a hiding place in his father's home; but basically because, as he says, "what is there that might compromise me in these pages? All is fiction as I have already explained, and all is written with a decency of reticence and reserve" (231). The pretense ends with a flourish: "it would not surprise me if I presently find myself committed to beginning another fiction" (233).

Various threads of ghoulish humor weave through this story of sexual mischief and other social transgressions. Ivan discovers that his straight friend Derek, a meter reader for the gas company, is still a virgin because of a case of undescended testicles. Derek has a crush on Ivan's always pregnant friend, Lucy. Her pregnancies are all the more remarkable since, he also learns, her husband, Leo, has such a small penis that he cannot truly penetrate her vagina. Thus she would welcome Derek's more sizable advances. But poor Derek, forced by Ivan to confront the truth that he is sterile, ends up in a psychiatric hospital, leaving Lucy's lusty fantasies unfulfilled. A spirited defense of pornography is worth quoting in full. Ivan has met his father at his club, to be joined by an army officer, an Australian customs official, and an American evangelist: "The army man pronounced himself not interested in questions about the control of pornographic literature which the other two were discussing. The operative words in use were undesirable and unsavoury, and I risked intervening to protest against the misuse of the English language. Obviously what was much desired by great numbers of people should not be described as undesirable. Surely too anyone was capable of the clear and simple understanding that since nobody would care to eat an unsavoury meal, nobody need worry one moment about *any* kind of unsavoury consumer-item. Clearly consumer-demand would register zero. And surely too it was clear that in a society committed to democracy and universal education nobody would argue on behalf of obstacles designed to prevent people from discovering in books anything they might have a mind to search for" (225).

Born Norris Frank Davey (1903–1982) in Hamilton, New Zealand, he was arrested in 1929 as the result of an encounter with a Wellington painter and given a suspended sentence on the condition that he live with his uncle, Oakley Sargeson, on a remote farm. Thereafter he called himself Frank Sargeson. In the mid–1930s he formed a liaison with a laborer and horse trainer, Harry Doyle, which they maintained until Doyle's death in 1971. Sargeson never came out, but he formed friendships with other gay writers, a number of his short stories are homoerotic to varying degrees.

King, Michael. *Frank Sargeson: A Life*. Auckland: Viking, 1995.
Sargeson, Frank. *Man of England Now, with I for One ... and A Game of Hide and Seek*. Christchurch, N.Z.: Caxton, 1972. *London: Brian & O'Keeffe, 1972. 151–233.
____. *That Summer. Penguin New Writing*, ed. John Lehmann, nos. 17–19. Harmondsworth, Eng.: Lane, 1943–44. *The Stories of Frank Sargeson*. Auckland: Penguin, 1982. 143–227.

38 W. Somerset Maugham: *The Razor's Edge*, 1944.

Though gay, Maugham carefully steered clear of introducing any gay characters into his work until late in his writing career. *The Razor's Edge* presents Elliott Templeton, a rich American expatriate living in France. His sexuality is never mentioned per se, but in his mannerisms and his type of snobbism, he is almost stereotypically gay. It is hard to like Elliott; it is even harder not to admire the manner in which he maintains his pretensions against all odds. However, even though he is constantly butting into his sister's and his niece's lives, he has absolutely no effect on the novel's straight hero, young Larry Darrell, who is searching for the meaning of life. To be such an ineffectual and actually relatively minor character, it is striking how many readers have commented on the powerful impressions he leaves behind.

According to Maugham's biographer Selina Hastings (476), "there was much busy speculation about Elliott's original, but in the end it was Maugham's publisher who revealed that the prototype was one Henry Chalmers Roberts, a retired American diplomat [and] pederast." Since Larry becomes involved in Hindu philosophy, there were claims that Isherwood, to his great annoyance, served as his model (and thus, by implication, that Denham Fouts, with a sex change, must have served as the addicted woman to whom Larry proposes marriage). Isherwood's biographer Peter Parker records (469) that he was consulted about the proper translation of the epigraph to the novel, taken from the *Katha Upanishad*, but his advice was then ignored. The novel has been filmed twice.

William Somerset Maugham (1874–1965) was born in the British embassy in Paris. He lost his parents at an early age and was reared by an emotionally cold uncle. He attended Cambridge and then qualified as a physician, serving with the Red Cross in World War I as well as being a government spy. Maugham became a highly popular playwright and a best-selling author (*The Razor's Edge* quickly hit the best-selling lists upon publication). His two great loves were the American Gerald Haxton (1892–1944) and Alan Searle (1905–1985), of cockney origins. Maugham fathered a child in 1915 and later married, and then divorced, the mother, Syrie Wellcome. He was promiscuous all his life. Some readers, most notably Gore Vidal, have also claimed *The Narrow Corner*, 1932, for gay fiction.

Hastings, Selina. *The Secret Lives of Somerset Maugham*. 2009. New York: Random House, 2010.

Maugham, W. Somerset. *The Razor's Edge*. London: Heinemann, 1944. New York: Doubleday, Doran, 1944. *New York: Vintage, 2003.

39   Tom Hopkinson: *Mist in the Tagus*, 1946.

On a whim Caroline Page, a young London copywriter, decides to holiday in Marinha, Portugal. Literally a self-made person (Caroline Page was not her birth name), she is seeking the next stage in her evolution. There she falls under the spell of a mixed but strangely united group of friends. There are Paul, an Oxford dandy having his "first love affair with a woman" (63); Hélène, a Savoyard dress designer working in Paris; Maxim, a Dordogne heir to a cutlery business; and Bettina, a German artist and a sensualist pursued by a Portuguese man of some standing in the community. And there are Robert Kranz, a German physician in exile because of the Nazis, and his lover, the charismatic poet Leo, who is absent in person until the final chapters, but who is very much present in everyone's mind throughout the course of the story. The two have been together for eight years, ever since Robert nursed Leo back to health in Berlin after he slashed his wrists. Robert has stuck with him even when Leo's sexual escapades have caused trouble (like the time he became too chummy with some of the Portuguese fishers' sons). Bettina holds that "Leo is not ashamed, for he knows that he is what he is. He did not make himself, and does not feel responsible or guilty. You cannot alter Leo, or make him into something different" (132).

Saved by Robert when she exhausts herself swimming, Caroline falls in love with him. They have sex and share secrets. But as soon as Leo reappears, Robert is his again. Again, Bettina seems to have the deepest insight: "I thought that underneath all this muddle, Robert was either one thing or the other, either an ordinary man or ... something different, just as Leo is. I see now that he is not one thing or other, he is double. And it's not because he's attracted both ways, but because he is repelled. He is divided in himself, and reacts always *against* the thing which is and wants the thing which is not" (213). Caroline returns to England, convinced that she has learned something about the nature of love but that Robert has not and will, as a consequence, suffer. But she also perceives: "since I have changed my name, I have lost my own identity, and so I cannot recognize things and people any more" (243).

The novel is simultaneously a dated prewar period piece and a timeless (as long as one ignores technology) story of rootless bohemians, expatriates, nonconformists, free spirits. Henry Thomas Hopkinson (1905–1990) was born in Manchester, the son of a clergyman and a schoolteacher. He graduated from Oxford and moved into journalism, being one of the foremost editors of photojournals—most remembered now for his stint on London's *Picture Post*, 1938–50, and South Africa's *Drum*, 1958–61. He was married three times and was the father of three daughters.

Hopkinson, Tom. *Mist in the Tagus*. London: Hogarth, 1946. *Boston: Little, Brown, 1947.

40   Ernest Frost: *The Dark Peninsula*, 1949; *The Lighted Cities*, 1950.

The Dark Peninsula describes Italy in 1944 as the Italian campaign is being fought in the north. The title is also, according to the poet Arnold Thompson, a private in the British Army, the metaphor for each individual's life (192). Two lives in the novel are of particular interest to the gay reader: that of Colonel Edward Judd, formerly a London publisher, and that of Lieutenant David Mulholland. Both men are haunted by their relationship, emotional and sexual, with a dead poet, called either by his initial "A." or by his first name only, "Anthony." A. left Mulholland for Judd because Judd was more useful to him. The day of his desertion remains engraved on Mulholland's memory: when "they had moved through morning like tall, handsome ghosts, finally ranging each other with flesh in an unmade bed" (146). Trying to recapture A., Mulholland finds himself drawn to Thompson, even as he recognizes just how shallow and dangerous the young man is, and to Judd who proves more powerful than he. Judd in turn is attracted to both of them because of their resemblance in different ways to Anthony.

A widower and a father, Judd has become the subject of gossip and of military cover-ups because of his pursuit of young men. Declaring that "history is a matter of repeated errors," he admits, "I've grown into error" (207). His latest is some sort of advance he makes to a young private named Kent, one which gets him reposted to the north. Judd goes for a last visit to Mulholland, who is recuperating in the military hospital from a tropical fever that has nearly killed him but that provides some cathartic liberation from A.'s influence. It also acts as some strange rite of passage into full-fledged heterosexuality. Mulholland thinks: "Their lives branched out in opposite directions: the Colonel's towards the past, to Anthony [...] and his towards the mute, upstanding future" (210) in which he will unite with the adulterous woman he has fallen in love with. The two men briefly acknowledge Anthony's influence on the two of them. Judd says, "Yes, he was worth it—the reality and the memory...." To which Mulholland replies, "Worth it if we could bear it, if we could live to that pattern. I can't any more, but you, sir—?" And Judd says, "I have to" (212).

An obsession with the letter *A* gets the best of the author in *The Lighted Cities*. (The title comes from the first of Spender's "Variations on My Life," 1939). Alexander Rainham is an elderly music teacher, hopelessly in love with his protégé, Arthur Godwin. Arthur has essentially taken the place of his dead lover, Adriano Confallodini. He is a sexless sponger, with less talent than everyone thinks, but is useful as a pawn in an academic rivalry between Rainham (who thankfully is called Alexander only part of the time) and Andreas Amenis, an art teacher. Andreas steals Arthur away from Rainham, but Rainham will not give up and persists in trying to find Arthur in order to win him back. Andreas, who enjoys wielding power over young men, picks up the writer Bernard Austel. Bernard (occasionally called Austel) falls in love with Andreas's wife and, unknowingly, impregnates her. Rainham, now senile, accidentally drowns, leaving his money to Arthur. Andreas agrees to play the father for Bernard's child. All this presumably has some point, but not only is it difficult to keep all the A-characters straight, it is difficult to care about them, they are so self-absorbed and unbearably dull.

Ernest M. Frost (1919–1986) served in the British Army 1940–46. After the war, he married and had a son. He became a teacher, first in schools in and around London and then in a teachers' college in Leicestershire. He published five more novels, the last in 1966.

Frost, Ernest. *The Dark Peninsula*. London: Lehmann, 1950.
_____. *The Lighted Cities*. London: Lehmann, 1950.
*New York: Harcourt, Brace, 1952.

41 Nancy Mitford: *Love in a Cold Climate*, 1949. Villiers David: *Love in London*, 1954. Pamela Hansford Johnson: *The Last Resort*, 1956.

Mitford's and Johnson's novels have many similarities. Both are narrated by married women who are more observers than participants in the action. Both have as a central character an unmarried daughter in conflict with her family. Both treat heterosexual adultery lightly. Both introduce characters who are flamboyant gay stereotypes. And both novels are content to use slurs about homosexuals. The endings do differ significantly: *Love in a Cold Climate* leaves a homosexual in the ascendency; *The Last Resort* permits the triumph of heterosexuality.

Love in a Cold Climate is the middle novel of a trilogy narrated by Fanny Logan Wincham. The parents of Fanny's cousin Polly Hampton are distraught because she shows no interest in marriage. After the death of Boy Dougdale's wife, it comes out that the cool, aloof Polly has been in love with the man, despite the great difference in their ages, ever since he fondled her while she was a fourteen-year-old girl. In fact, it turns out that not only is Boy fond of fondling all ages of both sexes, he was at one time the lover of Polly's mother. Ignorant of all this and headstrong in her passion, Polly maneuvers him into marriage, to her parents' horror. They cut off their allowance, and the newlyweds are forced to move to the less expensive Sicily. There, Polly's shallowness and xenophobia come to the fore. Meanwhile, her parents have invited Cedric Hampton, her cousin born in Nova Scotia, to visit the family estate. It turns out that he has been living in Paris, the kept boy of some baron. Cedric charms his hosts, if not their neighbors, and "London society, having none of the prejudices against the abnormal" (224), embraces him. He settles in as a permanent guest and quickly picks up a lorry driver, whose truck has broken down outside the estate's gates, "to do odd jobs" (194), including, presumably, special services for Cedric. Pregnant Polly, her marriage in tatters, returns to England. Seeking to make money, Boy takes on a book about dukes, including two whom Cedric knows. The two men get on "like mad" and start planning a visit "to Paris together to do some research" (244). Our last view of Cedric shows him resting on a wall, plucking out the petals of a daisy: "He loves me, he loves me not, he loves me" (245). Simon Raven adapted the novel for television.

The Last Resort makes for an unpleasant read, from its sly title (ostensibly meaning one thing; contextually another) to its smug heterosexual finale. (The novel was retitled *The Sea and the Wedding* in the United States.) The narrator is Christine Hall, a successful novelist married to a successful publisher. But the plot is provided by the muddled life of Celia Baird, the daughter of a surly physician and an overly protective mother. Celia has entered an adulterous relationship with Eric Aveling, an architect whose wife is confined to a hospital where she lies dying. Just before her death she reveals to her husband that she has known about his unfaithfulness. The couple's guilt drives them apart. Out of loneliness and something approaching desperation, Celia accepts as a last resort marriage to Junius Evans. He is tired of the fickleness of the young men he has being having affairs with. According to the narrator, Junius "was looking forward to this marriage, to the outward respectability that it would bring him, to not being alone any longer. It could not be a true marriage; but it might work. [...] In this strange and empty marriage there would be no sin for Celia" (284–85). Celia has the last word, triumphantly signing the postcards written on her honeymoon, "Celia Evans."

Sometimes muted, sometimes overtly antigay attitudes run throughout the novel. Celia's father is the most obnoxious, creating a scene worthy of the Marquis of Queensbury when two young aesthetes appear in his presence. Junius is Eric's partner in the firm, but Eric admits, "I've always found it hard to be tolerant, as the custom is nowadays, towards Junius's way of life" (244). The narrator has more than her share of intolerant comments, always ready with the subtle putdown for gays she runs into in clubs and at parties. She accuses Junius, as had Celia earlier, of being misogynous. When Junius admits that he does not approve of Eric and Celia's relationship, she implies that Junius lusts after Eric for himself. He points out to her: "You like men. I don't insult you by supposing that you want to go to bed with every man you meet" (173). Later the narrator keeps to herself that she feels "nothing but admiration for the persistence" of the mother who takes Junius's last lover away from him. But Junius understands well that she does not "really like people of my persuasion. All tolerance outside, all Pilgrim Fathers within" (261). Heterosexual adultery and deception of a dying wife can be condoned; homosexuality is, at best, distasteful.

The campy *Love in London* is of a different order, but it has enough of the same attitudes that it can serve as a kind of coda. It too has a daughter (Maria) in conflict with a mother (Lola), both of them lusting after the same man. In this case, the mother is the wife of the ambassador from Santa Cruz to the Court of St. James (José Calderon-y-Carrambas). The man is a London bobby, Tom English. He is a curiously sexless human who, nevertheless, impregnates a local girl and then seems willing to rent his body to a gay man in order to obtain the money needed for an abortion. The gay, a decorator who goes by the name Mr. Tristan (his unseen partner is called Isolda), is even more a stereotype than Cedric. When Tom flees the overly demanding Calderon women, Lola hires a detective to find him. He reports back how Tom has been seen in Tristan's company, and she uses the information to blackmail him out of presenting a bill for redecorating their official residence. The satiric novel is a soufflé, nothing more.

Nancy Freeman-Mitford (1904–1973) was born in London and brought up in Oxfordshire. Cedric was based on one of the bright young people, Stephen Tennant. Her own romance with a gay Scot, Hamish St. Clair Erskine, failed, and she married Peter Rodd, one of the models for Waugh's Basil Seal. They separated in 1939 and were formally divorced in 1958. During the war she had a relationship with De Gaulle's chief of staff and moved to Paris to be near him after the fall of Germany. She died in Versailles of Hodgkin's disease. A London native, Pamela Hansford Johnson (1912–1981) wrote twenty-nine novels, including two mysteries with her first husband, the Australian novelist Gordon Neil Stewart. The mother of three children, she married second the English novelist C. P. Snow. Villiers David (1906–1985) was a poet and a largely self-taught artist. The Villiers David Foundation was founded by his heir, Gerard Schlup.

David, Villiers. *Love in London*. London: Duckworth, 1954. *New York: Coward–McCann, 1954.
Johnson, Pamela Hanford. *The Last Resort*. London: Macmillan, 1956. *The Sea and the Wedding*. New York: Harcourt, Brace, 1957.
Mifford, Nancy. *Love in a Cold Climate*. London: Hamilton, 1949. New York: Random House, 1949. *New York: Vintage, 2010.

42 Norah Lofts: *The Lute Player*, 1951. Helen A. Mahler: *Empress of Byzantium*, 1952. Margaret Campbell Barnes: *Isabel the Fair*, 1957. Alfred Duggan: *Family Favourites*, 1960.

Four novelists chose a homosexual ruler as the subject for a historical novel: Elagabalus (c.203–222), Theodosius II (408–450), Richard the Lionhearted (1157–1199), and Edward II (1284–1327). And each used the strategy of viewing that ruler through heterosexual eyes. Nevertheless, they are commendable for their daring, considering the period in which they were writing. Lofts outed Richard I at a time when his sexuality was largely ignored. Moreover, her story, as well as Duggan's, contains an explicit defense of homosexuality.

Lofts plays her readers cagily. There is no indication that Richard I is sexually interested in only men until almost halfway through *The Lute Player*. His mother, Eleanor of Aquitaine, comes, unannounced, upon him in his tent in Sicily, when he is with Blondel: "And I looked into Richard's face and saw there [...] naked, hungry, lustful desire directed at another man" (248). She reflects, however, that "he was my best beloved son; flawed by a fault I had never suspected, less perfect than I had believed all these years, but no less dear" (254). Almost immediately the narrative responsibility shifts to Blondel, who remains oblivious to Richard's desires until after the Crusade has been lost. True, the attentive reader picks up hints he unknowingly drops and begins to wonder about Richard's relationship to a recaptured Christian, Raife of Clermont. But not until the two men are on road to Austria does Blondel record: "On the second night out from Seleucia I learned exactly what it was that Raife of

Clermont had tried to tell me on his deathbed, and I knew exactly why Richard Plantagenet had no love for or need of his wife. I swear I did not know until then" (417).

Blondel rejects Richard's overtures. But then the author has Blondel say, "I ask myself: Was he to blame because he had an inclination towards men rather than towards women? Surely no man would choose it any more than he would choose to be deformed, or cowardly, or diseased. [...] What does puzzle me about it all is the inescapable sense of shame which attends even the thought of the subject. It is, we say, 'against nature'—but then so are many things: patricide, matricide, infanticide—yet the mention of them brings no blush to the cheek. True, it is sterile, it defies God's order to 'be fruitful and multiply,' but the same is true of all monastic and conventual vows which are considered most honorable. It is not forbidden in the Ten Commandments; nor does it take rank with the seven deadly sins" (418). The final section is narrated by Queen Berengaria's half-sister, Anna, a hunchback who is in love with Blondel. Richard's—and supposedly Blondel's—secret is now known to the women in the household, though Anna feels certain that the rumors are wrong about Blondel. On his deathbed Richard begs pardon of Berengaria, then continues: "But god makes us, you know, and He did not make me—a lover of women—it was not my choice" (554).

Mahler's novel about Theodosius II, *Empress of Byzantium*, was written in German but was translated "by the author with the assistance of Leona Nevler." It is pure melodrama. Young Theodosius feels a deep passion for his lord chamberlain, the straight Paulinus. But once Paulinus forces Theodosius into a house of prostitution and he gazes upon a woman's naked body, he confesses that he has "been plagued since then by a yearning for women" (68), and he agrees to take a wife—without ever losing his passion for Paulinus. His choice of empress, Athenais, likewise falls in love with Paulinus. To add more complications, the Emperor's sister too is in love with him. When Theodosius realizes where his wife's true affections lie, he takes Paulinus sexually (229).

After several turns and various machinations, one of Paulinus's enemies, introduces Paulinus's illegitimate (and castrated) son to Theodosius. He looks so like the young Paulinus with whom Theodosius fell in love that they are soon sharing sexual favors. The emperor still feels betrayed by his wife, however, and ultimately decrees that Paulinus must be destroyed. As a result, he is left utterly alone and miserable.

Barnes's take on Edward II in *Isabel the Fair* provides a surprisingly fun read, not nearly as one-sided as one might expect from the author's decision to show the king and his two lovers from the viewpoint of his queen. She is not happy with the way her husband treats her, yet she is far from being a virtuous, misunderstood wife. Though sometimes she can be compassionate, caring about others' feelings, she is vain, impetuous, the sort that would have been less than easy to live with even had Edward's tastes been heterosexual. Edward and Piers Gaveston are portrayed as handsome, fun-loving men, obviously in love with each other. At one point Piers says to her, "But do you not realize, Isabel, that but for our mutual love for Edward you and I might have been very good friends?" (98). Once Isabel succeeds in securing Piers's death (only to realize that she did not really hate him), husband and wife split irreconcilably.

Envy, jealousy, and a hurt pride (plus her strong sex drive) propel her into Roger Mortimer's arms. Memories of Piers continue to haunt the rest of the action, but Edward now becomes enamored of young Hugh Despenser. At one point, he begs his queen: "Do not wholly condemn me, Isabel. My life has not been easy, either. You speak of urges which you do not understand" (215). She herself recognizes that "not even the Despenser's death could give her back her marriage—nor her clean, self-respecting soul" (273). The tragedy uncoils in grim deliberation: Mortimer and Edward are killed, and Isabel is imprisoned for life by her own son. The manner of Edward's death is cruelly detailed, without making anything of its possible sexual significance. Romantic as it may be, the novel allows one to reread both Marlowe's and Brecht's plays with new understanding.

Any reader who expects to be titillated by Duggan's account of the notorious Roman emperor Elagabalus, *Family Favourites*, will be sorely disappointed. Not that the author ignores the familiar stories that have come down to us. The emperor's relations with the drivers Gordius, some fifteen years his senior, and Hierocles, a youth his own age, are an important part of the story, as are his various gender performances and his near-nude athletic excesses. But they are recounted in such a matter-of-fact way by the narrator, a completely heterosexual, Gallic-born praetorian, that they have no shock value, and in fact many of his acts that have been labeled as decadent, Duggan shows to be an outgrowth of his deeply religious nature. Ceremonies, military and government affairs, and, above all, intrigues among the women in his family (Elagabalus and an equally young cousin are the only surviving males) take up a goodly portion of the novel.

Margaret Campbell (1891–1962) was born in Sussex. She married Peter Barnes in 1917 and had two sons. She wrote ten historical novels in all, with clearly a female audience in mind. She died on the Isle of Wight. Helen A. Mahler was born Anna Helene Askanasy (d. 1970?). She was Gustav Mahler's niece, an Austrian refugee who fled to Canada in 1938. Living in British Columbia, she was involved in the feminist movement there. Norah Robinson (1904–1983) was born in Norfolk. In 1933 she married Geoffrey Lofts, by whom she had a son; widowed, she married Robert Jorisch in 1949. She published well over forty historical novels, as well as mysteries under the pseudonym Peter Curtis. She died in Suffolk.

Alfred Leo Duggan (1903–1964) was born in Argentina but was still an infant when the family moved to London. His father had Irish roots; his mother, American. Widowed before her son was a teenager, she became the second wife of Lord Curzon. Duggan served in World War II. He married in 1953 and had a son. He was a prolific writer of both standard histories and historical novels, but this was the only one with a gay thread running through it. As a student at Eton and Oxford, Duggan, though heterosexual (he was expelled from Eton for all-night dalliances with a town girl), would have been familiar with homosexual scenes. It is easy to imagine his voice behind the narrator's when we read, "The Emperor's private life was his own affair, and it seems to me ridiculous to hold that it is more wicked to love boys than girls. But my own tastes lie in a different direction, and I could never understand the intensity of his feeling" (162).

Barnes, Margaret Campbell. *Isabel the Fair*. London: Macdonald, 1957. *Philadelphia: Macrae Smith, 1957.
Duggan, Alfred. *Family Favourites*. London: Faber, 1960. New York: Pantheon, 1961. *London: Phoenix, 2007.
Icks, Martijn. *The Crimes of Elagabalus: The Life and Legacy of Rome's Decadent Boy Emperor*. 2011. Cambridge, Mass.: Harvard University Press, 2012. Chapter 7.
Lofts, Norah. *The Lute Player*. London: Joseph, 1951. Garden City, N.Y.: Doubleday, 1951. *New York: Touchstone, 2009.
Mahler, Helen A. *Empress of Byzantium*. New York: Coward–McCann, 1952.

43 Michael Meyer: *The End of the Corridor*, **1951. Note on Graham Greene.**

Meyer's only novel, a schoolboy story, seems curiously broken-backed, uncertain of its direction. This is all the more disheartening since all the elements are present to have lifted it well above the usual fare. In particular, the final chapters explore the nature of love, including its relationship to the physical, in a deeper, more satisfying way than one finds in the majority of the genre. Young Adrian Derwent develops an unrequited crush on his schoolmate Peer Lang. Then he is visited one night by an unknown boy who reveals to him the physical pleasures of sex: "Love, Adrian had believed, was what he felt for Peer Lang: altruistic and absolute devotion [...] an aesthetic ecstasy. Physical desire had seemed to Adrian something distinct from, if not opposed to love. He had been unable to connect the two. But now, for the first time, he had actually slept with someone, and he felt no shame at all; only a great bodily peace and mental exhilaration. [...] he longed only for the unknown boy to come back and lay again his warm and naked body against his own" (176–77).

For a moment he thinks Colin Eliott, another boy in the circle of seven who have formed around a young master, Roger Woolley, may have been the one who paid him the nighttime visit. But he realizes that Colin is in love with an unknown. Adrian decides that the only way he can free the two of them is by unveiling who this person is. He discovers, to his astonishment, that it is Roger, whom he has never even considered because of his age (he is twenty-nine) and, above all, his ugliness. He and Roger have a long talk, invoking the symbol of the Golden Bough, preparatory to Adrian's leaving the school. For a rare moment in the schoolboy genre, we have several boys and a master who accept matter-of-factly that they are gay and that, even though finding love will not be easy, it is a worthy goal to pursue: "So, thought Adrian, I have come at last to the end of the corridor" (219).

For some reason, the author chose to tell Adrian's story at one remove. The story is narrated by his guardian, Paul Macrae, a stiff, unfeeling, womanizing bachelor. The device yields none of the richness it does in James's or Conrad's works. Macrae admits that he feels no love for the boy and operates only from a sense of duty, Adrian's mother, widowed by World War I, having begged him just before she dies in childbirth to take on the boy. Paul seems to understand little of the story's significance and to learn nothing from what Adrian reveals to him. He even gets the structure wrong when he claims that "Adrian's short career through life was a kind of inverted parody of Dante's journey through the lower regions; beginning in a dull kind of Paradiso, he passed through an even duller, but less agreeable Purgatory, and ended in the most violent section of the Inferno" (82). One wonders if the author himself grasped his failure as a novelist when he gratuitously kills Adrian off in World War II.

Michael Leverson Meyer (1921–2000) was born and died in London. He was educated at Wellington and Oxford. After service in World War II, he taught at Uppsala University in Sweden, the first step, as it turned out, to his becoming an authority on both Strindberg and Ibsen. He translated their plays and wrote a biography of each. He wrote an autobiography, *Not Prince Hamlet: Literary and Theatrical Memoirs*, 1989, focusing not on his life but on the people he knew, most notably Graham Greene.

Henry Graham Greene (1904–1991), incidentally, presents an interesting case. Though he would appear to have been straight, a certain homoerotic tension runs through much of his work. Michael Shelden in his biography devotes an entire chapter to the subject. He cites the following novels as worth reading from this perspective: *The Man Within*, 1929 (Andrews and Carlyon); *Brighton Rock*, 1938 (Pinkie); *The Ministry of Fear*, 1943 (Rowe's dream); *The Heart of the Matter*, 1948 (Scobie and Ali); *The Third Man*, 1950 (Martins); *The End of the Affair*, 1951 (Bendrix and Miles); and *The Quiet American*, 1955 (Fowler and Pyle). Sheldon also explicates ways in which a final memoir, *Getting to Know the General*, 1985, about a visit to Panama, is of gay interest. If nothing else, Greene's frequent use of the secret agent trope adds insight into the double life gays had to live throughout the period in which he was writing. The 1962 short story "May We Borrow Your Husband?" is, of course, gay in every sense of the word (as are the plays: *The Return of A. J. Raffles*, 1975, and the doubleheader *Yes and No* and *For Whom the Bell Chimes*, 1980).

Meyer, Michael. *The End of the Corridor*. London: Collins, 1951.

Shelden, Michael. *Graham Greene: The Enemy Within*. New York: Random House, 1994. Chapter 4.

44 Walter Baxter: *Look Down in Mercy*, 1951.

Here is another novel inexplicably missing from most gay literary scholarship, an exception being Paul Hammond's *Love Between Men in English Literature*. It deserves rediscovery. Set during the Burma campaign against the Japanese during World War II, it describes

Captain Tony Kent's growing awareness of his feelings for his batman, Anson, until his final capitulation and acceptance of his sexual and emotional needs. It is a tribute to the author's skill that one cares about the relationship, for Kent is not an attractive figure. He is callused, early on raping a Euro-Asian nurse in an attempt to prove that he is not homosexual, that he just misses his wife whom he has not seen for two years, and then blaming her for being "so easy" (48). He proves to be a coward when he faces death, even, to his humiliation, soiling his pants under Anson's gaze. He feels relieved to discover that Anson does not despise him as a result, that his rank still commands respect. As Hammond writes (222), "War has loosened some social constraints, throwing up new kinds of time and space where desire may find expression, but class distinctions still have an important influence over what turns out to be imaginable."

The two men escape the general massacre by the Japanese and literally walk back towards the safety of India. Kent "now knew quite clearly what he wanted to do but he was still struggling against himself, bitterly resenting the truth and terrified of the consequences, all his upbringing and fundamental ignorance shouting at him that what he was considering was unthinkable, beyond words dreadful" (231). But finally the two men embrace sexually, fully, tenderly. Their moment of happiness is threatened by the ironically named Goodwin, a soldier who derives pleasure from hurting others. He has earlier gratuitously murdered a leper asleep outside a Buddhist temple without being discovered. He now tries to blackmail Kent, whereupon Kent coolly shoots him. For once a gay man definitively eliminates an oppressor. But Kent finds he cannot eliminate his own social conditioning so easily. When they arrive to safety in India, Kent decrees that they must separate and forget what has occurred between them. As he sinks into depression, his Indian servant suggests he invite Anson to return: "Kent looked at him morosely. If any European had said such a thing to him he would have been instantly suspicious, but although he was fond of Sher Ali it never occurred to him that an Indian, of the servant class, could have the faintest suspicion as to the reason why he talked so much about Anson. 'I couldn't possibly do that, he's a private soldier, it would be unheard of for me to be seen going about with him, quite apart from the fact that it isn't allowed.' And Sher Ali sighed at what he considered to be Kent's stupidity and wisely held his tongue" (301).

Kent contemplates suicide. He decides to pitch himself out the window so his death might appear an accident. And now something amazing happens between the British and the American editions of the novel. In both he climbs up on the window sill; in both the wooden ledge breaks and at the last moment he tries to save himself. Providing the novel's title, the British edition ends, "As his body began to plunge towards the drive he held his arms in a grotesque attitude as though to break his fall and he cried out; but not for mercy" (288). The American edition ends, "He knew that he had solved nothing and he persuaded himself that there was nothing to solve, all he had to do now was to go on living and be with Anson. He resolved firmly to try and be brave and to try and be good; to do more than that, he told himself, was not in his power. Sher Ali came into the room and picked up his hat and equipment" (308). The American version also earlier permitted more physical rapport between the two men, including kissing. As of yet, there seems to be no explanation how the differences came about, but gay readers definitely want to read the American version.

Walter Baxter (1915–1994) served in Burma and India during World War II. Tennessee Williams encountered him and his lover in Rome in 1953. In his notebooks (July 8) he mentioned how much he had enjoyed the novel. Baxter's second, and last, novel, *The Image and the Search*, 1953, depicts a woman trying to find a love to take the place of the one she had with her dead husband. Its frankness resulted in its being charged with obscenity and brought to trial. Discouraged, Baxter floundered. Isherwood called upon him in

London in fall 1961 and recorded in his diary (October 6) that he "has become a rather tragic self-pitying drunken figure with a philosophy of failure." Baxter insisted that he could still write, but the "only thing that interested him [...] was to record some of his very early sex experiences; and those couldn't possibly be published." By then he had a French restaurant in South Kensington, The Chanterelle. In 1962 Baxter fell in love with Fergus Provan (1941–1997), newly arrived in London from Scotland. Provan opened his own restaurant, but when Baxter retired in 1978, he took over The Chanterelle until his own retirement in 1993.

Baxter, Walter. *Look Down in Mercy*. London: Heinemann, 1951.
_____. *Look Down in Mercy*. Revised. New York: Putnam's, 1952.

45 Desmond Stewart: *Leopard in the Grass*, 1951; *The Unsuitable Englishman*, 1954; *The Vampire of Mons*, 1976.

In *Leopard in the Grass* a young English archeologist, John Stirling, arrives in the fictional Mideast city of Cyropolis to pursue his love of the structural arch. There his life becomes intertwined with three very different types. He is pursued by Sophie Abbas, Jewish but apparently formerly married to an Arab. For her, sex is a drug, and John is willing enough to provide her a fix. He meets a homosexual sculptor and poet known only as Q., "more exotic, more bizarre than the Irishman of the anecdotes" (56). Universally disdained by the other Europeans, he would be for that reason alone appealing to John. The third is Q.'s former servant and lover, Nimr, a Bedouin, the leopard of the title, for whom the only fitting adjective, John says, is "beautiful" (57). His charismatic appeal changes John's life. Nimr now hates Q., "the man who had removed him from the anonymity of the desert, taught him profoundly a new language, seduced him, tired of him, thrown him equipped on the competitive heap of those who struggle for government appointments, of those who for money push down or are themselves pushed" (152). When an opportunity arises, he kidnaps Q., along with John and Sophie, planning to kill him. But soldiers intervene, and subsequently Nimr is hanged. Now in love with him or the idea of him, John vows to take up Nimr's cause. John himself is sexually ambiguous. There is Sophie. But he also recalls at length, and with pleasure, his sexual interactions with other boys at his public school (135–39). On a brief sojourn in Cairo he meets Rasul, who introduces him to hashish; it is mentioned casually that "he and Rasul had kissed goodnight outside the hotel" (99). One gets the sense that only the date of the novel prevented the author from being more explicit.

The Unsuitable Englishman is also set in Cyropolis, but with a new cast of characters. Jason, the title character, a young Englishman with a need for adventure, wheels his motorcycle into town and precipitates a cluster of events that portray the British in an even more unfavorable way than the first novel does. Having no desire to hang out with his compatriots, Jason makes friends first with Hassan, a taxi driver, and then with a journalist and a revolutionary, Dari Selman, whom he serves as chauffeur. He falls in love with Dari's friend, the singer Kareema Kareem. Life is all he wants it to be. But the resident English cannot abide one of their own going native and start creating problems. To complicate matters, Hugh Flodden, one of the members of the diplomatic corps, a married closet case who secretes a stash of Scouting magazines in an office drawer, lusts after the extremely good-looking youth. A perfect case of arrested development, poor Hugh has never managed to outgrow his public school days. Jason rebuffs Hugh, unleashing a murderous hatred. But in redirecting his fierce sexual energy, Hugh catches a case of gonorrhea, which leads to his own downfall. The novel ends with Dari and Jason's friendship intact.

Twenty-two years would pass before Stewart published his public school novel. *The Vampire of Mons* is a distinct letdown, its moral compass either confused or confusing (it's not clear which). It is narrated by the ostensibly heterosexual Clive Swinburne. Then why is he so jealous when one of the teachers—

Heinrich Vitaly, a refugee from Central Europe (the year is 1939)—takes up Darwin Corelli and Theodore Sturges as his special protégés? Clive stokes a myth that Vitaly is a vampire, a pederast, and in a final act he not only murders him but provokes a German pilot to strafe the campus. As a result, the school collapses as an institution. Clive tries to reestablish a friendship with Darwin and Theo, but is rebuffed: "Don't you realise, Swinburne? We're vampires. [...] We're poufs, Swinburne. If you don't get out, we'll sodomise you" (166). The novel ends with Clive's meeting an older student who compares what has happened at the school to what is going on in Europe. Summing up his feelings about Vitaly's death, he says simply, "I, for one, am sorry." To which Clive thinks, "Jealous, violent, sly, conformist, I might be. In this confession I was not hypocrite enough to join him" (169).

Desmond Stirling Stewart (1924–1981) belonged to that strange breed: rightwing gays. He admired the British fascist Oswald Mosley as well as Hitler (who is mentioned approvingly in all these novels); he was anti–Jewish and pro–Arab. Born in Leavesden, England, and educated at Oxford, Stewart spent the years 1948–58 teaching in Baghdad and Beirut and later settled for a period in Cairo. A correspondent for the *Spectator*, he spoke Arabic fluently and became an expert in the political history of the region, although his book on T. E. Lawrence was not well received. (The art dealer David Carritt nicknamed Steward "Florence of Arabia.") Two of his early books were written in collaboration with John Haylock and Gerald Hamilton. In his memoirs Francis King described Stewart (69), "Always charming, always bold, even brazen in his sexual behavior and his political views, and always adroit at looking after himself, however unfavourable the circumstances." Stewart died in London.

Stewart, Desmond. *Leopard in the Grass*. London: Euphorion, 1951. New York: Farrar, Straus, & Young, 1951. *New York: New American Library, 1953.
_____. *The Unsuitable Englishman*. New York: Farrar, Straus, & Young, 1954. London: Collins, 1955. *A Stranger in Eden*. New York: New American Library, 1956.
_____. *The Vampire of Mons*. London: Hamilton, 1976. *New York: Harper & Row, 1976.

46 Douglas Sanderson: *Dark Passions Subdue*, 1952.

An author courts danger if he assembles a cast composed almost entirely of unpleasant characters, all the more so if he leaves it up to his readers to infer his satiric intents. To Sanderson's credit *Dark Passions Subdue* remains very readable. The two major characters, Stephen Hollis and Miriam Sabel, are both self-delusional, never more so than when they think they are seeing reality. Miriam is an anti–Semitic Jew who envisions herself as an artiste and a patron of artists. Ignoring the fact that she has little talent and no real knowledge of the arts, she has talked her obliging husband into buying a home in the Westmount section of Montreal, only to suffer one disappointment after another in her attempts to establish a salon. But she always manages to reconstruct each incident into something favorable to her self-esteem.

Stephen is her male counterpart. It is emblematic that his only sexual experience is a fumbling attempt with her. He is a totally self-centered student at McGill University, a war veteran who passed his service behind a desk, the self-righteous son of a zealously religious father who mentally and physically abused him as a child and whom he now takes great pleasure in taunting, without ever having the courage to leave off his dependence on his family. Stephen is snobbish. And sexually he is either a virgin or very inexperienced. But just as Miriam fantasizes a new role for herself with each young male she picks up, Stephen envisions a totally new life when he meets a foreign resident in Montreal (known only by his first name, Fabien) and falls in love with him, certain that his feelings will be reciprocated. His conceit wreaks havoc, indirectly causing two deaths. Unlike Miriam, who seems to face hard reality as a result of cascading events in the novel, Stephen faces the world alone, unfulfilled at novel's end.

Fabien is the catalyst, attractive to both men and women, another Valentino (160). He has taken in a young Scot, another war veteran, who takes incessant baths (we discover the reason late in the story). In love with Fabien, Duncan McSurt wants to be a writer, and between enormous alcoholic binges he busily works at his manuscript. Stephen first encounters him selling men's goods at a department store and just assumes that he is lower-class, a parasite on Fabien. Then he comes to see him as his rival for Fabien's affections and is ready to concoct any story about Duncan that will put him in a bad light. As events unfold, Duncan emerges in many ways as the noblest and certainly the most tragic of all the characters. Their very likeable friend, Bill Prescott, another McGill student, seems the most stable. For whatever it might mean, he also seems to be asexual. He easily sees through Stephen's pretensions and understands the dangers he poses, but he is incapable of countering them effectively.

There are two flamboyant gays, also McGill students: Matt Lambert and his lover, Bobbie. Harrigan, another young man, tangentially associated with them, is more discreet but has an obvious crush on Stephen. There is another important woman in the novel, a medical student from Alberta named Crystal. When the reader first meets her, she seems to be relatively well adjusted, but gradually a number of unpleasant aspects of her personality begin to appear. She makes vicious fun of Miriam. In her last meeting with Stephen, she calls him a "lousy queer" who needs "medical treatment" (286). The novel ultimately teases the reader; what is it really showing us about the lot of post-war gays in Montreal? And what is the significance of its title coming from a very orthodox hymn that distills the spirit of the elder Hollis?

Ronald Douglas Sanderson (1920–2002) was born in Kent. He served with the Merchant Marine and the Royal Air Force during World War II. In 1947 he emigrated to Canada, where he attended McGill. He was naturalized in 1952. Disappointing sales of this, his first novel, made him turn to writing pulp mysteries under the pen names Malcolm Douglas and Martin Brett. These were widely successful, especially their French translations. In 1955 he moved to Spain, where he died in Alicante. Literary historians ignore his role in gay Canadian literature.

Sanderson, Douglas. *Dark Passions Subdue*. New York: Dodd, Mead, 1952.

47 Colin MacInnes: *June in Her Spring*, 1952. Hal Porter: *A Handful of Pennies*, 1958.

Between 1937, with Mackenzie's *The Young Desire It*, and 1965, with Neville Jackson's *No End to the Way*, Australian letters seem to have made little progress toward developing gay fiction in any meaningful way. Robert Dessaix (*Australian Gay and Lesbian Writing*, 12), attributes this failure to Australian's "political and social conservatism" and its tendency, even on the part of homosexuals, "to see gender as synonymous with sex" so that "basically there were only two kinds of human beings." As a consequence, he continues, no one stepped forward "to explore homosexuality as a normal variety of human sexual experience." Moreover, the main outlet for gay Australian fiction continued to be London publishers.

After Mackenzie's, the next novel with an Australian setting to have an important gay character is *June in Her Spring*. It was written by an Englishman who happened to spend ten years of his youth there. Colin Campbell MacInnes (1914–1976) was born in London but, as a result of his mother's second marriage to a Tasmanian army engineer, lived in Melbourne 1920–30. He then returned to Europe. During World War II he served in the army and was part of the occupying forces in Germany. Openly bisexual, he is most remembered for his London trilogy. The second volume, *Absolute Beginners*, 1959, has several gay characters, but none of them contributes significantly to the plot. His gayest novel, "Fancy Free," set in Australia, has never been published. MacInnes died in Kent of cancer.

June in Her Spring is a story of first love between teenagers, both of whom carry the heavy burden of their pasts. Sixteen-year-old

June Westley has been born into a family beset with a hereditary strain of mental illness. Seventeen-year-old Benny Bond (né Benjamin Murray) has taken the place of his dead father, a troubled alcoholic, in his "Uncle" Henry's bed. The two pledge to run away and marry. But she renounces the idea when her father commits suicide and her brother, independently, has another mental breakdown. Benny announces that he still plans to strike out alone, even as Henry tries to persuade him to let them go together: "Some men are born [...] who are not fit for women.... You are so like your father, Benny.... Be true to your own nature..." (173). Earlier Benny has admitted to June that Henry "treated me like a girl and I never stopped him. What's hateful to me is that I never stopped him..." (163). And even earlier he recalls "the longed-for hateful fingers of Uncle Henry in the night" (71). Given Benny's obviously ambivalent feelings about sexuality, one wonders about his future, especially since Henry has the last line of the novel: "Let him dream on of this girl June, but he will never escape from the man I loved with all my understanding" (174).

Six years later came Porter's *A Handful of Pennies*. It follows a number of Australians who are part of the occupying forces in (unnamed) Japan in 1950. Among them is a padre, Captain Stanley L. Hamilton, a "Nero on a bed, Heliogabalus alertly disconcerted and far too rosy" when caught preparing to penetrate a pants-less Japanese bartender from the officers' club in his room (78). The latter is "Brigadier, Yoshiharo Minato, naval officer's son, student of engineering, nineteen years old, heterosexual, dexterous bar-boy, intelligent, and anxious to do the right thing" (34–35). Another of the padre's conquests is Maxie Glenn, school captain, son of one of the occupying officers, who is even imprudently brought by the padre to officers' club as a reward because, the padre explains when questioned about the boy's presence, "he performed well tonight" (21). Another officer explains that "the Padre has been tutoring him in the ... the Padre's room. Latin, I hear." Then adds, "It may be Greek" (17).

The commanding officer summons both lads to headquarters. Brigadier admits freely, "Padre is having sex with me," but defends himself as an impoverished student, further justifying, "Is politeness, is democracy" (129–30). Maxie does not come off so well in his cross-examination, but then he has more to hide: "For the youth, too mature physically, the Padre's lesson had been undisturbingly coarse because, though an unpimpled adolescence gave him an ethereal air, Maxie Glenn was coarse also" (194). The padre is only one of several characters in the novel to stray beyond what might be considered proper conduct in an occupied country. But he is the only homosexual we get a glimpse of before he is deported. On the plane with him, however, is an interpreter who "had courageously trusted all the lift-boys at the Moat-Circle Hotel, when he should have trusted all except the last and most comely" (209–10). The novel is often disturbing in its portrayal of raw racism at work between occupiers and the occupied, but it is as often very funny, not least in the events leading to the padre's exposure.

Homosexuals (or at least men who have sex with men) show up in two later Porter novels: the actor Polidorio Smith in *The Tilted Cross*, 1961, set in the penal colony of Hobart, Tasmania, in 1847; Gavin Ogilvie and his nephew Alastair in *The Right Thing*, 1971, a family melodrama in which Alastair is killed. More a short story writer than a novelist, Porter published a number that were gay-themed. Harold Edward Porter (1911–1984) was born in Melbourne and grew up there and in Bairnsdale. Returning to Melbourne, he worked as a journalist, teacher, and librarian. He was briefly married. A close friend identified him as a pederast, but his last relationship was with a married man. He died as the result of being struck (for the second time in his life) by an automobile.

Jon Rose's fictionalized memoir, *At the Cross*, 1961, often gets mentioned in Australian literary histories for its depiction of drag parties. Although the Melbourne-born narrator is coy about his sexuality, he describes gay culture in Sydney during World War II in generally affirmative terms. By the time of the book's publication, Rose (dates unknown) was living in England, where he was Sandy Wilson's lover during the period when the latter was working on the musical *The Boy Friend*. (Rose's memoir itself inspired an Australian musical comedy by Alex Harding, *Only Heaven Knows*, 1988.)

Gould, Tony. *Inside Outsider: The Life and Times of Colin MacInnis*. 1983. London: Allison & Busby, 2003.

Lord, Mary. *Hal Porter: Man of Many Parts*. Milsons Point, N.S.W.: Random House Australia, 1993.

MacInnes, Colin. *June in Her Spring*. London: MacGibbon & Kee, 1952. *Harmondsworth, Eng.: Penguin, 1964.

Porter, Hal. *A Handful of Pennies*. Sydney: Angus & Robertson, 1958.

Rose, Jon. *At the Cross*. London: Deutsch, 1961.

48   G. F. Green: *In the Making*, 1952; *The Power of Sergeant Streater*, 1972.

Green's obviously autobiographical first novel, *In the Making: A Story of a Childhood*, is another schoolboy romance, one that is virtually sexless: a furtive kiss while lying atop another boy in bed is about it. Randall Thane falls under the spell of the older Charles Felton. The novel follows the vicissitudes of their relationship across several years, with Felton withdrawing and Thane effectively ending any physicality by his impulsive climb into Felton's bed, to be discovered by the matron. On the train, heading for the next stage in his life, he feels "as if he watched a crystal, within which his own life and the movements and the being of Felton gradually became ordered." He feels a poem stirring within his mind: "The poem and Felton possessed his mind. The two patterns of his life were achieved" (145). The novel has been much admired and has been reprinted in the Penguin Classic series. But it has nothing like the powerful punch that Green's second and last novel packs.

The Power of Sergeant Streater deserves (re)discovery. It is a dark, disturbing novel, experimental in form, set in an unfamiliar culture. The title character of the novel (also the title of the first section) is Military Policeman Sergeant Ronald Streater, aged twenty-four, stationed in wartime Ceylon, bored, hating his job, a virgin. Early on, there is a curious forewarning that he may be a catalyst for destruction. In looking at him, his office mate thinks of Marlowe's famous description of Helen of Troy—*Was this the face* ... (6). The gender-bending comparison also subtly prepares for the revelation of Streater's deeply buried sexuality. We quickly meet three men whom he will destroy. All have roots in the island, are in fact tied to the nascent nationalist movement that will convert Ceylon into Sri Lanka. All are at ease with their sexuality. Streater finally loses his virginity to one of them, the Euro-Asian Peter Lusaka, who brands him, so to speak, by passionately biting his lip and leaving a scar (52). But the encounter does not prevent the inexorable course of events. His office mate sums up: "If you'd left them alone, you know, Sergeant, none of this would have happened. I've wondered sometimes how you endure being yourself and doing what you do." But he acknowledges that the man will never change: "You've nothing in you to change" (57).

It is slightly disconcerting then to move to the second section of the novel, "The Last of the Snow." Without explanation we are thrust into the first person voice of David Sheldon, and back into time, 1929 to the mid–1930s, in an England seemingly caught in perpetual winter. As Robert Aldrich points out (*Colonialism and Homosexuality*, 205), "the interplay of race and desire is replaced by a comparable interplay of class and desire." Young David meets a slightly younger boy, Leonard Williams. He is keenly aware that Leonard comes from a lower class than his, but he pursues him, and they hang out together. The boys attend a crime film: "The murder took place. I felt Leonard's warmth beside me" (74). They hang out in a pub called the Eagle, so named because "an eagle stole a child here" (78). They hike. David feels trapped: "If we stripped off our clothes and lay naked in the street and performed every act of sex and the climax was over and we dressed and stood face to face [...] nothing would have changed. The insensate longing for all that I saw would still be there" (96). And so David too becomes a destroyer.

With the third and last section, the ironically titled "The Man Who Could Do No Harm," which makes up more than half the novel, we return to postwar Ceylon and the third person. Sheldon is now there as an acting Assistant Government Agent. We find that he has become insatiable in collecting gems and boys, but he remains cold and uncaring. The new Police Inspector is none other than Streater, now twenty-six. Sheldon hears all about Streater's former activities and his part in the deaths of the three men, and Streater discovers Sheldon's confessional manuscript, which we have just read. The two appear evenly matched in their ruthlessness, but Streater may now be the more vulnerable. He has fallen in love with the Malayan boy Mahmoud, whom he used to bring about one of the deaths.

Sheldon begins a path of destruction when he stubbornly refuses to admit that he was in the wrong about a supposed theft. He also quixotically decides he wants Streater to join him and maneuvers to get rid of Mahmoud. Aldrich sums up (206): "The extraordinary psychological cruelty of both men—using sex as weapon and reward—implies the impossibility of Englishmen to work out their sexual problems satisfactorily. Time and again, Streater and Sheldon are told that they are emotionally stunted. By contrast, natives engage in easy and uncomplicated sexual liaisons." Aldrich notes that the Ceylonese "use Europeans for political or personal ends, jousting with each other in rivalry. Yet the locals bear the cost of involvement with Europeans." As for the sexually charged duel for power between Streater and Sheldon, we are left with an ambiguous ending. The author sets up the strong possibility that one of the two will be killed in an "accidental" fall, but which will it be?

In a reminiscence published in the collection *A Skilled Hand* (73), the publisher John Lehmann recalls that Green gave him the original manuscript of the novel for his opinion. He records: "This early version was short, about fifty thousand words, but I was deeply impressed by the beauty of the writing." Still, Lehmann had reservations. He had even more about what subsequently happened to the manuscript: "Dick rewrote it and broke it up, thus, in my opinion, spoiling it, even if he provided a longer and more saleable novel for his publisher. But although it seemed not quite to fit the new scheme, it did give him the chance to insert one of his most perfect stories, 'The Last of the Snow,' in his old manner." Lehmann remembers that Green "was anxious about the homosexual setting," but, he says, "I told him that, even then—it was 1964—it was absurd to be bothered about that."

Underneath its sometimes flat tone, the novel is indelibly rich, not only in its creation of colonial and class tensions and its examination of the effects that a stunted emotional development has on everyone involved, but also in its subtle use of literary and biblical allusions. The language moves towards poetry in its descriptions of landscapes. The first section of the novel was published in 1969 in *Winter Tales*, no. 15 (which has led to some confusion about the date of the novel). In another reminiscence also published in *A Skilled Hand* (221), Paul Spencer reports that Green had hoped to do "a sequel, to be called *Streater's Prison*" (which reveals that Streater survives), to end back in Sheldon's home territory, where Streater becomes involved nonsexually with an autistic boy, but Green finally gave up on the idea.

George Frederick Green (1910–1977), "Dick" to his friends, was born in Derbyshire. He was educated at Repton and Cambridge. In 1940 he was called up for military duty and posted to Ceylon, where he was assigned the task of editing a magazine for the Ceylonese forces. In 1944 he was caught having sex with a Sinhalese rickshaw-puller, court-martialed, and sentenced to two years' imprisonment. The diary that he kept was published in *Penguin New Writing*, no. 31, in 1947, under the pseudonym "Lieutenant Z." After his death, his friends put together a selection of his writing interspersed with their tributes to him: *A Skilled Hand*. Of particular interest are five short stories published for the first time, four about the encounters of Englishmen with Ceylonese natives and one about an Englishman in Morocco.

Green, Chloë, and A. D. Maclean, eds. *A Skilled Hand: A Collection of Stories and Writing by G. F. Green with Memoirs and Criticism* [...]. London: Macmillan, 1980.

Green, G. F. *In the Making: The Story of a Childhood.* London: Davies, 1952. *Intro. Peter Parker. London: Penguin, 2012.

———. *The Power of Sergeant Streater.* London: Macmillan, 1972.

49 Robert Liddell: *Unreal City*, 1952. Lawrence Durrell: *Justine*, 1957; *Balthazar*, 1958; *Clea*, 1960.

Two very different British novelists were influenced by the Egyptian city of Alexandria and inspired by the commanding figure of C. P. Cavafy (1863–1933), the gay Greek poet who lived and died there. For gay letters *Unreal City* is the more important. Set in the city re-imagined as Caesarea, it recounts the friendship between a young English teacher, Charles Harbord, stranded there during World War II, and the aging Greek savant Christo Eugenides. Of the latter, "his reputation was so bad that respectable Caesarea held aloof from him. His best chance of friendship was with people from other countries, who possibly minded less about his private life, and who certainly minded less what Caesarea thought of it" (75). Charles, grieving for his sister, killed by one of the bombs dropped on London, becomes fascinated by the man and allows Christo to monopolize much of his spare time.

The reader must presume that Charles is by inclination gay, but temperamentally he is asexual. He feels simultaneously uncomfortable and yet at ease when Eugenides takes him to Chez Térèse, a gay bar filled with a cross-section of Caesarean society (many of whom we come to know) and military officers stationed nearby: "Charles, gaining courage, because the underworld looked very like the world, and proved to be little more than a selection from it, began to feel a little disappointed as well as relieved that he not going to see that dangerous (perhaps fabulous) thing, Life" (82–83). Eugenides is not so lucky. He catches a glance of a Canadian Air Force corporal who resembles the engravings of Antinous and loses his heart to him. To the amazement of some, Jim (that is Antinous's name) is content to enter into apparently a nonsexual relationship with the elderly Greek. Charles is bemused to find the two sitting happily together in Eugenides's apartment, Jim darning his socks for him. But even Charles is attracted to the man's vitality.

Unfortunately, Jim also is prone to drunken bouts. In one of these, in the same bar where they had met, "Jim turned, with his back to the bar, and with drunken solemnity told Eugenides just what he thought of him, and of everyone present. [...] It was cruel, and all the more cruel because it was not only vulgar abuse. Little failings of Eugenides, quite shrewdly observed, were being remorselessly betrayed. His vanity, his snobbery, his little economies. It was the worst kind of treachery, of which only a friend could be capable" (164). Many weeks pass before a reconciliation can occur. But just as the war is inexorably sweeping towards its end, so is the relationship. Jim is killed in a freak traffic accident; Eugenides submits to a surgical procedure that he does not survive. But Charles learns that he can live with his wound: "In a confused way he felt that, by dying, Christo had helped him to come through into the daylight again, to leave his grief and Caesarea behind him" (236). The novel ends with a victory dance in which men dance with women and men openly dance with men.

John Robert Liddell (1908–1992) was born in Tunbridge Wells, England. His father a retired military officer working for the Egyptian government, he grew up in Cairo. He graduated from Oxford and worked in the Bodleian Library. He taught at the Universities of Athens, Alexandria, and Cairo. He was good friends with Francis King, Ivy Compton-Burnett, and Patrick White, among others. King in his memoirs (145) noted that Liddell was always so discreet that he never admitted a Greek friend was his lover. Among Liddell's many critical studies, he wrote a pedestrian biography of Cavafy, 1974. He died in Athens.

Durrell's more highly praised, but far less interesting tetralogy, *The Alexandria Quartet*, follows the political and mostly heterosexual games engaged in by a group of Egyptians and expatriates who wind up in the city just before and (in the last volume) during the early years of World War II. In three of the novels (all narrated by the straight schoolteacher and aspiring writer L. G. Darley) homosexuals have significant roles, but one would hardly read the *Quartet* for its insights into gay men. In fact, it is questionable that Durrell had any insights to offer, given the kinds of homosexuals he portrays and their comments about themselves.

The aged expatriate Joshua Scobie is introduced in the first volume, *Justine*. He admits to Darley that in his past he did "quite a bit of scout-mastering" but voluntarily exiled himself from England: "The strain was too much for me. Every week I expected to see a headline in the *News of the World*, 'Another youthful victim of scoutmaster's dirty wish'" (104). To Scobie's amazement he is appointed to the secret service to root out potential dangers as war looms in Europe (127). He enlists Darley's aid, and the two become closer. In an explicit evocation of the Greek mythological figure Tiresias, Scobie confesses to Darley that at "full moon" he likes to dress up as a woman, especially "when the Fleet's in." He begs Darley to confiscate his clothes so that he will not bring disgrace upon himself (231–33). The plan does not work. Somewhat later Scobie is discovered, dressed in women's clothes, beaten to death by English sailors whom he apparently solicited (329–30). Scobie undergoes yet another metamorphosis after his death. He becomes the patron saint of his *quartier*, "El Scob" (714, 717), and the bathtub in which he brewed an alcoholic drink is "invoked to confer fertility upon the childless" (715).

We meet Toto de Brunel in the second volume, *Balthazar*. He is a procurer for "old society women too proud to pay for gigolos" (218): "his pederasty gave him a kind of illicit importance" (219). Although Scobie has composed an oral "saga" around the extraordinary exploits of one of his former friends, Toby Mannering (225–26), he does not approve of the way Toto is "an open nancy-boy" (223). At a masked ball Toto also comes also to a violent end while disguised as a woman (Tiresias is evoked yet again). He is wearing Justine's distinctive ring when he makes advances to her brother-in-law (374). In a fit of anger, he kills Toto with a hatpin "driven sideways into his head with terrific force" (360). Curiously enough, Toto is apparently the only gay who made it into the film version of the *Quartet*.

The most substantial of the homosexuals in the *Quartet*, Balthazar is a physician who darts in and out of all four volumes, giving his name to the second one. In speaking to Darley in *Justine*, he says, "Thank God I have been spared an undue interest in love. At least the invert escapes this fearful struggle to give oneself to another" (82). When he and an Egyptian policeman, Nimrod, compete over the "favours of a charming young Athenian actor known by the delightful name of Socrates Pittakakis," they "sensibly decided to bury our jealousy and frankly share the youth" (329). It is thus ironic that, a few years later, in *Clea*, Darley finds him aged, white-haired, on the verge of losing his practice altogether, as the result of his having fallen in love with another Greek actor, "the most disastrous [choice] that anyone could [have] hit upon." Balthazar says, "I became as weak as a woman," but he admits, "I enjoyed being debased in a queer way" (704). He has tried to kill himself, but was singularly unsuccessful, given his professional knowledge. After this talk, he pulls himself together. Balthazar is the accidental cause of the final casualty, the response to which brings this showy but often fuzzy experiment in narrative form to an end.

The spirit of Cavafy is constantly evoked. Balthazar was "a fellow-student and close friend" (79), and some of the straight characters in the novels initially come together as a result of attending Darley's lecture about him (297). But altogether gays (or, more precisely, characters whom Durrell labels as pederasts or inverts) appear on only a few pages of the nearly nine hundred that make up the tetralogy.

Lawrence George Durrell (1912–1990) was born in Jullunder, India, of an English father and an Irish mother. He was sent to England for schooling, but did poorly. Detesting the country, in 1935 he settled on the Greek island of Corfu. *The Black Book*, 1938, has a gay character, Tarquin. With the fall of Greece in World War II Durrell escaped to Alexandria, where he served as a press attaché for the British embassy. Working for the British government, he lived in various countries: Argentina, Yugoslavia, Cyprus. Married four times, he had two daughters. He spent his last decades in Languedoc, France, where he died.

Durrell, Lawrence. *Balthazar*. London: Faber & Faber, 1958. New York: Dutton, 1958. **The Alexandria Quartet*. London: Faber & Faber, 1968. 205–390.
_____. *Clea*. London: Faber & Faber, 1960. New York: Dutton, 1960. **The Alexandria Quartet* (see above). 655–884.
_____. *Justine*. London: Faber & Faber, 1957. New York: Dutton, 1957. **The Alexandria Quartet* (see above). 13–203.
Liddell, Robert. *Unreal City*. London: Cape, 1952. *London: Owen, 1993.

50 Angus Wilson: *Hemlock and After*, 1952; *Anglo-Saxon Attitudes*, 1956; *The Middle Age of Mrs Eliot*, 1958; *No Laughing Matter*, 1967; *As If by Magic*, 1973.

In James Courage's 1959 novel *A Way of Love* (q.v., 110), one of the characters says, "I've never understood why murder's considered a proper subject while love between two men definitely isn't. [...] I want to read a novel about queers that treats us as human beings like other people." A second character answers that it has been done: "At least one of the brighter post-war boys has tried it." Whereupon a third chimes in, "And personally I find his books not only sinister but depressing. That jeering satirical tone may be anti-sentimental but it's also inhuman, lacking in compassion, and to my mind utterly wrong-headed." The speaker may well be thinking of Wilson's second novel, *Anglo-Saxon Attitudes*, where his criticism is just. Nevertheless, starting with his first novel, *Hemlock and After*, Wilson ushered something new and important into British letters. First of all, he made his characters seem so ordinary. They do not defend themselves, question themselves, feel unnatural (though they know to be wary of the law). And whereas earlier writers, with a few notable exceptions, had pictured their gay characters mostly in London or abroad, Wilson found his also in small town England.

Bernard Sands, the fifty-seven-year-old protagonist of *Hemlock*, is a successful novelist, married with two children. His wife Ella has suffered some kind of a mental breakdown; he has accepted the sexual pull younger men hold for him and has taken a lover, Eric Craddock. He is also friends with the stage designer Terence Lambert, an earlier lover, and the gay play producer Sherman Winter. His life seems to be on an upswing. He gains the backing to establish a rural writing retreat for promising young poets. Ella finds her way out of the psychic morass she had wandered into (and emerges as the most likeable character in the novel). The two finally talk about their complicated relationship. Working together they thwart their neighbor Mrs. Curry from procuring young girls for pedophiles. But it is too late for Bernard to find happiness. He witnesses an arrest for solicitation: "He could trace now no kindness in his teasing exposure of Eric's ignorance, or in his witty rebukes of Terence's vulgarity; he could see only the white, frightened face of the arrested young man changing to the pink flush of Eric's embarrassment or the wincing tick of Terence's cheek, and could detect only his own answering shudder of pleasure" (189). He suffers from a weak heart, and the incident somehow hastens his final heart attack. Yet his spirit helps both Eric and Terence to make sound decisions about personal relationships. And in one of several comic moments, Mrs. Curry's accomplice, Ron Wrigley, who has been swept up in the arrests, finally achieves a goal: "Ron, though he much disliked the hard work of prison life, found in so monastic a community that success with the 'old one two" which had been so consistently frustrated in the course of this story" (244).

Wilson's biographer, the novelist Margaret Drabble, reports (205) that Wilson constantly worried whether subsequent novels were "too homosexual," but was determined to introduce gay characters naturally into them. *Anglo-*

Saxon Attitudes centers on Gerald Middleton, a straight historian in his early sixties. He is shaken out of his self-imposed lethargy and laziness to edit a medieval history, with the result that he finally confronts the nagging suspicion that an archeological fraud was perpetrated by people he knew at the beginning of his career. His gay son John, a television commentator, suffers from self-deception. He allows his enthusiasms to misguide his career and to damage his personal life. He becomes smitten with an Irish rogue, the sexually opportunist Larrie Rourke, and introduces him into his mother's home (his parents are estranged) despite warnings against the man. When Larrie is threatened with arrest, he and John depart on a road trip on the Continent. As a result of Larrie's careless driving, it ends with his death and the amputation of one of John's legs. Other gays appear. Vin Salad, a campy young waiter who has served time for solicitation, lodges in the same house Larrie did. Their celibate landlord turns out to have been the youthful favorite of a churchman involved in the archeological dig. The two are about the only likeable characters among the generally unsavory lot. The novel was adopted for the BBC.

After a third collection of short stories, several of which are gay-themed, came *The Middle Age of Mrs Eliot*. The title character must chart her path after her husband is killed in a South Asian assassination attempt. Her brother David Parker must do the same, first as he faces the impending death of his longtime partner, Gordon Paget, from cancer and then the aftermath. The two men run a nursery, "the sealing of a bond of their life together" (122). It is a curious life; David confesses to his sister, "I never had sexual relations with Gordon after the first few months that we knew each other" (296). He attempts "desperately to fuse into an indivisible trinity the three seemingly forever divided persons—David then, David now, David to be without Gordon" (231). But he seems to accept that "loneliness [is] the condition of man, a loneliness to be endured and fulfilled in the constant disguise of human contact" (166). The nursery provides no epiphany, and the novel ends on a dying fall.

A grandmother centers *Late Call*. After the death of his wife, her son invites both his parents to join his home in one of the new towns that sprung up across England after World War II. Ray Calvert, one of her two grandsons, is gay. After the police begin harassing his circle of friends, frightening Wilf Corney, a bank clerk, so badly that he kills himself, Ray comes out to his family and accepts the invitation of Geoffrey Lawshall to join him and his dress business in London. The father reacts with time-honored outrage; the grandmother responds stoutly, "Oh, Harold, you're talking about Ray. You can't wash your hands of someone you love" (311). As she herself, now widowed, begins to plan to get a place of her own, she maintains Ray made the right decision. But Ray himself plays only a small role in the story. It was adopted for the BBC.

No Laughing Matter is a long, complex, and experimental family chronicle about six children and their parents from just before World War I through 1967. The youngest son, Marcus Matthews, is gay. His story weaves in and out among those of his siblings. Taking advantage of the greater freedom given publishers, it is more sexually explicit than Wilson's earlier fiction. Failing to break into the film world, Marcus turns to prostitution. He thus meets Jack Pohlen while soliciting outside a theater (206). Jack takes him under his guidance and educates him in art. Marcus's taste makes them wealthy and brings them into contact with the cultural elite. At the same time, the two men having an open relationship, Marcus becomes involved with a lower-class lad, Ted (324). Because Jack is Jewish, he also becomes involved in politics as World War II looms and a fascist movement sweeps across England. His convictions do not curb his jealousy when he feels threatened by Jack's attentions to a moderately talented Jewish painter who has fled Germany (412). But the two forge a life that carries them through it all until Jack's death. Marcus then moves to Morocco and enters into a relationship with a Moslem named Hassan (453). Ten years later they are still together. The novel ends with Hassan contemplating the changes he will make to the factory Marcus has created there when he inherits it (496).

In *As If by Magic* Wilson retains the new frankness about sex but reverts to the satiric tone of *Ango-Saxon Attitudes*, evoking again James Courage's criticism of the author. We have two protagonists. Once more Wilson seems more sympathetic to his female character. Alexandra Grant is a young hippy, initially involved in a *ménage à trois*, who grows into a sense of responsibility. Her godfather is Hamo Langmuir, a plant geneticist who engineers a miracle rice that will quadruple production. He was in love with her uncle until the latter developed a five o'clock shadow (67). Now on a scientific junket around the world, Hamo seeks out ideal youths—ephebes, not boys—for his sexual pleasure. He is taken to a gay Japanese bar staffed with youths to satisfy old men (132), and there has sex with a young American deserter (the time is the late 1960s). In Indonesia, to his disgust, he attends a pederasts' orgy (161), which has moments that anticipate Pasolini's *Salo*, and brings down the wrath of the other men by being attracted to an older servant rather than the schoolboys they are serving up. The scene haunts him as he continues his journey (217), but his sexual itch builds. His pursuits in Ceylon and in Goa bring adverse results, including death, to the boys who arouse his desire (289, 303, 352). And bit by bit he learns that the Green Revolution is a two-sided sword, creating misery for small farmers as it provides better harvests for large estates. Trying to stop a protest, Hamo himself is killed in a riot that breaks out (368).

Wilson was comparatively out as an author from early on, but his novels are hardly posters for gay pride. I wonder what effect they have on straight readers. Angus Frank Johnstone-Wilson (1913–1991) was born in Sussex to a Scottish father and a South African mother. He attended Westminster and Oxford. He worked as a librarian for the British Museum with time out during the war to serve as a decoder for Italian naval codes. After the war he met Anthony Garrett (1929–), who was his lover for the rest of his life. He resigned in 1955 to devote himself full time to writing, but did serve as an English professor at the University of East Anglia, 1966–78. He offered to testify before the Wolfenden Committee, but if he did, the transcript no longer exists. In 1960 Garrett was forced to resign from his post as a probation officer because of his association with Wilson. The novelist died in a Suffolk nursing home.

Drabble, Margaret. *Angus Wilson: A Biography*. 1995. New York: St. Martin's, 1996.
Wilson, Angus. *Anglo-Saxon Attitudes*. London: Secker & Warburg, 1956. New York: Viking, 1956. *Intro. Jane Smiley. New York: New York Review, 2005.
_____. *As If by Magic*. London: Secker & Warburg, 1973. *New York: Viking, 1973.
_____. *Hemlock and After*. London: Secker & Warburg, 1952. New York: Viking, 1952. *Intro. Margaret Drabble. New York: St. Martin's, 1997.
_____. *Late Call*. *London: Secker & Warburg, 1964. New York: Viking, 1965.
_____. *The Middle Age of Mrs Eliot*. London: Secker & Warburg, 1958. New York: Viking, 1958. *Intro. Margaret Drabble. New York: St. Martin's, 1997.
_____. *No Laughing Matter*. London: Secker & Warburg, 1967. *New York: Viking, 1967.

51 Rodney Garland (Adam de Hegedus): *The Heart in Exile*, 1953; *The Troubled Midnight*, 1954. Note on Adam de Hegedus: *Rehearsal Under the Moon*, 1946.

The Heart in Exile is a milestone in the history of the gay British novel. From the beginning, its narrator accepts that he is gay. He is a psychologist, but he does not subscribe to the idea that homosexuality is an illness. He does distinguish between men who were born gay (as he asserts he was) and men who become gay for a variety of reasons and can be steered back to a straight course. His attitude about bisexuality is complicated. He acknowledges the need for discretion, given the legal oppression in Great Britain. As a result, he dislikes camp, effeminacy, and any actions that would draw the attention of London bobbies. He moves at times in the gay milieu in London, offering us more than glimpses of postwar gay life there (along with various foreshadowings of the way gay culture will develop in the 1950s and even 1960s). All the while he provides a running commentary on the sociological implications of the scenes before us. He remarks on the British class system and the attraction working class men hold for the upper class. There is a gay suicide, but it occurs before the novel begins and provides the basic plot, for *The Heart in Exile* is also a murder mystery, the very first gay detective story ever. It is also a romance: the main character knows that he suffers from "a stunted heart" (26), but he finally comes to understand how two humans of the same sex can forge a lasting relationship.

Dr. Anthony Page, the psychologist, receives a visit from Julian LeClerc's fiancée; not knowing that the two men were lovers before the war, she asks him to look into what could have led to Julian's suicide. Tony searches Julian's closed-up apartment and discovers the photograph of a man hidden behind the framed photograph of the fiancée. Convinced that the unknown holds the key, Tony tries to find out who he is. This search takes him to gay pubs, a party, and various encounters with other men. He ultimately uncovers the fact that, though Julian swallowed the sleeping pills of his own volition, he has in essence been murdered, betrayed in the worst way that a gay child can be. The discovery jolts Tony. All along he knows that he is hurting his factotum, the indispensable Terry, by not confiding in him, keeping him abreast of his investigation, by taking him "too much for granted" (177). But now he becomes keenly aware of Terry's importance to his own happiness; he confides, "He was the first human being who had ever really fallen in love with me. And now I knew I could return his love" (289).

Terry, an ur-clone, remains the least developed character in the novel. What little we see of him suggests that he is more grounded than Tony. The metaphor of life as a novel throws the differences between the two men into some relief. As Tony delves deeper into the mystery, he says, "I felt I was *living* a novel now" (134). Later he compares his adventure to "a real-life detective story" (167), even "a penny-dreadful, mystery story" (187). Terry raises the question "why all plays and novels dealing with queers have an inevitably tragic end." He argues "that's not so in real life" and goes on, "If ever I could write a book on the subject, I'd try to tell the truth" (185). When Tony finally accepts Terry as a lover, he foresees, "I should no longer have that mad craving for excitement the desire to 'live' a novel. [...] I should have to live my own life" (289). *The Heart in Exile* is required reading for anyone wishing to understand gay history in England.

This was not the author's first novel involving homosexuality. In 1946 he had published *Rehearsal Under the Moon* under his own name. Basically a satiric attack on the exclusory publishing industry, it describes straight, young journalist Paul Noley's ingenious, if fraudulent, scheme to prove his work is publishable. His former schoolmate, the gay Reggie Hoover, opens and closes the novel. His only narrative function is to pursue Paul, and when he discovers that Paul is impervious to his advances, the attraction evaporates. The last we see of him, he is happily picking up a sailor on leave to take to his flat. Paul catches on to Reggie's interest when he idly compares a young woman with whom he has become involved to Reggie: "he reflected that she could never give him the interest, the devotion, the understanding that Hoover had given him. [...] Well, of course, he thought. [...] How was it that he only saw it now, very suddenly and without any reason? That wasn't quite true, though. Last week he was reading *Si le Grain ne Meurt* and the week before that, he was reading Havelock Ellis." Then, in a passage that anticipates *The Heart in Exile*, he thinks: "he had solved a mystery that had not appeared to him as a mystery before. Elementary, my dear Watson. How he'd liked to be the intellectual detective when he was fifteen. It was one of his parts when he was a child. It still was for that matter" (151).

At one point in *The Heart in Exile* Tony observes, "The invert's whole life is spent hiding his real passion from the enemy. A double life becomes second nature to him; he learns the technique in his teens" (120). In May 1951 two

British diplomats suddenly disappeared. The government dragged its feet disclosing the matter, but finally admitted that Guy Burgess and Donald Maclean had defected to the Soviet Union, for which they had been spying for nearly twenty years. It also came out that the two were gay, a fact that would reverberate in all kinds of ways throughout the rest of the decade. Three years later a second Rodney Garland novel appeared, *The Troubled Midnight*. Transparently based on the case, it is apparently the first English novel about gay spies. It is narrated by the novelist James Edmonton. He is straight, but admits, "Men had never interested me, but inversion in itself always had. I found it absorbing and stimulating" (202). He also reveals that he has often been mistaken for a homosexual. Through a convoluted set of circumstances he inadvertently warns Eric Fontanet (the Burgess figure) that British intelligence is onto him. Eric persuades Alan Lockheed (the Maclean figure) to flee with him across the Channel. James is recruited by British intelligence to follow them to France, posing as their friend, to try to prevent their defection to the Soviet Union and to bring them back to justice.

Since the three had actually been somewhat close at Oxford (in actuality Burgess and Maclean were at Cambridge), James feels guilty about his deception, its being further complicated by the fact that he was in love with Alan's wife before their marriage. In any event, his ruse is penetrated and the two spies escape (not before a sexual interlude with Arab street boys in Paris). Two other figures in the novel are intriguing. Arthur Beaufort does not correspond as closely to Anthony Blunt, the third gay Cambridge spy, as do Eric and Alan to their real-life counterparts, but there are too many similarities to be accidental, most notably his connection to French culture and his expertise in art history. MI5 did not learn definitely of Blunt's duplicity until 1963, and he was not publically exposed until 1979. Then there is Jan Barton—either an Austrian or a Czech, though carrying a Czech passport: "His real name is something unpronounceable, and officially he's a journalist. He's made his home in London now for quite a few years" (138). He resembles Benjamin Britten (183). The novel is also interesting for its discussions of British intelligence, American infiltration of the European network of espionage, the immediate dangers posed by McCarthyism, and the long-term dangers posed by American technology coupled with American political naiveté.

Adam Martin de Hegedus (1906–1956) was born in Budapest. He worked in London as a foreign correspondent for various Hungarian papers beginning in 1927. After return visits to Hungary and brief stays in Paris, where he was friends with Gide, he settled permanently in England in 1939. He served briefly as a gunner during the war, before suffering a nervous breakdown. Peter Wildeblood has left a record of his meeting with the author just days before the latter's death; there he is disguised as Waldemar von Ochs. Ian Young records (67) that the publisher of Hegedus's final novel, *The Struggle with the Angels*, 1956, had a notice on the dust-jacket that the author died "at a tragically early age" just as the book was going to press; it added, "It can now be revealed that, under the name of 'Rodney Garland,' he was the author of two other novels which received wide notice: *The Heart in Exile* and *The Troubled Midnight*." Inside the book (which itself has no gay interest), opposite the title page, appears a list of the author's works, including these two novels dutifully credited to Garland. The dust jacket also had a photograph of the author, but it is impossible to tell whether he resembles Britten or not. The circumstances of Hegedus's death remain cloudy: suicide, accident, or other?

In addition to the spy scandal, the 1950s saw a number of high profile arrests and trials for homosexual offenses in England: Alan Turing, 1952 (who killed himself two years later); Rupert Croft-Cooke and John Gielgud, 1953; Edward Montagu and Peter Wildeblood, 1954; Ian Harvey, 1958. To gays at the time it seemed only too obvious that the British legal establishment was taking a leaf from the same playbook being used by U.S. Senator Joseph McCarthy. Cultural historian Patrick Higgins

(*Heterosexual Dictatorship*, 250) denies such assertions, but he does assent "that something important did happen in the early 1950s, but it [...] came about as a result of developments in Fleet Street, where newspapers reported homosexuality more widely and more frankly than at any point this century." In this atmosphere the Wolfenden Committee was created in 1954. Higgins (5) sums up its charge as to "study the operation of the laws relating to homosexuality as well as examine possible strategies for the treatment and the cure of homosexuality that the state might adopt." Composed of Jack Wolfenden, its chair, and fourteen other members, the committee submitted its report three years later. Its principal recommendation called for the decriminalization of homosexual activity between consenting adults aged twenty-one and older. It took ten more years for the Labouchère amendment of 1885 to be repealed.

Garland, Rodney. *The Heart in Exile*. London: Allen, 1953. New York: Coward–McCann, 1954. *Intro. Neil Bartlett, Jeffrey Simmons, & Peter Burton. Brighton, Eng.: Millivres, 1995.

―――. *The Troubled Midnight*. London: Allen, 1954. *New York: Coward–McCann, 1955.

Hegedus, Adam de. *Rehearsal Under the Moon*. London: Nicholson & Watson, 1946.

Wildeblood, Peter. *A Way of Life*. London: Weidenfeld & Nicolson, 1956. Chapter 3.

Young, Ian. "The Two Rodney Garlands: A Literary Mystery." *The Golden Age of Gay Fiction*. Ed. Drewey Wayne Gunn. Albion, N.Y.: MLR, 2009.

52   Mary Renault: *The Charioteer*, 1953; *The Last of the Wine*, 1956; *The Mask of Apollo*, 1966; *Fire from Heaven*, 1969; *The Persian Boy*, 1972.

David Sweetman in his biography writes (xii): "Mary Renault's novels helped millions of people come to terms with their sexuality, people who had never 'come out' or protested in public, but who, without her work, would have considered themselves alone and unnatural. One of her greatest achievements was to give homosexuals a place in history while offering non-homosexuals a sympathetic world where heterosexuality was neither the only nor the dominant sexual type." A bonus was that closeted gays could read her Greek novels in public without feeling they were outing themselves; after all, they were approved by respected historians and critics for offering a window onto the past.

Even before Renault turned to historical fiction, she had shown her interest in ancient Greek culture. *The Charioteer*, her first gay novel, gets its title from Plato's *Phaedrus*. The novel is a romance set mostly in a World War II military hospital in the days after Dunkirk. Laurie Odell—nicknamed Spud because of his Irish-sounding name—is the protagonist, the charioteer who must learn the true nature of his heart. He is torn between the innocent and sexless conscientious objector Andrew Raynes, who has been assigned to the hospital, and his former schoolmate Ralph Lanyon, the powerful naval officer who rescued him almost dead from the beach. The presence of the two opposing steeds in Plato's metaphor makes it too easy to see the two men as representing the horses. But, if I am reading Plato and Renault correctly, the tensions are *within* Laurie, not externalized onto the two men he loves. Fulfillment occurs only when the two horses work together, and Laurie can arrive at such maturity only with Ralph, not Andrew. For the thoroughly idealistic Laurie the course is rough.

The novel depicts an array of gay types of the time. Laurie and Ralph react against campy stereotypes. Ralph admits that he has attended a party composed largely of such in search of satisfying his physical needs. Laurie binds himself up more tightly. What to the reader may seem most stupid on Laurie's part is his unwillingness to choose Ralph over Andrew. Even he "couldn't pretend to himself that even this last loyalty of the heart to Andrew was innocent. It was withheld at the expense of someone who on his side had withheld nothing, and whose need of love was in its kind no less" (320). The underhanded manipulations of one of Ralph's former partners brings on the final crisis, testing Laurie and finding him wanting. The altruism of another of Ralph's ex-lovers, coupled with Laurie's accidental discovery of Ralph's hidden despair, finally forces him to accept that the deeper truths of the heart must be found in compromise, in yoking the opposing horses so firmly together that "they are reconciled" (347).

Sweetman (145) records that her London publisher was taken aback by the manuscript but gamely went ahead with publication. Her American publisher flat out refused, and it did not appear in the States until 1959. The author "never doubted" that the rejection "sprang from McCarthyism." Sweetman (146) notes that within a few weeks of the book's appearance in stores, John Gielgud was arrested, to Renault's distress, and gays became convinced that the Tory home secretary, David Maxwell-Fyfe, was on a witch-hunt.

Beginning with her next novel, all future Renault novels moved to safer ground: classical Greece. Perhaps for that reason they are even more subversive. Set in Athens during the time of Socrates (470?–399) and Plato (428?–348?), *The Last of the Wine* takes the form of a fictional memoir by one Alexias, an ephebe. In the first chapter he casually mentions that his older brother killed himself when the youth "with whom he was in love" died of the plague (2). Later he says, "I was old enough to have received some attentions from men, while still young enough to think them rather absurd" (30). A man named Kritias draws his ire: while Alexias is serving him at his father's table, Kritias spills wine on the youth's tunic and then uses the pretext of inspecting the damage to grope him. Alexias gives his heart to the noble Lysias. At first all Lysias asks for is a kiss (92), but during their first campaign together, clearly something more physical occurs (124). The author, however, is discreet. Throughout, the two men act like lovers and friends (even to bouts of jealousy), not like teacher and pupil, though Lysias models for him such abstract qualities as honor and courage. Both males have sex with women (but not with other men); Lysias argues that since Alexias must one day marry, he will "not know whom to choose" unless he gets "used to women first" (238). Lysias himself takes a wife. After Lysias is killed, coming to Alexias's aid in battle, the younger man marries her. The novel's action is more driven by various kinds of competition—war, athletic games, and rivalries among factions (including philosophical schools)—than by character. As a result, it is often plodding.

For three-fourths its length *The Mask of Apollo* is character-driven. The Athenian actor Nikeratos, "Niko," recounts his life in the theater during the time of Plato and his Syracusian disciple Dion (408–354). Niko grudging respects the former, though he does not understand him, and is angered when his teaching leads to the closure of the theaters in Syracuse. He is in love with the latter, but knows he is "too old for the love of a boy who reveres a man" (67); when he hears about his part in the closing of the theaters, he tells Dion, "I am a servant of the god, and though I honor you and love you, I will obey the god, rather than you" (160). Throughout the story Niko beds a variety of men and, after an extremely tense moment, a boyish-looking woman (320). But his constant lover is young Thettalos, whom he takes on as his protégé. Together, the two are faithful; when separated by tours, each "could do as we liked" (226). Even if the summaries of plays are sometimes tedious, the theater stories that Niko relates and the characters associated with them are fascinating. Toward the end, however, his movements seem forced by the author to get him oh the scene to witness the events leading to Dion's downfall. Then, in apparent anticipation of her next move, Renault ends the novel with Niko's encounter with Alexander, still a teenager. By now, even the antique mask of Apollo, which he wore when he had his first great triumph and to which he has always turned for divine help, seems to have lost the force it once possessed.

Renault's next novel, *Fire from Heaven*, takes Alexander (356–323) as its protagonist. It is a bildungsroman covering his life from early childhood until the assassination of his father, King Philip II of Macedonia. By making the person who most interested her the hero of her story, Renault no longer had a problem with focus. Here, even Thettalos's brief reappearance becomes germane to the plot rather than a gratuitous walk on. The reader follows

Alexander's education: formal (for a considerable portion of his youth under the tutelage of Aristotle), political, martial, physical, moral, and emotional. He is constantly pulled between his father and his mother as part of their toxic conflict. His refuge is his companion and lover, Hephaistion. Though sex, "his human needs," leaves Alexander feeling "profound melancholy after" (204), his peer in age provides him physical comfort and moral support. They discuss Plato's thoughts on love. After one especially trying moment with his father, Alexander grasps Hephaistion "in an embrace so fierce that it knocked the breath out of him, and said, 'Without you I should go mad.' 'I too without you,' said Hephaistion with loving ardour" (283). Philip's own series of erotic adventures is presented in contrast to the two youths' steadfastness; Hephaistion sees "in a divining moment the succession of King Philip's young men: their coarse good looks, their raw sexuality like a smell of sweat, their jealousies, their intrigues, their insolence. Out of all the world, he had been chosen to be everything which those were not: between his hands had been laid, in trust, Alexander's pride" (174–75).

Renault continued Alexander's story in *The Persian Boy*, where she returned to a first-person narrative. Part of the spoils of war, young Bagoas is castrated and sold in the marketplace to a gem dealer. His owner prostitutes him to important customers. As his royal origins become known, he comes to the attention of King Darius's court and is bought and trained for his pleasure. To keep the king entertained Bagoas learns to dance, but he cannot give him his heart. Meanwhile, Alexander is on his eastward march. After he defeats Darius, Bagoas is offered to him, and the young Persian falls in love, having his first erection with a partner (428). Thereafter he is unfaithful only once, the night of Alexander's marriage to Roxanne (510). Bagoas naturally sees Hephaistion as his rival. He says, "Often I wished him dead, as no doubt, so he did me; but we had reached an unspoken understanding. Neither of us would have robbed Alexander of anything he valued; so we had no choice" (446). They have only one true confrontation: when Alexander in drunken fury kills one of his men, Hephaistion forbids Bagoas access to the king until he has sobered up, fearing that the Persian will give the Macedonian the wrong message (495). When Alexander's horse Bucephalus dies, Bagoas divines that he needs Hephaistion at his side and goes to find him (544).

Despite his own need to feel that the king needs him, he recognizes that "it's with Hephaistion he will want to die" (579). But Hephaistion dies first, and Bagoas grieves: "He was the victor for ever, now" (617). Alexander goes mad with sorrow, and even though he and Bagoas share a bed again, when Alexander himself lies dying, he calls on the childhood friend who proceeded him. Still, Bagoas convinces himself that at the end Alexander knows him: "I will take my oath before the gods. It was to me that he bade farewell" (642). The novel, the most romantic of the historical novels, has been particularly appreciated by gay readers. Renault returned one final time to fictionalizing the Alexander story: *Funeral Games*, 1981, re-recounts his death and the political intrigues that follows on its heels. She also wrote a nonfiction study, *The Nature of Alexander*, 1975.

Eileen Mary Challons (1905–1983) was born in Essex. She was educated at Oxford and trained to be a nurse. Fellow nurse Julie Mullard became her lifelong companion. Her early novels flirt with lesbian relationships; she adopted her pen name to protect the two of them in their jobs. In 1948 they emigrated to Durban, South Africa. She died in Cape Town.

Renault, Mary. *The Charioteer*. London: Longman, Green, 1953. *New York: Pantheon, 1959.
———. *Fire from Heaven*. New York: Pantheon, 1969. Harlow, Eng.: Longman, 1970. *The Alexander Trilogy*. London: Penguin, 1984. 7–316.
———. *The Last of the Wine*. London: Longman, Green, 1956. *New York: Pantheon, 1956.
———. *The Mask of Apollo*. London: Longman, Green, 1966. *New York: Pantheon, 1966.
———. *The Persian Boy*. New York: Pantheon, 1972. London: Longman, 1972. *The Alexander Trilogy* (see above). 317–650.

Sweetman, David. *Mary Renault: A Biography*. New York: Harcourt Brace, 1993.

53 Jocelyn Brooke: *Gerald Brockhurst*, 1954; *Conventional Weapons*, 1961.

The narrators in both stories must be gay. After all, all their closest friends are, and they hang out in gay clubs. But both remain guarded, even coy about their sexuality. A typical subterfuge is to avoid pronouns: "I happened to meet someone by whom I was attracted, and who—much to my surprise—reciprocated my feelings. We left the party together" (*Conventional Weapons*, 85). While guarding his own emotions, each narrator asks the reader to take an interest in another person, male, whom he has encountered. Gradually it emerges that this figure is gay (albeit with an interesting twist in the second story). As a result, this secondary character becomes more vivid, more alive, than the person telling the story. The narrators' circumscribed emotions, meanwhile, may leave the reader annoyed at their inability to open up.

Gerald Brochurst, a novella, is the second and longest story in the collection *Private View*. The unnamed narrator—"a conscientious (and even a militant) aesthete" (36)—meets Gerald while out horseback riding. They are both students at Oxford, Gerald in pre-med. The narrator is wary of becoming friends with Gerald: they come from different backgrounds, different classes, and belong to different university coteries. He is completely oblivious to the fact that Gerald is not only attracted to him personally but also sexually, even after Gerald tries to get them to go swimming naked in the river (68–71) and then later, when they have both moved to London, suggests that they share a bed after a night spent carousing (80). Gerald's engagement to an actress seems to confirm the narrator's assumption that he is heterosexual. Therefore, he is taken aback when a gay friend informs him that Gerald has been having an affair with Teddy Boscombe (103–04). Gerald himself confirms that he is gay the next time they meet, both verbally (110–11) and visually, when he picks up a young soldier (112). In an ironic turn, Gerald loses his wife to Teddy, but he never ceases loving him. Since Brooke belongs to All the Sad Young Men school of gay writing, of course Gerald must come a cropper in World War II.

Conventional Weapons was called by the less misleading title *The Name of Greene* in the United States. The unnamed narrator becomes fascinated by a pair of brothers, his distant cousins. The older one, Geoffrey Tufnell-Greene, is a hearty bully who dominates his wife and makes a stink when he discovers his younger brother reading *The Well of Loneliness*, denouncing it as "filth" (87). Later in the novel he bursts out, saying all homosexuals "ought to be strangled at birth," or better, "castrated" (109). Nigel, who Geoffrey worries is gay, is the aesthetic one, vaguely dabbling in painting and composition. When one of the narrator's friends asks about him—"I suppose he's queer, isn't he?"—he answers that he doesn't know, then adds, "I doubt if he knows himself" (85). Geoffrey is arrested, tried, and acquitted of fraud. Nigel goes in for politics, specifically communism, and takes up with the proletariat, a cockney jack-of-all-trades. Then, the narrator loses track of both brothers, only to run into Geoffrey in the mid–1950s in Malta. The novel ends with a series of revelations; the narrator's understanding of the people he is observing proves to be untrustworthy, and sexuality is not as consistent as one imagines. he sums up, "I was aware [...] of a sense of shifting frontiers, of fixed categories becoming merged into an amorphous, dream-like unity" (189).

Bernard Jocelyn Brooke (1908–1966) was born and died in Kent. He was educated at Bedales and Oxford. During World War II he served in the Royal Army Medical Corps, treating venereal diseases among the enlisted; his experience led to his best known work, his semi-autobiographical *The Orchid Trilogy*, 1948–50, and the homoerotic *The Image of a Drawn Sword*, 1950. His novel *The Scapegoat*, 1948, describes a boy on the edge of puberty in an all-male variant of Henry James's *Turn of the Screw* and is often classified as a gay novel. An avid amateur botanist (he has an orchid named for him), Brooke wrote several books about wild flowers. He also wrote a study of Firbank and edited works by Denton Welch.

Brooke, Jocelyn. *Conventional Weapons.* London: Faber & Faber, 1961. **The Name of Greene.* New York: Vanguard, 1961.
———. *Gerald Brockhurst. Private View: Four Portraits.* London: Barrie, 1954. *London: Clark, 1989. 36–126.

54 Francis King: *The Dark Glasses*, 1954; *The Man on the Rock*, 1957; *A Domestic Animal*, 1970. Frank Cauldwell (Francis King): *The Firewalkers*, 1956.

Francis King is another openly gay writer with a long and distinguished publishing career, covering more than sixty years, who has received scant attention from gay critics. One searches in vain to find mention of him in standard gay literary histories. *The Cambridge Guide to Literature in English*, 1995 edition, is more appreciative. It sums up, "His fiction displays a careful, sensitive concern with the impulses of human action, a fluent narrative skill and a preoccupation with decadent, sometimes horrific, aberrations of behavior." A number of his novels have especial interest for gay readers.

In *The Dark Glasses* King pulls off having a major character be a homosexual hiding in plain sight. We meet sixteen-year-old Stavro before the newly arrived protagonist, Patrick Orde, and his wife have even unpacked their belongings in their home on Corfu (10). And his presence remains steady till the ill-fated end of the novel. Iris Orde is a physician, who was born there; her husband is a thirty-nine-year-old Englishman, an expert on Greek plant life. But, as she points out, he knows little about Greeks—or about people in general (11). While he engages in a dalliance with Stavro's fifteen-year-old sister, Soula, he (as well as probably all but the most astute readers) misses every sign that the boy is infatuated with him. Stavro's constant toy is a jackknife given him by a Danish sailor (36), a man he refers to often. He is jealous when Patrick, having bought a new pair, makes a gift of the dark glasses he habitually wears to Soula instead of to him. Patrick himself is jealous when he realizes a Greek officer-cadet is making subtle advances to Soula, but it takes an encounter in Naples—where he is, on the way back to England, the Ordes having conceded that the Greek experience has been a failure—to unveil the truth about Stavro. While he is sitting on a bench in the public gardens, a man sits beside him and asks for a light. When Patrick moves on, the man follows, exactly as the cadet had followed Soula, overtakes him, and then stands by a convenient tree, *psst*-ing to get his attention: "And suddenly [Patrick] understood: he understood it all" (121). His mother-in-law sends him a newspaper clipping recounting the outcome of the emotional mess he has left in his wake; "sometimes Patrick tried to imagine what kind of love it could have been that drove [Stavro] to commit that horrible, useless act of violence. What kind of love? ... And he had never guessed—had never suspected!" (122). The novel's title works on all kinds of levels.

In his introduction to the Gay Modern Classic reprint of *The Firewalkers* (v), King reports how his job with the British Council required his receiving prior approval for any publications he undertook while thus employed. The Council handed him an ultimatum for this novel: "I could resign and publish the book under my own name; I could stay in the British Council and publish it under another name." They objected to the fact both that it dealt with "distasteful aspects of sexuality" and that "it was all too plainly a *roman à clef*." King chose the second alternative, but wickedly used the name Frank Cauldwell because "it had been the name of the young man, in many ways identifiable with myself, who was one of the characters in my first (and, since it contained an incident of fellatio, then considered shocking) novel *To the Dark Tower*." As he explained, "I was vain enough to wish to leave a clue to my identity for anyone who cared enough to discover it. No one did." Only a specialist in the cultural history of the time would now recognize the characters' original models, but the story itself remains enjoyable.

With a touch of Isherwood (whom King discovered when he was thirteen and about whom he would later write a monograph), the novel's narrator is also called Frank Cauldwell, and the subtitle is *A Memoir*. Frank is a writer offering private English lessons in Athens. He becomes fascinated by Colonel Theo Grecos's infatuation with an exceeding ugly German photographer, Götz Joachim. The novel is a series of often comic vignettes recounting incidents in their life together: Theo's failure to establish himself as a composer, followed by an equally disastrous attempt to start a new art movement; Götz's pursuit of a Greek woman whom he encounters at the beach. Cecil Provender, a gay Englishman, becomes virtually a permanent houseguest. His pickups are instrumental in causing both Theo's failures, but Theo accepts his fate with stoic courage. We see a great deal of Athens society, including the world of British expatriates, The title comes from a rural ceremony that brings the four men together. As Theo lies dying, his having suffered a series of strokes, he refers to the occasion: "You remember the firewalking—the firewalking, Frank? [...] Well, for someone like myself—someone so *different*—life is like that firewalking. If one has absolute faith in one's own rightness and the wrongness of the world—as those firewalkers do—then one can get across without being burned. [...] Well, thank God, I've had that faith: I've managed to get across with no more than a minor blister or two" (211).

In the introduction to the novel (vi), King also gleefully recounts his encounter at a cocktail part with a member of the British Foreign Office just returned from a post in Greece. The man accosts King, asking him if he is the author of *The Man on the Rock*. When King verifies the fact, he announces, "I read it the other day and I'm afraid I must tell you that I don't think you've understood Greece and the Greeks *at all*." He then continues, "Now there's one novel about Greece and the Greeks that really *gets* them. [...] It's called *The Firewalkers*."

The Man on the Rock (the title comes from Blake's poem "The Mental Traveller") is narrated by Spiro Polymerides, its egoistic antihero who betrays all those who love him. Irvine, a repressed American homosexual, finds him working as a gardener in a public park in Athens and assumes the role of Pygmalion to reshape the teenager's life. There is nothing sexual between the two men—not that Spiro would have objected (95) as long as it appeared that he was the one in command (118). He has an affair with a married woman, without losing Irvine's support. But when Irvine begins to cultivate a new Greek teenager, Spiro jealously destroys his reputation (233–34), leading to his dismissal from the Consulate (247). Spiro indirectly brings about the deaths of first his mistress and later his wife and their unborn child. By then his life has spiraled so out of control that he ends up destitute. He contemplates, as his next step returning to the park "to begin where I began," this time as a male prostitute: "What else?" (248).

A Domestic Animal is another account of a male homosexual's obsession with a heterosexual man, but it differs from the Greek novels not only in being set in England but also in having the gay male as its narrator. Despite the author's declaimer that "the 'I' is not I" (vi) the novel is heavily autobiographical, as King candidly admitted in his autobiography (214–21). With a change of names, the novel tells the story of writer Dick Thompson's infatuation with an Italian graduate student, Antonio Valli, who becomes a boarder at his home. Though married and the father of two children, his family having remained in Florence, Antonio begins an affair with a young Australian woman, Pam Mason. Dick becomes jealous of her to the point of madness, while Antonio accepts the homage paid him as his natural due. The novel is painful to read, leaving one wanting to shake some sense into the narrator. But Dick argues, "Pam and I were unhappy; but ours was the unhappiness of those who have acknowledged the deepest needs of their natures and have achieved the perfect freedom that comes from service to those needs, however fruitless that service. Antonio was unhappy because he only knew obscurely what those deepest needs were, and because he was ashamed of them and frightened of them" (209). The novel also reflects the new frankness in language permitted during the 1960s; genitals are finally on display, even if not shown in use.

Francis Henry King (1923–2011) was born in Adelboden, Switzerland, his father being in the British civil service. He spent his early years in India, coming to England only when he was nine. He was educated at Shrewsbury and Oxford. During World War II, as a conscientious objector, he worked on a farm. For nearly two decades he worked for the British Council, posted to Florence, Salonika, Athens, Helsinki, and Kyoto. In this position he met many people of note in both British culture and that of the countries in which he was working. His autobiography, *Yesterday Came Suddenly*, 1993, is a trove of information about the period. For twenty years he lived with David Atkin, who died of complications due to AIDS in 1988. King was president of PEN International, 1986–89. Many of his short stories also have gay interest.

King, Francis. *The Dark Glasses*. London: Longmans, Green, 1956. New York: Pantheon, 1956. *Intro. Jonathan Fryer. Kansas City, Mo.: Valancourt, 2013.
_____. *A Domestic Animal*. Harlow: Longman, 1970.
[_____.] *The Firewalkers: A Memoir* by Frank Cauldwell. London: Murray, 1956. *Intro., author. London: GMP, 1985.
_____. *The Man on the Rock*. London: Longmans, Green, 1957. *New York: Pantheon, 1957.

55   Edith de Born: *The Imperfect Marriage*, 1954. Gillian Tindall: *No Name in the Street*, 1959.

Two novels have in common a woman hurt by the infidelity of a bisexual Frenchman. *The Imperfect Marriage* recounts Louise de Castillac's bizarre relationship with her husband, Roger Warnier. The two meet at a party in 1936, fall in love, marry, and have two children. Roger is interred by the Germans throughout the war. Upon his return, he suffers erectile dysfunction. When Louise asks about the problem, he informs her that he is now gay and cannot be sexually aroused by any woman. He insists, however, that he still loves her and expects the marriage to continue. Roger becomes close friends with journalist Robert Perrin, and they go on holiday to Morocco without her. He takes up sculpture and invites handsome young men to serve as his models. He cannot understand why Louise is unhappy; she *is* married to him. So she has a sexual rendezvous in Paris with the local school teacher. She then visits the gay designer who was in the same internment camp Roger was. Roger hastens to Paris. Louise admits that she is still in love with his money. They have sex again. And one of Roger's aunts sums up, "So long as there is the will of the spirit to dominate nature, nothing serious can go wrong" (222).

The painter and journalist Vincent Lébert is seen through the eyes of his female English lover in *No Name in the Street*. A student in Paris, the uninteresting passive-aggressive narrator, aptly named Jane (without benefit of surname), attracts a bevy of friends and would-be lovers, though it is impossible to discern why. Vincent, who is almost twice her age, woos and beds her. Cocooned in her happiness, she is dismayed to discover him in bed with a male English student her age. In a series of passages scattered across the remainder of the novel, the reader is presented an etiological explanation for his condition. Earlier in the novel Jane and one of her suitors have checked out a gay bar. Now she qualifies her first reaction: "There was, I was growing to realize, a very wide gulf between the 'real article' such as I had seen at the *Cabriolet*—and the secret, unrecognized Vincents of this world. [...] Those elegant figures in the pretentious, over-sexed twilight of the *Cabriolet*, they had self-consciously created their own world, had formed their own defensive secret society. But Vincent was far from being a member of this eclectic society with the fellowship it must bring of pansy jokes and the pansy sense of superiority to the rest of the world. Not for him, the compensations of 'camp' slang and 'camp' intrigues [...]. So Vincent had no place where he entirely belonged" (198–99).

One of Vincent's oldest friends explains to

her that "the type of affliction, perversion, whatever name you like to fix to it, to which Vincent has this regrettable tendency, *is* a kind of childishness" (146). His development to normalcy was arrested, the friend explains, by the death of his best friend, Henri, during the war. The two of them had been, "genuinely, in love" (148). Now, Vincent is in "a genuine halfway house" (146), the true bisexual. His explanation leads Jane to conclude: "Had Henri lived, [Vincent] would very possibly have outgrown the fluid sexuality of youth: there would have been discord between them, a sad breakdown in their relationship—and then they might both have hardened in the direction of normality, and time would have washed over the past.... But, by dying, Henri had preserved for ever in Vincent's mind, as in amber, the bright, brief day: and Vincent would always, consciously or unconsciously, be seeking for it" (224). One leaves the novel wondering what point the author was trying to make. Was she asking, in some strange way, for tolerance or understanding? Was her novel an attempt to work through something personal, even if she insisted (according to the dust jacket) that it was not autobiographical? Was she simply capitalizing, like Born, on a trendy topic? Or is there actually a vicious attack on gays concealed beneath the placidly of the novel's prose style? Neither the British nor the American title provides any help.

Edith de Born (1901–1980s?) was born in Vienna. She married French banker Jacques Bisch; they lived in Brussels. Waugh and Francis King were among her friends. Born wrote her novels in English, but according to King's memoirs (278), "somewhere in East Anglia there lived a clergyman's wife [...] who, over a period of many years, had corrected almost every other sentence of every one of Edith's books for her." So, actually, it is stretching it to call her "British." Gillian Elizabeth Tindall (1938–) was born in London and educated at Oxford. Married to clinical psychologist Richard G. Lansdown, she has a son.

Born, Edith de. *The Imperfect Marriage*. London: Chapman & Hall, 1954.
Tindall, Gillian. *No Name in the Street*. London: Cassell, 1959. *When We Had Other Names*. New York: Morrow, 1960.

56   Audrey Erskine Lindop: *Details of Jeremy Stretton*, 1955.

Published the year after the Wolfenden Committee was formed, a *roman à thèse*, the novel is deadly earnest, dull, and now outdated, but there can be no doubt that its author meant well. She brings forth the enlightened theories of the day about the causes and the nature of homosexuality. The novel is even prefaced by an unnamed "consultant in psychiatry" willing to vouch for its "understanding and compassion," its "sincerity and truth" (ix-x). Throughout, however, she confounds homosexuality with gender confusion.

The dice are loaded against Jeremy from birth. His mother dies; his father, a minister in the Church of England, through ignorance turns his child's care over to his self-righteous sister, with the results that Jeremy grows up thinking no one loves him. Sent away to boarding school, he falls for the headmaster, John Osborne. John, and even less his wife, come little closer to understanding the child. Lindop indicates it is a problem endemic to education. A sexual relationship between the music teacher and one of his pupils is disclosed. The masters conduct an interview to discover if other boys are involved. In doing so, they reveal the huge gap that exists between the way adults view the world and the way children do and the incalculable harm that may come as a consequence. Under goading from his wife, John comes to believe that Jeremy has rekindled a homosexual desire that briefly flamed during his own prep school years. As a result he kills himself in his beloved Lake District, and the school closes down.

Having finished his military service but not yet of age, Jeremy determines to marry a local girl who was his best friend when they were children. His lack of desire for her forces him to acknowledge that he is, in fact, gay. Fighting the realization, he comes under the sway of a physician whose gay brother-in-law killed himself rather than face prison. The author depicts Dr. Louis Presnor as one cut from a heroic mold; for the present-day reader he seems part of the problem with his blind faith in the curative powers of abstinence. After having fought his urges for years, poor Jeremy finally has his first sexual experience with Gorwin Simpton, the man whom Louis seizes every opportunity to denounce and to warn Jeremy against. The two briefly live together, until Louis searches out Jeremy's father and convinces him to save his son. Taking a cue from Osborne, Jeremy decides to kill himself, only to discover that his wife has beaten him to it (though her attempt is clumsy enough to fail). Once again, Jeremy falls under Louis's influence. The doctor literally has the last word in the novel.

Audrey Erskine Lindop (1920–1986) was born in London. She also wrote crime and historical fiction and film scripts. She was married to the playwright Dudley Leslie. She died on the Isle of Wight.

Lindop, Audrey Erskine. *Details of Jeremy Stretton*. London: Heinemann, 1955. *The Outer Ring*. New York: Appleton–Century–Crofts, 1955. *The Tormented*. New York: Popular Library, 1956.

57 John Taylor: *Shadows of Shame*, 1956.

Apparently rumors long swirled about the African big game hunter's homosexuality, though his biographer, fellow hunter Peter Capstick, said he had no inkling until he read Taylor's one novel, published only as a paperback original in the United States. One finishes *Shadows of Shame* wondering how autobiographical it is. The cover is typical of pulps at the time in the way it sends mixed signals: "shame" acts as a code word to suggest homosexual content (think of Douglas's famous poem), but the illustration shows a provocatively posed white woman with a bare-chested black man gazing at her. The blurb on the back reads: "To wait on them by day, to share their beds at night—this was the corrupting role of Dumba the houseboy, who served white men and women with a dog-like devotion only to be betrayed by their unnatural desires." The novel is much better than one would anticipate from such hype.

Dunba describes in his own voice his series of encounters with Europeans: two men and a woman who defy white mores. After his mother's death, he and his twin brother, Aliki, are given shelter by the Irish hunter Bwana Jack. He, however, is killed in World War II. Eventually Dunba meets another young Irishman, only a few years older than he: Bwana Ted, who is looking for a native to share his bed with. Finding him likeable, Dunba has no hesitation to take up residence with him: "I was kindly treated and was genuinely happy with my Bwana. He was very different from most white men. He was not unkind, he did not force me to do things or submit to things against my will, he was not brutal. Why, oh why, cannot other white men, especially the officials, see these things through our African eyes? Where lay the crime or the sin in Bwana's dealings with me? Was I unwilling? Did he force me against my will? Did he lead me astray?" (58–59).

The idyll cannot last. Aliki is arrested and sentenced to die when he kills a white policeman attempting to rape their sister. Then the English officials go after Ted on trumped up charges of "indecent assault" and sentence him to hard labor. At this point, halfway through the novel, Dunba repeats himself: "But just as the whites do not understand us, frankly, we cannot understand the whites. For instance, we believe in allowing every man and woman, youth and maid, to live their own lives in the manner that best pleases them. We do not attempt to insist that they do exactly as we do if they would rather not. [...] Why, oh why, can't the whites see such matters as we do? Why must they insist that everyone conform to what they consider right? Do they really think that they and their judgments are infallible?" (92–93). This outlook, however, does not mean, Dunba insists, that he himself is homosexual (99). And indeed in the second half of the novel he becomes the lover of a white woman who deliberately seduces him. They are caught naked in bed by one of her white lovers, and Dunba is arrested. At the trial the woman refuses to give evidence against him; nevertheless, he is found guilty. However, since the jury recommends "mercy," taking into account "the accused's youth," the judge reduces the maximum sentence of seven years to "five years imprisonment with hard labor" (191).

It would be easy to dismiss the novel, but for the 1950s it was courageous. An author's note at the beginning stresses his long association with Central Africa and his fluency in various languages and insists that he "made it a point to get right into their skin, to think as they thought, to speak as they spoke," then translating it back into English (2). Born in Dublin, John Howard Taylor (1904–1969) led a checkered life even before he found his calling in Africa. There he was awarded the nickname "Pondoro," Zambian for "lion." He was deported from Kenya in 1957. It remains uncertain whether Taylor's sexuality, his defense of the native Africans, his sometimes illegal activities, or a combination of these was behind his being exiled. He settled in London, where he ended his life in poverty. He also wrote four nonfiction books for readers interested in his hunting experiences.

Capstick, Peter Hathawayck. *A Man Called Lion: The Life and Times of John Howard Pondoro Taylor*. Long Beach, Calif.: Safari, 2003.
Taylor, John. *Shadows of Shame*. New York: Pyramid, 1956.

58 James Mitchell: *Here's a Villain!*, 1957. John Cantwell: *Never a Closing Door*, 1958. Michael Hastings: *The Frauds*, 1960. Colin Wilson: *Ritual in the Dark*, 1960; *The Glass Cage*, 1966.

Five very different novels have in common that they pair a straight and a gay man. The two characters sometimes serve as slightly distorted reflections of each other; they sometimes complement each other. There is nothing sexual between them. They were written as the debate about homosexuality continued in the media and in legal and psychiatric circles, but they made little, if any, contribution to this discussion.

In *Here's a Villain!* Michael Bourke, a gay chemist, is the best friend of Alan Gregg, a straight schoolteacher whose wife has left him because he will not let her mother's money support them. Most of the comic novel details her petty attacks on him, his convoluted love life with the school's secretary, and the general pettiness of educators. But Alan also pays some attention to Michael's strange *ménage à trois*, consisting of him, Bill Murray, a nineteen-year-old manic composer of unclear sexuality, and Anne Hutchins, an aspiring painter. Alan seems simultaneously to know that Michael is gay and to be ignorant of the fact. The book ends with Michael's being accused of trying to seduce one of Alan's young students and running from the police. The reader never learns what really happened, but Alan says, "You had to know Michael and be with him to realize what he was, to know that he would never 'retire' from helping others, even if it, or they, killed him" (263). It now does: Michael deliberately wrecks his car, killing himself. He leaves the bulk of his estate to Alan, a sum large enough to recoup his wife. Alan sums up his friend: "Michael was a saint, a latter-day saint. That was the only queer things about him" (267). The American title, *The Lady Is Waiting*, presumably refers to the wife, though she never appears in the novel. The British title, taken from Shakespeare's *Henry VI, Part II*, could refer to either Alan or Michael.

Never a Closing Door brings together Robert Clover, an Australian solicitor working in London, and Alastair "Buck" Jones, an aspiring Canadian novelist, both in their early thirties. They meet on a boat taking them to a Spanish island resort and decide to rent a house together. They are both Catholics, and both guard a secret. Clover is seeking a miracle, the restoration of his fertility, a test having confirmed what his estranged wife suspected. Buck is fighting his homosexual urges. Clover's prayer is granted, as he discovers when he impregnates Nieves, a local woman. But as a good Catholic he feels he must now return to his wife, their marriage being again valid. Buck finds Paco, Nieves's fiancé, too attractive to resist and has his first homosexual experience with him (89), only to be blackmailed by the greedy Spaniard (94). About the same time two German tourists are arrested, having been surprised in bed together. Their plight awakens pity and, even more, fear in Buck. There is no chance now that he will accept himself as gay. The novel ends with Paco killing Clover as an act of honor (the town conspires to pass the murder off as an accident), and Buck, having blackmailed Paco in turn, proposing marriage to Nieves, with a pledge to accept Clover's child as his own.

The Frauds is an even stranger novel. Nicholas O'Manney is a twenty-two-year-old Lambeth native of Irish descent. He has just been demobbed from service in Cyprus, where he accidentally killed his best friend during a night attack but covered up his responsibility. His guilt continues to haunt him. Gerry Volk is a thirty-seven-year-old Christian Science minister working in London, a gay South African born of an English father and an African native. As a child he suffered from stigmatas. A homosexual journalist seized the opportunity to adopt him and parade him around the countryside for gain. He also used Gerry for sexual satisfaction. Now Gerry has impregnated Nick's former girlfriend and has become too tight emotionally with his younger brother, fourteen-year-old Tommy O'Manney. The truth comes close to bubbling out when Gerry tries to tear off the teenager's clothes, causing him to fall and damage his leg (100). It does come out when the girlfriend takes Nicholas to court (229) and Nick blabs. Straight Nick and bent Gerry reflect each other: "They were, each in their separate ways, self-deceivers of the first rank" (275).

Young Tommy becomes increasingly important in his own right. He begins to accept the fact that he is gay. He enjoys "the secret he and Gerry held between them" even thought "he didn't understand at all what drove Volk to attack him as he did" (130). When Tommy meets Old Bill, a pedophile, he allows himself to be seduced: "He wanted to shrink from the reality of it, but there was no going back; he had to go through with it" (222). As a result of their continuing encounters, Tommy moves on: "He had made some new friends in school too—a couple of sensual girlish fellows more than a year his senior. They had led Tommy quite a dance; he enjoyed the new-found pleasure in his body, the warmth of their silly relationship with one another, the odd meetings in outlandish places to play games of extraordinary enticement—three young smooth-faced warriors of perversion, finding, under a hot sun, a warm loving hand for sustenance of the flesh, outstaring each other's trespassing gaze or lying together, contentment-bound, beneath the streaming azure sky" (239). Tommy's alcoholic father, in predictable fashion, tries to beat the perversion out of him, but fails. Is Tommy the one character who finally is not a fraud? Perhaps.

Wilson's two novels about gay serial killers leave me uncertain what the writer was trying to achieve. Austin Nunne, in *Ritual in the Dark*, in some bizarre homage to Jack the Ripper kills women in the same Whitechapel section of London where the earlier murderer found his victims. Meeting the novel's protagonist, the straight Gerard Sorme, at a Diaghilev exposition, Nunne feels an attraction to a fellow lover of ballet and instantly takes him up. On his part, Sorme, a self-proclaimed existentialist, feels he has found a troubled but kindred spirit and maintains his fidelity to the man even as he learns, first, that he is a sadist and, then, that he must be the killer. In his introduction to the 1993 reprint, Wilson says that in order to explains why Nunne would involve himself with Sorme, he decided to make him homosexual. But he admits, "I have since then wondered occasionally whether this was the correct solution, since few sadistic homosexuals select women as their victims" (5). The novel obviously has pretensions to some kind of philosophical truth, but it offers no insight into Nunne's mental state, and his homosexuality seems irrelevant—as contrived as Wilson admits that it was.

The same may also be said of George Gaylord Sundheim, the serial killer in *The Glass Cage*. He kills both women and men, leaving their bodies along the Thames, sometimes with a quotation from William Blake scrawled nearby. In accordance with one psychological cliché, he is the offspring of a bullying father, who made him learn Blake's poetry by heart, and a smothering mother. Blake expert Damon

Reade is called in by the police to aid their investigation. He becomes fascinated by the strange figure and remains faithful to him even after he witnesses Sundheim nearly kill a hapless man in a sleazy club. The title refers to the container in which Sundheim keeps a boa constrictor—which Reade rescues at the end, throwing out a quotation from the gay Comte de Lautréamont.

James Mitchell (1926–2002) was born in County Durham, England. Educated at Oxford, he obtained a teaching diploma from King's College, Newcastle. He created three different crime series under his own name or a pseudonym. Married, he had two sons. John Kenneth Cantwell (1924–1966) was born in East Greta, N.S.W. During World War II he served in the RAAF. He graduated from the University of Sydney and, unmarried, vagabonded around the world. According to a web source, his family was "sensitive" about the circumstances of his death at Potts Point. Michael Gerald Hastings (1937–2011) was born and died (of cancer) in London. He trained at the Royal Court Theatre in London as an actor and a playwright. His best known work is *Tom and Viv*, 1984. He also wrote biographies of Rupert Brooke, 1967, and Richard Burton, 1978. Married, he had three children. Colin Henry Wilson (1931–2013) was born in Leicester. He got out of performing national service by claiming to be gay, but from then on insisted that he was straight. Throughout his life, however, he was fascinated by homosexuality. He became friends with Angus Wilson, who used him in his short story "A Bit Off the Map." One of the first English existential thinkers, he wrote several studies of crime and of the occult. Married twice, he had four children. He died in St. Austell, Cornwall.

Cantwell, John. *Never a Closing Door*. London: Putnam, 1958. *Miracle on San Jaime*. Philadelphia: Chilton, 1959.
Hastings, Michael. *The Frauds*. London: Allan, 1960. *New York: Orion, 1961.
Mitchell, James. *Here's a Villain!* London: Davies, 1957. *The Lady Is Waiting*. New York: Morrow, 1958.
Wilson, Colin. *The Glass Cage*. London: Barker, 1966. *The Glass Cage: An Unconventional Detective Story*. New York: Random House, 1967.

———. *Ritual in the Dark*. London: Gollancz, 1960. Boston: Houghton Mifflin, 1960. *Intro., author. Berkeley, Calif.: Ronin, 1993.

59 Kenneth Martin: *Aubade*, 1957; *Waiting for the Sky to Fall*, 1959.

Aubade remains an astonishing debut. Written by a not yet seventeen-year-old lad from Northern Ireland who had never been outside the area and published under his own name, it records a bittersweet summer romance. The teenager Paul Anderson feels an intense attraction to John Knight, an older medical student whom he first sees in church and imaginatively dubs "Gary." The feeling grows when they finally meet each other the summer Paul works for a tobacconist and Gary has a temporary job in the factory across the street. Paul allows himself to be seduced by a girl from his school: "When it was over, he felt completely disgusted" (81). But when Gary tries to kiss him, he balks (113). And when Gary declares his love, Paul is terrified: "I love you, too, but people say that it's evil. It makes you an outcast from society. People would never have you as a doctor if they thought you were having a love affair with another man" (129). And so Gary decides they should stop seeing each other.

It takes the death of Paul's father to reunite them. Gary stops by the tobacconist's to express his sympathy. He also tells Paul that he has accepted a research fellowship in Southern Rhodesia. This time when Gary pleads for them to spend the week they have left together "and have the time of our lives," Paul accepts: "'Gary, I don't care if loving you is wrong. It can't be, and even if it is, I don't care any more. If I let you go now, without telling you, I should regret it for the rest of my life.' He put his arms round Gary's neck, then leaned his head on his shoulder. He heard and felt Gary sigh, and he said, 'Strangely enough, I think this makes me more manly. This is the first time in my life when I've made a decision that needed courage'" (148). They spend a night together, in Gary's car. The novel ends with Paul rereading a Sanskrit poem he loves (quoted by John Steinbeck in *Cannery Row*), and he thinks, "But I have never been happy" (158).

The novel's honesty is all the more astonishing when one considers that, according to the author's 1989 introduction to a reprint (v), the men's declaration of love was something that "I'd never experienced."

Waiting for the Sky to Fall is structurally more complex; it holds up equally well. It describes a year in the London lives of various people loosely associated with the straight Irish-born brothers Simon and Perkin Young, respectively a painter and a writer. Most of the characters are heterosexual, but one series of vignettes follows the intense but short-lived affair between Jonathan Moore and George Tench. Jonathan is a poet who never writes poetry, a repressed gay who "seemed to know all about the loss of innocence without having experienced it" (7). George is "the kind of boy you stared at in the street" (21), an accomplished liar, the owner of a successful nightclub and a series of male brothels. Perkin brings them together on a whim, even though he knows that George will quickly tire of Jonathan and Jonathan will then want to kill himself (62-63). George offers Jonathan a room in the house he owns, where he has his own flat and the club, and occasionally spends the night with him there. For Jonathan they are "making love"; George's own choice of verb is more accurate (71). Helping out in the club, Jonathan meets Derek, George's former lover, now barman. He is present when George encounters his replacement in Trafalgar Square: Charles, a French-Canadian student pilot. George tries to comfort him: "Look, honey, don't be hurt. [...] You don't know enough about our world to understand, but it means nothing. Two people living together get bored. Actually these little affairs are a good thing" (215). Jonathan decides to kill himself, using the gas oven, but when he checks to see if his head will fit inside, he emerges "covered with black grease." Cleaning up, he concludes, "Oh God, why bother" and goes to sleep (218). Because Charles does not love George, he proves to be more adept at handling him (229).

After the comparative failure of this and his next novel, the author abandoned fiction for journalism. An adopted child, Kenneth Martin (1939–) was born in Belfast, Northern Ireland, but grew up in nearby Bangor. Upon the acceptance of *Aubade*, he moved to London, where he was on the fringes of a culture in transition. In 1970 he moved to the United States and trained to become a clinical research psychologist at Columbia, Minnesota, and San Francisco State Universities. Off and on he lived with architect Richard Oliver (1942?–1985). He became an American citizen in 1977 and settled in San Francisco, where he still lives. In 1989 he returned to fiction, publishing *Billy's Brother*, followed by *The Tin Islands* in 1996.

Martin, Kenneth. *Aubade*. London: Chapman & Hall, 1957. New York: Citadel, 1958. *Intro., author. London: GMP, 1989.

———. *Waiting for the Sky to Fall*. London: Chapman & Hall, 1959. *Intro., author. Kansas City, Mo.: Valancourt, 2013.

60   C. H. B. Kitchin: *Ten Pollitt Place*, 1957; *The Book of Life*, 1960.

At the end of a long career—chiefly remembered today, if at all, for his detective stories—Kitchin published two novels, in rapid succession, with boys at their centers. The one is physically deformed; the other is emotionally warped. *Ten Pollitt Place*, set in the present time, has the more appealing cast of characters, despite their numerous cruelties. *The Book of Life* is less successful. Set at the very end of the Edwardian era, it presents a sometimes appalling view of people, and the first person narration creates an almost claustrophobic feeling.

No. 10 Pollitt Place has been divided into four flats. On the top floor lives the owner, Miss Tredennick, an elderly spinster who becomes obsessed with the sexual life of the young woman living in the corresponding flat directly across the street. The next floor down lives the bachelor Justin Bray, obviously a fictionalized self-portrait of the author. We learn little about his emotional life other than his dismay about his fading career as a novelist. The ground floor holds the Fawley couple: a wife of independent means, a husband in research—who also is having an affair with

Magda Muller, the daughter of the housekeeper. The Mullers live in the basement flat. Young Hugo, fifteen, a humpbacked Gandymede with disproportionate limbs, plays a defining role in all their lives. Robert Fawley identifies him as "a bloody little pervert," saying, "He looks at me as a woman looks at a man" (88). But Hugo is in love with Bert, the thirty-three-year-old red-haired dustman. With almost preternatural self-knowledge, he knows "the kind of person I want to love me" and "the way I want to be loved" (113). He instinctively picks up on the "latent abnormality" of a younger boy he meets (152). He is upset when Magda denounces him for being "*abnormal*," not because of what she said—"nothing I'm ashamed of" (201)—but because she has upset their mother. The siblings' final confrontation has repercussions across all the occupied flats.

In the second novel, ten-year-old Francis Froxwell, orphaned, is taken into his grandfather's gloomy mansion. The old man rules his family through their greed; he calls his record of investments, and their slated allotments to each family member, his Book of Life. In this unhealthy environment young Francis becomes thoroughly materialistic; he is also misled to believe the grandfather will receive the title of baronet, which will then come to him as the son of the oldest son. Emotionally, he is drawn towards two men. Of his Uncle Demetrius he says: "I felt towards him all the emotions which a dutiful son is supposed to feel towards his father, with a mixture of others which are not normally filial" (24). His relationship with James Waring, whom he meets one day in town, is innocent yet fraught with dangers, as he dimly senses. Waring was once a school master, until some sort of relationship with a student led to his being brought to trial. A scene in which the police try to determine whether Waring ever abused Francis (182–83) vividly captures the damage ill trained officials can wreak upon a child. Demetrius falls for a twice-married woman with flexible morals, who happens to be Waring's half-sister. The tensions among the adults precipitate a catastrophe that will be fatal to young Francis's dreams of wealth and title. A weakness of the novel is that the reader is given no hint of the effects events have on Francis's future, even though the novel is being narrated by him from an adult perspective.

Clifford Henry Benn Kitchin (1895–1967) was born in Harrogate, Yorkshire, and died in Brighton. He attended Oxford and served in World War I. He made his wealth as an astute investor in the stock market. He lived fourteen years with Clive Preen, until the latter's death in 1944. His second lover was a married man with children. He was friends with T. S. Eliot, Leslie Hartley, and Francis King, among others.

Kitchin, C. H. B. *The Book of Life*. London: Davies, 1960. New York: Appleton–Century–Crofts, 1961. *Intro. Francis King. Kansas City, Mo.: Valancourt, 2009.
———. *Ten Pollitt Place*. London: Secker & Warburg, 1957. *Intro. Simon Stern. Kansas City, Mo.: Valancourt, 2013.

61 Martyn Goff: *The Plaster Fabric*, 1957; *The Youngest Director*, 1961; *Indecent Assault*, 1967.

Goff's three novels are widely different in character types and backgrounds, situations, and even the areas of London in which they are set. They have in common the arguments typical of gay novels of the period that homosexuality is normal for some people. The third novel in particular lets drop the specific names of gay writers, musicians, and artists. At the same time the portraits of homosexuals, particularly the secondary characters, tend to be negative, stressing casual seductions, infidelities, jealousy, backstabbing, and short-lived affairs. There are no gratuitous suicides or convenient deaths, but there are no positive role models or even people one would particularly care to have as friends.

The Plaster Fabric is centered on a weak, vacillating young gay. Feeling all too acutely his difference, Laurie Kingston runs scared most of the time and, as a result, pretty well muddles his life: "He wanted to tell and live the truth. He wanted to be a whole person, not just half a one and the rest filled in with lies, exaggerations and imagined virtues. From time to time he strove sincerely to achieve his wish, but the plastic fabric of his life hung over him always, and sooner or later a flake would chip from it, flutter down and mar his new-found honesty" (78). The novel records his painful steps over a period of two years to a renunciation that serves perhaps as a breakthrough in his efforts to find himself. The difficult, and often muddled, journey begins when he picks up a guardsman, Tom Beeson. That encounter leads to a strange *ménage à trois* with his friend Susan, which leaves him as odd man out. A lie leads to his leaving his job in a bookshop and moving in with bookseller Norman Wayne. An infidelity while on vacation in Florence brings that relationship to an end. Then fifteen-year-old Martin Rogers, with whom he is infatuated, unknowingly tells him the right thing to do when Susan leaves Tom and Laurie could have him back. Even before that defining moment, "he seemed to have a better measure of himself. His life was beginning to fall into a more orderly pattern and so yield greater security and less loneliness. [...] Some people knew about him and others did not, but in neither case was he lying any longer" (245–46).

In *The Youngest Director*. Leonard Bissel suffers likewise from homosexual angst, here magnified by differences of class and culture and aggravated by middle-class heterosexual oppression from the firm in which he has just been promoted as the youngest director. His supervisor and colleagues pressure him to marry. But Leonard has fallen in love with John Cramer, a relatively uneducated hotel clerk, eleven years his junior. Ignoring his friends' advice—Tony Newman, his closest friend says, "I shall never understand how someone can be as brilliant as you in business and such a delayed adolescent privately" (114)—he is determined to create a life with John that emulates heterosexual marriage. Then, Leonard violates his every principle by succumbing to jealousy when he thinks John has bedded Tony and is having sex with one of John's old friends. Tony called it adolescence; as the novel progresses it looks increasingly like stupidity, sometimes even hypocrisy. True, certain matters are out of Leonard's control. John is wrongfully entrapped by the police and accused of solicitation. Leonard's lawyer saves him by having him plead guilty, but then the hearing makes the newspaper and effectively outs Leonard and John alike to their families and their bosses. Leonard discovers that he has been unwise trusting a seemingly heterosexual colleague, who actually is a closet homosexual with a longtime crush on him. Even Leonard's idealism, diluted as it is by his unreasonable jealousy and an unacknowledged class consciousness, undermines any hope of permanence with John. The novel seems to end on an upbeat, but Leonard's final renunciation carries none of even the limited promise that Laurie's does.

Indecent Assault, published the year the Wolfenden recommendations were finally approved by Parliament, would have done little to support gay arguments for its passage. It reverts to the old ploy of having a heterosexual narrator, David Coulsdon. An art student, he is the son of a politician aspiring to the position of Prime Minister. His father urges him to move in with his brother, Julian Coulsdon, an open homosexual living with an actor. Belatedly, David realizes that the motive is the hope he will keep the errant uncle in check. Few people, however, know that Julian secretly hankers after young boys. Then, "the Stratford police rang to say Julian had been charged with the indecent assault of a thirteen year old boy" (135). The novel has an epigraph taken from *Lolita*. It would seem that Goff wants the reader at least to think about the ambiguities of intergeneration sex. David's girlfriend asks, "And how many *innocent* boys have ever been perverted because they've been seduced once, twice or ten times? [...] For all we know, it might have done the wretched child good!" (149). But then Goff undercuts any meaningful analysis when he gratuitously ends the penultimate chapter thus: "At one instant I stood there, hand on Julian's shoulder, feeling desperately sorry for the good, kind man who had slipped up—*if* he had. At the next my slimy, crawling uncle had unhooked my zip and slid his hand into my crutch" (217).

Martyn Goff (1923–) served for thirty-six years as administrator of the Booker Prize. Before that, he was a bookseller and a reviewer, both of books and of music recordings. He was the son of Russian emigrants (his birth name was Gulkov), manufacturers of fur coats. He served as a radio operator for the RAF during World War II, stationed in what was then Transjordan. His novel *The Youngest Director* brought a fan letter from a Scandinavian student named Rubio T. Lindroos; they fell in love and set up housekeeping. Goff dedicated his fourth gay novel, *Tar and Cement*, 1988, to him. The story of a long-term couple's reaction to urban renewal in their London neighborhood, it is only marginally more uplifting than the earlier works.

Goff, Martyn. *Indecent Assault*. London: Deutsch, 1967.
———. *The Plaster Fabric*. London: Putnam, 1957.
———. *The Youngest Director*. London: Putnam, 1961.

62 Angus Heriot: *Orphan's Progress*, 1957. Anonymous (Michael Nelson): *A Room in Chelsea Square*, 1958.

Two naifs, both named Nicholas, are more than a little uncertain about their sexuality. The first, Nicholas Bristowe, appears in Heriot's story of a wealthy but more or less dysfunctional family. He remains heterosexual through public school, the army, and his first ventures into society. But late in the novel he falls in love with Earnest Allsop, a figure who owes something to Wilde's character, even to living in the country and coming up to town for pleasure. Although Nicholas has no problems sexually with women, he finds that, as before when he has tried to be with a man, "I can go a certain way and enjoy it, and want to go further. But then when I do ... I suddenly can't bear it" (199). Yet with women he feels "nothing of that charm of mutual understanding that he had felt with Earnest, [...] nothing, even, of emotion" (201). He feels forlorn when Earnest breaks to him that he has found another partner, but ultimately decides that the rupture was for the best (239). He later takes up with Philip Stratton, "a remarkably charming and handsome young man, too superficial ever to be depressed for long," whose "entire world was the theatre" (242). Nicholas quickly loses interest in him. He tries marriage, sires a son, but they divorce, and Nicholas throws himself into becoming a writer. It's a charming book, quite gay in the ordinary sense, not very gay in the special sense.

Born in London, Angus Heriot (1927–1964) went to Eton. He then served in the army for three years in Egypt and Greece. He worked with the Council of Europe, moving to Paris. His partner was the mystery writer Neil Macmillan. He was friends with Angus Wilson and the French writer and illustrator Philippe Jullian, one of whose novels he translated. His most enduring book is his history of *The Castrati in Opera*, 1956. The novels *Four-Part Fugure*, 1962, and *The Island Is Full of Strange Noises*, 1963, are also of interest to gay readers. Heriot crashed his car and died in Morocco on his way to a rendezvous with a local youth he had met.

In Nelson's much gayer novel, Nicholas Milestone, a small town reporter, catches the eye of an overly wealthy patron of the arts down to attend a funeral. Patrick sets his mind to seducing him. To lure him to London, he pulls strings to get Nicholas a job working for one of the tabloids. Meanwhile, Patrick's former lover, the bisexual painter Ronnie Gras, convinces him to back a fashion magazine he wants to start up. Fellow painter Christopher Lyre will come on board to help with the venture. Patrick decides that Nicholas, instead of working for the tabloid, should be a part of the new project. He meets him at the train station and whisks him off to a hotel rather than to the room he has taken in Chelsea Square. Nicholas realizes, "It was no good pretending that he didn't know why Patrick was taking such an interest in him" (47), but he cannot give in, even as he tries to reason with himself: "What did sex matter anyway? It was a small price to pay for all the things that Patrick could offer him in exchange" (89). So he proceeds to do everything wrong, including allowing a pilot friend to use the apartment (while Patrick is away) to seduce Ronnie's mistress. Within a week Nicholas is being shown the door, his luggage literally packed by his replacement, the aptly named Victor. His destination, after all, will be the unfashionable Chelsea Square: "Poor Nicholas! Somehow he had failed to grasp what was expected of him" (188).

Published anonymously, the campy novel is a *roman à clef*. The author was not identified until a GMP reprint in 1986, but his name must have circulated earlier. Nicholas Milestone is Michael Nelson's stand-in (notice the play between the two names when reversed). The author's peripheral involvement in the creation of the influential literary journal *Horizon*, 1940-49, guarantees that his novel will always have a footnote in literary history. Ron Gras is a caricature of its editor, Cyril Connolly; Christopher Lyre is Stephen Spender; and Patrick is Peter Watson, a wealthy patron of the arts. The novel was originally written towards the end of the 1940s, but no publisher would take it. Having published another novel in the mid-1950s, Nelson returned to the manuscript and revised it at the insistence of his wife, updating the references to fit in with the time of publication. Michael Harrington Nelson (1921-1990) worked as a journalist, also as a secretary to John Lehmann during World War II. While living with his lover in Winchester, he met Rachel Holland, who married him even though she knew he was gay.

Heriot, Angus. *Orphan's Progress*. London: Secker & Warburg, 1957.
[Nelson, Michael.] *A Room in Chelsea Square*. London: Cape, 1958. Garden City, N.Y.: Doubleday, 1959. *Intro. Philip Core. London: GMP, 1986.

63 Lennox Cook: *No Language but a Cry*, 1958.

Martin Henley, twenty-six, once a star cricket player at Oxford, has spent eighteen months in prison because he was, in his own words, "drunk and lonely and weak and hopelessly innocent" (86). We learn, "His imprisonment had not only shocked him, it had instilled in him an awful dread of going back; but it was clear it had not succeeded as a corrective; it had not changed this queer and frightening twist of character; and sometimes he would think bitterly that unnumbered years of deceit and loneliness would surely be punishment enough: but no, the law had to make him a criminal as well. People liked him. He believed there were none he had known who would have sent him to prison for what he had done, and yet in part they had all been a little responsible" (186-87). Haunted by memories of his incarceration, trying to get away from everyone who knows about it, Martin accepts a job as clerk with a firm of timber merchants headquartered in Bangkok. But he discovers the impossibility of getting away from his past. Another member of the British colony and a fellow Oxonian, Nigel Benson, was in England at the time of the arrest. Out of mixed motives (including the fact that he had a crush on Martin at Oxford), the rather effeminate Nigel spreads the story within the British colony, from where it leaks out even to the Thais who work with him.

Martin tries to fit into the heterosexual world. He starts dating a young woman attached to the embassy; she is certain that she can convert him. But to Martin's shock, he realizes that he has fallen in love with his chief, Malcolm Steel. When he discovers that Steel is fully aware of his imprisonment and does not care, he starts feeling hope. Much of the novel is taken up with Martin's work for the firm, which has an all-important contract being placed in jeopardy by a power struggle among the native laborers. In the process Martin is forced to acknowledge that he is out, whether he wants to be or not. Then just as he seems to be achieving a breakthrough in self-acceptance, he allows Steel's refusal of his declaration of love to crush him. Martin resigns his post and sinks into a permanent state of lethargy, attended only by his houseboy. The novel is sad; it is also believable.

Born in Richmond, Yorkshire, John Lennox Cook (1923-) attended Oxford. He created the Lennox Cook School of English in Cambridge. He is married and has two daughters. An earlier novel was published by the Fortune Press: *Dark to the Sun*, 1952, is a quasi-gothic tale about a struggle between a sadistic schoolmaster who possesses a student's psyche and another who tries to save the boy, ending in the deaths of all three.

Cook, Lennox. *No Language but a Cry*. London: Hamilton, 1958.

64 Iris Murdoch: *The Bell*, 1958; *A Fairly Honourable Defeat*, 1970; *Henry and Cato*, 1976.

Religion and sexuality drive the plot of Murdoch's fourth novel, *The Bell*. Michael Meade decides to form a lay religious community in his ancestral home, which is adjacent to a convent of nuns. It attracts a number of people for varying reasons. They include Dora Greenfield, whose husband is researching medieval manuscripts that belong to the convent; eighteen-year-old Toby Gashe, who plans to pass a month there before enrolling at Oxford; and the now grown Nick Fawley, whom Michael had loved when Nick was a student at the public school where he taught. Though he felt physical desire for the boy, "they did nothing but hold hands and exchange the gentlest of caresses" (110). Then an evangelist was invited to the school; as a result of the fervor he stirred up, Nick went to the headmaster and embellished what had occurred between him and Michael. Dismissed from his post, thereafter, "though sometimes plagued by his inclinations, he avoided amorous adventures" (114).

The reappearance of Nick, now apparently openly gay, and the entrance of Toby into his life reawakens desire. Michael is a master of self-deception and rationalization. Thinking about what a relationship with Toby could mean, "he felt a serene confidence in his own most scrupulous discretion" (166). And then he kisses the boy—and does so just as Nick arrives on the scene. Toby is left perplexed, wondering if he somehow attracts gays and is therefore gay himself. Thus he is open to Dora's scheme to substitute the ancient abbey bell, which Toby has discovered while swimming in the lake, for the new one, not yet put in place. As for Michael, he worries that Nick will feel betrayed, that he has damaged Toby, and that he has "done something worse to himself" (176). In a sense, Nick cuts through the muddle, in a replay of his own actions thirteen years previous, by compelling Toby to confess to the most puritanical member of the community. In what Michael perceives as a gratuitous act of perfect revenge, Nick then shoots himself. The community dissolves. Dora's plan for the bell also fails, but she has finally gained a sense of her selfhood apart from her suffocating husband. And for Michael, "Very slowly a sense of his own personality returned to him. The annihilating sense of a total guilt gave way to a more reflective and discriminating remembrance" (335).

"Every novel she wrote after *The Bell*," according to her biographer Peter Conradi (424), "has at least one homosexual character." That would mean at least twenty-one more. In some, as in *The Bell*, the gay is a central character; in others he has only a walk-on role. Lesbians also populate her fictional world, having an important role in *An Accidental Man*, 1971 (in which a gay schoolboy has only a minor comic role). A kind of dialectic about homosexuality runs through the novels taken as a whole. A straight character in *A Fairly Honourable Defeat*, speaking of his brother and of a colleague, argues that "being homosexual doesn't determine a man's whole character any more than being heterosexual does" (8). But Michael holds that "God had created men and women with these tendencies, and made these tendencies to run so deep that they were, in many cases, the very core of the personality" (220). Murdoch's word choice is sometimes strange, even for her time. For example, the authorial voice tells readers that Toby knew Latin but no Greek, and therefore "his acquaintance with the excesses of the ancients was fragmentary" (171). *Excesses*? Still, because of her prestige, possibly she introduced more readers to gay men than any other author at the time.

A Fairly Honourable Defeat is about trust and honesty in a relationship. The members of the Forsters' extended family are tested on this score entirely at the whim of Julius King, the complete cynic, evil almost to the core. He wagers a bet with his ex-lover, Morgan Browne, that he can break up any relationship, and the two settle on simple Simon Foster (225). Playing upon Simon's weaknesses and his fears of disappointing his lover, Axel Nilsson, Julius first confuses Simon and then threatens him. Axel is too prickly a character to genuinely admire, though he is the most able spokesman for honesty and trust (23), but the reader's heart goes out to Simon. One feels a rush of relief when Simon decides that the truth cannot possibly make anything worse than it already is and discloses to Axel the machinations that Julius has set into motion. The heterosexuals are not so lucky. The only one who escapes is Morgan's ex-husband, one of the family's saner members. Julius leads Morgan to feel she is in love with her brother-in-law, Simon's brother. When the sister leaves him, he kills himself, either deliberately or accidentally. Leaving the wreckage he has caused behind him, Julius moves on.

Axel and Simon are Murdoch's most attractive gay couple. They are quite different from each other. Axel needs monogamy and, prior to Simon, has always been wary of commitment. He detests anything smacking of camp. At the same time, "He made Simon understand for the first time that it was perfectly *ordinary* to be homosexual." Until that point Simon had been happily promiscuous and has viewed homosexuality "as a peculiarity, something rather nice and even perhaps a bit funny, something rather like a game, but definitely odd, to be concealed, giggled about, and endlessly discussed and inspected in the private company of fellow oddities" (29–30). Simon's nephew first points out to Axel that he is not all that honest, however, asking, "And why don't *you* tell the truth! [...] Why don't you tell everyone in Whitehall that you live with another man? Are you afraid of losing your precious job? Afraid of being called a pansy?" (129). After Simon's confession, Axel accepts his part of the blame: "It was a failure of love. You held nothing back, but I played for safety. I haven't deserved your full and absolute faith" (423). Just a bit earlier, he also has admitted, "I think we should see more people and live more in the world. [...] I think if we'd been living more in the open we mightn't have been involved in this terrible muddle" (421–22).

Henry and Cato is a painful read. The thirty-one-year-old Cato Forbes is a lay priest who has fallen in love with one of his flock, the seventeen-year-old Joseph Beckett, "Beautiful Joe." Cato has never had sex with anyone and cannot decide even if he is homosexual. He both desires and is afraid to make advances to the boy, but like the self-deluded Michael, he is certain he can be a positive force in Joe's life. He decides to leave the priesthood and invite Joe to set up a home with him somewhere other than London. But it is Cato's role as a priest that has caused Joe to fall in love with not him but his idea of him. He says of the divested Cato, "All the—all the sort of—magic's gone—what made me care—Now you're just a queer in a cord coat" (211). In a melodramatic climax, Joe fabricates a gang that kidnaps Cato and forces him to ask for ransom from his newly rich friend, Henry Marshalson. He next stipulates that Cato's sister must deliver the money, whereupon Joe tries to rape her. Cato, having finally broken out of his cell, hears her screams and rushes in to kill Joe with a blow to the head. In an ironic echo of the opening scene, Cato is last seen carrying a heavy crucifix to his new home.

Jean Iris Murdoch (1919–1999) was born in Dublin but was taken by her parents to London when she was only a few weeks old. She studied philosophy at both Oxford and Cambridge. Bisexual, she had a number of lesbian relationships even after she married John Bayley in 1956. She suffered from Alzheimer's at the end of her life.

Conradi, Peter J. *Iris Murdoch: A Life*. New York: Norton, 2001.
Murdoch, Iris. *The Bell*. London: Chatto & Windus, 1958. *New York: Viking, 1958.
———. *A Fairly Honourable Defeat*. London: Chatto & Windus, 1970. *New York: Viking, 1970.
———. *Henry and Cato*. London: Chatto & Windus, 1976. *New York: Viking, 1977.

65 James Courage: *A Way of Love*, 1959.

At the end of the first chapter, the narrator—a middle-aged London architect named Bruce Quantock—places himself as one "among men of my kind" (13) Throughout the rest of the novel the label "my kind" or some variant occurs so monotonously that one almost expects the author to announce that he is writing a case history of one example of *homo sapiens homosexualis*. The story recounts his affair of a few years with a man half his age, an insurance clerk and aspiring landscape architecture named Philip Dill. Philip fights against becoming "one of your kind" (95) but finally moves in with Bruce. For a while they isolate themselves from Bruce's old friends. When after many months they accept invitations out, Philip is repelled. Eventually he decides that he really wants marriage and children, and the two men break up. At novel's end Bruce consoles himself by planning to become the perfect uncle to his sister's teenage son coming up to London to study.

The reader meets various types of London gays ten years after the war, including a happy long-term couple, but gains no sense of the political climate of the time, nor much of the cultural atmosphere. Various bromides are dropped about the need for masks (55), the problems of fidelity among men (87, 246, 249), the positive qualities of physical attraction (96), the naturalness of homosexuality (103, 137, 145), queer people's loneliness (112), the need for self-acceptance (154) and for social interaction with other gays (156), My difficulty with the novel is caring about the two main characters. I applaud when Bruce finally has the courage to say, "For goodness' sake, Philip, grow up a little" (193). Whether I believe Bruce or not, at least he ends his story on an upbeat: "No less profoundly than before, I cherish physical desire for its own sake, for its power to alleviate the solitudes of my kind and as it may expand into love" (255).

James Francis Courage (1903–1963) was born in Christchurch, New Zealand; he grew up on his family's farm near Amberley. In 1923 he entered Oxford. He remained in England, making only one long return to his native country in the mid-1930s. During World War II he served as a fire warden. Throughout the 1940s he managed a Hampstead bookstore. Chronically depressed, he was under psychiatric treatment for much of the remainder of his life. This was his only novel to address homosexuality specifically, but gay themes can be discerned in other works of his: *Fires in the Distance*, 1952, which has been compared to Pasolini's *Teorema*, and, his best known, *The Young Have Secrets*, 1954. Courage died in Hampstead. The New Zealand PEN society celebrates November 14 as Courage Day.

Courage, James. *A Way of Love*. London: Cape, 1959.
*New York: Putnam, 1959.

66 Paul Buckland: *Chorus of Witches*, 1959.

By the mid-1950s, when the novel is set, "the vogue," we are told, for campy drag shows "was waning. For a while its colourful extravagance appealed to the public [...], but eventually the original purpose of all such shows—the presentation of ex-services talent to a wider, peace-time audience—had become meaningless. The supply of genuine ex-service performers had run out long ago, and in many instances their places were taken by players [...] who otherwise would never gain admittance to the professional stage" (214–15). In many ways, the secondary characters, who have been known by their female stage names for so long that their male birth names have been almost forgotten, hold as much interest as the principals.

These are three in number: the young Englishman Colin Ford and two Scots, Alan Kendrick and Jock Macmillan, who both are attracted to Colin but who at novel's end are instead contentedly with each other while Colin has gone off on his own pursuits. The reader should feel grateful for a happy ending, but the characters' arrival at that point seems problematic. The author's handling of characters is inconsistent. Although Colin proves to be flighty when it comes to jobs and dishonest in his relations with his parents (who painfully discover his new profession when they attend a performance), he is initially presented as a caring, concerned friend to Jock. After one too many furious outbursts from the dour Scotsman, one hardly blames Colin for wanting to distance himself. Thus, the reader finds it difficult to believe Jock when he tells Alan that Colin's "a cruel boy and hasna consideration or love except for himself. [...] He'll take care he's no' hurt. He'll no' be the one to suffer" (196).

Jock insistently claims that he is the way he is because he is so fearful, having "been inside" as a result of being "caught wi' somebody" (166). But while the two were earlier riding an Edinburgh tram together, "Without thinking of the danger he was inviting, he drew Colin into his arms" (139). Alan met his first lover during the war, "and Bill had simplified the whole problem of transition, and a great burden has been lifted from him" (55). Yet Alan holds himself aloof from gays, more out of snobbism then fear of legal dangers. Males who dress like females are totally outside his social pale. It is not quite believable to read that, when Alan and Jock become lovers, "Between them both there was perfect accord, devotion, and respect" (222–23).

As in many gay novels throughout the 1950s, arguments supporting the naturalness of homosexuality are set forth. One of the funnier scenes depicts Alan as a verbal juggler "tossing authors and composers into the air; trying to keep Gide, Whitman, and Tchaikovsky spinning, while casually disposing of George Eliot and Bach" (149) as he tries to find out the obvious about Colin. Paul Buckland's identity remains unknown; this is his only novel. The dust jacket merely observes, "The author evidently knows both his major subject and his show-business." Many of the photographs in James Gardiner's *Who's A Pretty Boy Then* could serve as illustrations to the novel.

Buckland, Paul. *Chorus of Witches*. London: Allen, 1959.

67 David Caute: *At Fever Pitch*, 1959.

Mixing European and African viewpoints, the West African novel depicts a country in its last days of colonial rule. With a large cast of characters, the homosexual thread that weaves through the story is only part of the whole cloth. Still, the work begins and closes with a picture of twenty-year-old subaltern Michael Glyn, a closet case who destroys his African manservant, Sulley Azambugu. He uses Sulley for sexual release but is careful to keep him out of his bed, as that would symbolize some sort of equality. When he realizes that Sulley is in love with him, "Glyn felt the nausea flood up into his head" (91). He throws up and then orders Sulley to clean up his vomit. "An intense realization of his own guilt hammered at this head, a guilt which he had no intention of facing" (126). He lusts after another European, Hughes, the district officer, and feels betrayed when he sees Hughes leave with a woman.

Meanwhile, Brigadier Charles Ridley-Smith begins making advances on Glyn. He argues, "One of the secrets of life is to find out what are the things you just can't conquer, and then to accept them. You're trying to fight against life itself. That's not a sign of strength, you know, it's simply crass stupidity. No man can fight life itself" (174). The brigadier becomes indirectly responsible for Sulley's death. Glyn seeks out a brothel and has his first sexual experience with a woman. And then he begins sentimentalizing Sulley. Dimly remembering their first time together, Glyn massacres Africans. The implication seems pretty clear: denial of one's sexuality leads not only to self-destruction but to destruction of others. In the end, Glyn is due to stand trial under the new native government, but the brigadier insists on a court martial: "The loved one must be saved. At all costs" (250). Our last glimpse of him is in his cell thinking about Sulley.

John David Caute (1936–) was born in Alexander, Egypt, where his father, a military officer, was stationed. Educated at Oxford, he became a political historian as well as a political novelist. *At Fever Pitch* was his first work, based on his own military experience in the Gold Coast as it was on the verge of becoming Ghana. Simon Raven, whose own African military novel came out the same year, praised it. *At Fever Pitch* won the John Llewellyn Rhys Memorial Prize. Caute spent much of the 1960s teaching in the United

States. He has been married twice and has four children.

Caute, David. *At Fever Pitch*. London: Deutsch, 1959. *New York: Pantheon, 1961.

68 Simon Raven: *The Feathers of Death*, 1959; *Fielding Gray*, 1967; *The Judas Boy*, 1968.

A common theme dominates the three novels: love and betrayal. *The Feathers of Death*, Raven's first published novel, is the story of a British regiment sent in 1956 into an eastern African country to put down a native uprising led by a powerful new leader. Narrated by Captain Andrew Lamont, it recounts the fatal consequences of his friend Lieutenant Alastair Lynch's seduction of Malcolm Harley, an eighteen-year-old trooper under his command. Harley's mate, the equally young Simes, lectures him on the immorality and unnaturalness of the relationship. As a result, Harley tells Lynch that their relationship must end, and the two quarrel—after Lynch seduces the youth again. The next day Lynch assigns Simes to a party to return to headquarters to seek reinforcements and more ammunition against an imminent attack. Harley, drunk, demands that he take Simes's place to prove he's "not just a little pouf," "a nancy boy" (161–62). When Lynch refuses, he darts out against orders, potentially endangering their position, and Lynch shoots him. Court-martialed, on the stand Lynch defiantly admits that the two men were sexual partners and asserts that he was in love with him (222–23). As he has earlier explained to his friends, "In the circumstances one needed what comfort one could get. And by this time Malcolm meant more than comfort. In the hills at any rate he meant everything there was. Even if I hadn't loved him as much as I did, even if he had been only a plaything he would still have been a substitute for everything I hadn't got there" (186–87). But Lynch reveals to Lamont the circumstances of their last evening together; clearly feeling some kind of guilt, he muses, "I don't think I killed him because of that" (243).

The presiding officers at the court martial accept Alastair's justification for his action and exonerate him. Enraged, Simes darts forward as he emerges from the court and stabs him with a bayonet. In a muddled way, Lamont tries to assess blame, only to conclude that it really does not matter: "For this was all it came to: Harley, whom Alastair had loved like a woman, was dead; Alastair, whom we had all loved as a man, was dead; and Simes, whom Harley in some way or other had loved, would be dead within six weeks" (247). Lamont himself remains an indistinct figure. And since we see Lynch at one remove, it is difficult to empathize with him. It is left up to Colonel Sanvoisin to voice the social significance of the tale: he stresses that the overt homosexual is an "offense openly given to Mrs. Smith of Birmingham, to our 'young and lovely Queen' in Buckingham Palace, to trade-union leaders, to good-form conservative politicians—to everything and everybody in the Mediocrity State" (208). But then his observation may smack just a bit of class snobbery of the public school kind.

A public school is the setting for Raven's eighth novel, *Fielding Gray*, set in 1944–45 and therefore the first chronologically in *Alms for Oblivion*, his ten-volume *roman fleuve* that covers the period 1944–73. Here the title character narrates his own story. The crucial incident grows out of his romance with the slightly younger Christopher Roland. He himself is unsure what he feels for him—"love Platonic or love Romantic, agape, eros or caritas" (32). But he shies from the physical with him. Circumstances lead the two to sneak off to a hayloft. They undress and embrace each other; excited, Christopher ejaculates (69). The youth's loss of innocence perversely fills Gray with a sense of antipathy. Christopher senses the change. Home for the summer vacation, yearning to find someone "to be with and hold" (173), he starts hanging out at the gates of a nearby army camp, where he is reported to the police for soliciting (147). Dismissed from school, assigned a psychiatrist, he takes his father's gun and kills himself. Even before Christopher's expulsion, a classmate, Peter Morrison, has voiced what must be considered one of the book's messages: that "it's not what two boys do together in private which does the permanent damage, but the hysterical row which goes on if they get caught" (53). Gray's reactions to both the expulsion and the death are decidedly unsympathetic, but then he has already acknowledged at least three times his feelings of kinship with Dorian Gray (27, 88, 108). Morrison, speaking to him, sums up: "You failed in love" (201).

A sense of guilt for that betrayal still clings to Gray seventeen years later in *The Judas Boy*. The sixth in the series, its very title is telling. He is now a rising novelist, his latest book clearly based on the incidents recounted in *Fielding Gray*. He has also had his face nearly destroyed in 1958 in a bomb explosion in Cyprus. Multiple plots intertwine. On Gray's part, he accepts a BBC assignment to return to the island to assess the present situation and is caught up in dangerous political intrigue. Gaining information about Christopher—and his striking resemblance to a statue on the Acropolis in Athens—the mastermind recruits a youth named Nicos to deter Gray from his mission. Gray falls hard, sexually and emotionally, for the look-alike. Then, learning that BBC has canceled the project, the plotter recalls Nicos. Drinking himself into a stupor, Gray reflects that "there had been appropriate revenge. Years ago he had betrayed Christopher; now Christopher had risen up from the dead and betrayed him. And again: he had used Christopher to make a tale, he had exploited him, in [his latest novel], to get money and a little fame; and now Christopher had come back as Nicos to exploit him in return—to exploit his love and turn it into money, to use his anguish to make a career. Fair's fair, he told himself: paid out in your own dud coin" (150).

Betrayal of love recurs in at least one other novel: *Sound the Retreat*, 1971, set in India 1945–46. Lieutenant Barry Strange kills his former Indian commander, Captain Gilzai Khan, with whom he shares a bed while he is a cadet. International politics and British class snobbery, elements that show up throughout the series, motivate the murder. When one of the soldiers from the camp where Christopher hung out hitches a ride with the headmaster and Gray after the boy's funeral, Gray suddenly realizes "that this was the first time in my life (since the nursery) that a conversation between myself and a member of the lower classes had been other than merely administrative, and that I had no idea whatever how to proceed with it" (164). Derogatory terms fall easily from upper class British lips in all these novels. Some editions of the *Alms* series include a list of characters: more than a hundred, although only nine are given top billing. Other homosexuals make their appearance in *The Rich Pay Late*, 1964, and *Friends in Low Places*, 1965.

Born and dying in London, Simon Arthur Noel Raven (1927–2001) had a checkered career. He was expelled from school for his homosexual activities. After serving in the army, he enrolled in Cambridge. He briefly married in order to legitimize his son. Not being able to make a living as a journalist and finding no publisher for his first novel, he rejoined the army in 1953, serving in Germany and Kenya. He was allowed to resign in 1958 to avoid court martial for not meeting his gambling debts. With publisher Anthony Blond as his patron, he returned to writing. He scripted the teleplay for Nancy Mitford's *Love in a Cold Climate*, 1980. For a time he lived with Blond's former lover, the writer Andrew McCall. A collection of nonfiction, *The World of Simon Raven*, provides insight into the author's mindset across three decades.

Barber, Michael. *The Captain: The Life and Times of Simon Raven*. London: Duckworth, 1996.
Raven, Simon. *The Feathers of Death*. London: Blond, 1959. *New York: Simon & Schuster, 1959.
_____. *Fielding Gray*. London: Blond, 1967. *New York: Beaufort, 1985.
_____. *The Judas Boy*. London: Blond, 1968. *London: Panther, 1969.

69 John Rae: *The Custard Boys*, 1960.

William Golding's *Lord of the Flies* was published in 1954. It was not the first by far to portray how savage children could be, but it left a powerful impression on the public mind. Rae's schoolboy novel fits the same category. Set in 1942, it portrays a bunch of ordinary grammar schoolboys whose general barbarism reflects the "universal perversion" of war (161). They are evacuees from London, removed to the safer confines of Norfolk. The narrator, thirteen-year-old John Curlew, is one of seven boys who chafe at the fact that they are too young to enlist and have banded together to court danger as an escape from boredom.

When Mark Stein, a Jewish refugee from Austria arrives at their school, the headmaster assigns John the responsibility to show him the ropes. John instinctively likes him: "The friendship that I had sought but not found in the community of the gang; the love that my puberty was beginning to manufacture; perhaps more simply the need to nurse and protect something more animate than my [bicycle]—all these flying seeds of my disintegrating childhood settled and took root in my friendship with Mark Stein. [...] The world was not a better place because it had witnessed our love for one another; on the contrary, most people would regard our friendship as disgusting and immoral because we touched one another, held hands in church and once in the garden of the deserted manor house at Elbery-cum-Wooten we made shy inquiry into the strange secrets of our developing bodies" (73).

Their mutual masturbation—"our gauche exchanges of physical love" (93)—is witnessed by the leader of a rival gang of local boys, leaving John confused about his feelings. Thus, he has not the courage to stand up to the rest of the gang, who regard Mark as an enemy and who he knows will not hesitate to expose him as "a pervert" even though "such relationships between boys were accepted as quite normal by the majority of other boys" (177). Events escalate. In a battle between the rival gangs, Mark comes across as a coward. The gang decides to court-martial him. Found guilty, they sentence him to be shot at dawn. As the community at large becomes even more gripped by war hysteria, the boys prepare to frighten Mark with blank cartridges. One live round does not get exchanged, and Mark falls dead.

John at least has the courage to insist on calling the police and telling the truth. Xenophobia and religious prejudice carry the subsequent hearing: two boys are placed on probation; the rest are conditionally discharged. As narrator-historian, John concludes his story by recounting what has happened to all of them. He discloses that he himself registered as a conscientious objector when called up for national service and that he has become a schoolteacher. What is missing is any revelation about his sexuality. He only admits, "I still think that my love for Mark was the most natural unnatural emotion of my life" (177).

Having published his parable, the author went on to endorse two film versions, one of them with his own screenplay, and appeared in cameo roles in both. John Malcolm Rae (1931–2006) was born in London. He was educated at Cambridge and the University of London. He taught in various public schools, most notably Westminster. He married and had six children. He died in Haslemere, Surry.

Rae, John. *The Custard Boys*. *London: Hart-Davis, 1960. New York: Farrar, Straus & Cuduhy, 1961.

70 Hugh Ross Williamson: *A Wicked Pack of Cards*, 1961.

Adrian Musgrove, a young London schoolteacher on holiday, is struck by an inn-sign for The Four Kings. It was painted by John Adam, an itinerant sign painter, just before his death in a fall from a nearby cliff. Adrian questions the innkeeper, Evelyn Smith; the four men whose faces are reproduced, Tarot-fashion, on the sign; and an inn employee, Brian. Only late in the novel do we discover that Adrian is gay, that he was intimately connected with John in London, and that this is the reason he feels driven to discover whether John's death was an accident, suicide, or murder. In the process, he speaks often with Eve, who uses the Tarot as her basis for understanding life. Nothing special, however, is made of the fact that he, John, and two other characters are gay. It is simply one piece of information among others discovered in solving the mystery.

The detective story becomes an examination of the nature of love. John has left behind his diary, which includes the following passage: "'I love you too much to try to hold you against your will' sounded magnificent. But now I know it's the deepest lie, because no one who truly loved could say it. 'I'll kill you rather than let you go' is what ought to be said." The protagonist reacts to the passage, "Until this moment, it had never occurred to me to doubt that the distinguishing mark of all genuine love is unselfishness. By definition, 'to love' is 'to will the good of the beloved': and it is obvious that the 'good of the beloved' may be by no means the same thing as the wishes, or even the good, of the lover. The lover's conquest of his selfishness to ensure that the beloved may be free is the act of will which determines the genuineness of the love. Or so I have always insisted." But here "it was the theory itself that was attacked. "Unselfishness was the evidence not of true love but of the lack of it" (75–77). The novel ends with several twists, the most unexpected being Adrian's falling in love with the murderer. From his perspective, because he failed in love, he is as guilty as the murderer, who did not fail.

Hugh Ross Williamson (1901–1978) was born in Hampshire. He attended the University of London. He served as the editor of various magazines, the director of the London General Press, and as a minister in the Church of England. He wrote plays, novels, histories, and literary criticism, including an early study of T. S. Eliot, 1932. (*The Waste Land* is the source of the novel's title.) Ross Williamson used the stage name Ian Rossiter when he appeared as an actor. Married, he had two children. He died in London.

Ross Williamson, Hugh. *A Wicked Pack of Cards*. London: Joseph, 1961. *Washington, D.C.: Guild, 1965.

71 William Drummond (Arthur Calder Marshall): *Victim*, 1961.

Before the advent of home video players, it was common for studios to commission novelizations of films based on original screenplays, particularly if they thought the film would garner publicity. These were printed as inexpensive paperbacks, often with several pages of stills from the film inserted at the center of the book (though none were included in *Victim*.) Novelizations tried to remain true to the spirit of the film, if not always to the letter. Some differences came about because of alterations in the script during the shooting and editing process. Names got changed when someone worried about possible libel, so Melville Carr becomes Melville Farr in the film. Sets and costumes make subtle differences so that a viewer might infer one of the blackmailers is himself gay. (In the novel he hates gays because he was the victim of a Scout master's advances.)

Victim was deliberately written as propaganda in support of the Wolfenden Report, whose recommendations had yet to be passed by Parliament. In securing an actor with the status of Dirk Bogarde, it insured that its message would be heard. For the first time, a gay—or perhaps more accurately, a bisexual—is the hero of a film. Vito Russo wrote (129): "The film portrays the screen's first homosexual character to choose visibility and thereby challenge the status quo. The issues of repression and enforced invisibility were equated, for the first time, with the law's relegation of homosexuals to a lawless subculture in which they become victims of their own ghostly status." Earlier Parker Tyler weighed in (65): "One motive of the film is to present the homosexual 'side of the argument' as morally, legally compromised, sometimes tragically so, and yet exonerated by nature."

The novelization holds its own without having reference to the film. It begins with Jack Barrett seeing a police car pulling up at the construction site where he is working. He realizes that his embezzling has been discovered. He makes a run for it, all the while trying vainly to get in touch with barrister Melville Carr, on whom he has a crush. He has used the money to pay off blackmailers who have an incriminating photograph of the two of them. Taken into custody, Jack hangs himself. Carr, whom the police have now linked up with Barrett, is with them when they find the body. He realizes too late that Barrett was not trying to blackmail him, as he had thought, but to protect him. Feeling guilty, he decides to fight back, even though it may jeopardize his career and his marriage. Carr, with the help of Barrett's friend Eddy Stone, makes contact with others who are being blackmailed. A surprisingly understanding police inspector provides him backup, while he speaks eloquently in support of passing the Wolfenden Report's recommendations.

Carr—"this utterly uncertain, unreliable homo-heterosexual creature poised on the brink of ruin" (146)—is unusually complex. He himself dimly realizes that he may have married Laura Hankin because she so resembles her brother, Scott, "with whom in a common schoolboy fashion he had been sentimentally in love" (44). While at Oxford another student, Paul Stainer, had fallen in love with him and had then killed himself when he was rejected. Carr told Laura of his homosexual tendencies before their marriage and now swears he still loves her. But he also confesses to her that he was falling in love with Barrett (90). When he finally sees his face in the photograph the blackmailers took of the two of them, he confronts the truth that "there was no doubt he was laboring from [...] a whole mass of complicated and conflicting emotions: lust, desperation at discovering that he had not grown out of the feelings which he thought were dead, pity for the boy, fear for himself" (126). When the blackmailers are caught, it turns out that the mastermind had been in love with Paul Stainer also. Carr returns to Laura. Heterosexuality has won out on the personal level, but homosexuals have been vindicated.

Victim was the second of five novelizations that Arthur Calder Marshall (1908–1992) wrote under the pseudonym "William Drummond." He was born in Surrey and died in Kent, but he travelled widely, both as a child (his father was an engineer) and an adult. A graduate of Oxford (where he was part of Stephen Spender's circle), he married and had two children. His novel *Dead Centre*, 1935, is another public school story. Calder Marshall also wrote about Aleister Crowley, whom he knew (*The Magic of My Youth*, 1951), and *Havelock Ellis: A Biography*, 1959.

Drummond, William. *Victim*. Adapted from the original screenplay by Janet Green and John McCormick. London: Trasnworld (Corgi), 1961.

Russo, Vito. *The Celluloid Closet: Homosexuality in the Movies*. 2d ed. New York: Harper & Row, 1987.

Tyler, Parker. *Screening the Sexes: Homosexuality in the Movies*. New York: Holt, Rinehart & Winston, 1972.

72 Eliot George (Gillian Freeman): *The Leather Boys*, 1961.

Anthony Blond, its original publisher wrote in his introduction to the Gay Men Press reprint of *The Leather Boys* (2–3): "I knew of no book which told the story of love between two 'working-class' boys. Who better (I thought) to author such a theme than my old friend and former client Gillian Freeman? [...]. 'Romeo and Romeo in the South London Suburbs' was my prescription." The results were published under the playful pseudonym Eliot George, though the author wrote her screenplay of the novel under her own name. Blond went on to identify the main characters: "The leather boys are the boys on the bikes, the boys who do a ton on the by-pass," the rockers. Two eighteen-year-olds, Dick Smith and Reggie Rogers, meet up when Dick comes to his just widowed grandmother's home. Reggie is married, because it is the expected thing to do, but unhappy. He hangs out at a café "for the boys on motor-bikes." Being with them "gave Reggie his only sense of belonging and being part of society" (17). Dick reorients his life.

Sharing a bed one evening after having become pals, Dick has his first sexual experience with anyone. Their emotional dependence on each other quickly grows, and they accept with surprising ease that sex is not a matter of convenience but an expression of love. It is even important to the two of them that they are both male. Dick asks Reggie for reassurance, "When you kiss me and that [...], you don't pretend I'm a girl or anything?" Reggie replies, "Don't be daft. [...] 'Ow could I pretend you was a girl? You're the wrong shape." Dick muses happily, "It's funny, isn't it. I mean we don't want to put on lipstick or anything like that, do we?" (99) The two contemplate joining the Merchant Marine in order to have a life together away from their peers. Dick, however, is "less moral than Reggie" and takes easily to shoplifting and burglary, happy to get easy money (109). The local turf is ruled over by biker Leslie Green. Expecting his cut from any illegal gains, he prepares to retaliate when Dick and Reggie move on their own. Trapped one evening, Dick is badly beaten, and Reggie is killed. Dick feels guilty: "He felt that he was the one who was ultimately responsible for Reggie's death, because if Reggie hadn't fallen in love with him," none of what followed would have happened. "He thought he would never, never get over loving Reggie" (155). But with the passage of time, the trial and its aftermath, he discovers that his memory is becoming blurred. The novel ends ambiguously with Dick's acceptance of a race between his and a newcomer's motorbikes: "both machines roared away in union" (176).

Gillian Freeman (1929–) was born in London. She graduated from the University of Reading. Married to novelist Edward Thorpe, she has two daughters. In both her screenplays of *The Leather Boys*, 1964, and Richard Miles's *That Cold Day in the Park*, 1969, she muted the gay elements. She also wrote a novel *The Alabaster Egg*, 1970, which used in part the life of Ludwig II of Bavaria.

[Freeman, Gillian.] *The Leather Boys* by Eliot George. London: Blond, 1961. Washington, D.C.: Guild, 1965. *Intro. Anthony Blond. London: GMP, 1985.

73 Julian Mitchell: *Imaginary Toys*, 1961.

The novel of ideas follows the interactions of four friends at Oxford at the end of the 1950s. The bulk of the narration is given to Charles Frederick Hammond. Straight, he is a frustrated young man who pursues love, incarnated for the moment in a fellow student whom he claims is "immoral in that she allowed people to fall in love with her, and then used them" (16). He watches the troubled romance between Jack Evans, a Welsh coalminer's son, and Elaine Cole, the daughter of very class-minded parents. The two are wrestling with desire and religious prohibitions against sex before marriage. The fourth narrator, who both stands somewhat apart from the others and yet acts as their sounding board, their gadfly, even their catalyst for change, is Nicholas Sharpe, openly gay and openly socialist. The reader gets five long sections from his notebooks in which he muses about a variety of topics, among them the difficulties a gay man faces in England at the time. Nicholas and Giles Mangles, another Oxford student, forge a life together for a while (though we learn from Charles that they later broke up while still remaining friends). Charles gets the last word: "We were all beginners in those days, we hadn't, as we used to say, a clue, we were all learning. And what we learnt, I suppose, is what we now are" (208). The glimpses that the novel gives us of a changing England provide its greatest value, but it is unlikely that a reader will be struck by any particular insights that the characters, engaging as they may be, have to offer.

Charles Julian Humphrey Mitchell (1935–) was born in Epping, England. He attended Oxford and served in the British navy. He wrote a series of six novels, including some others with gay interest: *A Disturbing Influence*, 1962; *As Far as You Can Go*, 1963; and *The Undiscovered Country*, 1968, a postmodern exercise in which the two main characters are Julian Mitchell and Charles Humphries. He will probably be most remembered, however, for his play *Another Country*, 1981. He also wrote the screenplay for the resulting film starring Rupert Everett, 1984, as well as screenplays for *Vincent & Theo*, 1990, and *Wilde*, 1997, and the teleplay for the documentary *Consenting Adults*, 2007, about the relationship between John Wolfenden and his gay son, Jeremy. He has been partners with moral philosopher Richard Rowson for nearly fifty years.

Mitchell, Julian. *Imaginary Toys*. London: Hutchinson, 1961.

74 John Broderick: *The Pilgrimage*, 1961; *The Fugitives*, 1963; *The Waking of Willie Ryan*, 1965; *The Trial of Father Dillingham*, 1974 (French edition); *The Pride of Summer*, 1976; *London Irish*, 1979.

Given the high quality of his writing, it is impossible to understand why Broderick has been so undeservedly, inexplicably excluded from the gay canon. One looks for him in vain in gay literary references and anthologies in the English language. The 1984 French anthology *Les amours masculines* (edited by Michel Larivière) had no trouble placing him firmly within its selection of major writers from "l'époque contemporaine." In fact, the novel from which the excerpt was chosen, *Cité pleine de rêves*, 1974, was published in translation there a full eight years before the original manuscript (*The Trial of Father Dillingham*) finally saw light in England. One of the remarkable things about Broderick's novels is the way they so often depict older gays.

His very first published novel has gay characters at its center. Set in a town in the Irish countryside, *The Pilgrimage*—perhaps more felicitously titled *The Chameleons* in its U.S. edition—is told in the third person largely from the perspective of Julia Glynn. But it is the separate actions of her closeted husband, Michael, and his bisexual manservant, Stephen Lydon, that drive the novel's plot. Michael married Julia partly for a cover, partly in a half-hearted attempt "to reform his nature" (23), even as he continued to have affairs (they were accompanied by Helmut, a German boy, on their honeymoon). She married him for his money and his position, while she continues to have an affair with his nephew and physician, Jim Glynn. Now crippled by arthritis, Michael contemplates a pilgrimage to Lourdes to seek a cure. Then, Julia begins to receive a series of letters detailing her affair. She suspects young Stephen, so she proceeds to seduce him. Julia reflects that her life has become akin to a French farce and enjoys the comedy. Stephen has written a series of incriminating love letters to Tommy Baggot, though their friendship seems to have been sexless. For Stephen, Tommy is the reincarnation of the first man he fell in love with, who drowned, along with a priest in a boat with him. Tommy kills himself after he is apprehended trying to pick up an undercover policeman, and the letters fall into the hands of Tommy's gay roommate, posing a threat to Stephen. It turns out that Michael set Tommy up in the same house where Jim lives. "She thought again of how everything repeated itself: Michael in Stephen, [a former lover] in Jim, the letters she had received, in the letters the police had found in Dublin. Only miracles were complete and new in this life: all else was a twice-told tale" (119). And that is just what occurs at Lourdes. The novel should have made Broderick's reputation; it seems mysterious that it did not. But it is no wonder that it was banned in Ireland, containing as it does adultery, marriages of convenience, homosexuality, bisexuality, an outwardly respectable woman with as strong a sexual drive as men have, an attack on hypocrisy, blasphemy, and not only a happy ending, but a divine miracle.

The Fugitives continues the author's fierce analysis of the nature of love and belief, but it moves into the political arena. At times we may feel we are inhabiting "Greeneland" as much as Ireland—for example, when we read such statements as this (chosen almost at random): "She had never discovered, as bolder spirits always do, that virtue is a great deal more ruthless than lust" (160). The Northern Ireland Under-Secretary is assassinated in London, and Paddy Fallon is implicated. His sister, Lily, returns to their Irish home, knowing that he will flee there to hide. They are joined by Paddy's IRA minder, the sinister but charismatic Hugh Ward. The two men wear identical signet rings on their little fingers, but their exact emotional relationship is never defined. Clearly, Hugh holds young Paddy in thrall; he also exerts a strange fascination over the sister. The author leaves the reader to interpret Lily's final words to her brother about Hugh—"Do you know that [...] you could have bought your freedom anytime if you had given him the filthy thing he was looking for? Do you know what he thought you were, do you, Paddy? He doesn't give a damn about Ireland, or freedom, or martyrs or all the rest of that nonsense. He only wanted you..." (199)—as well as her final action. The novel is as dark and inexorably tragic as *The Pilgrimage* is comic.

The Waking of Willie Ryan shows the author at full strength. After a heart attack and a continuing decline in health, the sixty-one-year-old title character faces death. He wants to die in his own home. He has been incarcerated twenty-five years earlier in a mental institution, ostensibly because he was dangerous (he kissed his sister-in-law), but in reality because he is a homosexual and a religious nonconformist. During these twenty-five years no one in his family ever visited him—especially not his brother, who used him sexually, before marrying the wife his brother offended, and certainly not the sister-in-law, who continues to see Willie as a danger not because she believes he is violent but because he threatens her social status. Nor did Father John Mannix, the priest who went along with the scheme to have him committed, have any interest in checking up on Willie's state. And his lover, Roger Dillon, was soon dead after he was committed, and their mutual friends were afraid to come out of the closet. Willie simply walks out of the asylum and returns home on foot. His nephew Chris takes him in, and in face of his opposition to returning Willie to the asylum, his parents cave. But Chris's allegiance to blood ties strains his relationship to his fiancée, for she too is more concerned about public appearances than anything else. One of the officials at the institution, Peter Halloran, checks up on Willie and continues to monitor his condition until the end. Others sympathetic to Willie as a person are the nonconforming Susan Carroll, who is also interested in Chris (but hasn't a chance because of his mother), and Roger's sister. Meanwhile, Father Mannix sees Willie's approaching death as an opportunity to show the church's power by reclaiming Willie's soul. The last part of the novel explores the ramifications of Willie's final mass, forced upon him by priest and family, throughout which Willie maintains his integrity and, in a personal confrontation, shows his moral superiority and greater understanding of the meaning of love. Broderick's choice of titles is often curious. Does *The Waking of Willie Ryan* refer to his return to the world, to his confrontation with his still living past, to the long wait for his death, to the ironic fact that there is no wake over his dead body (as his brother remarks in an alcohol-induced observation that concludes the novel), or to all?

The Trial of Father Dillingham (another curious title) was finished in 1968 but did not find an English publisher until 1982. Yet it represents Broderick at his wisest, his most assured in his exploration of the meaning of love and mutual trust, not only between two men but between heterosexual couples as well. Maurice O'Connell and Eddie Doyle are lovers, but they are so discreet that they have separate apartments in the same building (homosexuality was not decriminalized in Ireland until 1993). In the first half of the novel they must face Maurice's impending death from leukemia. After he dies, Eddie discovers that not only did all their friends know of their relationship, but they approved. Maurice's spirit continues to affect all of them and helps direct their lives in positive ways. Others in the building are Jim Dillingham, an ex-seminarian vaguely attracted to Eddie sexually, and Maria Keeley (née Mary Jane Kelly), a retired opera singer. After Maurice's flat is vacated, it is rented to Patrick Lord Bellington and his lover, Kate Vale, a dangerous criminal; their relationship serves as a foil to that of the other couples. Because their own relationship was built on trust, Eddie can return to gay bars without guilt to seek the physical relief his body desires; for the same reason, he is saved from becoming too involved with one of the men whose moral fiber has been so compromised that he has served time for pedophilia. *The Trial* is more ragged in execution than the earlier novels, but it is not only his most heartwarming piece of fiction but perhaps his most enduring achievement.

Gays have very minor roles in *The Pride of Summer*, but the novel, among the author's other usual attacks on Irish society (here, religion, politics, violence, hypocrisy), makes a savage and ironic indictment against homophobia. The plot is set in motion when Olive O'Reilly leaves her husband, having realized that she no longer loves him or their two children. Two minor characters, Shaun Lucey and his sister Theresa, have not one redeeming quality between them. Years before, she stood silently by while he repeatedly molested their younger sister. He now procures women and preadolescent girls for men and gigolos for wealthy women, as well as arranges abortions. But both siblings sneer at gay men and lesbians: Theresa calls them, "Filthy degenerates [...]. No wonder the Lord rained fire and brimstones upon them, the rotten outlaws" (68). She refuses service to one, saying, "We don't want your sort here. This is a respectable establishment" (70). The five homosexuals whom we meet, including Olive's son, are all deeply closeted, and, admittedly, none is very likeable behind his handsome exterior.

London-based Danish journalist Gunnar (Johnny) Hansen becomes involved in an Irish family's maneuvers to secure an inheritance in *London Irish*. He is a friend of a young American, Nancy Cook, who is engaged to marry a rich Irishman, Andrew Pollack, in a May-December romance. Pollack's niece and nephew show up as soon as they learn about the proposal; Michael Pollack instantly suspects that Nancy is less than faithful and, rather improbably, tracks Hansen down. A competent columnist, much respected in Copenhagen, Hansen enjoys queening it up with the others, but his role is relatively minor. All the characters are strongly drawn, but the plotting often creaks, making this the weakest of Broderick's books.

John Broderick (1924–1989) was born in Athlone, near the geographical center of the island. The French connection began in 1951. He became friends with Julian Green, and also met American expatriates Ned Rorem, Gore Vidal, Truman Capote, James Baldwin, and even Hemingway. His fiction became respected enough in Ireland to gain him election to the Irish Academy of Letters, but he also had run-ins with the Irish Censorship Board for his books' sexuality (of all sorts) and supposed blasphemy. In his personal life he had to battle alcoholism. In 1981 he self-exiled himself to Bath, England, where he died eight years later. His novel *The Rose Tree*, 1985, is set there and has a significant gay character. His personal life he kept private; there is no evidence he was ever in a relationship. When an interviewer raised the question of his sexuality, Broderick labeled himself a bisexual and then deflected the discussion.

Broderick, John. *The Fugitives*. London: Weidenfeld & Nicolson, 1962. *New York: Obolensky, 1962.
_____. *London Irish*. London: Barrie & Jenkins, 1979.
_____. *The Pilgrimage*. London: Weidenfeld & Nicolson, 1961. *The Chameleons*. New York: Obolensky, 1961. *The Pilgrimage*. Dublin: Lilliput, 2004.
_____. *The Pride of Summer*. London: Harrap, 1976.
_____. *The Trial of Father Dillingham*. London & Boston: Boyars, 1982.
_____. *The Waking of Willie Ryan*. London: Weidenfeld & Nicolson, 1965. *Dublin: Lilliput, 2004.
Kingston, Madeline. *Something in the Head: The Life & Work of John Broderick*. Dublin: Lilliput, 2004.

75 Stuart Lauder (David Leslie): *Winger's Landfall*, 1962; *Camp Commander*, 1971.

Though it takes the reader some time to realize it, *Winger's Landfall* is actually a mystery. A twenty-four-year-old table steward (a "winger"), Harry Shears, creates a last-minute opening on the ocean liner *Cyclamen* by breaking the present holder's jaw while onshore in Sydney. Slowly we learn that his younger half-brother, Danny Shears, with whom he was in undeclared love (86), mysteriously went overboard from the ship while working as a bellboy, apparently a suicide. Suspecting some kind of foul play, Harry is determined to uncover the circumstances leading to his death. Because of the way the wine steward, Bernard Norrie, reacts to his last name, he starts to focus on him and his mysterious hold over various youths working on the ship. He suspects it is sexual, but he learns that instead it is spiritual. Bernard is a member of a religious group, based in Ceylon, seeking to unite Christ and Buddha. The youths he has gathered around him are actually in search of enlightenment.

The ship's galley has a large set of gays who freely camp, using feminine names and pronouns. Harry himself has learned how to hide behind "protective coloration" (120), but in his attempt to ferret out the truth about Bernard, he seduces a bellboy (junior waiter),

Danny Prince, and the two become lovers. Bernard himself seems to be asexual. He obviously suspects Danny Shears of having taken to sea to escape his brother's advances (219), and he feels that Harry was somehow implicated in the boy's death (232). He now warns him off Danny Prince. In retaliation, after the ship docks in England, Harry lures Bernard apart and brutally assaults him, perhaps even kills him. But it occurs to him that the two of them are alike: "We talk very big about 'affection.' But what we mean is 'possession'" (271). Meanwhile, an explanation has emerged for his brother's erratic behavior: it turns out that epilepsy runs in the Shears family, and the novel ends, inconclusively, with Harry suffering a seizure in the pub to which he has retreated just as the police arrive.

Camp Commander is a completely different type of novel. Set during the last fourteen months of World War II on an imaginary Portuguese island in the South Atlantic, it aches to be a romance between two airmen in their early twenties: the narrator, Roger Gough, and Peter Parrish, nicknamed Blondie because of his light-colored hair. Instead, we see at a distance the homosexual dalliances of the grossly overweight, sybaritic camp commander, Seymour Floss ("Flossie"), with an array of good-looking airmen, including Peter. Hut 21 also turns out to be an epicenter for homosexual activities, including a number of airmen who enjoy drag. Their sexual activities spill off the base into the town. Roger and a mate witness a blowjob in progress behind a partially open door, leading the latter to declare that the entire "camp's turning bent" (166). Inevitably, an unstable recruit who has found religion concludes that it is his mission to expose everyone, and a disgruntled officer who feels he should have been the camp commander forces a witch-hunt.

Flossie loses his post but does not face court martial. One of those who do is a former dancer, Tim Blackburn, who earlier brushed off Roger's warning that he was attracting attention, saying, "I'm twenty-three ... I'll never be twenty-three again. [...] And I'm going to live my life as best I can. [...] They can't take away the life what I've had" (118). After the war is over, the military returning to their hometowns, Flossie and Roger have one last encounter. Flossie sums up the kind of life Roger has led and contrasts it with his own: "Poor Roger. All those years in the emotional desert. [...] At least we had affection, our golden days, a *life* of sorts." He goes on, "Peter was very fond of you [...]. But of course it got him nowhere. He couldn't break through the ice." He sums up: "To love is a necessity. And it doesn't greatly matter whom you choose" (212). In a final bleak comment Roger seems to equate his failure to those of his entire generation.

David Stuart Leslie (1921–1999) was born in Croydon, Surrey. When he was eight, his family emigrated to Australia. He served in the RAF during World War II. He wrote a series of novels, some with homoerotic elements, under his birth name, including *The Man on the Beach*, 1957; *The Green Singers*, 1958; *Two Gentlemen Sharing*, 1959; and *In My Solitude*, 1960; the last two were filmed. He also wrote other novels under the Lauder pseudonym. He died in London.

Lauder, Stuart. *Camp Commander: A Novel of the Second World War*. Harlow, Eng.: Longman, 1971.
_____. *Winger's Landfall*. London: Eyre & Spottiswoode, 1962.

76 Michael Power, *Holiday*, 1962. Laurence Eben (Michael Power): *Shadow Game*, 1972.

Holiday was Power's first novel. Set on the Natal coast, it is narrated by sixteen-year-old Jeremy Herschfelder. Immature and self-dramatizing, Jeremy loses his virginity this summer with the girl in the beach cottage across the way, leaving him with mixed emotions. It is even less clear what impact his witnessing his uncle's quarrelsome relationship with his ex-lover has on him; it is not even clear whether he realizes they are a couple. The grownups seem to understand that Uncle Edward is gay. Jeremy must receive inklings. He witnesses him breaking the country's rigid caste roles to be seen in public walking and laughing with a young Indian—when he had said he was going up the coast fishing (73–76). Later Edward takes the boy on a day trip to Durban. There he gets him drunk. And there they run into Edward's former lover, Louie Allison. Pieces start to fall into place: Louie was the brother of the woman to whom Edward was engaged for six years, who mysteriously killed herself (presumably because she realized that her brother and her fiancé were lovers). The two men lived together for ten years, with Louie largely sponging off Edward. Now Louie wants to resume the relationship. On their way home, Jeremy falls asleep; he awakens to find the car stopped and his uncle leaning over him, then moving away and crying. Jeremy wonders if "he had been trying to kiss me" (129).

A few days later, Jeremy having given Louie the clue how to locate Edward, he turns up at the family's beach home. Edward orders him to leave; Edward's mother offers him hospitality and a part of her son's bedroom. Louie proves how irresponsible he is. He sneaks Jeremy and his girlfriend off to a mixed party in Durban—racially mixed, sexually mixed. Jeremy is thrown in with a young gay couple for a moment, "aunties." ("We're as gay as two daisies in May," says one.) He seems oblivious, however, even when one of them asks him to dance (154). They return home, to find Edward waiting. Sexual tensions build. Everything comes to a head the evening of a proposed night swim. Edward pushes Louie off the high rocks where they are standing into the ocean, and he is killed. Since the reader is dependent on what Jeremy knows, the motive remains as murky as everything else about the relationship. He does record that Edward says, "Oh, the relief now" (207). Edward is arrested; Louie is buried; Jeremy decides to break with the girl: "There didn't seem to be much left in the world for me that was worth doing" (215).

Power published another novel the next year, and then he seemed to go silent. It was many years before it became known that he published a third novel under the pseudonym Lawrence Eben. In both his acknowledged novels he shows something of the racial prejudice and the caste system binding South Africa. In *Shadow Game* he attacks apartheid and sexual prejudice full on, resulting in a novel banned in his home country until recently. It is a bleak work; it is also unforgettable. Lovers living in Johannesburg, Ray Starle, the narrator, is white; Victor Butele is black. Ray works in public relations, Victor is an announcer for a native languages radio station. The two men met at rehearsals for a show being put on by a group working to preserve and promote native cultures. They fell for each other instantly. Such a life as they try to create is, of course, pure folly under apartheid. Not even understanding friends can help.

Ray sums up their problems and foreshadows the tragic end at the very beginning: "There were almost no places where we could be together: a web of laws had been spun to keep us apart. If we had not continually used our inventiveness to put up smokescreens between ourselves and other people, we would hardly have seen each other at all. Like all black people in South Africa, Victor had always been obliged to lie. Quite soon I picked up the habit, though I lied less efficiently than he did." He goes on, "No matter how you tried to simplify it in your mind, life for us could not be worked out in ordinary terms. All that we wanted to be able to do, really, was what other people did, yet without those other people being aware that we were doing so. The likelihood of our being able to pull this off, however, was scarcely possible. Nevertheless we persisted in our illusion. No other method of living seemed bearable" (3–4). The moment that Ray's neighbors become aware that the black seen at his place is not a servant, the relationship is doomed. The state police arrive; permanent exit visas are offered in an attempt to forestall scandal; but for Victor the crisis is insurmountable.

Michael Power (1933–) was born in Pietermaritzburg, Natal. He was educated at the University of Natal and Oxford. Beginning in 1962 he worked in public relations for a Johannesburg firm, part of the time based in Rhodesia. Power has credited the English publisher Anthony Blond for pushing him to write *Shadow Game*. I can find nothing about his life after the novel, save that he still resides in South Africa.

Power, Michael. *Holiday*. London: Cassell, 1962.
[_____.] *Shadow Game* by Laurence Eben. London: Joseph, 1972. *Johannesburg, S.A.: Penguin, 2008.

77   David Storey: *Radcliffe*, 1963.

A contemporary gothic novel with more than a touch of Dostoevsky's *The Idiot*, the title "The Fall of the House of Radcliffe" would not have fit exactly, but something like "The Decline of" or "The Dissolution of the House of Radcliffe" would have worked well. Its protagonist is Leonard Radcliffe. He lives with his parents and his sister in the ancient family home, Beaumont. The decaying house suffers from strange sounds and fearful tremors, caused in part by the trains running through the tunnel that has been cut under its foundations. For Leonard: "His habitation of the Place was like his habitation of his own brain, its cellular structure disposed around him as the endless ramifications of his thoughts. The identity of the building itself, its size and the scale of its architecture, its sense of duration, seemed to be that exact image he now possessed of his own mind. As he took on the identity of the Place, and became the building in the sense that all his feelings were invested in it, the aristocratic form of its dark shape became that essence which occupied every cell and atom of his brain" (116–17). Leonard is given to hallucinatory visions of an unsettling kind. Nearly all the scenes in the novel are wrapped in darkness, shadows, fog.

Victor Tolson is intimately interlocked in his destiny. Leonard is irresistibly pulled to him from the time they first encounter each other in school, an attraction that becomes physical when, as adults, they become fellow workers for a contractor putting up marquees for festive events. The married Victor makes the first advance when they share a tent pitched near "the broken stump of a small castle" (60) so they can guard the equipment they have set up (71). But when the next morning Leonard throws himself onto Victor and runs "his hand up again between Victor's thighs, pressing himself forward," he recoils (80). The two men engage in a strange sexual sparring throughout the rest of the story. At one point their relationship takes a bizarre scatological turn. One of their fellow workers, a man named Shaw, crudely asks Leonard, "What've you been doing the last few days, then? Stuffing it into old Tolson's chocolate box? Rooting it about amongst the raspberry creams?" (106). In retaliation Leonard grabs the sandwiches Shaw is eating and dumps them into the temporary latrines set up. Days later, Leonard is eating his sandwich when he realizes something is wrong: "Pressed into the buttered bread were two pieces of excrement, one bitten off at the corner" (147). He moves to attack Shaw, to be stopped by Victor. Later, he confesses that he was the one who defiled the sandwiches—"It was my shit you ate! *Mine!*" (188)—just before he attacks Leonard with one of the hammers they use.

Denis Blakeley makes their love-hate relationship more tortuous. A comedian who performs at various venues, he has just been released from prison for an unspecified crime. He is the father of three children by his own daughter. (Is he the unnamed singer with whom Leonard's uncle Austen was friends? Earlier we heard that the two men had a rendezvous that the singer missed: "Austen went in search of him with a recklessness that not only surprised but profoundly excited him [...]. When, some time later, he heard that the man had been arrested and subsequently imprisoned for a kind of behavior which, tormentedly, had been at the back of his own mind, he felt that a part of his body had been torn away" [53].) Denis is in love with Victor and, consequently, jealous of Leonard. Denis warns him, "Vic sees everything in term of *victories*, of his assimilation of other people. He consumes people" (170). He goes on, "it's *spiritual* things Tolson seeks to possess most of all. Things he can't acquire through his own temperament" (173). His daughter accuses Victor of being a vampire (199). Following the two men, Denis witnesses their love-making in the family church attached to the estate (222–23). But Leonard insists that, whereas he himself has no conscience, Victor does—though "all his actions are directed against admitting it" (233). (Austen also often has shadowed Leonard's movements and generally taken what seems to be an unhealthy interest in his nephew.)

In a tumble of events, Leonard's extended family meet and decide it is time to abandon the family estate. The next day Leonard and Victor have another sexual encounter in which the author's description emphasizes the bodily (257–58). Victor also takes Leonard's sister and impregnates her. After Victor forces himself on Leonard again, Leonard murders him with a hammer. Thereupon, Denis proceeds to kill his entire family and then take his own life, leaving behind a confession that *he* killed Tolson. Leonard hides his guilt, but Shaw goes to the police and "described in some detail the nature of the relationship that had existed between the accused and the victim" (365). Leonard tells his father, "Vic was my body, and I was his soul. We were one. Or could have been.... It's the division that separates everything in life now" (367). He continues the argument at his trial, before going on to say: "You've got to *accept* that there is a love that exists between men which is neither obscene nor degrading, but is as powerful and as profound, and as fruitful, as that love which bears children. [...] Politics, art, religion: these things are the products of men's love" (371). He is sentenced to a mental institution, and there he becomes subject "to the continual and open soliciting of other prisoners, and to fits of incoherent moralizing whenever he was confined for his behaviour" (374). He dies there. The house is abandoned, and finally it and the church are leveled, leaving no mark save "a slight undulation of the ground" to mark where they stood (376).

David Malcolm Storey (1933–) was born in Wakefield, Yorkshire. He attended the Slade School of Art at the same time that he was playing rugby for a local team. He has said that *Radcliffe* grew partly out of his own angst about the split between the physical and the aesthetic. An award winning playwright, one of whose plays (*The Contractor*) consists of putting up and taking down a marquee like the ones in the novel, he also wrote other novels, screenplays (including an adaptation of his first novel, *This Sporting Life*), and teleplays. Married, he has four children.

Storey, David. *Radcliffe*. London: Longmans, 1963.
  *New York: Coward–McCann, 1964.

78   Colin Spencer: *Anarchists in Love*, 1963; *The Tyranny of Love*, 1967; *Lovers in War*, 1969; *The Victims of Love*, 1978.

The tragic-comic four-volume *Generation* series chronicles the Simpson family and some of their intimates across several decades. Narrative chronology is nonlinear, and characters seem fated to repeat wearisome variations on the same act. A prominent thread shows the impact the mercurial Reginald Pearson has on them. Reg is bisexual, or at least acts that way. When we first meet him in *Anarchists in Love*, however, we learn that "he felt there was something false about his passion and desire for women, while when he had sex with youths his own age it was all so off hand, so casual, that in fact it seemed quite natural." He wonders if homosexuality is "really a kind of passion for oneself," if there is "a larking Narcissus in all of us searching for our own image to love." At the same time, he is aware that "all the root of all his homosexual encounters was the desperate wish, the lust to hurt, to commit an act that was criminal against the heart." He blames his father: "What that bastard had done to him" (30–31). When asked point-blank if he is "queer," he shrugs and answers, "I just love sex, that's all" (199). But since Reg is the consummate liar, even to himself, it is impossible to be certain that anything he states is true.

Sundy Simpson meets him in a Brighton bar and takes him home with her. She is a struggling painter; he is a struggling novelist. They fall in love and begin living together. What Sundy does not yet know is that all the while Reg is being kept by a retired major in the Guards, Benjamin Balchin, and that he has just ended a relationship, playing the "deaf and dumb" Simon with her Brighton neighbor Steven Addison. Becoming suspicious, however, Sundy follows him and witnesses part of a quarrel between Reg and Benjy. She hears Reg confess to (or fabricate a story about) incest with his father, but she leaves before he tries to strangle the major. Reg is convinced he killed him; actually Benjy suffered a heart attack and is in the hospital, where Sundy visits him. Finally fed up with Reg, Sundy aborts their baby. But after a retreat with her mother and her brother, Matthew, to an Anglican abbey, where she is pursued by a boring clergyman (as is her teenage brother, by another, more randy member of the clergy), she returns to Brighton and marries Reg. When her father learns that she has married the "bloody pansy boy," as usual he goes for a cheap laugh and professes that he will "be afraid to bend down when he's around" (281).

Matthew comes to the forefront in *The Tyranny of Love*. Tied into "a psychological knot" (181), he tries at various times to kill his father, his mother, and himself. Reg holds that he is in love with Sundy. A neighboring girl, Jane Harrison, pursues him even though she, like many other people he encounters during his military service and later as a hospital orderly, thinks he is gay. Reg, in his usual way, cuts through Matthew's defenses (with Bizet's *Les Pêcheurs de perles* playing in the background) and takes him to bed: "Matthew felt no shame, no guilt, no revulsion or nausea. For the first time he felt free, the ultimate release of all fears." On Reg's part, he "felt that he found himself again: the dark part of his soul that he had lost and ignored" (259–60). When Reg proposes that brother and sister share him, however, Sundy lashes out, and Reg chooses her. Matthew gives himself up to promiscuity, knowing "that in every encounter with some young man he was search for the image of Reg" (277). But then Reg starts vacillating. The two men get back together in Vienna, where Reg is editing a journal and Matthew is working in a refugee camp; again Reg abandons him. Upon Matthew's return to London, Jane steps in and proposes marriage.

The marriage takes place in *Lovers in War*, but the vacillation continues. In many ways Matthew comes to resemble Reg: "he only had to see Reg and he became his shadow" (287). Matthew and Jane have a son, Nicholas. Stephen reappears in Matthew's life. Jane, suffering from postpartum depression, is certain that he is encouraging Matthew "to indulge in homosexuality" (264). In truth, it her nagging that makes gay life seem enticing. Sundy moves in with Jamey Best-David, a married man whose Catholic wife will not countenance divorce. Reg reappears, and once more both Matthew and Sundy succumb to his charm. Brother, sister, and lover-in-common, together for a moment, "Matthew was acutely aware of the three of them like heroic figures out of an ancient drama [...] acknowledging the other's presence and isolated history, which had been knitted together in ecstasy and anguish so that this moment was like a loose pullulating knot where tears and torment changed timelessly into satisfaction and bliss" (286). Reg fathers Sundy's new son, "Boyo." He convinces Matthew, by now an accomplished painter, to fake drawings by various artists. Reg will then sell them in the United States, and Matthew will have the money to buy a home for his family in Brighton. The sudden wealth raises further suspicions in Jane's mind. The tensions between them reach a new level of fury when he finds her unmailed letter to Reg, in which she writes, "What I most deeply fear is that when Nicholas is fourteen, Matthew will fall in love with him and attempt to seduce him" (338). Confronted, Jane blames Reg for ruining their marriage. Matthew answers, "No. We ruined it" (371).

The opening of *The Victims of Love* finds them still together, still quarreling, but soon thereafter Matthew becomes involved in a passionate affair with Jamey's brother, Roland, at whose art gallery he shows his paintings. Jane starts divorce proceedings and, in her devious way, cuts Matthew off from Nicholas. The tensions between them affect his relationship with Roland, especially when the latter finds out that he is going to be named in the divorce proceedings. And all it takes is Reg's reappearance for Matthew to follow him docilely home for a one-night fling. Roland asks Matthew to leave. Meanwhile, he discovers that a short story of his, containing a barely disguised portrait of Stephen, has deeply wounded him. Roland's new lover describes Matthew as "pink and soft" (248). He tries to kill himself (again) but only manages to destroy the beam to which he has tied the rope. Sundy loses Boyo even more brutally, drowned in a freak flood that immerses their home. Reg has been to Paris with his daughter and returns only after the funeral. Almost the last we see of him, he is on top of Sundy, "his unclothed posterior moving energetically" (301). Matthew, on Roland's money, is off to a Greek island to lick his wounds. One gets the feeling that were there a fifth volume, it would be more of the same.

This family saga also chronicles the lives of the parents: the father's shady dealings and rip-offs and his comical series of adulterous relationships; the mother's retreat into piousness. The second sister and her family receive attention, as does Reg's father. The author, in the first volume of his autobiography, *Backing into Light: My Father's Son*, 2013, reveals how autobiographical the series is. He describes too the problems he and his publisher had with the *Anarchists*'s printer. Complaining that the book was obscene, he refused to print it unless the offending portions were cut. The publisher caved in, but Spencer reports that he restored all the cuts in the Panther paperback. Colin Spencer (1933–) was born in London. He was a pacifist during World War II, serving with the Royal Army Medical Corps. A painter as well as a writer, he has also lived in Austria and Greece. An avowed bisexual, he has been twice-married and has a son. In addition to other fiction and drama, all of which have gay interest, he has written about food and cookery, flatulence (*Reports from Behind*, with Chris Barlas, 1984), and homosexuality (*Homosexuality: A History*, 1995; *The Gay Kama Sutra*, 1996). In 1990 he published his and John Tasker's love letters, *Which of Us Two? The Story of a Love Affair*.

Spencer, Colin. *Anarchists in Love*. London: Eyre & Spottiswoode, 1963. *Revised. London: Panther, 1967. *The Anarchy of Love*. New York: Weybright & Talley, 1967.
_____. *Lovers in War*. London: Blond, 1969. *London: Panther, 1970.
_____. *The Tyranny of Love*. London: Blond, 1967. *London: Panther, 1968. New York: Weybright & Talley, 1968.
_____. *The Victims of Love*. London: Quartet, 1978.

79 Nicholas Monsarrat: *Smith and Jones*, 1963. Anthony Firth: *Tall, Balding, Thirty-Five*, 1966. Peter Leslie: *The Gay Deceiver*, 1967.

In 1962 John Vassall, then a clerk in the Admiralty in Whitehall, was exposed as a spy for the Russians, having been threatened by the KGB back in 1955, while he was serving in Moscow, with exposure as a homosexual. Gay historian Patrick Higgins (*Heterosexual Dictatorship*, 313) points out that Vassall's conviction "confirmed the connection that existed in the minds of many that homosexually inclined men were peculiarly susceptible to treason. His case was added to those of Redl, Casement, Burgess and Maclean to support this prejudice." In 1963 Kim Philby fled to Moscow. Though he was straight, the news revived memories of the earlier defections of the gay Guy Burgess and bisexual Donald Mclean. Burgess died in Moscow the same year. Thus gay spies were very much on people's minds during this tense period in the Cold War recently inflamed by the Cuban missile crisis.

Smith and Jones fits right into the temper of the time. Narrated by a government security officer, the case discloses his government's efforts to get back middle-aged career diplomat Ivan Percival Smith and his much younger lover, Peter Paul Jones, a cultural attaché, after they defect and request political asylum of the country in which they are serving. This narrator tells us early on, "Like nearly all other governments, our position on homosexuals was one of extreme caution. It was not prejudice so much as hard experience. We had learned, over many years, that however gifted they might be, the chance was scarcely worth taking. They attracted trouble; they made trouble; they were exceptionally liable to cause public scandal [...] they invited the kind of blackmail which must inevitably destroy their usefulness" (20–21). There ensues a comedy of errors, one that will result in the deaths of both defectors. Only in the novel's last four sentences do we learn that all the names are aliases, that Smith and Jones are actually Russians, and that they have defected in Ottawa, Canada. It's clever, but in looking back through the text, one discovers that the author has played far from fair. The novel was selected by *Reader's Digest* for its condensed novels series.

In *Tall, Balding, Thirty-Five*, the Irish photographer John Limbo, Third Lord Killinchy, becomes accidently ensnared in cold war maneuvers taking place around Ludwig II's Bavarian castle, the Herrenchiemsee. He has chosen the king's castles as the subject for his next book. First mistaken for a spy, then cleared and pressed into service, he proves more adept than the professionals at uncovering the double-crosser in their midst. However, the enemy perceives his own deep secret: that he is a virgin closet case. They use a seventeen-year-old German boy, Christian Brandt, to seduce him. The experience changes John. He reflects, "When he could be more detached he felt that the most interesting thing he would have learned would be how other people could make you feel guilty for doing something you believed to be right" (144). But it does not necessarily liberate him: "Would he ever dare, even if he wanted to, join the shrill freemasonry of the London gay?" (162). Our last glimpse of him, back home, suggests that he has sunk back into his old comfort zone.

In response to the highly popular James Bond movies, American television took the camp elements implicit in the series and created *The Man from U.N.C.L.E.* Peter Leslie wrote a number of spinoff novels, and *The Gay Deceiver* was heavily marked by the show's basic concept. Everything is going wrong in the British secret service. Sources are drying up because agent David Charter has fallen in love with a Russian double agent, Igor Schelgatseff, and become sloppy in his work. At the same time, another Russian agent is sabotaging their equipment, and instructions are going crosswire so that a scheme is set in motion to assassinate the president of the U.S.A. instead of the U.F.A. (United Federation of Arabs), whom the British want killed because he is jacking up oil prices. The plan is passed by mistake to a television contestant, Herbert Crisp, who thinks it is his final test for the grand prize. Meanwhile, the Russians are not faring much better. They believe a heterosexual brothel specializing in caning and other tastes peculiar to the British is the foreign branch's secret headquarters and are bewildered by the "coded" talk they overhear. David is assigned the job of ferreting out the miscreant in their service, whereupon he and Igor begin an elaborate intrigue to fool all sides. Trailed by journalists, agents, and double agents, Herbert sets off for Monaco, where the president is speaking. He is in the company of Ursula Inlet, a young woman he has met at a party. After Herbert, at the final moment, calls off the attempt, she guards the secret that she is a Russian agent but reveals that she is transgendered. She asks Herbert, "Do you mind very much my being a man, darling?" And in a moment reminiscent of the ending of *Some Like It Hot*, he replies, "No, it doesn't matter, really" (207).

The three novels share a deep suspicion that espionage in itself verges on the absurd. The agents appear to be uniformly myopic, self-deceiving, curiously provincial in their outlook, but (as Firth writes) "they were still sinister. All over the world, issues that would make for peace or war were in their meticulously inept hands" (164). They show less clearly that the double lives gays were forced to lead at the time were akin to the double lives spies have to lead. Already famous for *The Cruel Sea* and *The Tribe That Lost Its Head*, the Liverpool-born, Cambridge-educated author, Nicholas John Turney Monsarrat (1910–1979), seems to have had fun with his exercise in reader entrapment. Anthony Firth (1937–1980), according to the dust jacket, was born in Kent, attended Cambridge, was married, and had a son. His name appears on the Internet Movie Database as a producer during the 1960s. Peter Leslie (1922–2007) was born in Cornwall. Trained as a geologist, he made a total career change and became a London journalist and record reviewer, editor of a jazz magazine, actor, and writer. He died in France.

Firth, Anthony. *Tall, Balding, Thirty-Five*. London: Hutchinson, 1966. *New York: Harper & Row, 1966. *The Limbo Affair*. New York: Lancer, 1968.
Leslie, Peter. *The Gay Deceiver*. London: Macgibbon & Kee, 1967. *New York: Stein & Day, 1967.
Monsarrat, Nicholas. *Smith and Jones*. London: Cassel, 1963. *New York: Sloane, 1963.

80 Montague Haltrecht: *Jonah and His Mother*, 1964; *A Secondary Character*, 1965. Richard Chopping: *The Ring*, 1967.

As the debate about the Wolfenden recommendations continued, climaxing with the change of the law in 1967, many gay novels were curiously depressing, populated with downright unsavory characters. Certainly, none of these three is an edifying read; their portraits of gays dominated by domineering mothers, addicted to relentless cruising, driven to self-destruction contribute nothing to any construction of gay pride. Even more curious, some of the most disagreeable gay characters were created by writers who were comparatively open about their own lives. In addition to Haltrecht and Chopping (both of whom were among the first to take advantage of same-sex civil unions when they were legalized), we have Angus Wilson, Simon Raven, Robin Maugham. It leaves me wondering if these novels appeared differently to readers at the time.

Jonah and His Mother is a dark comedy with five characters and a relatively simple plot. Having been picked up by Gray Linton, a middle-aged antiques dealer, eighteen-year-old Jonah moves in with him, to be joined by his mother, Frederika. She has been down on her luck, but manages to recoup nicely by using Gray's generosity to the max. Her motherly advice to Gray simultaneously promotes and undermines the men's sexual happiness. Jonah grows restive and decides to adventure out. He starts to date Susan, a twenty-two-year-old who lives above them. A clerk at Harrods, Susan is also pursued by her boss, the married Leo. He just happens to be one of Frederika's former lovers. So it is an easy step for her to expose her son's sexuality to him, knowledge which Leo then uses to convince Susan to become his mistress. Gray accuses Frederika midway through the novel: "You're obsessed with [your son....] It's ridiculous. He's grown up. I tell you, it's more than ridiculous, it's downright obscene." To which Frederika retorts, "I count on having him for ever!" (100–01). And so apparently she will.

Divided into three parts, *A Secondary Character* tells the story of a cold-blooded young man named Christopher. In the section titled "Flashes," we get just that: quick views of Christopher at age twenty-four trying to extract himself from his dominating parents, having sex with a Spanish female prostitute, irrationally slapping a boy in the class where he serves as a supply teacher, taking a bath, following a man in the streets. In the second section, having fled to the Mediterranean, he comes under the domination of Léon, a homosexual. Though Léon beds any number of black males whom he picks up, he and Christopher seem never to have sex together. An alcoholic and a drug-user, Léon is dying. Too late, Christopher realizes that "Léon didn't want a victim, though Christopher had willfully offered himself as one" (122). In the third section, "Madness," back in London he enters a life of promiscuity (a bit of comic relief offered when he has to be treated for crab lice). He returns to Spain full of disgust for "Men who prowled foreign cities like scavengers. [...] Queers, filthy pansies, with the hidden lusts. Hidden, but not from him" (141). Whereupon, he picks up a teenager, takes him back to his hotel, and proceeds to murder him: "The boy was in his way, he was between Christopher and the quest for perfection" (153). His last act is to take care of "the serious business of directing his unspoilt body towards the open sea" (160).

The Fly, 1965, the first of Chopping's two novels for adults, was recommended by his friend Angus Wilson to his publishers; it left the book editor feeling queasy. Dominated by flies, which, as in Sartre's play, represent both the furies and fate, it is not a gay novel in any sense of the word. One of the protagonists of the intertwined stories, is the Irishman O'Flattery, who is troubled by sex in general and whose pornographic fantasies included both heterosexual and homosexual couplings. Driven to the brink of insanity when his first sexual encounter with a woman brings on a fatal heart attack, in his flight from her dead body he runs into a rent boy who offers him a blowjob on the train (167–68). He encounters a gay teenage couple on the riverbank: "He wanted desperately to talk to them. For some extraordinary reason he felt that to do so would be his only hope of salvation from the dreadful fate which he was beginning to feel must inevitably overtake him" (199). They become a symbol of innocence and purity for him (the only glimpse we get of such in the novel). But it is too late. O'Flattery is committed to an insane asylum, where—so we learn in the second novel—he catches flies and eats them.

Though a family returns from *The Fly* in a minor role, *The Ring* otherwise introduces a whole new set of characters. Taking advantage of the relaxing of censorship, sexual scenes are more graphic. Here we have the only appearance, among all the novels in this guide, of the gay bathhouse culture. The protagonist is Boyde Ashlar, thirty-four years old, independently wealthy, tied to his aging mother. The authorial voice says of him, "Never did he yearn to be heterosexual, balance was what he hoped for but could never attain" (61). But he tells his best friend, Grahame Whiteley, "I get so terribly depressed by it all, [...] it's all so very unsatisfactory. I'm sick of queers, sick of the way we never stop hunting, sick of what we do in bed." He does indict the legal system for creating his malaise: "We live permanently in corsets of controlled behaviour" (177). He worries about "his constant preoccupation with sex" (201), but continues compulsively to cruise. He becomes besotted with Tex, a straight masseur at the baths, but moves into a troubled relationship with Roddy, a teenaged sexual opportunist.

In contrast, Grahame enjoys "his unscrupulous promiscuity" (142). He reports back to Boyde with gusto about his holiday in Tangier; he pursues every appealing man of color he encounters in London; and Boyde knows that he will make a pass at Roddy the moment he has a chance. When Boyde asks him if he never worries about his pickups, he responds, "Not really. I think I believe that one is rather like a magnet; if you expect that kind of thing, in some curious way, you draw it towards you" (178). But, in general, the description of the penises on display at the baths is typical of the authorial voice's outlook on sex in both novels: "The human equivalent of the gentle, the maggot, the larva of the flesh-fly or bluebottle, used as bait by anglers" (49). When Boyde recalls the time he has spent with Roddy, he writes in a letter: "I can only look into the past months and see them as a horrible scarred battlefield sprouting phallic monoliths, monstrously diseased, putrid, obliterating everything, dripping with stinking ordure, spunk and decay..." (249). Unfortunately for him, one Mr. Crypts serves as manservant at the house next door. Incarnate evil, seemingly omnipresent, he witnesses every major transgression that occurs in the novel. Boyde becomes the magnet. Living up to his name, Crypts precipitates the crisis that will lead ultimately to the protagonist's sordid death.

Montague Haltrecht (1932–2010) was born in London, one of four sons of a Polish immigrant father. After graduation from Oxford, he managed his father's dress shops, worked as a script reader, acted, modeled, and wrote radio and television scripts. Colin MacInnes was instrumental in getting his first book published; *A Secondary Character* was revised when the publisher became fearful that a character in it (probably Léon) was based too closely on MacInnes. Haltrecht published two other novels. His husband was the actor Nicolas Amer (1923–). Richard Wasey Chopping (1917–2008) was born and died in Colchester, Essex. He was also an author of children's books and natural histories, but is now most celebrated for his illustrations of the covers for the original James Bond novels. His friend Francis Bacon painted two portraits of him. His husband was the landscape painter Denis Wirth-Miller (1915–2010).

Chopping, Richard. *The Fly*. London: Secker & Warburg, 1965. New York: Farrar, Straus & Giroux, 1965. *New York: New American Library (Signet), 1966.

___. *The Ring.* London: Secker & Warburg, 1967. *New York: Bantam, 1970.
Haltrecht, Montague. *Jonah and His Mother.* London: Deutsch, 1964. *London: Mayflower–Dell, 1966.
___. *A Secondary Character.* London: Deutsch, 1965.

81 Maurice Leitch: *The Liberty Lad*, 1965.

The Liberty Lad is reputed to offer "the earliest description of a gay bar in Irish literature"—the Royal Avenue (RA) Bar in Rosemary Street, according to cultural historian Jeff Dudgeon. But the novel offers readers a good deal more than that. Frank Glass, its narrator, is a straight schoolteacher who, through education, has pulled himself out of his working class origins; his best friend is Terence Butler, who is by necessity discreet but unashamedly gay. Frank muses at one point, "Just how *normal* was our relationship anyway? Most people would jump to one conclusion, only, if they could overhear most of the conversations we have, for most people, I have discovered, although they don't talk about it, are terrified of even thinking of *that* subject. I don't know if I have the same sort of fear myself deep down, because old Terry and I, we've talked about it so much and he's told me so much about *his* side of things, that it's hard to imagine what a "normal" reaction is like. So that makes *me* not 'normal'...." (27)

When Terry takes Frank to the gay bar, he does not at first recognize what kind of place they are in. He notes that the customers are a mixed lot: "teds, ratings and labourers in clean blue serge donkey jackets with leatherette shoulders sat beside quietly dressed middle-aged men and a lot of thinnish younger men who looked like clerks or shop assistants" (153). When finally the truth dawns, Frank realizes, "I was seeing Terry in a light I'd never seen him before. Here he was with his own kind. Before that night I'd always thought of *him* as being different, as the misfit in the society in which we moved back at home, but now it was me who was out of place. It was a strange feeling to have" (159–60). Later Terry explains the purpose of the games Frank has witnessed: "*We* have to have somebody. The sex part is nothin.' Believe me, *nothin*.' But it's the only way to meet someone. That's what all of us are searchin' for" (170).

One of Terry's sexual partners is a Member of Parliament, Sam Bradley. When Terry finds out that Frank is up for the post of school principal, he suggests that Frank ask Bradley, whose son attends Frank's school, to pull some strings in his favor, it being understood that sex will be involved in the transaction. Surprisingly, Frank goes along with the idea. He is amazed to discover that he initially responds, before the "unreality" of it all leads to his losing his erection (188). Unfortunately, in playing his part, Frank leads Bradley to think that the utterly discreet Terry has been loose-lipped about their relationship. When Bradley finds out that the police are on the verge of a crackdown, he warns Terry of its imminence, but when Terry turns to him for greater reassurance, he is coldly told that he "couldn't be trusted," for he "talked too much" (202). Terry departs for Australia, leaving behind a conscience-stricken Frank. Attending his father's funeral, Frank summons up all the losses he has suffered during the past year. He realizes that his biggest loss has been himself as he once was. For the first time he weeps.

For someone so honored and so involved in public media, Maurice Leitch (1933–) manages to be fairly elusive concerning his private life. He was born in Northern Ireland. Without forsaking his Antrim roots, he moved to London in 1969 to work for BBC radio. Frank Glass returns in the novel *Stamping Ground*, 1975, but not Terry.

Leitch, Maurice. *The Liberty Lad.* London: Macgibbon & Kee, 1965. *New York: Pantheon, 1965.

82 Neville Jackson (G. M. Glaskin): *No End to the Way*, 1965.

Robert Dessaix (in the introduction to his anthology of gay Australian writing, 13) asserts, "In a real sense *No End to the Way* was the first Australian gay novel." By Gerald Glaskin—but brought out, at his publisher's insistence, under a pseudonym—it was the first to be told from a gay man's perspective—

although, in an unusual move, the second person pronoun ("you") replaces the conventional first or third person. It was the first about an affair between two adults. (There are memories of the protagonist's being introduced to sex as a child by his teenage uncle, a relationship that was cut short by a motorcycle wreck.) And it described gay life in Perth during the early 1960s, surprising many readers who, again according to Dessaix, had no idea that any kind of a gay culture existed there. It is also the saddest novel, not to have any other death, mugging, or similar plot thread.

Ray Wharton owns an advertising agency in the never-named city. One evening he meets Cor van Gelder, an immigrant from the Netherlands, and it is pretty much love at first sight. Only later does Ray discover that he holds an uncanny resemblance to Cor's first major love back in his native country. By then, he has also learned that Cor is married and an expectant father. Against all odds the two men try to set up life together, Cor even abandoning his wife and unborn son. But everything seems stacked against success. A jealous rival begins a whispering campaign that almost costs Ray his agency. A bout of hepatitis does finish it off. All along Ray has doubts about Cor despite the man having given up more than most people would to stay with Ray. The novel ends on a melancholy note, but not a despairing one.

The finest achievement of the novel is its very realistic depiction of the protagonist in all his multiple aspects. The use of "you" is ingenious, forcing the reader in essence to become one with a character who is all too understandable if not that admirable. Even a straight psychiatrist accuses Ray, "I do think you might have made more of an effort over it. Frankly, I think you might have at least considered him to be worth that much" (235). But because of "you" the reader must ask whether he himself would have done any better in the situation. Too, as Ray notes several times, the problem is with the "so-called normal people who are always trying to deprive you of your own chance of some kind of life together, amongst yourselves" (145). One of Ray's friends is entrapped by the police and sentenced to three months in prison. "*And* the infamy of course" (172), which will destroy his job opportunities, not to think about what the other prisoners may do to him first. As Ray says, "it take a good deal of character to be a decent homosexual" (231). One could wish to see more of Bruce Farnham, who appears twice briefly. He seems to have achieved that balance, but the reader has no idea at what cost to him.

Gerald Marcus Glaskin (1923–2000) was born and died in Perth. He served in the Royal Australian Air Force. He lived for some time in Singapore and later Amsterdam. In 1968 he met Leo van de Pas (1944?–), who would be his partner until his death. According to his biographer, John Burbidge (211), his favorite gay work was not this novel, but a short story published in 1968, "The Asking Price."

Burbidge, John. *Dare Me! The Life and Work of Gerald Glaskin*. Clayton, Vic.: Monash University Press, 2014.
Jackson, Neville. *No End to the Way*. *London: Barrie & Rockliff, 1965. New York: Macfadden–Bartell, 1969.

83 John McIntosh: *Blood Brothers*, 1965.

A daring work for its time, the novel depicts an eroticized adolescent interracial friendship in a country governed by the principle of apartheid. Set in the early 1960s, it draws a savagely negative portrait of whites, whose stronghold on the country is under escalating threat. The Sharpeville Massacre of 1960, though never mentioned in the novel, was a defining moment in the country's uneasy history. As a result, nonwhites became increasingly militant. The armed wing of the Pan Africanist Congress, Poqo (the Xhosa word for "pure"), formed in 1960, began its violent campaign to eradicate white rule. Even Nelson Mandala, a member of the African National Congress, who had advocated nonviolence, changed his stance; in 1962 he was tried and sentenced to life imprisonment. By then South Africa had become a republic, severing it ties to the British government and (until 1994) the Commonwealth. Yet, as the novel shows, even amid such racial unrest, whites accorded blacks varied treatment depending on their economic status. This is the background against which Francois Groenewaldt, nearly twelve, and Zonk, thirteen, form their unlikely alliance.

Zonk is the son of one of the workers on Petrus Groenewaldt's ironically named farm, *Mon Repos*. The Groenewaldts are hardly model parents. He is a bank accountant. One fatal day, while the manager is away, he lets his innate bigotry dominate and bodily ejects one of the bank's most prominent black customers. He is fired, and his life begins to careen downward. Matie Groenewaldt dwells in exaggerated memories of having been a beauty queen and a stage actress. The only other nearby whites are the meddlesome Macauleys, who own a country store down the road. They look with disapproval upon the boys' intimacy, while Francois's parents, caught up in their perpetual bickering, are oblivious. It remains mysterious how the friendship developed, though Francois mentions several times that Zonk is the only boy his age within walking distance. He takes delight in sneaking food to the inadequately nourished boy, and he passes on the lessons he has learned in school. The two also experiment sexually: "On a number of occasions they had played with each other's dinguses in the manner Francois had learnt from the older boys at the farm school, in the bushes behind the lavatories during break" (18). An image of Zonk's "dingus" often comes to Francois's mind whenever he misses his company (32).

They walk together holding hands, which naturally arouses Mrs. Macauley's suspicions. Late in the novel she spies on them and reports what she sees to Francois's parents: "I saw them take off their clothes ... and ... Oh. And *play* with each other" (90). When the Macauleys leave, his father uses his belt on him. As a result, "a kind of release came out of his pain. Or relief, rather: the relief of knowing that he now had something specific to hate them for" (95). The boys' secret hideout is a natural rock formation rising above a river and given the fanciful name Lovers' Rock: "The legend in the valley was that years and years ago two lovers had drowned themselves at this spot" (15). There they cut their fingers and let their blood mingle (20). Nearby Zonk discovers a cave in whose recesses he finds a skeleton. Alongside the body is a weapon used in the Boer War: "The soldier must have been wounded by the bloody British and he crept in here to escape them and died here" (49). The boys treat the remains like a holy relic, adorning it with flowers and cloth. The rock and the cave, love and death, become emblematic.

At the very beginning of the novel, Francois stumbles upon a meeting being held outside Zonk's home. When he later questions what was going on, Zonk reveals casually that the leader "was saying that we Africans must kill all the White people in the valley" (21). It briefly worries Francois whether he should tell his parents, but after listening to another of his mother's interminable drunken reminiscences about her glorious past, he decides, "No. No—he would not tell his parents. Definitely not" (28). As events escalate, policemen pop in, government helicopters swirl overhead, and his own parents mistreat their workers, his resolve to stay silent gains reinforcement from the heartless acts he witnesses on both sides. The Poqo begin their campaign of intimidation by killing all the whites' animals. Petrus can prove nothing against his workers, but he drives them off the farm. Later, in a particularly humiliating scene, the Groenewalds accuse their house servant of numerous thefts that actually Francois has committed and turn her out. While Francois's parents are at a meeting to discuss their plan of retaliation, Zonk sneaks into the house.

It is an emotional meeting. Francois vows never to hate Zonk. "Then, feeling as if he were condemning himself for ever, he said, 'I love you, Zonk.'" And he invites the boy to bed. He "cleaved to the body next to him, wishing to melt into it. Slowly, like milk on a low fire, he came to the boil. There was no pain, no aching this time. It was all new. He felt as if the whole of him was flowing out, and he was carried on a thundering wave to a region of warm darkness. He gave up a few drops" (129). Coming down from their momentary union, they accept that they will never again be so joined emotionally and physically. But the moment has marked Francois's rite of passage: "The door on his childhood had been shut and locked and he was outside, in a strange and unfamiliar place" (130). And so the novel moves to its inevitable but enigmatic ending.

John McIntosh (1930–1970) was born in Southern Rhodesia (Zimbabwe) but grew up in South Africa, the son of a bank manager. He attended the Universities of Cape Town and the Witwatersrand. Fluent in both English and Afrikaans, from 1953 until 1961 he worked for a Johannesburg newspaper, being briefly dispatched to London in 1957. From 1962 until his untimely death from cancer he taught English at Boys Town, Magaliesburg. McIntosh's last novel was posthumously awarded South Africa's CNA Literary Award.

McIntosh, John. *Blood Brothers*. London: Blond, 1965. *London: Panther, 1969.

84 Wole Soyinka: *The Interpreters*, 1965.

The inclusion of Soyinka's first novel on a list of gay Commonwealth novels, can be debated. Its one gay character, Joe Golder, plays only a small role. The bulk of the novel focuses on five Nigerian friends who are trying to find their place in their newly independent country. Two are university lecturers, two are civil servants, and one is a journalist. Golder intersects their lives beginning with the art lecturer, who is working on a massive canvas depicting the Yoruba pantheon. Golder is his model for the god Erinle. We learn a bit more about him in each of his successive appearances: that he is American, three-quarters black, disgusted by his white skin (102), a university lecturer in history (136), a tenor (186), gay (200), always on the prowl (216), a fan of James Baldwin (200, 217); and that one of his overtures led to a boy's leap to his death from a balcony (236). But in the end he remains a one-dimensional figure. That does not prevent critics from interpreting his purpose in the loosely plotted novel in all sorts of ingenious ways. Briefly, Golder enters into the ongoing African political argument denying that homosexuality is indigenous to the continent. When the journalist snorts, "I happen to be born into a comparatively healthy society," Golder attacks: "Don't give me that. Comparatively healthy society my foot. Do you think I know nothing of your Emirs and their little boys? You forget history is my subject. And what about those exclusive coteries in Lagos?" (199).

The playwright and poet Akinwande Oluwole Soyinka (1934–) was born in Isara, Nigeria. He was educated at the Universities of Ibadan and Leeds. He has been imprisoned for his political beliefs and suffered exile numerous times, living for long stretches in the United States. Married, he has four children. He was awarded the Nobel Prize for literature in 1986.

Soyinka, Wole. *The Interpreters*. London: Deutsch, 1965. New York: Collier, 1970. *London: Heinemann Educational, 1970.

85 Desmond Cory: *Deadfall*, 1965.

Diamonds are pure; human lives are messy and anything but. Michael Jeye, a Scot, straight, is recruited by Richard Moreau and his wife Fé to team up with them to pull off a jewel heist in Spain. Michael recognizes at once that Richard is "queer" (39); his current lover is a young poet, Antonio, of whom we see little. As Michael and Fé fall in love, Richard's past comes out little by little. He is nearly sixty years old. During the war he played a double game. A policeman in occupied France, he caught a young and accomplished cat burglar, Dubos. Falling in love with him, he let him continue his profession. Any useful papers Dubos discovered, Richard passed on to the Resistance. The Germans made catching Dubos a top priority and recruited Richard to help: "So Richard caught him. Dubos was caught one night in the act, and at dawn next morning they shot him dead. On Richard's orders. That was in the winter of '43. The year after that, just before the Normandy landings, Richard left for Spain" (184). So Fé tells Michael. Still later he learns that she is actually not only Richard's wife but also his illegitimate daughter. Michael's last job goes wrong and he falls. Fé saves him. Richard fatally shoots himself, leaving behind a letter, partly written to Dubos. The novel was adapted as a film.

Chapter 4 contains a relatively long, and rather muddled, meditation on the "affinity" between homosexuality and criminality. It begins, "Of course, in many countries all homosexuals are criminals, in the sense that the practice of homosexuality is proscribed by the law. It doesn't follow that all criminals are homosexuals; naturally not. But the knowledge that homosexuals are, in that one essential respect, very like themselves is bound to have an effect—to establish, if you like, an identification. [...] The struggle in the criminal's mind is against authority, against all established order and custom; and in that struggle, the homosexual and the pervert are also joined." In trying to define qualities peculiar to the homosexual alone, the author writes, "It's a *refusal* to dominate. It's an insistence on equality, even in sex." The author goes on to note that prison "encourages homosexuality among people who are already criminals. And two men who are able to share—so to speak—both their work and their play are in an enormously strong position; both socially and professionally, they're a self-contained unit," making it all the harder for the police to catch such a team (110–12).

Desmond Cory was one of the pennames adopted by Shaun Lloyd McCarthy (1928–2001). He was born in Lansing, Sussex. After serving in the Royal Marines, he entered Oxford. In 1953 he moved to Cordova, Spain, where he married and became the father of four sons. He taught at the University of Cardiff, where he was awarded a doctorate in 1976. He also taught in several Arab-speaking countries and in Cyprus. He retired to Malaga, Spain, having authored some forty-five thrillers, as well as screenplays and radio scripts.

Cory, Desmond. *Deadfall*. New York: Walker, 1965.

86 John Pollock: *The Grass Beneath the Wire*, 1966.

Michael Richmond is in love with John Bachelor. That is established from the beginning, and nothing is going to change the fact. Michael will leave Oxford to be with him in London. He will pass any number of bogus checks to provide John the entertainment he desires on the nightclub circuit. He will refuse to report for military service, though it is 1943 and he has volunteered for the Senior Training Corps. He will go AWOL to return to him when he is seized by the military police: "When he was with John, he could not believe that he had done anything wrong, anything for which he should be punished. The love that he bore him made the war seem of no importance whatsoever. It was worth any amount of suffering afterwards, as long as he could be with him for just a little longer" (65). He suffers when he discovers that the rich Mary Arbuthnot has successfully bedded John behind his back: "John Bachelor obviously went to the highest bidder" (56).

But his love does not waver, not even when he is court-martialed (for passing bad checks) and sentenced to the glasshouse, where he is assigned the task of pulling the grass out from under the wire fencing that surrounds the detention camp. Being in love is not to be confused with being faithful. Michael is only too happy to seek comfort nights from Alf Tappit, who has the adjacent bed. He adjusts to the loss of an eye during a prison brawl, a condition that finally obtains his release, and he returns to search out what has happened to John, "whom he still loved" (192), even though straight Alf had fallen in love with him. And John, once found, proves to be more affectionate than ever—at least until Michael's money once again runs out. The idea of changing, getting a job, leading a more orderly life never occurs to either of them. Michael is defiant to the end: "'We will manage,' he said" (224).

The story is a rollicking frolic. Here is an author who has taken to heart Wilde's dictum: "There is no such thing as a moral or an immoral book. Books are well written, or badly written. That is all." Information about John Pollock himself (dates unknown) eludes me. One gets glimpses of him in Francis King's and Anthony Blond's memoirs. Pollock attended Oxford. According to Blond (92), who published his three novels, "After a desolate career, which included stays in various asylums, he ended up supported by his brother in a large chilly house in Belgravia."

Büssing, Sabine. *Of Captive Queens and Holy Panthers: Prison Fiction and Male Homoerotic Experience*. Frankfurt am Main: Peter Lang, 1990. Chapter 2.3.

Pollock, John. *The Grass Beneath the Wire*. London: Blond, 1966.

87 Rodney Garland (Peter de Polnay): *Sorcerer's Broth*, 1966. Peter de Polnay: *The Permanent Farewell*, 1970.

The dust jacket for *Sorcerer's Broth* gives as its author "Rodney / Garland / Author of / The Heart in Exile." Just the author's name is given on the title and copyright pages. No one seems to have explained why the publisher would perpetrate a hoax for the third novel it published under the Garland name after Adam de Hegedus's death. Just as the first Garland novels introduced the first gay sleuth and the first gay spies, so this last Garland novel seems to have the first gay British criminal. Though the notorious London East End gangster Ronnie Kray immediately comes to mind whenever the subject of gay criminals pops up, I see no indication that he colored the author's imagination in creating Major Ray Watkinson.

Sorcerer's Broth is narrated by Don Apps. Though proud of the fact that he has "artistic tastes and inclination" (5), he claims, "I never flaunted my apartness, which was mine and those like me" (133). He disdains "simpering little queers" (16), but no one that he meets seems to mistake his sexuality. What seems mysterious is the way no one seems to recognize how utterly callous and pretentious he is. The middle-aged Ray Watkinson falls in love with Don at first sight and plucks him from the men's clothing store where he works as a salesman. All kinds of mysteries and misinformation swirl around Ray's head, but all the evidence points to the idea that he is telling the truth when he claims that he has become a bank robber in order to avenge himself against a society that used him in World War II, then dropped him when it had no further use for him: "They were willing, in fact had spent money on it, to let me kill, murder, burgle in their name, yet they would spend nothing on finding me the sort of employment to which my rank and the authority I wielded, and the responsibility they had given me, entitled me to" (55–56).

Besotted with Don, he does not recognize that the youth feels no real attachment to him. Convinced, in fact, that Ray is hoaxing him, Don shows up at the bank he plans to rob in time to witness Ray inflict a shoulder wound on one of the young tellers who stupidly tries to stop the robbery. Don now takes on the role with the teller, Benjy Baxter, that Ray has played for him, with the differences that Benjy is his own age and a true innocent, fearful of his sexuality, whereas Don had been sexually active with many other men. Ardor wins over Benjy though, leaving Don a number of lies he has meanwhile told to clear up. The novel ends with Ray dead, shot by the gangsters whose number he refused to join, and Don back as a clerk in a clothing store, albeit one of a higher class. He is still callous and still pretentious. It is to the author's credit that he maintains the irony between what Don thinks of himself and what we see of him, but more comedy than that provided by his "pansy" hating sister would have helped.

The author of *Sorcerer's Broth* has been identified as another Hungarian expatriate, Peter de Polnay. Four years later he published *The Permanent Farewell* under his own name. As with *The Heart in Exile* a suicide has occurred before the novel opens. But there are no other similarities. Set in 1969 Paris, an English lesbian and heroin addict takes too many sleeping pills. Aidan Duncan, the father who never really knew his daughter, sets out to find out why. By novel's end he realizes that he will never know for sure, though he himself has transformed from his encounters with one sector of the Parisian demimonde. Two of its prominent members are young lovers: Francis Ruellan, a poseur who professes to support Maoist propaganda while supporting his drug habit by taking money from his rich industrial father, and Ralph, a Belgian posing as an American, brought back from India by a German drug dealer, Kurt Wanger, for whom Ralph now works. After Kurt's arrest, Ralph becomes totally dependent on Francis for money and drugs, but a petty criminal, Michel Tivier, threatens to supplant his position with Francis. Francis comes up with a scheme to rob a bank, one that he himself aborts. Then he concocts a new plan to rob his father, using Michel's safecracking skills, a harebrained idea that Ralph join in with disastrous results. Other plots, mostly involving lesbian contretemps and a bourgeois *ménage à trois*, intersect Aidan's and Francis's paths. Aidan tries to formulate a moral to their stories: "One is given a line to follow, and if one deviates one comes a cropper" (193). This thought occurs to him after his own love affair with his daughter's former lover has come a cropper, just as his daughter's had before her fatal overdose.

Peter de Polnay (1906–1984) was born in Budapest. He farmed in Kenya during the early 1930s, but moved to Paris before the war began. He joined the French resistance, was captured, but managed to escape to England, where he had already established himself as an author. Married three times, de Polnay had one son. He died in Paris.

Garland, Rodney. *Sorcerer's Broth*. London: Allen, 1966.
Polnay, Peter de. *The Permanent Farewell*. London: Allen, 1970.

88 George Moor: *The Pole and the Whistle*, 1966. Royston Ellis: *The Rush at the End*, 1967.

Despite having created the modern paperback book before World War II, there was nothing comparable in England to the vast outpouring of gay pulp fiction that occurred beginning in the mid–1960s in the United States. Mainstream English publishers seem to have been unreceptive to gay paperback originals, and there was no equivalence before the 1990s to the American erotic publishing houses which sustained gay pulps for two decades and beyond. Moor's and Ellis's paperback originals are thus a rarity. Though they have completely different plots, they even share certain elements in common. Both are comical romances ending with a union, both are coming out stories, and both are quite frank, for the period, about the sexual aspect of homosexuality. Finally, both end with a flight from England.

John Anselm, the twenty-five-year-old narrator of *The Pole and the Whistle*, is "a sedate young accountant" for a chicken hatchery (17). One evening he walks into The Pole and Whistle (the second *the* appears only on the title page of the novel), gets picked up by Frank Jeffers, a petty criminal, and falls in love with him. But Frank cannot stay out of trouble and gets sent back to jail. John bursts out, "It's a waste of money sending you to prison. You should be in the hands of a psychiatrist" (67). After a spell John returns to the pub, this time to be picked up by Les Barron. But Frank remains his love, and when he breaks out of prison, John happily harbors him until he is taken prisoner once more. The story becomes darker: six of the pub's regulars get drunk on New Year's and rape and badly assault John. A Japanese savior, one of a delegation inspecting the advanced methods of the hatchery, unexpectedly offers John a job with his father's company back home. Once in Japan, John finds a Japanese lover, but he continues to care for Frank, now a fugitive in Ireland.

The novel suggests how England is changing in the 1960s. At one point Frank takes John to a Famers' Ball. The two men dance together, and "it felt so natural that [...] I forgot anyone could think otherwise." In fact, the other people's reaction is "a look not of aversion or disgust, surprise or anger, it was a look of not seeing us. People simply pretended that our bodily images were not there." John thinks, "I was grateful for a tolerance which could ignore us" (47). Frank's mother meets John in the streets and tells him: "He loves you [...]. He pays attention to what you say. I only wish you could put up with him. [...] he'll never change for me. But he just might for you" (79). John's own mother comes searching for him when she finds out he has been assaulted: "'I came,' said my mother simply, 'as soon as I heard you were in trouble through being a homosexual.' [...] There had been nothing of exclusion in my mother's tone; I was still her son" (107). In fact, he discovers that she has known for years. John sums up: "There is a turmoil and tranquility when at last our inmost secret is wrested from us" (108).

George James Moor 1927–1992) was born and died in Lancashire. He was educated at Cambridge, where he began publishing poetry and wrote the libretto for a puppet masque and a chamber opera with Wilfred Mellers. After a stint teaching English in North Wales, he worked for a time as a farmer. He then taught English in Japan, Saudi Arabia, and Iran. A note at the beginning of *The Pole and the Whistle* compares the novel to Japanese *shishosetsu*. Moor also published two gay novellas: *The Heat of the Sun*, 1976, is a savage satire against "Soddy Arabia" in which the Arabs are depicted as despicable, but the story does permit some sort of romance to grow between Tony Stockings, a would-be English teacher there, and Inspector Saleh ben Yusif, in whose custody he lands after being repeatedly raped just before the muezzin's call to prayer and left naked during it. *Bowl of Roses*, 1978, a more sustained work, recounts a relationship between the unnamed narrator, an English teacher in Tehran, and Feredun, an Iranian student-activist campaigning against the Shah whom the narrator helps escape the country just as he is about to be apprehended.

Ellis's *The Rush at the End* charts the rocky but growing acceptance on the part of fifty-eight-year-old Arthur Darby and twenty-four-year-old Andrew King of their sexual natures and of their relationship to each other. Arthur falls for Andy almost as soon as they encounter each other on a London commuter train. But seducing the man—young enough to be his son he realizes—is not easy. Arthur is married, with a daughter, Jane. Andy shares a flat with Chris, a former classmate with whom he is in love and with whom he has occasional sex. Then several things happen. He discovers that Chris intends to get married. On a holiday to Brighton he allows himself to be seduced by a well-known television script writer. After an invitation to Arthur's home, he allows Jane to seduce him. And finally, in exchange for Arthur's paying Chris's part of the rent after the marriage, Andy allows Arthur to have him. At first, Andy finds that, "when encouraged," he is "powerless to do anything but sing along with the music being strummed on his body" (147). But as he gathers more confidence from his bisexual experiences, he becomes the aggressor with Arthur. Andy even supports gay marriage—this in the 1960s!

The climax of their relationship comes as a result of taking a trip together to the Canaries. As a result of going to a gay nightclub in Las Palmas, Arthur discovers that one of the heads of his firm has a Spanish boyfriend, a fact accepted by the rest of his business partners. In turn, as a result of their finding out about Arthur, the last obstacle to their asking him to join the firm as a partner is removed. Arthur is left exalting: "Had it really happened? Had he met a boy one day and fallen in love with him, against all the norms of nature and against his own moral code? Had he gone away with boy and had a time unequaled by anything he could recall, even his honeymoon. [...] Had he done all this and returned to find his wife knew, forgave, and even approved? Had he been discovered only to be offered a position and money more than he had ever thought could be his in a lifetime? Had all this happened with the complete acceptance of what he was and what he felt for Andy? Not only that, but with the complete acceptance of Andy? Had all this happened, and didn't anyone care? Yes. Yes. Yes!" (218–19).

As a measure of Arthur's new freedom, an identical scene told in identical language occurs near the beginning and again at the end of the novel. Finding he has a bursting bladder, Arthur makes use of a public facility. He chooses the last urinal and has no more started to use it than he becomes aware that someone has moved into the adjoining stall. "He glanced at the person next to him. It was a boy in a white raincoat. To Arthur's amazement, he found himself looking to an enormous grin." Arthur looks away, then back again: "There was the boy as bold as brass standing with his penis in his hand and caressing it. The boy looked at Arthur and winked" (10). The first time Arthur buttons up and flees. The second time, "Arthur glanced around, gulping. There was no one else in that corner of the toilet. He put out his hand quickly, grasping the boy's penis" (219–20). And with that they adjourn to a toilet cubicle, where Arthur sucks off the youth.

Christopher Royston George Ellis (1941–) was born in Middlesex. He alternated between manual labor, working in the film industry, reviewing, and writing. He was associated with the American Beat movement and befriended the Beatles before they became famous. He has lived mostly outside England: Berlin, Moscow, Canary Islands, Maldives, Dominica, and, since 1980, Sri Lanka. An earlier novel, *The Flesh Merchants*, 1966, is a comedy recounting the way an enterprising young (and straight) Englishman, Klin Xavier Dunbar, sets himself up as the go-between for a gang of Canary Island beach hustlers and the men and women tourists who wish to avail themselves of their services. Ellis now writes mostly travel guides.

Ellis, Royston. *The Flesh Merchants*. London: Anthony Gibbs, 1966.
_____. *The Rush at the End*. London: Tandem, 1967
Moor, George. *Fox Gold, Nightingale Island, Bowl of Roses*. London: Calder, 1978. 137–76.
_____. *The Heat of the Sun. New Writing and Writers 13*. London: Calder, 1976. 147–95.
_____. *The Pole and the Whistle*. London: Four Square, 1966.

89 Leonard Cohen: *Beautiful Losers*, 1966. Scott Symons: *Combat Journal of Place d'Armes*, 1967.

Two post-modern novels created something of a national scandal when they appeared in Canada in the mid–1960s. They share many similarities. Their overt sexuality and explicit language mark a new freedom for Canadian authors. Both play fictional games with their readers. Both have Anglophone protagonists in Francophone Quebec. Both are trying to understand what it means to be Canadian, *Beautiful Losers* looking to the country's Native American heritage, *Place d'Armes* to its French heritage in their search for definition. Both seem to see personal identity, and thus sexual identity, as fluid—though one of Symons's characters does complain that people always ask "'what do you do?' […] Always 'what are you?' Never 'who?'" (59). Both seem ambivalent about what (or who) it means to be homosexual. In short, both books are for readers who relish intellectual games, but are tough slogging for someone looking for insight (or *insite*, as Symonds would have it) into gay identity.

Beautiful Losers consists of three parts. The first, which takes up a bit more than half the novel, is a first-person narration by an unnamed folklorist. He is an authority on an almost extinct Native American people, one of whom, Edith, he has married. The second part is a letter written by his best friend and sex buddy, a male politician known only as F. The third, very short part is "An Epilogue in the Third Person." The novel opens as a meditation on the late seventeenth century Native American saint Catherine Tekakwitha. It becomes a *tour de force* about the triangular relationship between Edith and the two men, severed when she kills herself in a bizarre manner. It sometimes evolves into a madcap narrative about the men's friendship and their explicitly described sexual play: "filthy activities" by "fairies" (84), mostly lots of mutual masturbation, at its funniest when F. tries to link the little death with the big one in a staged car wreck. In his letter, however, F. does describe their "queer love" in more noble terms: "I was your mystery, and you were my mystery, and we rejoiced to learn that mystery was our home. Our love cannot die" (136). Despite its homosexual acts, however, *Beautiful Losers* is not a gay novel. A *queer* novel, yes. The unnamed narrator insists, "Homosexuality is a name" (21). His statement seems to define it as simply an empty label, not a meaningful act or an orientation. The same could be said for all the other sexual possibilities in the novel.

Despite its title being listed in full as *Combat Journal for Place d'Armes: A Personal Narrative*, Symons, as well as critics, consistently referred to it as simply *Place d'Armes*. Its narrative structure is far more complex. Covering a period of slightly more than three weeks, it is the record of Hugh Anderson's abandonment of his Toronto wife and two children to go to Montreal and come to terms with the multiple aspects of himself, to find his "assoul," by writing a novel about a character named Andrew Harrison, a novelist whom it turns out has come to Montreal to write a novel about a character named Hugh Anderson. We are given their diaries, notes, Combat Journals, novels, all in different typefaces, though it ultimately makes little difference as author and characters merge into one. In his introduction to a posthumous reprint (16), Christopher Elson describes the original publication: "*Place d'Armes* was published in hardback in a format that reflected the nineteenth-century journal used by Anderson in the story, including jacket pockets containing marked-up maps, postcards, et cetera. There is a page at the end that is simply the reproduction of a notebook page with phone numbers, appointments, notes, and lists. Stan Bevington of Coach House Press designed the book and contributed immensely to its originality."

Unlike Cohen's novel, *Place d'Armes* is a gay novel. Symons evokes homosexual acts as a means for penetrating knowledge. Two of the more powerful scenes detail encounters with other men: Andrew's with Yvon and Pierrot, two teenage prostitutes, on Day Two and Hugh's with André Germain, a "blond beatlenik" (319), on Day Nineteen. Yet already the narrator has declared that "it is not the homosexual I want ... it is the sentient man. A new kind of man. The man who thinks at the end of his fingertips. Like the homos. And to this end I am prepared to take some cue from them ... just as I am prepared to admire and respect them for their dedication. Their dedication to Heaven, and their witness of Hell. And take some cue from them the way I take some cue from the heteros; or from the neuters—the professors, priests, psychiatrists. But I no more want to be mere homosexual than mere heterosexual" (301). Terry Goldie (*Pink Snow*, 114) records that the novel's publication was a *cause célèbre*. And then, "after all the furor, the novel almost disappeared. Unlike other controversial texts, such as Leonard Cohen's *Beautiful Losers*, it was not considered to be emblematic of the disruptions of the 1960s or even of the flamboyant directions nationalism took at the time of the Canadian centennial." Goldie ponders whether the neglect stemmed from Symons's "overt homosexuality," his status soon thereafter as an expatriate, "or because, even in comparison to *Beautiful Losers*, the novel was just too weird." He concludes that, as of the time of his writing, it remained "definitely outside the canon."

Better known as a singer, songwriter, and poet, Leonard Norman Cohen (1934–) was born in the Westmount quarter of Montreal. He graduated from McGill University. The father of two children, he has never married, though living for long periods with four different women. He has spent much time on the Greek island of Hydra. Hugh Brennan Scott Symons (1933–2009) was born in Toronto in an established and culturally important Canadian family. He was educated at the University of Toronto, Cambridge, and the Sorbonne. He worked as a curator at the Royal Ontario Museum as well as the Smithsonian in Washington. He married and had a son. Divorced, he began living with John McConnell. After they broke up, he lived for a time in Mexico and then Morocco with Aaron Klokeid. These experiences led to his writing *Helmet of Flesh*, 1986. He returned alone to Toronto in 2000, where he died in a continuing care facility.

Cohen, Leonard. *Beautiful Losers*. New York: Viking, 1966. London: Cape, 1970. *Toronto: McClelland & Stewart (First Emblem), 2003.

Symons, Scott. *Combat Journal of Place d'Armes: A Personal Narrative*. Toronto: McClelland & Stewart, 1967. *Intro. Christopher Elson. Toronto: Dundurn (Voyageur Classic), 2010.

90 David Griffin (Robin Maugham): *The Wrong People*, 1967. Robin Maugham: *The Link*, 1969; *The Last Encounter*, 1972; *The Deserters*, 1981.

Peter Burton, in notes to an interview (*The Boy from Beirut*, 128), proposes that "Robin Maugham's literary career falls conveniently into three phases." The first period he dates as roughly the years between 1943 and 1950, with *The Servant*, 1949, being the best known. The second period Burton labels "the pre–*The Wrong People*" or "the pre-homosexual period," dating it from 1950 to 1970 by ignoring that this novel had first appeared under a pseudonym in 1967. He lists *The Second Window*, 1968, whose major gay character seems to have invented much of his story, as the culminating novel from this middle period. The third period Burton calls "the post-*The Wrong People*" or "overtly-homosexual" phase, dating its beginning from Maugham's republication and acknowledgment of his authorship of that pivotal novel. No one of the homosexuals in these novels, until the very last one (a German), is at ease with his sexuality.

The Wrong People actually dates from 1958. Burton notes (135–36), "Maugham had already used homosexual characters in several of his novels, notably in *Behind the Mirror*, 1955, but *The Wrong People* was his first wholly homosexual novel." He showed it to various friends, including Michael Davidson and Harold Nicolson, and to his uncle, Somerset Maugham; they all advised against publication. However, he could not let go of it, and in 1967 he published it with an American pulp paperback press under the pseudonym David Griffin. The novel was translated into German in 1969 under his own name. The next year Heinemann brought it out in somewhat revised form, to find they had a best-seller. Maugham dramatized the novel in 1970, but the play was apparently never performed. Sal Mineo hoped to bring out a film version, one with a happy ending, but that project ended with his murder in 1976.

It is a chilling tale. Ewing Baird, a wealthy English expatriate living in Tangier, meets a repressed vacationing English schoolmaster in a gay bar. Arnold Turner teaches in a school for youth who have run afoul of the law. Realizing that he may be a means for achieving his own desire, Ewing begins an elaborate game of manipulation that comes perilously close to undermining Arnold's moral integrity. Recognizing that the two share an interest in teenage boys, Ewing introduces a fourteen-year-old Berber into Arnold's bed and then uses him as bait to convince Arnold to return to his school and talk a vulnerable thirteen-year-old student there to run away and join Ewing in Tangier. At the last moment Arnold's sense of responsibility leads him to thwart Ewing's plan even though he realizes it means prison time for him. Various other homosexual characters have their roles in the story, most prominently Tim Deakin, Ewing's former lover who could take his niggling instruction no longer and left him, and Jack Stobart, a vicious schoolmaster who, Arnold discovers, has raped the boy he has selected to become Ewing's protégé. At the end Ewing is sitting alone in the same bar on the lookout for a new victim. The irony is, as the barman has already observed to Arnold, "he passionately resents the fact that he's a queer. You see, at heart Ewing's deeply conventional" (185).

The Link: A Victorian Mystery is, as its subtitle suggests, a historical novel inspired by the Tichborne case. The heir to an English baronetcy, Roger Tichborne, presumably died in a shipwreck in 1854, but in 1866 an Australian claimant came forward. In 1874 a court dismissed his claims and sentenced him to prison for perjury. Maugham uses multiple narrators for his improvisation on the case. We begin by following James Steede, the heir in the novel, from his brutal prep school through Eton to Cambridge, witnessing his growing awareness of his sexuality and increasing discord with his possessive mother. After she prevents a marriage that he feels offers him his only chance at following a heterosexual life, he flees the country. Changing his name to Jimmy Smith, he takes a ship bound for Mexico, where he meets a sailor named Clint. After a series of adventures he eventually lands in Australia and into a doomed sexual and business relationship with the man. Later, Ben Ashby, an Englishman who has become intrigued by rumors that he and Jimmy share an uncanny resemblance, shows up; he turns out to be Jimmy's illegitimate half-brother. Dying, Jimmy wants Ben to return to London in his guise and claim the estate. That scheme (which occupies half the novel) fails. Ben's last words to the mother, rather enigmatic in the context, are,

"You weren't the only one that loved him" (283).

The Last Encounter is another historical novel, about the last weeks of General Charles Gordon's life and his death at Khartoum in the Sudan. It takes the form of his lost journal detailing the days from December 14, 1884, to January 26, 1885, in which he also reminisces about the events in his life that have brought him to this moment. In the entry for January 16 the virginal general finally confronts his long fight to resist the temptation of adolescent boys and asks himself, "Can this be what it has all been about? Did I come out here to Khartoum only because I was yearning for death, but was afraid of accepting my nature and because I was afraid of committing the crime before God of killing myself?" (103). At the last moment a final temptation shows up in the figure of the hero-worshiping youth Trooper Willie Warren, who is only too ready to offer his body to the man. The general resists and instead welcomes the final encounter with death. Though begging the boy to destroy it, one of his final acts is to give Willie his journal and to help him escape the besieged fort. Sick of the world's hypocrisy, Willie guards it, however, and leaves it to his heirs. The imaginary editor of the book sums up its moral: "denial *or* indulgence can make the whole difference to a man's life and—in the General's case—to the fate of a whole country" (145).

In a note (157), the author remarks that the germ for the novel *The Deserters* came from an incident that happened to him during the desert campaign of World War II. He first worked it out in dramatic form in a play titled *Enemies*, the name used for the U.S. edition of the novel. The play premiered in 1969. Peter Burton persuaded him to turn it into what became his last novel. It tells the story of an encounter between two stranded soldiers, the English driver Ken Preston and the German gunner Paul Seidler. As they talk, they gradually become friends. Ken is straight, but Paul was the lover of a German actor who, seized by the Nazis, died in a concentration camp. He is clearly now falling in love with Ken. The latter blurts out, almost in sorrow, "you and me ... we're on different tracks" (127), but he accepts Paul's simple declaration, "Maybe we are on different tracks. But the tracks can still run side by side" (133). When a jeep shows up with a jingoist English officer , Ken attempts to hide Paul, but the officer kills the German. Throughout the novel Maugham attacks the excesses of patriotism and xenophobia. Paul's lover has said, "Men and women who are different from the mass of the population are viewed as an enemy; they are looked upon as deserters from the community at large" (104). To Ken's honor, he proves capable of respecting difference.

Robert Cecil Romer Maugham (1916–1981) was born in London. His father, Viscount Maugham of Hartfield, served briefly as Lord Chancellor. He was educated at Eton and Cambridge. Maugham served in North Africa during World War II, before receiving a head wound. He published his autobiography, *Escape from the Shadows*, 1973, and followed that with an account of his travels, *Search for Nirvana*, 1975. He died in Brighton after a long illness.

Maugham, Robin. *The Boy from Beirut, and Other Stories*. Ed. Peter Burton. San Francisco: Gay Sunshine, 1982.
———. *The Deserters*. London: Kimber, 1981. *Enemy*. San Francisco: Gay Sunshine, 1983.
———. *The Last Encounter*. London: Allen, 1972. *New York: McGraw-Hill, 1973.
———. *The Link: A Victorian Mystery*. London: Heinemann, 1969. *New York: McGraw-Hill, 1969.
[———.] *The Wrong People* by David Griffin. New York: Paperback Library, 1967. Intro. Cyril Connolly. London: Heinemann, 1970. Without intro. New York: McGraw-Hill, 1971. *Intro. Peter Burton. London: GMP, 1986.

91 Michael Campbell: *Lord Dismiss Us*, 1967.

A new headmaster, Philip Crabtree, accompanied by his wife and his seventeen-year-old daughter, arrives at Weatherhill school with the mission to bring it out of the slump it has fallen into. That mission soon encompasses also stamping out "moral laxity" (143). Even some of the faculty have come to agree that the school has become "an emotional hothouse" (235). But when the head announces his campaign, the French master asks, "What do you propose [...]. Castration?" (144). Certainly a lot of handholding, much kissing, and some mutual masturbation are taking place, at times practically in public view. Crabtree appoints the school physician, the aptly named Dr. Boucher, to root out the offenders. Four students are dismissed. In a final confrontation between Boucher and the school chaplain, the chaplain says, "I am fully acquainted with your morality. You may well have destroyed four young lives" (358).

Eric Ashley, the French master, is a product of the school, an aspiring literary critic much marked by Forster, Yeats, and Eliot. Doomed from the beginning, he is frustrated in both his scholarly life—having failed to get an appointment he had counted on at Cambridge—and his emotional life—unable to get over an adolescent attraction he had to another Weatherhill boy, who has married and gone into the ministry. Ashley is the only one to stand up to Crabtree when he becomes tyrannical; he is the only one to come to the defense of two teenagers set upon by the student body with the full complicity of the headmaster. And yet he is incapable of understanding himself: "How is it that I find myself empty, perverted, without hope, dead inside, dark inside ... with that sense of futility near to panic?" (327). For all his defiance, he does not even seem comfortable with his sexuality. He sets himself up for further failure by falling in love with a graduating student, six years his junior. This is Terry Carleton, who aspires to be a writer and begs Eric's help with a short story he has written. Terry is also wrestling with the link between profane and sacred love. He accepts a wank (136–37) from his fellow altar boy with whom he has "been conducting a humorous flirtation" and who "neither encouraged or dissuaded" him (60), but he is dismayed when he has an involuntary ejaculation while cuddling the boy he is in love with (319–20)—to such a degree that he sends the younger Nicky Allen the wrong signals so that Allen cuts off their relationship for good. Just as Carleton tries to cope with what he has inadvertently done, Ashley unfortunately declares, "I love you" (331). For Carleton, Ashley is his teacher, his creative writing mentor whom he looks up to, and to have him suddenly transformed into a sexual creature is too much. What saves Carleton is his self-acceptance that he is a writer.

At one point, Ashley's mother says, "There's something I never dared ask *you*. Are some of these children as romantic, to put it politely, as one reads in books?" Ashley answers, "More so than in any of the books I've read" (246–47). The novel is a serious examination of the nature of adolescent love, including its relationship to the physical, and the possible link between sexuality and creativity. There is much more going on, however, than love and sex in the novel. There are, as always, cricket, lessons, choir practice, a disastrous visit from a nearby girls' school, and the end of the school year play. There are the foibles of the faculty, the machinations of the Crabtree daughter, and the incredible kleptomaniac activities of young Gower. Though often called "the fiend," he is more a Loki-like character (possessing "the largest organ than anyone had ever seen" [30]). Not only stealing but sometimes craftily revealing matters others want hidden, he serves at times as a plot device. Though probably no more complex than other school novels, *Lord Dismiss Us* is infinitely more complicated than most, having constantly shifting points of view. Students' names are dropped—nearly forty, the last one only a few pages from the end of the novel—the majority never appearing a second time. Masters are referred to by both their real names and their nicknames. Yet if one doesn't worry about trying to keep everyone straight, the novel can sweep the reader along. It is by turns satirical, savage, sentimental, and hilarious. Dirk Bogarde hoped to bring out a film version, but Lindsay Anderson's *If...* preempted the project.

Michael Mussen Campbell, Fourth Baron Glenavy (1924–1984), was from Dublin, the brother of the humorist Patrick Campbell. He attended St. Columba and Trinity College. He served briefly as a lawyer and worked for a time for the *Irish Times* in London. He published five other novels; *Nothing Doing*, 1970, in particular has strong gay interest.

Campbell, Michael. *Lord Dismiss Us*. London: Heinemann, 1967. *New York: Putnam's, 1968.

92   Christopher Dilke: *The Rotten Apple*, 1968.

Godsell School, founded in the early years of Victoria's reign, lies at the edge of town. Its moral code has remained little changed since then. Behind it on the Downs is the prehistoric chalk carving of an imposing white horse. At one time the image sported a huge phallus, but school officials, deeming such to be offensive, covered over the offending member with turf. Before the end of the novel the figure will once again display its rampant glory to the world. In the words of one of the characters, a psychiatrist, its restored "message is that we shouldn't allow ourselves to be cheated out of our fun, whatever sort of fun it may be" (206).

The discovery of two students in bed together, Tony Picton and Philip Mallaby, sets the chain of events into motion that will lead to this restoration, as well as to major changes in the lives of faculty members and a few students. The Webb house matron, Joan Harrington, seems to have a vendetta against homosexuals. (Late in the novel we find out that her husband was arrested "for some business in Leicester Square" and "decided to skip the country" [170].) Tony is one of the three boys that the housemaster, Rodney Webb, had decided to appoint as house monitors to fill vacancies. According to school rules, he should report Tony, who would then be expelled. Holding more progressive views (homosexual acts between consenting adults have just been decriminalized in England), he decides to say nothing to the morally hidebound headmaster, Cecil Dormer-Wills, and to stick with the appointment, only demanding that Tony and Philip have no repeat encounters. Tony warns him that he is "making a mistake" (37). Heterosexual actions on the part of the other two appointees cause complications. Webb catches Gavin McBain and Frank Pooley when they sneak out to be with two girls and, inconsistently, reports them to Dormer-Wills. Frank defends their transgressions as perfectly normal and protests that when homosexuals are "discovered nothing's done about it and it's all hushed up" (52). Homophobic to the point where some connected to Godsell wonder if he is a closet case, Dormer-Will seizes on his statement and sets forth his position: "Boys in school are like apples in a basket. If one goes rotten, it infects the others unless it's immediately removed and thrown away as rubbish" (53). He is already on the scent: "His phrase about the rotten apple in the basket had not been employed in the abstract. He had a particular fruit in his mind's eye" (56).

Joan Harrington ingeniously and maliciously reports that Tony and Philip have been together again, and Dormer-Wills and Webb head into a career-changing showdown, which takes up most of the novel. As a result of the clash, the gamut of British thought about homosexuality at the time is aired, without a dialectic ever quite developing. Home for the Christmas holiday, in response to his mother's remarking on Webb's report that her son should try to overcome his "weaknesses," Tony sums up: "Yes, and the Headmaster would like to flog them out of me. Neither of them can see that I'm just what I am. They want to justify their wretched systems, whether they're liberals like Rodney Webb or fundamentalists like old Dormer-Wills." The mother replies, "I don't want to prove any system, Tony. I want you to be happy, if that's possible" (131). And she invites Philip to spend the holiday with them, but she and Tony concur that he is just too boring and pack him back to the Midlands.

Christopher Wentworth Dilke (1913–1987) was educated at Winchester and Cambridge, without taking a degree. He worked in journalism and publishing. During World War II he served as lieutenant colonel in the Royal Artillery. Immediately after the war he was assigned the task of creating a democratic press in Germany. He worked for BBC and also wrote film scripts. Married, he had four children.

Dilke, Christopher. *The Rotten Apple*. London: Macdonald, 1968. *London: Pan, 1971.

93   Angus Stewart: *Sandel*, 1968.

Critics have compared *Sandel* with Roger Peyrefitte's *Les amitiés particulières*, 1944. One of the characters in *Sandel* even owns a copy (as well as one of Peyrefitte's notorious 1955 attack on the pope as a closet case). The rather manipulative fourteen-year-old protagonist of Peyrefitte's novel becomes infatuated with a younger student at their Catholic boarding school. When his attentions are not returned in kind, he starts "a special friendship" with a twelve-year-old. A priest intervenes to end the amorous but nonsexual relationship, with the result that the younger boy kills himself. The oft comical *Sandel* can be seen as a corrective to the very earnest and tragic French novel. Book One serves as prologue, recounting incidents from David Rogers's life between eight and seventeen. He is attracted to a series of boys at his public school; contact with one of them provokes a spontaneous ejaculation while fully dressed. He develops a special crush on fourteen-year-old Peter Greaves, whom the school's "Thought-police" arrest for a "routine admonishing" (22–23). Much later in the novel the reader discovers that Peter has died (132) and, even later, that it was, as in Peyrefitte's novel, suicide (159, 199). At the same time, we meet David's oldest friend, Bruce Lang, later to become a converted Catholic, who serves throughout the novel as David's moral conscience. He will try to reason with David, accusing him of trying to resurrect Peter by falling for another boy, but when David persists, unlike the French priest, Bruce reluctantly aids his pursuit.

Book Two recounts David's ardent relationship with Antony Sandel. David is now a nineteen-year-old student at Oxford, and Tony is a prepubescent thirteen-year-old member of the chapel choir. Gifted with an extraordinarily pure voice and a range from soprano through most of alto, he is sought out by a recording company for a solo album. In this case the younger boy is the manipulative one. He maneuvers to seduce David, unafraid to use his physical allure. He voluntarily strips naked for a photography session (121) and invites David into the bathroom when he bathes (184). His voice becomes an added enticement, since David is an amateur composer. At one point, he asks David for the definition of *homosexual* and *pederast* and then asks, "What's the *specific* term for a boy who loves a man?" (109–11). Though sometimes wise beyond his years, Tony is essentially a naive youth, about whom David refrains from being judgmental.

Two accidents, both involving engine oil, rather bizarrely punctuate the narrative. The first occurs when David engages in an illegal car race. The car in front of him throws a connecting rod through the crankcase and floods the ground with oil. David's car skids and overturns, breaking David's back and sending him into a coma. He regains consciousness over ten weeks later to find he has been dismissed from Oxford for infraction of rules. He becomes a teacher at Tony's school, displaying a natural flair for being able to reach the boys. His posing as Tony's half-brother, the rest of the world sees their affectionate relationship as natural. Under this guise they take various excursions together, go shopping for clothes. Even the headmaster's wife, the only thoroughly unlikeable person in the novel, in maneuvering to get rid of David, misses the obvious and believes that he is using Tony's room to have an affair with a school matron, forcing the boy to sleep in David's bed. The truth, of course, is that he and Tony finally begin sharing a bed. Bruce insinuates that there must be a sexual component to the friendship. David tells him: "There was one night. There couldn't not have been ... I see that now ... But not since then [...]. It was simply premature" (232). He never apologizes for his feelings and, to his surprise, finds that Tony's guardian aunt thoroughly approves of their involvement (153–54). Still, he and to a lesser extent Tony are aware of society's condemnation even as the nation wrestles with the Wolfenden Report. (The novel is apparently set in 1960). Yet the author makes no special pleading. In fact, David contemns another teacher for being a pansy: "Flirting with young boys the way Wallace did was indeed pathetic" (219).

A series of Tony's actions precipitate the beginning of the end of the affair. It turns out that he has connived for David to be dismissed from his job so that they can leave school together. He voices too much feeling for David during an interview with two journalists about the release of his record album. (Tellingly, the first thought to cross Bruce's mind is not moral rectitude but the danger of blackmail.) The two, with the aunt's blessing, prepare to depart for Italy. But when the journalists reappear at the airport, Tony pulls away, and the second accident occurs, with consequences. He slips on a patch of oil and breaks his leg. David succumbs to an attack of unexplained hysteria, and three days later departs for Spain to enroll in a goldsmithing course. Book Three functions as an epilogue. David visits Tony at his public school. He learns that Tony's pubic hair has begun to grow and that he is contemplating experimenting sexually with one of the maids. But the boy affirms, "I still love you [...]. One night I'll let you do what you want to me. All right?" (255). The declaration is followed by an unsatisfactory kiss, and David departs: "He was alone now. Nothing dramatic. And perhaps only for a bit" (256). To the end, the beloved, in his eyes, has done no wrong.

Angus John Mackintosh Stewart (1936–1998) was born in Adelaide, Australia, the son of the Scot-born J. I. M. Stewart. The family moved to Belfast in 1946, when the father became a professor there, and then to Oxford in 1949, when he became a fellow of Christ Church. Young Stewart spent long periods of time in Morocco. His second novel, *Snow in Harvest*, 1969, recounts the collisions of various Europeans and Arabs in Tangier, many of whom turn out to be secret agents for both sides in the Cold War. It has some gay interest. This was followed in 1972 by a collection of verse and by a memoir, *Tangier: A Writer's Notebook*, which offers brief portraits of other gay expatriate writers there. Stewart published no further works.

His father, John Innes Mackintosh Stewart (1906–1994), has a number of novels, rather Jamesian in style, of marginal interest in a survey of gay fiction. In *An Acre of Grass*, 1965, friends conspire to protect an author's widow from discovering that his last novel fictionalized his early attraction to other men, including her deceased brother, only to discover that she already knows what is in it. In *Avery's Mission*, 1971, an art expert's "kept boy" turns out to be his illegitimate son, and everyone is heterosexual after all (though the unmarried narrator may be suspect). Two friends in *Mungo's Dream*, 1973, engage in a nude wrestling match, comparing their sport afterwards to the scene in *Women in Love*. Stewart also wrote crime fiction under the name Michael Innes. Some of these works, Anthony Slide writes in his survey of mystery novels (96), reveal "a curious fascination with the male body, innocent yet suggestive." After his wife's death in 1979, his son Angus moved into an annex to his home in Oxfordshire.

Kauffmann, Walt. "Discovering Angus Stewart (1936–1998)," with a follow-up by Alexei Delaine (online).
Stewart, Angus. *Sandel*. London: Hutchinson, 1968.
———. *Snow in Harvest*. London: Hutchinson, 1969.

94 Maurice Capitanchik: *Joseph*, **1968. Andrew McCall:** *The Au Pair Boy*, **1968. Richard Green:** *Street Boy, Swinging London*, **1972. Peter Kortner:** *Breakfast with a Stranger*, **1975.**

Bisexual authors and characters pop up regularly in British letters. Sometimes the character's sexual nature is of no importance to the plot; sometimes, as with these four novels, it drives the action and precipitates the crisis. Before the end, each bisexual protagonist is forced to choose between heterosexuality or homosexuality. In only one cases does he opt for homosexuality as his norm. Of the four protagonists, intriguingly enough, the male prostitute comes across as the most likeable and the most honest (and the only one who continues to be somewhat bi).

Joseph Ashley, in the first-person narrative *Joseph*, alternates serially between sex with men and women. While at school at age sixteen, he falls in love with Ted and has his first sexual experience. At the art school where he is a model, he falls in love with a female student, Anna. His experience with her leads him to reflect, "I did not feel that there is anything innately desirable about heterosexuality as such, but I benefited from it" by becoming "one of the sexual majority" (20). Their relationship lasts until he meets the male impresario Dachs, who stirs him "to an extraordinary pitch of passion, resentment, desire, almost fury" (29) and who launches his career as a writer. Their life together lasts until another female artist, Maggie, falls for Joseph. The two brave Dachs's anger and marry. But soon Joseph begins to "feel hemmed in by her, trapped" (69), and the strain threatens their marriage. Maggie tries to make him jealous by inviting an old flame, Tom, to share their former bed. On his side of the house Joseph throws himself into writing his latest novel, as he feels a growing attraction to Tom. After much vacillation, during which most of Joseph's mental arguments favor homosexuality, along with many fights with Maggie and her mother and an appeal from a dying Dachs, Joseph confesses, "I'm in love with her—and with you, Tom [...], but I've chosen her" (154). The novel begins with Joseph's looking back on the story he is about to tell: "I do not regret anything, except that we should not be allowed, or allow others or ourselves, to live openly and freely according to our natures, to live spontaneously, as only man is able, and as only he refuses to do" (9).

Jacques Deschamps, the au pair boy of the title, is essentially a gigolo, most of whose experiences are with women. Born in Cahors, France, he is hired by a London couple, the Framptons and quickly becomes the wife's lover. Through a series of turns, she cuts him off, and he comes under the influence of Daniel Last, whose lover has to flee England when his affair on the side turns out to be only nineteen. (Even after the decriminalization of same-sex relations, the age of consent was defined as twenty-one.) Although Jacques and Daniel never have sex, Jacques does permit himself to become part of a sexual tangle at an all-male orgy. Victoria Turnbull, a teenager whose enormously wealthy father opposes their union because of Jacques's family, pursues him. After the father hires thugs to beat up Jacques, Victoria blackmails him into letting her have her way. Poor Jacques tries to assert some measure of independence, to no avail: "Once again, he had allowed events to take charge of him" (252). The novel ends with him a virtual prisoner of his wife and his in-laws.

Street Boy, Swinging London is presented as a memoir, but the work uses all the tricks of fiction to tell the story. Richard acknowledges several men who come to mean a great deal to him emotionally, but he insists that "this does not mean that I was queer, homosexual, for I was not. Perhaps I was and still am bi-sexual" (19). He has his first sexual encounters with schoolmates, a teacher, and a man at a nude beach while growing up close to the Welch border. He also falls in love with a local girl. In London, under the tutelage of one of his mates, he becomes a successful prostitute. He takes pride that he has "helped people, helped men that had all sorts of tensions and conditions which could only be relieved by sexual stimulation" (74). Among his many faithful clients is a peer of the realm; another is a literary agent. One of the most touching scenes is his introduction of two young men from rural England to gay sex (Chapter 8). Because of his good heart, he becomes heir to the literary agent, he makes a success in a new job selling accident insurance, and he becomes a serious painter. In the end he marries his girlfriend, though he does not entirely give up going with boys. "Did we live happy ever after," he asks, and he answers, "not quite, but almost" (149). In its contents (and typos), though not its physical appearance, the work is virtually indistinguishable from the novels being published by American erotic publishing houses at the same time, right down to having a foreword by a "psychologist" to inform us about the work's social value.

In *Breakfast with a Stranger* forty-eight-year-old Kurt Heller, a self-absorbed cad and former Hollywood television producer, has fled the American scene to live in London. After five years of living with Dennis, his British lover, he leaps, one weekend, into an affair with the twenty-two-year-old Nancy Williams while her husband is in Brussels and Dennis is visiting his mother. It is Kurt's first heterosexual experience, and he becomes obsessed with the relationship. All the while he is also remembering his discovery of his sexuality and its promiscuous evolution to this point, so that as much of the novel is set in the past as in the present. The reader has the legitimate expectation that the two plotlines will come together in some sort of epiphany. Instead we get a kind of pseudo-insight on Kurt's part as the result of a literal fall down the side of a cliff and greater understanding on Dennis's part even as he remains ignorant of Kurt's and Nancy's adulteries. The heterosexual couple splits up; the homosexual couple will probably remain together because of Dennis, of whom we see far too little.

Joseph was Maurice Capitanchik's only novel. He was a book reviewer, primarily for *The Spectator*. Otherwise, I can find nothing about him. Nor can I locate any information about Richard Green (or the psychologist who wrote the introduction). Peter Kortner (1924–1991) was born in Berlin, the son of Austrian actors Fritz Kortner and Johanna Hofer. The family fled Germany in 1933. He served in the U.S. Army during the war, becoming an American citizen, and then attended UCLA. He was a television writer and producer. He spent the years 1966–75 in London. His other two novels are both set in Hollywood. Kortner died in Sonoma, California. Andrew McCall (1941–) was born in Penang, Malaya, from which his family fled to New Zealand just weeks after his birth. He attended Cambridge. For fourteen years the publisher Anthony Blond was his lover. After they split up, he formed a liaison with Simon Raven, until 1984. He appeared in the film *Blueblood*, 1973. He is now remembered chiefly for his cultural history, *The Medieval Underworld*, 1979, but McCall admitted to Raven's biographer, Michael Barber (208), that he really "didn't enjoy writing."

Capitanchik, Maurice. *Joseph*. London: Olive, 1968.
**Friends and Lovers*. London: Sphere, 1971.
Green, Richard. *Street Boy, Swinging London*. Intro. Laurence Ray [Lawrence Ray, on cover]. London: Silver, 1972.
Kortner, Peter. *Breakfast with a Stranger*. London: Allen, 1975. *New York: St. Martin's, 1975.
McCall, Andrew. *The Au Pair Boy*. London: Blond, 1968. *The French Boy. New York: Putnam's, 1969.

95   Charles Dyer: *Staircase*, 1969.

In Charles Dyer's novel *Staircase, or Charlie Always Told Harry Almost Everything*, Charles Dyer and Harry C. Leeds, both now in their late sixties, have lived together for thirty years. Charlie used to be an actor in pantomime. They met when Charlie rented a room from Harry's mother. Then he disappeared for two years (having been sentenced under the Criminal Law Amendment Act, we later learn), to return and offer to help Harry in his barbershop. They moved in together to share a bed. A crisis arose when suddenly all of Harry's hair fell out. But mostly the two men have tended to their business, looked after their aged mothers, and camped it up. At least, until now. Charlie has been arrested and is to be tried for solicitation while dressed as a woman outside the nearby cemetery. For the rest of the novel he worries about what will happen to him and plots how to defend himself against the charges. He is also in search of his father, whom he thinks he has never known, but it turns out that his mother's brother is both uncle and dad. Harry is the one who points out that Charlie's search for identity is intertwined in a bit of metafictional play. Protagonist and author have the same name. But then Harry C. Leeds is an anagram for Charles Dyer. Does Charlie inhabit a solipsist universe? All this would be more interesting if one could just like Charlie, but he is about as wearisome a character at one can imagine. The novel might be better were it about a third its length.

According to a blurb by Isabel Quigly at the front of the Corgi edition, the novel came before Dyer's 1966 play, even though it was published three years after its premiere—undoubtedly as a tie-in to the release of the film version, with a screenplay by the author. If so, it was revised between manuscript and publication. A policeman is upset with the "consenting Males Law Codswallop," an obvious reference to the decriminalization of same-sex acts in 1967. And there is a reference to Pope Paul's encyclical of 1968 against the use of contraceptives (85). The play has a much tighter structure than the novel; for one thing, it cuts the incest angle altogether. But the character is no more likable. Charles Raymond Dyer (1928–) was born in Shrewsbury. During the war he served in the Royal Air Force. He has been a vaudeville comic, a dramatic actor, a playwright, and a director. Married to an actress, he has three sons.

Dyer, Charles. *Staircase, or Charlie Always Told Harry Almost Everything*. London: Allen, 1969. *Staircase.* New York: Doubleday, 1969. *London: Corgi, 1971.

96 Marc Deschamps: *Homo*, 1969. Jonathan Lynn: *A Proper Man*, 1976.

Two ruthless scam artists—the first of whom is "ambidextrous," the second, straight—abuse a renowned gay artist to the point of his losing everything. But whereas the gay character in the second novel becomes a total victim, at least in the first, he does rise above his misfortune. Reading both books is akin to receiving a punch in the stomach.

In *Homo*, Waldo Emerson, a famous novelist, becomes Alec Smith's prey. Alec dreams of becoming a major figure in world cinema, though he clearly does not have the necessary talent. In his latest attempt to get ahead, the con artist moves in on Waldo, one of whose novels has just been turned into a successful film. Tracking the retiring author to his Italian home, Alec quickly realizes that the married father is gay and sets out to seduce him, quite willing to use his body to achieve his aims. Waldo's wife, his two children, even his cat see that Waldo poses a threat. "This man is a danger, the [local] priest decided sadly. He has *got* to win. He is one of the world's predators, lonely prowlers who must use other people for lack of stable resources of their own" (95). Only Waldo is blind. Before the novel is over Alec has killed the cat, watched the wife drown (in an accidental fall), and wrested Waldo's estate from him. Yet, remarkably, Waldo manages to emerge bloodied but unbeaten: "His reputation, his life, remained intact. [...] He would try to survive, and to work. He had taken a beating, but he was what he was. An old queer. Was that so evil? It was only evil if a felony had been compounded. He had committed a moral felony by turning a blind eye to the wife who loved him, ignored his responsibility to his children. Yes, he had done wrong, made himself a pawn to lust. [...] Somehow, he felt, he would survive" (191–92).

In *A Proper Man*, both George Whyte, a celebrated pianist, and, indirectly, Michael Feather, his lover, are Jim Kinnear's victims. Jim is a sociopath who enjoys inflicting pain, even death, on others. He is just out of prison, after serving ten years at Dartmoor. By happenstance he comes upon George just after his car breaks down and Michael has left to find help. He immediately starts playing games with George—who has always prided himself on being "a proper man"; that is, as masculine as any heterosexual could be, as well as a gentleman, "correct in all his behaviour" (128)—and first excites him by the possibility of "making love," to the point of George's "getting an erection" (161), and then reduces him to "a rabbit mesmerized by a snake" (213), "a hunted fox" who is trapped by his own ego (214). The novel is at base the tragedy, albeit one with loads of melodramatic trappings, of two people who cannot be open and honest with each other. Both George and Michael are at fault, but George must bear the brunt of responsibility. He is older (fifty-nine to Michael's twenty-six) and more powerful because of his wealth and fame. He has also allowed himself to feel vulnerable, to be frightened of being exposed as bent (even though gay liberation has already arrived in England), scared of rejection, egoistic. Unlike Somerset Maugham, whom he met, George is incapable of openly admitting that "I know just where I stand—in the very front rank of the second-raters" (50). The last chapter seems gratuitous, out of character for Michael. Even so, though far from being as fine a novel as *Homo*, it remains a powerful work, not easily forgotten.

Homo is the only novel Marc Deschamps published. It is such an accomplished work that one suspects the name is a pseudonym concealing a known author. A movie version, *A Lick of Cream*, was scheduled for production but was apparently never made. Jonathan Adam Lynn (1943–) was born in Bath. He attended Cambridge. He was an actor, appearing in the first London production of *Fiddler on the Roof*, and a director, most notably for *My Cousin Vinny*, and has written numerous award-winning screenplays and television scripts. Married, he is the father of a son. He now lives in Los Angeles.

Deschamps, Marc. *Homo*. *London: Leslie Frewin, 1969. *A Lick of the Cream*. London: Sphere, 1971.
Lynn, Jonathan. *A Proper Man*. London: Heinemann, 1976.

97 Michael Porcsa: *Under the Brightness of Alien Stars*, 1970.

The novel is so earnest that one sorely wishes it were better written. As it is, it is unbearably painful to read. The blurb on the back of the first edition, presumably written by the author, sums up the novel and illustrates its problems: "Robert Morieau, a self-torturing homosexual is pleading [sic] his Hungarian friend who will lead him to the road of self-acceptance and fulfilment [sic]." The protagonist is an Alberta journalist who goes to Europe. Covering the Hungarian uprising of 1956, Robert rescues young Peter Koltay, who is suffering from amnesia (Robert calls him Paul) and takes him back to Alberta. Peter in turn saves Robert when he tries to kill himself, teaching him finally to think with the heart (229). The novel, understandably, had no impact on gay Canadian letters. Michael Porcsa (dates unknown) was a refugee from the Hungarian uprising of 1956. He came to Canada and settled in Alberta, receiving a degree from the University. He appeared in several theatrical productions during the 1960s. I can learn nothing more about him although this appears to be his real name.

Porcsa, Michael. *Under the Brightness of Alien Stars*. *Montreal: Sans le Sou, 1970. New York: Vantage, 1971.
Young, Ian. Untitled. *The Body Politic*, Aug. 1979 (online).

98 Rupert Croft-Cooke: *Exiles*, 1970.

A comic novel about expatriates in the imaginary North African city of Bentarik, Mangeria, during the 1950s and 1960s, its setting was obviously inspired by Tangier, just as its central character, Miranda Pluck, was patently modeled on Barbara Hutton, the identification made all the more evident by the author's emphatic denial (iv). One would assume that many of the other characters also had real-life models (the noted photographer "Beryl Seaton," for example, being instantly transparent). What plot there is grows out of the machinations of the foreign colony to obtain an in with the rich heiress as she discards one husband or lover for another, all the time lavishly entertaining those who have obtained her favors. It ends with a party planned to outdo all earlier parties, at which she will announce her engagement to a bogus prince. By now, however, she has made enough enemies who manage instead to turn it into a complete and hilarious fiasco.

As is usual with such novels, it has a large cast of characters, several gays prominent among them. There is Tommy Weigall, who "had been one of those noisy and vigorously pleasure-seeking people who inspired Evelyn Waugh's *Vile Bodies*. He had known, and frequently mentioned, Harold Acton, Cyril Connolly, Beverley Nichols, Cecil Beaton, Noël Coward, Daphne Vivian, Nancy Cunard, various Sitwells, Guinnesses, and Tennants, Elizabeth Ponsonby, Brian Howard, Patrick Balfour." We are further told, "His emigration to Mangeria had been made advisable by a pre-war scandal in London but the highly-coloured rumours current about this in Bentarik were to say the least of it exaggerated." Tommy introduces Miranda to the one man who loves her rather than her money: Harry Day, a deserter from the Royal Navy who is "totally irresponsible, amoral and good-natured" (91) and who briefly shares Tommy's home "like a brother" (93). Tommy's chief social rival is Ray Lewin, some people "even suggesting a comparison between the two of them and Miss Mapp and Lucia" (29–30).

Hubert Clayton is another prominent member of the colony: "He had charm of a somewhat sardonic kind and was successful with women but on the whole preferred youths [...], eager male prostitutes who had learned their trade in a hard school" (17). To everyone's surprise, he and George Knight move in together after Hubert saves George from a general arrest made by the local police on the occasion of a mass nude swim: "among the more hardened critics in this town the only aspect of the relationship which attracted any attention was that it seemed to be a lasting one. This was unprecedented" (81). When George's father unexpectedly appears on a mission to rescue his son, having heard rumors that he is behaving in a way that might affect his own personal aura of respectability (165), Hubert takes him on with aplomb, comparing him to the Marquess of Queensberry, criticizing the etymologies of *homosexual* and *sodomite*, and parrying the father's thrust, "To imagine sexual acts between men is horrifying," with the counterthrust, "Isn't the thought of any sexual act pretty repulsive unless it's one own? Like excretion, I mean" (167–69).

Joe Lauder is an American, the owner of one of the two principal bars patronized by the English colony. The women are particularly attracted to his establishment because of the attention he gives them, advising them "how to dress and what jewellery to wear" (83). His closest friend is an eighty-year-old British dowager. But it becomes increasingly obvious that he is closeted. Only in the inner recesses of his home "Joe let himself go with all the camp he concealed elsewhere" (145). He loses his self-confidence when the owner of the rival bar calls him a "big poof" (117) and slides into a decline, dying in his bar of a heart attack. Hubert proves his mettle this evening, all the more noteworthy because no one ever knows what he has done for the dead friend. And there are still other gays. During the 1960s "hoards of shrill young men" descend on the town "because of a certain reputation it had earned in recent years" (162). Then too there are men like the American nicknamed "Ditchwater," who "pursued very small Mangerian boys" (197). Two gays are particularly important to the plot, both of them hired by Miranda. As she says philosophically at one point, "It takes a fruit to understand a girl like me" (58). Martin Gee is "an English interior decorator known as the Reine Blanche" (53) whom Miranda engages to decorate for her engagement party. She likewise brings in Ronald Pipler, "an avant-garde sculptor whose fame rested on a curious pillar of clay called The Erection" (85). After their falling out, his skill at forging handwriting is instrumental in helping destroy her big party. The novel makes a pleasant divertissement.

Rupert Croft-Cooke (1903–1979) was born in Kent. He studied at the Universidad de Buenos Aires, where he founded and edited a weekly, *La Estrella*. He served in the British army during World War II. A prolific writer, including novels, mysteries (written under the name Leo Bruce), histories, biographies (including Wilde and Douglas), and food books, he has over a hundred titles. In 1953 he was arrested for indecency and sentenced to six months in prison. Upon his release, he wrote an account of his ordeal, *The Verdict of You All*, 1955. He spent fifteen years in Morocco and then sojourned in other countries. He died in Bournemouth.

Croft-Cooke, Rupert. *Exiles*. London: Allen, 1970.
Stewart, Angus. *Tangier: A Writer's Notebook*. London: Hutchinson, 1977. Chapter 15.

99 C. J. Bradbury Robinson: *A Crocodile of Choirboys*, 1970; *Bare Knees, Boys Knees*, 1971; *Young Thomas*, 1971; *Arabian Boys*, 1972.

British publishers having turned down Bradbury Robinson's first novel because of its subject matter, it was brought out by Greenleaf Classics, an American publishing house specializing in erotica in its Pleasure Reader series. It sold so well that Greenleaf brought out three more novels. They are all celebrations of pederasty, though the author insists they are moral works. They came to the attention of William Burroughs, who at the time was living close to the author in London. Burroughs volunteered to write an introduction to a fifth novel, *Williams Mix*, and to arrange for Olympia Press to publish it. Before it could be brought out, the press folded, and the galley proof was stashed away, not to appear until forty years later, with revisions of two of the earlier novels. I cannot discover much about Christopher J. Bradbury Robinson (date unknown). He attended Cambridge in the 1960s, where he wrote his first novel. He presently lives in London.

The Greenleaf novels are interconnected literary *tours de force*, postmodern works involving all kinds of narrative play: metafictional games, parody, invective, doubling and tripling of characters, changes of sex, along with much word play and an inventive use of incremental repetition. Within the books, the author acknowledges his stylistic indebtedness to Burroughs and Samuel Beckett, with an occasional mention of Laurence Sterne, Gertrude Stein, and Jean Genet. He cites the novels' predecessors in subject matter: Petronius, Antonio Rocco, Byron, Rimbaud, Forest Reid, Gide, Thomas Mann, Firbank, James Hanley, Peyrefitte, Tony Duvert, Angus Stewart, and, in a bit of metafictional play, C. J. Bradbury Robinson. Such varied writers as Swift, Yeats, Eliot, Pinter, and John Lennon also have a presence, as in a sense does Nabokov, whom he repeatedly denounces, specifically attacking *Lolita*, *Pale Fire*, and *Ada*. Lawrence Durrell also draws his scorn.

A Crocodile of Choirboys describes a day in the lives of three Cambridge males. Steven Maldoror (a nod to Comte de Lautréamont) teaches at the boys' choir school. Stephen is a university undergraduate studying psychology. Stephan is one of the choirboys, a pupil in Steven's class, whom both men lust after. The three go through their usual daily routine. Steven and Stephan are both in classes. Stephen spends time in the university library in the Arcana section (i.e., "sex books"), to which a copy of a book titled *A Crocodile of Choirboys* has been consigned. Interspersed with descriptions of their day are Steven's memories of trips to Morocco in search of boys, horrendous descriptions of sexual assaults on boys culled from books and newspapers the two men read, and various other digressions. Two other characters have roles of some importance. Simon is Stephan's best friend; the two boys play a game of chess and later engage in innocent sex with each other. Deidre, "a female heterosexual paedophile," is the matron; her joking with Stephan about cutting off his foreskin, according to the narrative voice, triggers a castration complex that makes him in later life a full-blown pedophile (147–48). The day ends with Steven taking the boy into bed with him. Depressed, Stephen deliberately overdoses on sodium amytal. Another flashforward tells us that Steven will be sentenced to prison for pederasty but then freed, unrepentant, on a technicality.

Bare Knees, Boy Knees, the second Greenleaf novel, is a wholly different narrative experiment. The protagonist is named Deidre. But everything about her or him is fluid—sexuality, age, profession, location, situation—the only constant being a desire for prepubescent boys. The dominant setting is a New York City mental hospital where Deidre is being treated with LSD (though one of the doctors incongruously refers to Guy Fawkes Day). One could rationalize that great swathes of the novel are her inventions under the influence of the drug. She metamorphoses into a transgendered goth (to use an achromatic label) hanging around gay bars, a Polish witch who procures boys for use by villagers stricken with a venereal disease who believe intercourse with an innocent will cure the malady, an English maid who seduces the boy of the house and then aids the butler in having his way also, an American male sunbather who rapes a young boy who stumbles upon him, a Parisian brothel-keeper who caters to old men's schoolboy fantasies, an English school matron in love with a boy named Stefan, and a French-born proprietor of an American clothing store for children. Cutting across these stories is a memory of a traumatic experience involving her and another boy when she was twelve and he was ten.

The psychiatrists attending Deidre need help as much as she does.

In his preface to *Young Thomas*, its "editor," William Graffiti, tells the reader how he came into possession of the papers of his friend Stephen, who was working on a novel before his death: "The novel, which was to have been called *Little Fingers*, tells of a certain Steven, writer, and his sexual passion for Stefan, the small son of the landlady of his lodgings. Steven is quite clearly the alter ego of Stephen, uncomplicated by moral doubts and inhibitions, less of an intellectual, and Stefan [is] perhaps Thomas in another pose. Who knows? Steven himself is trying to put together a novel called *Little Toes*, about a shy schoolmaster brought into full bloom by a seductive pupil. Both books are intercut with writing from lavatory walls, of which Stephen was an avid collector, and author." Graffiti goes on, "Often it will not be clear whether you are reading Stephen's journal, Thomas's diary, or one of the novels. It matters not. They are all words. And my selection was as random as your understanding will be" (6–7). The novel is a rush of words which the reader must read "as you would listen to the music of Webern" (5). The prep schoolteacher's infatuation with one of his pupils concerns the student's father enough for him to request a meeting. With surprising equanimity, he says, "I'm not making any comment about your character nor am I saying that homosexual relationships can't be happy. I'm not competent to pass an opinion on that, but we are afraid of Tom becoming dependent on you" (94). Therefore, he requests, "I just want you to undertake not to see Thomas along again" (97).

In *Arabian Boys* the authorial voice constantly breaks into the story to ponder the nature of pederasty, including its darkest side as exemplified by Gilles de Rais and Albert Fish. The voice concludes, "The only pornography is the pornography of violence" (163). The story itself follows two Englishmen into the Mideast. The ruler of Arcana, in a fervor of westernization, has decreed homosexuality a crime. In an extended parody of Christ, a new messiah has arisen there, preaching revolution and a return to the acceptance of pederasty. Inspector No, a member of the Scotland Yard vice squad, is invited by the Arcanan government to aid its efforts. He is obsessed with his mission, without realizing what his mania reveals about his own hidden desires: "All bent things obsess the straight, especially those who aren't as straight as they think" (8). After the messiah is crucified, No picks up one of his young followers and takes him back to his hotel: "No's first sexual experience with a small boy had been followed by a massive surge of guilt [that] returned him next day to England, repressed and depressed" (200). Flipping out, "the first conscious manifestation of what was happening inside him was a swelling hatred for all little boys. It was their fault he was feeling like this" (201). He joins a sadistic couple who film their abuse of children. In contrast, the second Englishman, William Graffiti, goes to Perana for the express purpose of finding boys; he remains there, "teaching and happy" (202). Both men keep encountering a book called *Arabian Boys*. Graffiti is the hero of the fifth novel, *Williams Mix*.

Bradbury Robinson, C. J. *Arabian Boys*. San Diego: Greenleaf Classics (Pleasure Reader), 1972.
_____. *Bare Knees, Boys Knees*. San Diego: Greenleaf Classics (Pleasure Reader), 1971.
_____. *A Crocodile of Choirboys*. San Diego: Greenleaf Classics (Pleasure Reader), 1970.
_____. *More Please No More: Williams Mix and Other Writings*. Intro. William Burroughs. London: Out Now, 2011.
_____. *Young Thomas*. San Diego: Greenleaf Classics (Pleasure Reader), 1971.

100 L. P. Hartley: *My Sisters' Keeper*, 1970; *The Harness Room*, 1971.

The Harness Room recounts the emotional and physical attraction between seventeen-year-old Fergus Macready and his father's chauffeur, the twenty-eight-year-old Fred Carrington. It develops while the father is on his honeymoon after his December–May marriage to the twenty-three-year-old Sonia Verriden. The father wants his bookish and rather frail son to follow in his footsteps into the military. To prepare him, he asks the chauffeur to engage Fergus in physical training while they are away. Fred is eager to provide his services. Of him the reader is told at once: "He was bisexual, as he was quite ready to admit; he had had affairs with men and women, boys and girls; he preferred his own sex in these relationships, because it led to less trouble" (5). The garage is a converted stable (the novel seems to be set between the World Wars); Fred has turned the old harness room into a private gym. There they exercise. And there one kind of physical contact leads to another. Fergus for the first time yields to the "happiness of the flesh" when Fred, "with the practical hand and a face suddenly grown grave (for even the smallest introduction to sex is no laughing matter) [...], succumbed to Fergus's fumbling advances" (76).

Though we are never treated to details, the two seem to move into an easy relationship with each other. Their time together will culminate with Fred's recognition that the boy was "perhaps the only human being he had ever really loved" (117). Their happiness is cut short, however. The father and the stepmother return from their honeymoon, and a new but not unexpected motif sounds as the ancient Phaedra archetype once again plays out. The house servants, even Fergus himself, all suspect that the stepmother displays an unnatural affection for the stepson. But in the final analysis it is the father's pigheaded insistence on forcing his son into his own preconceived notion of what the boy should be that indirectly precipitates the catastrophe that destroys his house. The novel is slight, yet it leaves the reader much to mull over, perhaps because of its unfinished quality.

A novel published the year before, *My Sisters' Keeper*, also has gay interest. Basil Hancock feels he should warn his elder sister, Gwendolen, that the man she has chosen to marry, Terry O'Donovan, had repeatedly but unsuccessfully tried to seduce him while they were in school together but had succeeded with other boys. Being the bungler that he is, Basil goes about his self-appointed task all wrong and alienates Gwendolen before he can tell her the truth. Several years into their marriage Terry is caught trying to pick up a teenager in an Earl's Court Road public toilet. Upon talking to Terry, Basil realizes that he was entrapped. With help of one of their former schoolmates, he sets up a rather improbable scheme to entrap the entrappers and pulls it off. The whole plot gimmick does not bear sharp scrutiny.

Leslie Poles Harley (1895–1972) was born in Cambridgeshire. Educated at Harrow and Oxford, his university life was interrupted by World War I service. A social snob, he ran with various literary circles between the wars, but seems to have always been regarded as an outsider. His friend Clifford Kitchin, introduced him to Venice. He was sometimes joined there by the biographer and historian David Cecil. Francis King in his memoirs (203), wondered, "If Leslie had not been so nervous about his homosexuality and so desperate to conceal it, would his novels have been better or worse? I suspect that they would have been worse, since it was precisely the damming of all the strongest and deepest emotions in his life behind a barrage of conventional propriety that gave those novels much of their force."

The Go-Between, 1953, Hartley's best known novel, provides a good example of what King is talking about. It describes the crucial summer early in the twentieth century when its narrator, Leo Colston, becomes thirteen. Invited by an upper class schoolmate for an extended visit to his ancestral home, Leo is used by his sister, who is engaged to a nobleman, to carry clandestine messages to her working class lover, a farmer. Some readers have derived added pleasure from the novel by claiming a homoerotic subtext. Even so perceptive a reader as Colm Tóibín willfully ignores text in order to sustain an argument that Leo is emotionally (read: sexually) pulled between the sister and the farmer. Leo is, if anything, more attracted to the titled fiancé, though he was terribly scarred in the Boer War, than to the farmer, though the farmer does display more flesh. The novel has everything to do with the shattering discovery of sex and little, if anything, to do with sexuality. The hopelessly innocent youth is actually more akin to the boy in Graham Greene's short story "The Basement Room" who is forever maimed by being thrust into the midst of adult passions before he is psychologically equipped to deal with them. And, as King knew, *The Go-Between* is a much better novel than *The Harness Room*.

Hartley, L. P. *The Go-Between*. London: Hamilton, 1953. New York: Knopf, 1954. *Intro. Colm Tóibín. New York: New York Review, 2002.
_____. *The Harness Room*. London: Hamilton, 1971.
_____. *My Sisters' Keeper*. London: Hamilton, 1970.
Wright, Adrian. *Foreign Country: The Life of L. P. Hartley*. 1996. London: Tauris Parke, 2001.

101   Paul Bailey: *Trespasses*, 1970; *A Distant Likeness*, 1973; *Peter Smart's Confessions*, 1977.

Bailey has a penchant for male characters whose lives have become fragmented, directionless, death-oriented. Largely, they have arrived at this state for no very clear reason, although absent or ineffectual fathers, overbearing and loveless mothers, and wives that the protagonists are incapable of loving are often implicated. A gay male has a part, either a positive or a neutral one, in the story of their plight. The protagonists are aware of their predicament and try to make sense of their condition, not always successfully. Their accounts, however, are highly readable and often humorous.

The pattern is established in Bailey's second novel, *Trespasses*, whose very form is itself fragmented and repetitive. Ralph Hicks, writing from his ward in a psychiatric institution, assembles the bits and pieces of his life. He totally unraveled when his wife killed herself. At one point he imaginatively takes on the personas of others he knows, including his wife's best friend, the campy Bernard Proctor. Bernard's life parallels Ralph's in ways. His life also once unraveled, when his lover died in a POW camp in Germany in World War II. In deliberate opposition to Forster's adage, he says: "'Only disconnect,' became my motto" (120). Jim and he had met "in a dark and gloomy lavatory in the vicinity of Blackfriars Bridge" (115). With the news of his death, he begins looking for quickies once again. His cruising becomes obsessive upon his mother's death, delivering him into the hands of the law and a fine (125). He copes now by deliberately playing the role of "a parody pansy" (51, 120). Does Ralph's creative excursion into Bernard's life help him? Perhaps. At least the novel ends on a positive note.

For multiple reasons Inspector Frank White, the protagonist of *A Distant Likeness*, has lost his sense of direction. A childless marriage led to a loveless marriage, and his wife has left him for another man. His momentary fame as the officer who tracked down a serial killer who preyed on little girls has skewered his sense of proportion. He now identifies too much with Jim Belsey, who butchered his wife and son. That misguided sense will stupidly lead to the tragic end of his own career, though he does manage to perform one decent act for his wife before then. Somewhat surprisingly, Frank also has one very brief but entirely pleasant connection with a gay passerby. Piers literally picks up Frank, after he has fallen into a drunken stupor in the street, and sees him home. Frank had engaged in adolescent circle-jerks (15–16), but this seems to be his first encounter with a man as an adult. They end in bed together. Conflicted at first, Frank's mind succumbs to the attraction of a living, warm being and discovers he can even show affection. After first telling Piers, "I can't kiss you," he works to a different position: "With so many excuses, it was easier to kiss" (119).

Peter Smart's Confession, which was short-listed for the Booker Prize, seems yet another variation on the pattern, but evolves into the eponymous hero's unexpected acceptance of himself as homosexual. Peter's memoirs begin with an account of his latest failed attempt to kill himself. This time he decides to write out his autobiography to see if he can "make some sense" of his life (13). We meet his unbearable mother, who will not stop talking, and hear about his father, wounded in the war. Later we meet the woman he will marry after saving her from killing herself (ironically they are on the bridge together as Peter himself has decided to jump) and then impregnating. There is also the gay best friend, Neville Drake. He is a flamboyant actor whom Peter meets when he goes on stage. Never lovers, they board in the same house when performing outside the capital; in London Peter is Neville's lodger. Neville accepted his sexuality in his early teens as a result of being presented a copy of *Corydon* by "a would-be seducer." His admiration of the book led him to write Gide while on holiday in France, whereupon the author invited him to tea (120). New to the narrative pattern is a doctor who has written his own memoirs. Something of a charlatan, he hires Peter's mother as his housekeeper and sexual partner. He also takes Peter to a brothel for his first sexual experience at age sixteen. And his library provides a literary education for the boy.

Neville's weakness is Germans; as he puts it, "I enjoy mastering the master race" (122). He picks them up at the National Gallery, having found Leonardo's *Virgin of the Rocks* to be useful since one can make eye contact with another person via the reflection in the glass protecting the painting. One of those Germans is Wolfram Bonn, who appears in Peter's bedroom one morning after Neville has departed for work. Peter puts up the feeblest of resistance: "As I entered him, I thought: I shouldn't be doing this. After all, I'm a man." The results are, "We had breakfast in the late afternoon" (125). Years later, after Peter returns from a tour with an acting company in the provinces, his wife confronts him with a letter that she has read from Wolfram, accusing him of being queer. She also informs him that "the postman's a very good lover" (174). When the postman, not realizing he is back, shows up at their front door the next morning, Peter invites him in: "the smiling postman lowered his trousers" and soon Peter's "mouth was full." This scene segues into his meeting with Wolfram. The two do their best, but find it is impossible "to recapture the enchantment of yesteryear [...] despite the fierceness of our love-making" (177). Still, Peter has moved to a new stage in his quest to find meaning in life. In an epilogue written after Peter's death from cancer, Neville informs us that "his precocious promiscuity" led Peter and his son to meet one time "by accident in a V.D. clinic, to Son's considerable amusement" (189). Neville further informs us that Peter "foolishly abandoned acting and became a singularly inept social worker. He fell in love with a tattooed young thief named Freddy" (190–91). On the other hand, in a surprising twist, we discover that Neville has married and fathered twins, though obviously not without now and then a twinge of regret.

Peter Harry Bailey (1937–) was born in London. In his memoirs *An Immaculate Mistake: Scenes from Childhood and Beyond*, 1990, he talks about growing up in a working-class neighborhood, closeted by necessity for survival. (Along the way, he also explains the relationship between "Peter" and "Paul.") He worked as an actor before becoming an award-winning novelist. He has taught at Newcastle, Durham, and North Dakota State Universities. He published a second volume of memoirs in 2003, the delightful *A Dog's Life*. In it he talks about his twenty-two year relationship with costumier David Healy, until his death, and then his continuing relationship with the publisher Jeremy Trevathan.

Bailey, Paul. *A Distant Likeness*. London: Cape, 1973.
———. *Peter Smart's Confessions*. London: Cape, 1977. *London: Fourth Estate, 2000.
———. *Trespasses*. London: Cape, 1970. *New York: Harper & Row, 1970.

102 T. C. Worsley: *Fellow Travellers*, 1971.

Whether seen as a fictionalized memoir, the way Worsley presents it in his author's note at the beginning (7), or as a *roman à clef*, the way most readers will probably view it, *Fellow Travellers* takes as its form a collection of notes for a novel rather than a finished product. We have interviews, letters, the author's recollections and annotations, and excerpts from one of the character's own novel. There are five main characters, four gay men and an aristocratic woman. Martin Murray is a novelist who keeps trying to convince himself he is bisexual. His lover is Harry Watson, who left the Scots Guards to live with him. Lady Nellie Griffiths's teenage nephew Pugh Griffiths is sent down from his school after he is discovered with "the school tart [...] his trousers down" and Pugh's "open," so "there wasn't much to be said in our defence" (118). He takes up with Harry, is courted by Martin, and ends in the company of Gavin Blair Summers. Gavin will compose his own novel about the events. The person who has accumulated the files is a sixth character, speaking often in the first person, but, since he insists on the role of "an anonymous editor" (10), he remains insubstantial.

Though the materials are presented in rough chronological order, it is left up to the reader to fashion the novel. He is given some guidance: "What these five characters all had in common was that they all landed up in Spain during the war in various capacities, and it was to be one aim of my novel to trace the pattern which landed each of them there" (10). Three topics dominate the notes: the men's sexual relations with each other, the appeal of communism during the 1930s, and the ideologies of the Spanish Civil War. Because of the fragmented nature of the story, a reader probably has to have an interest in one or more of these topics to enjoy the work. An interest in Stephen Spender will also carry the reader along, for he is the model for Martin, and his lover Tony Hyndman is the model for Harry. Somehow, though, a postmodern historical novel just does not work very well.

Thomas Cuthbert Worsley (1907–1977) was born in Durham. He was educated at Marlborough and Cambridge. He worked first as a schoolteacher and then as a literary editor and critic for the *New Statesman* and later the *Financial Times*. He was a friend of the playwright Terrence Rattigan, to whom he dedicated *Fellow Travellers*. For thirty years he and John Luscombe were lovers. Worsley published his candid autobiography, *Flannelled Fool*, in 1967. Suffering from acute emphysema, he killed himself in Brighton.

Worsley, T. C. *Fellow Travellers: A Memoir of the Thirties*. London: London Magazine, 1971. *Intro. Paul Binding. London: GMP, 1984.

103 Susan Hill: *Strange Meeting*, 1971; *The Bird of Night*, 1972.

Two works of historical fiction may be more about male bonding than about gay relationships. But since one character in each book uses the word "love" (without ever defining it, thus leaving the reader to assume it has sexual connotations), the two novels need to be considered. *Strange Meeting* is the story of two English officers in World War I, John Hilliard and David Barton, who strike up a close friendship. Part two ends with David declaring, "I love you, John," and John responding simply, "Yes" (160). Yet there is no indication of anything overtly genital between them. In many ways, their relationship resembles more that of brothers. John comes from a cold, emotionally distant family; he finds the family he desires in David's warm, loving one, evinced first through the letters they exchange and promised by his visit to them at the end when he carries the news of David's death.

The Bird of Night, set some fifteen years or so after the war, recounts the deep friendship between Harvey Lawson, an Egyptologist and the novel's narrator, and Francis Croft, a sometimes insane poet, who may or may not have been pushed over the edge by the war. They spend twenty years together, though it is never clear whether they so much as hold hands. Harvey is intensely jealous when Francis is taken under wing by a California professor while he is a visiting teacher in the United States, and he does defend the way he cares for the poet to a physician, saying he does so "Because I love him" (176). Francis's father merely comments, "You live a rather *irregular* life" (146). By 1970s' standards both works are pretty tame. The second novel won the Whitbread Award for that year. Each book, incidentally, has a gay link to the outside: the title *Strange Meeting* comes from a poem by Wilfred Owen; *The Bird of Night* is dedicated to William Plomer.

Susan Elizabeth Hill (1942–) grew up in Scarborough and Coventry. She graduated from King's College, London. In 1975 she married Shakespearean scholar Stanley Wells; they have two daughters. A number of her short stories are also homoerotic.

Hill, Susan. *The Bird of Night*. London: Hamilton, 1971. *New York: Saturday Review, 1973.

_____. *Strange Meeting*. London: Hamilton, 1972.
*New York: Saturday Review, 1972.

104 Reginald Hill: *Fell of Dark*, 1971; *Another Death in Venice*, 1976; *A Killing Kindness*, 1980. William McIlvanney: *Laidlaw*, 1977.

Gay characters were important to two mystery writers. From Hill's first on, they often play major roles. In each case, the gay male is fairly complex psychologically and never falls into stereotypes. Admittedly, they all, at least in the early novels, are either mentally unstable or physically unattractive, but then the straights that Hill portrays are much the same. McIlvanney opened his trilogy with a gay killer.

In *Fell of Dark* two friends, the straight narrator, Harry Bentink, and his gay companion, Peter Thorne (suggestive names, if one thinks about them), decide to take a walking tour of the Lake District. Harry's marriage is undergoing a strain, in part because of the couple's innate differences, in greater part because of Peter's neediness, Harry's over-solicitude about his friend's health, and the wife's jealousy. Peter has had a nervous breakdown after the parents of one of his students discovered incriminating letters he had written the boy. Unfortunately, the two become chief suspects when two women hikers are raped and strangled to death. Even more unfortunately, Harry goes along with a lie Peter signals he wishes to maintain: that they did not encounter the two women on the trail.

He now discovers that Peter has been cruising and often bedding young hotel employees, one of whom turns viciously against him. And Peter, his nerves stretched to the breaking point, confesses to the murder he most certainly did not commit. Harry impulsively escapes the police headquarters when he is left alone and goes on the run. Aided and threatened by a number of women he encounters, including his wife, he stumbles onto the truth about who was actually responsible for the murders. Thus, for the greater part of the novel, Peter is physically absent. But psychologically, he continues to dominate the story. When the guilty are apprehended and Harry rejoins his wife, she gives him an ultimatum: either he drops Peter, or she is leaving him. By this point in the story, the reader is not surprised by Harry's choice.

Another Death in Venice, with its obvious title reference to Thomas Mann's novella, assembles three English couples on vacation in Italy, in the cities of Rimini and Venice, who are so clueless about their surroundings and about each other that no con artist could possibly resist trying to victimize them. A gay couple, Sydney Dunkerley, an Englishman some fifty years of age, and his very young lover, Aristide Roussel, a Frenchman, are ready to move in. The stupidity of the six tourists is great enough, however, to suck even them into their inimical vortex. It is never clear why the three couples remain so tight since basically they cannot stand each other. Throughout we follow the thoughts and movements of either Sarah or Michael Masson, but we are not privy to all that goes on; even they seem to experience great gaps in their consciousness, he is so wrapped up in his world of imaginary films and she in her passion for liberal causes.

We finish the novel with many unanswered questions to muse about. Who killed the young man on the beach at Rimini? Was it Aristide or Michael, or some unknown individual? And was it the same young man whom Michael accosted when he misunderstood a situation? How exactly did Michael get the scratches on his face? There is no reason not to believe his story, but we are given no confirmation that it is true either. And who beat him up in Venice? Did Aristide try to kill one of the wives as Sarah watched, or was it truly an accident when they fell out of the gondola together? And how exactly are we to take Michael's outcry when Sarah suggests he needs treatment? Much of what he says is nonsense, but is there any truth when he bursts out, "Ah! God, yes! It's all clear. I'm a repressed homosexual! That's how I got beaten up in Venice. I was trying to pick up a boy in a red shirt and he got angry and attacked me" (219). There are no questions, however, about the final death, and what we learn is chilling.

In 1970 Hill began his series starring Superintendent Andrew Dalziel and Sergeant Peter Pascoe of the Mid-Yorkshire Criminal Investigation Department. In the fifth novel, *A Pinch of Snuff*, 1978, the reader is introduced to Sergeant Wield (called V. K. in the next novel and Edgar thereafter). In his early thirties, his extreme ugliness is stressed. We discover that he is well liked in the town, and Pascoe begins to appreciate his worth. The case itself concerns the murder of the part owner of an adult cinema club, intertwined with Pascoe's dentist being accused of impregnating a minor. We hear nothing of Wield's sexuality. But in the next case, *A Killing Kindness*, the reader is informed: "Wield's self-containment and reticence were not linked, as the amateur psychologist might have guessed, to his fearsome appearance. They derived from his early recognition that the best way to conceal one thing was to conceal all things, to have so many secrets that the only important one would not be suspected. And this was that he was wholly and uncompromisingly homosexual" (49). He is realist enough to believe that the police would not accept him if they even thought he might be gay. Now, his ten-year relationship with a post office executive is coming unraveled as the result of his lover having been transferred a hundred miles distant and becoming interested in another man on place.

The closet to some degree aids Wield in his investigations: "As a long-established expert in putting up fronts, Wield had a sharp ear and eye for uncertainties of tone and manner" (186). The closet also sensitizes him to other people's woes. A Romani enclave becomes caught up in the case. The reader is told that Wield "felt a sneaking sympathy with them as outcasts and envy of them as defiant outcasts" (58). Having his own brand of humor, he is a welcomed relief to the Laurel and Hardy team under whom he works. This case involves a serial killer attacking women, who telephones the local newspaper with a telling quotation from *Hamlet* after each murder. Wield takes a more active part in this investigation and turns up several important clues on his own. In fact, because of an impulsive action of his, the murderer is identified in the opening line of the novel—just no one recognizes the fact.

Wield plays greater or lesser roles in the subsequent sixteen mysteries in the series. His most important appearances occur in *Deadheads*, 1983; *Child's Play*, 1987; *Bones and Silence*, 1990; *Pictures of Perfection*, 1994; *The Wood Beyond*, 1996; *On Beulah Height*, 1998; *Dialogues of the Dead*, 2001; *Death's Jest Book*, 2002; *Good Morning, Midnight*, 2004; *The Death of Dalziel*, 2007 (U.S. title, *Death Comes for the Fat Man*); and *A Cure for All Diseases*, 2008 (U.S. title, *The Price of Butcher's Meat*). Other gays show up across the various novels, and in *Pictures of Perfection*—a pastoral novel no gay reader wants to miss—he falls in love with an antiquarian with whom he later enters a civil union.

Laidlaw, set in Glasgow, has been credited with creating "tartan noir." From the beginning we know that young Tommy Bryson has brutally murdered a girl and left her body in a park. Gradually we learn that in trying to prove to himself that he is straight, he failed and killed her in some weird streak of retaliation. Tommy turns to his older lover, Harry Rayburn, the owner of a nightclub. Of Harry, we are told, "He had been taught despair but he had learned defiance. Out of its tension he had earned his own sense of himself. He wasn't a poof, taking his identity from a failure to be something else. He wasn't gay, publicly pretending to a uniformity that had no meaning in private. He was a homosexual, like everybody else one of a kind." But he realizes that "Tommy was where so many people wanted homosexuals to be, trapped in a ghetto of self-loathing" (112). As far as Harry is concerned, "the viciousness of public virtue" (114) has caused the murder, and he will do anything to help Tommy escape. Detective Inspector Jack Laidlaw instinctively understands Harry's existential position. Laidlaw snaps back at his homophobic police partner's "crappy attitudes" (210) and, curiously, cites the example of Marlowe (presumably Christopher, not Philip). Later, when the police discover that Harry has cut his throat, Laidlow asks the partner, "How many people have you ever loved like that?" (217). The novel won the Crime Writers Association Silver Dagger.

Reginald Charles Hill (1936–2012) was born in Hartlepool, Durham, the son of a professional football player. While still a child, he moved with his family to Cumbria. Educated at Oxford, he served as a schoolteacher for many years, before committing himself to becoming a fulltime writer. He received the Crime Writers Association's Diamond Dagger for lifetime achievement in 1995. He took no part in the television film of *A Pinch of Snuff*, which he hated. As a result he almost did not permit the popular BBC television series *Dalziel and Pascoe* to be launched. He was married, but childless. He died of a brain tumor. William Angus McIlvanney (1936–) was born in Kilmarnock, Scotland. He attended the University of Glasgow and then taught school until he retired to become a fulltime writer. He is married and has two children.

Hill, Reginald. *Another Death in Venice*. London: Collins [Crime Club], 1976. *New York: New American Library [Signet], 1987.

———. *Fell of Dark*. London: Collins [Crime Club], 1971. *New York: New American Library [Signet], 1986.

———. *A Killing Kindness*. London: Collins, 1980. *New York: Pantheon, 1980.

———. *A Pinch of Snuff*. London: Collins [Crime Club], 1978. *New York: Harper & Row, 1978.

McIlvanney, William. *Laidlaw*. London: Hodder & Stoughton, 1977. *New York: Pantheon, 1977.

105   V. S. Naipaul: *In a Free State*, 1971; *Guerrillas*, 1975.

This is the kind of fiction that leaves one feeling no better for having read it, despite the great symbolic and psychological values that critics profess to find. Admittedly, these two works are not as bad as one might expect from an author who, in an August 2001 interview in the *Literary Review*, attacked Forster for his homosexuality, what he labeled his "nastiness," accusing him of knowing nothing about India save "the court and a few middle-class Indians and the garden boys whom he wished to seduce." *In a Free State* is the last story in a three-story cycle published under the same title.

Bobby is an English civil servant working in a southern African state on the verge of revolution. The story details his return by car from the capital to the headquarters where he works. He is coerced into taking Linda, one of his colleague's wives, along with him. We initially meet him at a bar in the capital city, where he has been attending a conference. He tries to pick up a Zulu, but the African very publicly spits in his face. Much later in the novel, he thinks he has scored with a native barman in another bar, only to discover that he has again misread the situation. The bulk of the story is about the various mishaps he and Linda experience. Bobby alternately ignores her, taunts her, shares gossip with her, and confides in her. He obviously feels conflicted about being homosexual. In one outburst, he exclaims, "I hate English queers. They are awful and obscene." Then he admits that he was arrested for importuning (154). The novel won the Booker Prize.

Guerrillas is set on a Caribbean island. Four characters engage in a deadly dance: Peter Roche, a white South African do-gooder; his lover, Jane, a Canadian-born Englishwoman who has no clue how superficial she is; Jimmy Ahmed (né James Leung), a mixed-race revolutionary, a would-be writer, and a bisexual; and Bryant, his teenage black follower and lover. There is much talk and a good deal of violence, leading to Jimmy's anal rape of Jane before he turns her over to Bryant to hack up with a cutlass. The two men toss her body into the pit that has been dug out for the septic tank and cover it up. Arriving later that day, Peter deduces that they have done away with her somehow; he returns to the hotel, destroys her passport and return ticket, and lets out that she has departed early. The novel comes across as homophobic, racist, and misogynist.

Vidiadhar Surajprasad Naipaul (1932–) was born in Trinidad of Indian ancestry. Educated at Oxford, he writes both fiction and travel literature. He was awarded the Nobel Prize for literature in 2001.

Naipaul, V. S. *Guerrillas*. London: Deutsch, 1975. *New York: Knopf, 1975.

———. *In a Free State*. London: Deutsch, 1971. New

York: Knopf, 1971. *Harmondsworth, Eng.: Penguin, 1973. 103–238.

106 Leo Madigan: *Jackarandy*, 1972.

As its title indicates, the novel to a large extent considers the power of sex—"not so much the act as the *need*" (158). Keiron Dorrity is a merchant seaman convalescing in a London convent run by nuns after surviving his ship's explosion in the South China Sea. Eddie Coulson, his best friend on board ship, did not make it. Keiron's call on Agnes Coulson, the widow, leads to an affair with her. The comical short story he writes about the outcome of a homosexual encounter Eddie had in New York leads to his meeting the editor of *Gandymede* and his subsequent introduction into London's gay demimonde, including a stint working as a model and a call boy for rich tourists and businessmen. Early on he sums up: "Life has fallen into a fairly regular pattern—*Manicomio* [the novel he is drafting] mornings, Agnes afternoons and whoring at night" (81). And the whoring introduces him to Rufus, a mysterious American with whom he falls in love. Among the many other characters introduced in the course of the novel are his best London friend, the heterosexual Peter (whose wedding he nevertheless forgets), the sexually ambiguous Father Michael, and a Chinese woman living at the convent, whose death brings claims that she possessed a cache of rich jewels. The story is told in the form of a journal, interrupted periodically with extracts from Keiron's fiction and poetry, ending with a newspaper clipping and a letter to Father Michael. Keiron concludes, "A bird's still best for sex (it never was much cop with a fella) but somehow they don't interest me too much any more" (174). He goes on to say, "That day-trip I took to Sodom came to be a regular journey. Not just Sundays but Mondays, Tuesdays, Wednesdays ... I don't even commute any more ... I'm a citizen" (175). Though the sex is never detailed, the language is explicit. Something new and fresh has entered gay British letters.

Leo Madigan (1939–) was born in New Zealand. He joined the British Merchant Marine at age sixteen. He was a graduate of London University and taught in London and Izmir, Turkey. According to the dust jacket, "By 21 he had tried being an actor, a Horse Guardsman, a husband, a monk, a psychiatric worker," before returning to sea. He appeared in Ron Peck and Paul Hallam's film *Nighthawks*, 1978. He moved to Fatima, Portugal, and has written several books about the shrine.

Madigan, Leo. *Jackarandy*. London: Elek, 1972.

107 Hunter Davies: *Body Charge*, 1972.

Reading the novel is akin to entering the funhouse at the park. One is never quite sure where he's going or what's coming next, but it's fun. The author himself, in his introduction to its first U.S. printing, confesses that he had a good time rereading it. The narrator is Franko Baxter. A mini-cab driver, formerly a hairdresser, he cannot make up his mind whether he is bent, bi, straight, gay-curious, or confused. Nor can he decide whether his present divided state derives from his having allowed the gay hairdresser with whom he lived for a while to have his way with him, nor whether it explains his inability to make it with women. It's a problem he doesn't solve until the final lines of the novel. Franko has as much difficulty trying to suss out the sexuality of the people he meets in his business, though some are so obvious that even he is not left in doubt. They include footballer Hugh (Shuggy) Gallacher; Zak, an habitué of the dole, and his wife Sally; closeted but promiscuous BBC personality Jonathan (Joff) Howard (né Bates) and his more open but monogamous lover, Eddie; and two hoodlums, Ginger and Vince. One of these acquaintances is brutally murdered on Hampstead Heath. The police suspect Franko. Though he's a bit slow, Franko finally realizes that not only was it a gay-bashing but that he knows the perpetrators. With no clean plan in mind about what he is doing, he puts himself in harm's way and is almost killed for his efforts. Two *deae ex machine* put all right, and the novel swiftly winds up on a humorous note.

Davies credits his gay agent for introducing him to "some of his boyfriends," whose "world and language" he found fascinating. Born in

Scotland, Edward Hunter Davies (1936–) moved with his family to England at age eleven. He attended Creighton (which he later wrote a book about) and the university in Durham. This was his fifth and final novel, but he is probably better known for his biography of the Beatles and his nonfiction books about football than for his fiction. He is married to Margaret Forster, the author of *Georgy Girl*. They have three children, including the author Caitlin Davies.

Davies, Hunter. *Body Charge*. London: Weidenfeld & Nicolson, 1972. *Intro., author. Kansas City, Mo.: Valancourt, 2013.

108 Laurence Collinson: *Cupid's Crescent*, 1973. Mark Harris (Carl Ruhen): *Society Stud*, 1973; *The Gay Way*, 1974. Robert Adamson and Bruce Hanford: *Zimmer's Essay*, 1974.

Despite two lively scenes in a park cottage and an all-male orgy in a hotel room, it is difficult to label *Cupid's Crescent* a gay novel. Its protagonist, Frank Bailey, has dedicated himself to the task "to purify humanity" (12); that is, to stamp out sex. He decides to start on a small scale. By chance he discovers that the five houses on Cupid's Crescent, St. Albans, are all connected by a subterranean tunnel with secret panels permitting entrance into each domicile. He and his virgin wife, Vida, live at number one. From there he methodically eliminates the married couple in number two for their multiple infidelities, the elderly man in number three for pedophilia, and the hermaphrodite twins in number four for their devotion to S/M practices. He begins work on the two married couples in number five, who have marriages of convenience to conceal that the men are gay and the women lesbians. Though Vida has started complicating his plots (out of desperation for affection, she accepts an invitation to a lesbian party), the men and one of the lesbians are easy to weed out. The other lesbian is not so simple a matter. The novel is summed up at the beginning: "It was a journey of only a few hundred yards; it took two years; it ended in an orgasm" (13)— to his "horror," we are told at the end (143),

Detective Inspector Betty Steen of number five triumphs. The reader makes of it what he will.

Laurence Collinson (1925–1986) was born in Leeds, Yorkshire. His family moved to Australia when he was five. He attended school in Brisbane and Melbourne and taught English and mathematics in various Melbourne secondary schools. In 1958 he unsuccessfully attempted to establish a homosexual law reform society. He had already begun his literary career as a poet, playwright, and television script writer. He returned to England in 1964 and worked as a gestalt therapist. In 1973 he conducted an interview with William Burroughs, which was printed in *Gay Sunshine*. He died in London. According to bibliographer Ian Young, the novel was rejected by several English publishers—"Too dirty," "too kinky"— so this satire against censorship had to be self-published. But Collinson would probably have fared no better had he remained in Australia. Bruce Hanford in his preface to *Zimmer's Essay* reports that the first printing of the novella, in 1972 in the Melbourne alternate journal *The Digger*, was censored by the government because of its graphic homosexual rape scene. Co-written with Robert Adamson and based on his experiences in prison, the original version was finally published along with some of Adamson's poems by a small press two years later.

The novella recounts Robert Zimmer's growing love for his fellow inmate in the Maitland Prison, the New Zealander Lawrence Glaister. Glaister has fled his parents for undisclosed reasons, but proves to be incapable of making his way in Sydney. Arrested for stealing, he is sent first to Long Bay. Unfortunately for him, prison culture "is strictly heterosexual"; it "rigidly enforces two separate codes of conduct upon its members, who are either masculine or feminine. Butch partners are not considered homosexuals in this culture; they are the *men*," while "Queens are treated and spoken of as girls. [...] When the roles are sorted out, prisoners can do time easy. When their sexual identity is in doubt, they do time hard" (31). Poor Glaister falls into the latter category. He is raped by his two cellmates and, because "she sang so good" (60), given the name Carol. Assigned to Maitland, Zimmer takes him under his protection, "two queens, getting it together" (75).

Zimmer is driven to educate Carol. Being the "runner" for the prison library, he has access to books. He steers Carol to Shelley and then Rimbaud (as seen by Rogier Van Aerde). When Carol denounces both Verlaine and Zimmer as manipulators, Zimmer tries to get him to read Machiavelli. In love, "Zimmer had in fact blown it. From the comfort of poetry and the self-assurance of pedagoguery, he had blown through to a need for meaning, and Carol was it." As a result, "Zimmer's world began to disintegrate" (75). He writes Carol an ambiguous note, which a guard seizes. Zimmer is removed from the library to the laundry; Glaister is sentenced to chopping wood. Unable to take the physical and emotional hardships dumped upon him, Glaister manages to accumulate enough paint-stripper from the maintenance crew to self-immolate. The novella ends: "What impressed Zimmer most about Glaister's entire existence was how it had changed almost nothing in anyone else's life, except for the fact that Glaister had cost Zimmer his job in the library" (85).

Bruce Hanford (date unknown), American by birth, studied pre-law and anthropology at Portland State University in Oregon. He came to Australia in 1966 to escape the American draft during the Vietnam War. He has been credited with introducing the "new journalism" of Tom Wolfe and Hunter S. Thompson into Australia while working on *The Digger*. He also edited the Australian edition of *Rolling Stone*. He is now executive director of a firm serving businesses and the government. Robert Adamson (1943–) was born in Sydney. He spent most of his teenage years in a home for juvenile offenders. While in prison in his twenties, he discovered poetry and went on to become an award-winning poet. In 1993 he collaborated with Dorothy Hewett on *Zimmer: A Mock Opera in Two Acts*.

According to gay Australian scholar Jeremy Fisher ("An End to the Way," 304–05), though a number of pulp publishers sprang up in Australia in the 1950s and 1960s, they never developed much of a homegrown market or authorship. Because of Australia's strict censorship law, there was no opportunity for erotica to develop along the lines that it did in the United States. The nearest was the Horwitz Publishing House's Scripts imprint, under the direction of Stanley Horwitz, which published an Adult Only line 1969–74. Even then there was no attempt to find a gay market. The New Zealand born author Carl Ruhen (1937–2013) turned out the only two novels with a substantial gay content that Fisher has located so far. Both were written under the pseudonym Mark Harris.

In *Society Stud* the womanizing Talbot, drunk, is taken home by Kirby, a man he has met at a party. While passed out, Kirby performs oral sex on him. He apologizes the next morning, fearing that Talbot will now "despise" him, but Talbot asks, "Why should I despise you?" (96). When Kirby tries to have sex with him again (after having proposed to accompany Talbot on his restless travels), Talbot, however, rebuffs him: "I resented him, not so much for what he was doing, but for the demands he was making on me" (100). Interestingly enough, in the midst of the failed seduction attempt, Talbot's mind flashes to his friend Duncan, killed in guerrilla action beside him. Later when he hears that Kirby is in a coma, having been beaten up by rough trade, he wonders "if I should make an effort to see him, then decided it would serve no purpose" (125). Talbot makes no real judgment, one way or the other, on what has happened.

I have not seen *The Gay Way*. Fisher records that it follows nineteen-year-old Danny as he is pulled between his girlfriend, Erica, and his current boyfriend, Gerald. Danny invites her to a gay party, at which she sees the two men kissing. The next day Danny and Erica go to the beach, where he tells her he is invited out to dinner with Gerald that evening. She insists on accompanying him. There "she confronts Gerald and triumphantly leaves with her man." There are indications that trouble may lie ahead, though she intends to be a "tower of strength" and he insists, "It wasn't serious. It never was." Fisher says that "some sympathy" is offered Gerald, even as the girl gets the boy.

Adamson, Robert, and Bruce Hanford. *Zimmer's Essay*. Sydney: Wild & Woolley, 1974. 11–99.

Collinson, Laurence. *Cupid's Crescent*. London: Grandma, 1973.

Fisher, Jeremy. "An End to the Way: Pulp Becomes Classic Down Under." *1960s Gay Pulp Fiction: The Misplaced Heritage*. Ed. Drewey Wayne Gunn & Jaime Harker. Amherst: University of Massachusetts Press, 2013.

Harris, Mark. *The Gay Way*. Sydney: Scripts, 1974. [not seen]

———. *Society Stud*. Sydney: Scripts, 1973.

109 Yulisa Amadu Maddy: *No Past, No Present, No Future*, 1973.

Three teenage friends forge a bond at a mission school. Joe Bengoh is an orphan, the sole child of a shiftless pair who literally blow themselves up manufacturing gin. Ade John is the son of rigidly moral *élites* who turn their back on him when a girl accuses him of impregnating her. Santigie Bombolai is disappointed not to be chosen chief of his tribe, following in his father's steps when the latter dies. They find solace with each other, "Brothers Three." But strains develop quickly in their relationship when they leave for London in an attempt to better themselves through education. Partly circumstances are against them, but they also sabotage their own advantages. In the end they split, and each seeks happiness in a different way.

All the time Joe is in his homeland Bauya (i.e., Sierra Leone), he is having sex with women. Only late in the novel does Ade let drop that Joe may also have been having sex at the mission with Father O'Dan (115–17). The reader's first inkling that he is gay comes when Joe leaves Africa: "Before coming to London, he had been to Paris where he spent two lovely months with his French boy-friend" (77). At drama school (Joe wants to be an actor) he falls in love with Michael, a fellow student from Wales. Ian is another school friend, apparently also gay. But Joe gets hooked on drugs and runs up more debts than he can repay. As a result, he is dismissed from school and has a mental breakdown. At novel's end he is on the way to Rome to rejoin Michael, who has a teaching job there. But it is disappointing that at no time do we ever see Joe with his gay friends or gain any real insight into the way he views his life as a gay man.

The playwright, dancer, and director Yulisa Amadu Maddy (1936–2014) was born and died in Freetown, Sierra Leone. He was educated in London and worked in England, Denmark, and his native country. He was imprisoned and then exiled for his political outspokenness. Married, he had six children.

Maddy, Yulisa Amadu. *No Past, No Present, No Future*. *London: Heinemann Educational, 1973. Washington, D.C.: Black Orpheus, 1974.

110 Aubrey Menen: *Fonthill*, 1974.

"Fonthill or Beckford?" one of William Beckford's former lovers says to the prospective buyer of his estate. "They're the same thing, really" (164). The insight becomes the central conceit unifying this engrossing, if sometimes inaccurate tale about the author of *Vathek* (1760–1844). The setting is Fonthill Abbey during the late summer and early fall of 1822, when Beckford, once the richest man in England but now destitute because of changing economic times, faces the fact that he must sell his creation, along with his vast collection of art and books. Trying to avoid seeing his creation parceled out at a Christie auction, Beckford is trying to tempt the rich John Farquar, who has made a fortune from gunpowder, to buy the house and its contents entire. The ensuing conversations and inspection of the estate provide a thread on which to string a recall of the events in Beckford's life that have led to this fateful moment. Throughout the narrative appropriate passages from *Vathek* are introduced.

Beckford and Farquar have in common that they are both "boy-lovers," though no longer sexually active. Beckford is seen as still a boy himself (103), an adult who has refused to grow up, and "Fonthill was his sand castle, the biggest any boy had ever built" (20). The idea for his home was launched by his tutor Alexander Cozens, who seduced the fourteen-year-old by pulling him into an elaborate oriental fantasy set in an imaginary city of their joint creation. Public reaction to Cozens's deviation from accepted social standards provided Beckford his first visceral encounter with English Puritanism The scandal that erupted when he was found in bed with the youth William Courtenay deepened his hatred of his fellow citizens. In an attempt to divert the Courtney scandal, Beckford was pushed to marry Lady Margaret Gordon. Wisely tutored by her worldly aunt (the mistress of the future George IV), she became, in Beckford's own words, "the best wife a sodomite could have" (86). In a surprising development, when he found that he could not consummate the marriage, Courtenay stepped in and fathered her first child. Beckford connived with Gregorio Fellipe Franchi, the Portuguese boy he had made part of his household, to help him preserve an erection long enough to father a second child. And then, Franchi says, "slap me, if Beckford didn't take to the thing" (176). Margaret confessed to her husband, "Because now that you love me, I can understand how you love Courtenay and Franchi and—oh, all the other boys" (178). But Margaret died in childbirth, and that was the end of Beckford's heterosexual experiences. Her death drove him back to England and the beginning of his creation: "Fonthill was to be a retreat, but also a shrine" (192).

The tower that dominates Fonthill Abbey serves as a recurring motif in the novel. Its prototype was actually built in miniature one winter with Cozens, and it was always part of their emotional connection: "after making love, each would lie still, each would go into the tower. Each would be protected from a world that, if it knew of what they had done, would destroy them" (74). Later Beckford tells Farquar, "Yes. It is my tower, but its 'onlie begetter' is really Cozens" (190). Reminiscing about Courtenay, Beckford claims, "Hadrian raised a monument to his boy lover because he was faithful [...]. I raised that tower because of a boy who was the very reverse" (154). Soon after Farquar takes up occupancy of Fonthill, the tower collapses, "but Beckford was unruffled. He was busy building another tower in Bath" (223).

Salvator Aubrey Clarence Menen (1912–1989) was born in London to an Indian father and an Irish mother. He attended University College, London, where he was friends with Duncan Grant. Via him, he came to know the Bloomsbury group. He was a drama critic and playwright. He lived variously in India, Italy, and England. His partner was Graham Hall, a photographer. Menen died in Thiruvananthapuram, India.

Menen, Aubrey. *Fonthill: A Comedy*. *New York: Putnam's, 1974. London: Hamilton, 1975.

111 John Batchelor: *Breathless Hush*, 1974.

Written with the new frankness granted novelists in the 1970s, the novel delves deeper into the physical and emotional aspects of homosexuality in the British school system than usual. We follow the education of Matthew Smollett from the age of twelve to his very early twenties, a prolonged "adolescence which had been by turns wretched, complex, equivocal and lyrical" (165). Prep school is the time in which he discovers his passion for music, religion, and masturbation. His fumbling apprenticeship into sex with another boy is refined at public school almost out of existence: "Homosexuality was the natural climate of the school. Although no one seemed to practise it, it was part of the scenery and the life style of the place in a way far more insidious than if there had been a bull-calf orgy of mutual masturbation every Saturday night. We assessed each other in terms of beauty, charm, precocity [...] the school was a forcing house for homosexual sensibility" (36).

As a result of playing Viola in the school production of *Twelfth Night*, Matthew comes to the attention of one of old boys of the school, now an Oxford don, Dr. Paul Havapandria. When Matthew arrives at Oxford in the early 1960s to pursue a degree in music, Paul becomes his dark angel. His nemesis, as Paul recognizes and Matthew does not, is a post-graduate student, Rupert Hope-Jocelyn. He is the first man to kiss Matthew—"on the mouth, [...] in the open, at three in the morning" (47)—with the results that "Oxford had become actual in a way that it had not been before" (48). As he meets all sorts of gays, Matthew reflects, "If one had to be queer, and it had not yet occurred to me that I might be otherwise, then Oxford was a good place to be queer in" (52). At the same time, he finds himself "at a loss how to begin to put the theory into practice" (58). Rupert takes the initiative. But he warns Matthew, "I admit that I like to be screwed stupid just occasionally, but that's all there is to it" (75). Matthew does not heed the forewarning and falls in love with him.

The privacy permitted for their bedding has been provided by the enforced stay of Rupert's lover in the hospital to await the delivery of their twins. Melanie Tufnell is an heiress, older than Matthew, simultaneously more spontaneous and more culturally conventional. As she and Rupert begin to drift apart, his ruthlessly cultivating "the queer clique in the broadcasting, arts and literary world of London" (94) to forward his career, and as Matthew gains heterosexual experience with a fellow music student, he begins to question just how queer he is and to shift his emotional needs from Rupert onto her. Viola undergoes a gender identity change; Matthew essays a sexual identity change. Curiously, his discovery that Rupert is, in Paul's words, "sociopathic; [...] driven to act destructively towards those with whom he has been intimate" (141), seems not to affect Matthew. The novel ends inconclusively with Matthew in Birmingham, where he has taken a post as music teacher, standing outside the cathedral, smelling the stink of "a sulphurous pit" (167).

John Batchelor (1942–) was born in Hampshire. He received his degrees from Cambridge. This was his only novel. He has subsequently dedicated his writing career to biography, especially studies of late Victorian and Edwardian authors. He taught at the Universities of Birmingham, Lancaster, and Oxford, and is now professor emeritus of the University of Newcastle. Married, he has three children.

Batchelor, John. *Breathless Hush*. London: Duckworth, 1974.

112 Clive Murphy: *Summer Overtures*, 1976.

The spirit of Ronald Firbank hovers over the novel. Marcus Denton, an Irish teenager, newly arrived in London, is walking through the Serpentine when he spots Barnsdale Livingstone, who was in love with Marcus while they were schoolboys together. Trying to get away, Marcus is stopped by the painter Medway Phipps. He is reading: "'The book?' 'Firbank.' Marcus winced. He had never heard of Firbank" (12). Phipps invites Marcus home and introduces him to his Negro manservant, the sexually insatiable Panther. Later, Marcus meets the novelist Frinton Purbeck. (Purbeck, Firbank.) It is in his chambers that Marcus evolves his theory about the association between bacteria and faith that will render him a three-day wonder. Purbeck is murdered by a failed writer, another Irish youth named Charles Mulligan, who will try, unsuccessfully, to frame Marcus. Livingstone sums up Purbeck: "He was a snob, obsessed by penises and pedigree. He was a stickler for precedence and liked to dine off silver. Excessive success combined with successive excess impairs the intellect." Charles adds, "He had a turgid literary style which harmed a generation of writers including myself" (136). Is this the author's final say on Firbank—and on *Summer Overtures*? Perhaps. One doesn't read this novel for the story, not even for the characters. Language and style are everything. Firbankian innuendo has given way to plain speech, but surprise and shock still carry their part.

The wellsprings of what action there is are four: ambition, sex, writing, and teaching. The last enters the novel halfway through, when yet another Irishman, Dominic O'Dwyer, shows up. He is the only heterosexual man in the novel, a tutor for rich youths and a potential lover for their mothers. As such, he enters the Livingstone household for a spell, until he literally loses their hare-lipped son in Paris while on a trip. At novel's end, Marcus, Livingstone, Charles, and Dominic come together to form a fraternity of countrymen in Dominic's rooming house, under the benevolent eye of his elderly landlady, Miss Peach. Charles sums up their first evening in a letter to his mother: "It was a celebration during which, if there pertains to 'love' an intensity which 'liking' lacks, I evinced love for Dominic, Livingstone for me and Marcus, Marcus for Dominic and me, and Dominic for what he terms his 'belle laide.' That Dominic was at last sufficiently mature, or sufficiently drunk, to permit liaisons other than the kind to which he normally subscribed was, for me in particular, the cause of profound gratification." He concludes, "I recall that Marcus gave forth on how he, Livingstone, myself and Dominic were aspects of the one character, how together we made a symbiosis" (140–41).

Clive Murphy (1935–) was born in Liverpool, but was reared in Ireland. He attended Trinity and was admitted to the Dublin bar in 1958. He worked in marketing and public relations, mostly in London, before becoming a London primary school teacher. After publishing two novels, he began a highly successful series of oral histories with uneducated people. He has lately turned to writing satiric and gay verse.

Murphy, Clive. *Summer Overtures*. London: Dobson, 1976.

113 Eleanor Spence: *A Candle for Saint Antony*, 1977. Barrie Hughes: *The Martini-Henry*, 1978.

Two novels about Australian adolescents came out a year apart. They could not be more different. Spence's, written for young adult readers, is about the loss of innocence, with melancholy (perhaps because it occurs too soon) but basically positive consequences. There is nothing overtly sexual in the attraction between the two boys. Hughes's, written for older readers, is set in the fallen world, and the consequences of its characters' actions are left undetermined but seem hardly positive. Sex pervades the story.

A Candle for Saint Antony records a year in the life of two teenage schoolboys: the popular and quite boyish Justin Vincent and the studious Rudolph Mayer, a new student at his school. Rudi is Austrian by birth but has lived in Australia for some eight years. Justin initially bullies the frailer youth, jeering at his origins and his Roman Catholic religion. But after a confrontation in which Justin acts more than usually mean, the two become fast friends: enough so that the other boys remark upon their relationship and Justin—perhaps sensing something in himself, perhaps not—perceives that they could be accused of being gay (61, 107). One of his pals, Greg, becomes jealous of the attention Justin now pays Rudi. Their German class arranges a trip to Vienna. The three boys will be part of it. Greg, however, comes to feel even more excluded, "a complete outsider—literally and figuratively" (122). He is thus eager to report to the other boys the end of an exchange he overhears. Having taken shelter from a storm, Rudi asks Justin "to stay here in Austria with me," for here "we can be together as much as we want without people noticing, or saying stupid things, when all along the truth is so simple." And when Justin asks Rudi, "What *is* the truth, then?" Rudi replies simply, "I love you" (119).

It is left hanging exactly how Rudi is defining *love*, but that evening Greg attacks the two as only a confused, still immature boy could. Under pressure to decide publicly where his allegiances lie, Justin blurts out that he will return to Australia: "For many years to come, Justin would regret that he had let [Rudi] go" (126). Rudi is perhaps even more scarred. But he finds unexpected comfort in a poem by Goethe in *Wilhelm Meister's Apprenticeship*: "Wer nie sein Brot mit Tränen ass" (139), an illustration of the adage "Nothing venured, nothing gained." Saint Anthony (here spelled *Antony*) is Rudi's special saint. One of his favorite pieces of music is Brahms's *Saint Anthony Chorale*, which his dead father, a musician, loved. When Justin's father tells him he can take the trip only if he earns high marks in *all* his studies, Rudi lights a candle for St. Anthony. And he declares his love for Justin in a ruined chapel that had been dedicated to the saint. Nothing is made, however, of the life of the saint.

The Martini-Henry is set on an island up for sale just off the Australian coast. There are four male characters: two teenagers and two adults. Bill Green is the elderly caretaker. He lives on an adjacent island but regularly sails the narrow channel to check on the property. David Fairfax, whose deceased father owned the island, uses it as an escape from the Catholic school in Sydney that he attends. He sometimes brings one of his schoolmates, Peter Vanderleur, along. The fourth character is their English teacher, the grotesquely overweight Tony Carmichael. He is driven compulsively to pick up younger men for sex, even when he knows his pursuit will lead to bodily harm (44). He falls in love with David and begs him for his affection. David invites him to the island. He "had never been in love and he had no idea how he should feel, but if the man loved him, then he enjoyed it." But "he soon understood the power that such an emotion could give to the second, the desired, person in a relationship which remained unfulfilled and unreciprocated. [...] though in his own way the boy loved the man [...] he wanted to be able to control, and if necessary, hurt the man" (91). At the moment that he finally succumbs and allows Carmichael to kiss him, Peter bursts in on them. It turns out that Carmichael, even as he was pursuing David, was paying Peter for sexual favors. He blabbed to Peter, as the two of them were coming down from sex, about how he loves David. Peter's own feelings for David remain murky, but jealousy may well play a part in what ensues.

The novel's title might well have been "The Hunters and the Hunted." The four males become locked in a gothic dance of death and desire. Peter is a sociopath, whose ambition is to graduate from killing reptiles and other small animals to humans. He has bought a modified Martini-Henry for its deadly power. Now he announces that it is time for the game to begin: Carmichael must hide on the island, and Peter, armed, will come in search of him. But the equally murderous Green has also been watching the events unfold. A World War I veteran who was at Gallipoli, he has retained a souvenir of the battle: the skull supposedly of one of his Turkish enemies, which he displays on his mantel. Actually (as we learn late in the novel) the skull is that of his company commander, whom he shot in the back when ordered to go to his own certain death. Married but childless (a son who died fighting the Japanese seems to be an invention on his part), he is contemptuous of the "bloody sodoman" (159), "the fat English pansy" (181), but he is ready, even desiring, to bring down the armed boy. One of the four will not survive the evening.

Eleanor Rachel Kelly (1928–2008) was born in Erina, N.S.W. She graduated from Sydney University and then worked as a librarian in Canberra. In 1952 she married John Spence. They lived for two years in England, before returning to Sydney. They had three children. After their divorce in 1988, she moved back to the area where she had grown up. Spence wrote altogether twenty-one books for young adults. Barrie Hughes (1944–) was born in Melbourne and grew up in Malaya and Borneo. He attended the University of Sydney, the London Film School, and the Royal Academy of Dramatic Art. He has written one other novel.

Hughes, Barrie. *The Martini-Henry*. London: Weidenfeld & Nicolson, 1978. *The Martini-Henry Modification*. New York: Norton, 1978.
Spence, Eleanor. *A Candle for Saint Antony*. Oxford: Oxford University Press, 1977.

114 John Bruce: *Airscream*, 1977. Thomas Keneally: *A Victim of the Aurora*, 1977.

Two Australasia detective novels indicate how gays were apparently becoming trendy. In both the character is killed off early in the novel, however, and neither work contributes anything of significance to an understanding of gay lives. In *Airscream*, Captain Harry James Standar is a closeted New Zealand airline pilot, pretty much a stereotype, who is being blackmailed: "One of the 'ashamed' brigade—timid and frightened of it. A good guy to hook into: someone who would pay well for silence in the long run" (5). Harry is at the controls of a plane involved in a midair collision. When the widow of the pilot of the small plane involved in the accident brings suit against the government, the question of Standard's state of mind at the time becomes germane. Was he mentally distracted by the threat of exposure? In order to track down the young blackmailer, Philip James, a private detective, pays a visit to a Wellington gay bar, "the smart Gay Lib place," where he finds the owner "in full drag" (289–90). From there he tracks James to Auckland. The boy's testimony, along with secret audiotapes he has made of their lovemaking, creates a media sensation. But Harry's sexuality turns out to be irrelevant. The collision was caused by a simple mistake in the control tower.

A Victim of the Aurora has a quasi-closeted journalist, Victor Henneker, as a member of a fictional 1909 New British South Polar Expedition. Since the novel is narrated by another member of the expedition, Henneker remains indistinct. One of the men describes him as "a closet queen" (31), an anachronism perhaps excused by the fact that the narrator is recalling the story some seventy years later. He himself remembers wondering if "Henneker might be the first sodomite at the pole" (44). The distinction is rendered impossible when he is brutally murdered. The supposition immediately arises that he may have made an unwanted advance on one of the thirty-some men, who had reacted in an early example of homosexual panic. However, it turns out again that Henneker's sexuality is a red herring. He was killed for quite other reasons.

John Bruce (1938–) is a New Zealand author of two novels; I can find nothing more about him. Thomas Michael Keneally (1935–) was born in Sydney. He is best known for his novel *Schindler's Ark*, 1982, which became the basis for the award-winning film.

Bruce, John. *Airscream*. Auckland, N.Z.: Collins, 1977. London: Collins, 1978. *New York: Atheneum, 1978.
Keneally, Thomas. *A Victim of the Aurora*. *London: Collins, 1977. New York: Harcourt Brace Jovanovich, 1978.

115 David Watmough: *No More into the Garden*, 1978.

"Oh, Davey Bryant, if the artist in me had not created you, the coward in me would have had to invent you. How grateful I am for the fictional fact of you and your world" (viii). Thus David Watmough's "first novel," *No More into the Garden*, opens. "Novel" in quotation marks because the work is made up of eleven self-contained portraits (two of which were published previously as independent short stories) of Davey Bryant at different stages in his life, and at different places, forming a picaresque novel, with each chapter preceded by a brief meditation pondering the relationship between the creator and his character. And "first" in quotation marks because there is little difference between this book and Davey's earlier appearance in the author's first collection, *Ashes for Easter and Other Monodramas*, 1972. As a short story cycle, it resembles a novel as much as does *No More into the Garden*. In fact, from *Ashes* through *The Moor Is Dark beneath the Moon*, 2002, there have been, so far, twelve volumes in "The Chronicles of Davey Bryant."

As has long been acknowledged, there is a complex intertwining of autobiography and fiction in Watmough's creation of the character. In a statement written for Dennis Denisoff's short story anthology *Queeries* (201), the author notes that he and his alter-ego "have much in common but there is substantive difference, too. As a gay author, I need the freedom to fabricate and distort experience—in other words, to write fiction. I do not write autobiography, distancing myself by fictional event from the roughly parallel life-experiences of my character, who always appears in the first-person. So although my own life—and, by extension, the lives of those I've met in the course of it—provide the motherlode of material for my fiction, it doesn't prove a mirror for it. [...] Woe betide those who blithely confuse David with Davey or search for inner consistency over details in book after book." The bare biographical facts though for both David and Davey correspond closely. David Arthur Watmough (1926–) grew up on a farm in Cornwall, England. He served in the navy. He was arrested and jailed for three months for "gross indecency." He studied theology at King's College, London. He worked as a reporter, then an editor for Ace books. He met his companion of more than fifty-seven years, Californian Floyd St. Clair, in Paris. Watmough came to the United States in 1952, living in New York and San Francisco. He moved to Vancouver upon being offered a job with CBC in 1961 and was joined by St. Clair in 1962, when he secured a position with the French department at the University of British Columbia. Watmough first wrote plays, including one-man "monodramas." These became the basis for the *Ashes for Easter* collection, followed by *Love and the Waiting Game* and *From a Cornish Landscape* (both 1975), before the "novel."

The eleven chapters of *No More into the Garden* take Davey on a peregrination from Cornwall to the Royal Navy, to London, across to Paris, then Villefranche, back to England, then on to Victoria, Vancouver, and finally Cornwall once again. The period covered is from the early 1940s through the mid–1970s. The novel begins with Davey receiving a pair of binoculars as a Christmas gift; he prophetically looks west toward Canada, all the way to Vancouver he asserts. Next, he is hauled before the Navy brass after his "return from civilian detention," having been arrested "for importuning and soliciting one evening when on shore leave" (19). Sent to an observation ward, he is promptly hit upon by one of the attendants and makes "a sighing return to the land of self-degradation [...], finally free of responsibility, as convicted pervert, as male prostitute" (25). Mustered out, he has an interview with the Reverend Symes Monk, who convinces him to study for the priesthood. At Kings College he is more interested in sex, trying both men and women, than in his studies. We next see him in a comic interlude in Paris, where he is teaching English to young wards. By happenstance, he runs into the Archimandrite Alexei, who teaches Davey's charge two words that result in the teacher's dismissal when the boy uses them before his mother, whereupon Alexei sets him up with a rich giantess from Alabama.

Next, Davey is kept" by a jealous UNESCO librarian; that is, until he catches Davey making out with a French priest. Another comic interlude follows with Davey being hired most improbably by an English school as a "teacher of French and master in sports and athletics" (113) in order to make enough money to join his lover, Ken, in California. There he is tempted by the nubile pleasures of one of his female students. Much later he has a sad encounter with a grieving friend, one of his former fellow editors at Ace Books. In Canada again, Davey reunites with the woman who initiated him sexually, who turned out to be his father's mistress. Next, in a repeat performance, he has sex with a female student in the Creative Writing Program he is directing. Finally, Davey returns to Cornwall for his father's funeral. In his final meditation on the meaning of Davey's meandering search through life's possibilities, the author asserts that both of them have finally laid to rest their Cornish past.

Watmough, David. *No More into the Garden: The Chronicles of Davey Bryant*. Garden City, N.Y.: Doubleday, 1978.

116 Eve Zaremba: *A Reason to Kill*, 1978.

Building on Zaremba's introduction to the second edition of *A Reason to Kill*, Judith Markowitz (*The Gay Detective Novel*, 110) notes that the protagonist, Helen Keremos, "was not only the first middle-aged lesbian main character, she was the first lesbian PI, the first gay Canadian detective, and the first lesbian or gay detective with Native American heritage." (This last, however, does not appear in the first novel.) Given the political climate in Canada at the time, Zaremba's choice of a heroine and of a plot was a bold decision. Encyclopedists Steve Hogan and Lee Hudson (*Completely Queer*, 119) records, "More gay men and lesbians have been arrested on sex-related charges in Canada since 1969 than in any other English- or French-speaking country—despite the fact that 1969 was the year the Canadian government technically decriminalized private sexual acts between two consenting adults over 21." Three years after Zaremba's novel appeared, there was "a brutal raid on Toronto bathhouses, in which a record 286 men were arrested." The resulting riots have been commemorated as "Canada's Stonewall."

The victim is a gay teenager and the series of events that led to his murder was set off by homophobia. His lover is frightened enough to retreat to the closet, but he is there at the final showdown, as are two important gay men who have aided Helen's investigation. The plot does not bear close scrutiny, in particular the events surrounding the actual murder. A professor at the University of Manitoba hires a private investigator from Vancouver to look into the disappearance of his son in Toronto, where the boy's mother lives with her alcoholic lover. Such an extraordinary trans–Canadian investigation becomes plausible when it comes out late in the story that the father has hired her because she is lesbian since he suspects his son was gay. And in fact, eighteen-year-old Martin Millwell was in love with his best friend, Oscar Borg. In May 1976 they attended the Mariposa Folk Festival, where Martin, an aspiring musician, met a gay agent, Nate Ottoline. And then Martin disappeared, and Oscar, under pressure from his deeply homophobic father, retreated deep into a protective shell.

The reader must follow Helen through a dizzying series of twists and turns before the truth is out. At the final showdown Martin's mother bursts out, "I see, and it just blows my mind. That you could calmly plan to kill a human being! Because he was gay and loved [...]! Is that a reason to kill?" (178). Curiously enough, however, it is envy, bumping up against homophobia, that actually led to the murder. All the gay men are deeply closeted, and on the evidence of the novel, there appears to have been no gay community in Toronto at the time. On the other hand, based on Helen's interactions with other women, one would gather that a lesbian network of sorts existed. In aspiring to be no more than a good pool read, *A Reason to Kill* offers a fascinating window onto the time.

Eve Zaremba (1930–) was born in Poland. She emigrated with her parents at the start of World War II to Britain. In 1952 she relocated to Canada, where she eventually graduated from the University of Toronto. She was an early lesbian activist, helping create the review *Broadside* as well as being one of the founders of the Lesbian Organization of Toronto. This was the first of six mysteries in the series. Nate reappears, with his lover, in *Work for a Million*, 1987, and again in *Uneasy Lies*, 1990, where we learn that he is HIV-positive and his lover has died of AIDS. Even though there is a sleazy side to Nate, he seems to be the first gay male to play an important role in a Canadian crime novel.

Zaremba, Eve. *A Reason to Kill*. Markham, Ont.: Paperjacks, 1978.

117 Roderick Grant: *A Savage Freedom*, 1978.

Set in Malaya in 1951, the novel has two protagonists, both in their twenties: Peter Gordon, a police lieutenant, Scot, straight; and Roger Pierce, an assistant manager on a rubber plantation, English, gay. The two become something like friends as a result of circumstances forced upon them. It is a period in which Chinese ethnics, under the aegis of the communist party, are resorting to terrorist tactics to drive the British off the peninsula. Amid these dangers, Peter is seduced by the lusty wife of a Royal Air Force officer, disillusioned by her marriage. And Robert is working to seduce Hussan, a plantation clerk—when the youth asks matter-of-factly: "Roger? Do you want to go to bed with me?" To which the only answer is, "Yes, I do" (77). From that evening, the two men are lovers. The author is discreet about the physical aspect, the raciest comment permitted being one made by Hussan the first evening as he slips his hand down over Roger's body: "you are indeed the big white tuan" (78).

Malaya is presented as tolerant of homosexuality. The first evening Hussan and Roger are together, Hussan asserts, "In Malaya when two men want to sleep together they do not waste time looking and waiting and going around in circles. They just ask each other and have done with it" (77–78). Later, Peter says to Roger (thinking also of himself, at least in his first statement): "You're not the first person—man or woman—who's let love or sex or whatever rule their heads. And in Malaya, leastways among the Malay race, there's no shame in loving another man. In fact, they encourage it. There's something of the Ancient Greeks about the whole Malay race—their customs, culture and so on" (171). He goes on to cite the example of his corporal, who "has a wife and two little kids whom I know he loves dearly tucked away up-country in Kota Bharu and a young man in Temerloh whom I also happen to know he loves equally dearly as a brother and as a friend" (173). Nor do the other British care that Roger is gay. Again Peter sums up: "Life's too short—and in this part of the world, even without a war, too precious—to spend time wasting it by worrying about other people's sex lives" (173).

What Roger does not realize, despite some slips that Hussan makes, is that he has been blackmailed into working for the communist party in order to protect his politically outspoken parents. Hussan is gathering information about the rubber compound to pass on to the terrorists. There is the suggestion that his first overture to Roger was calculated; at least, his party boss remarks, "It was fortunate for all of us that your young manager friend was so kind, as you say, fortunate indeed that his tastes are for handsome boys such as you" (105). What the party boss does not anticipate is that Hussan and Roger will fall in love and that, when the raid occurs, Hussan will feel compelled to make a choice. Roger is devastated. But at the end he and Peter survive one final bloodletting instigated by the terrorists; mysteriously as a result, Roger finds reaffirmation of himself out of the tragedy he has been dealt and decides to remain on the peninsula. The novel is violent and cruel; it is also tender and uplifting.

Roderick Grant (1941–) was born in Morayshire, Scotland. He became a journalist and travelled widely in Southeast Asia. He writes both fiction and nonfiction. He seems to prefer to keep his private life private.

Grant, Roderick. *A Savage Freedom*. London: Hale, 1978.

118 David Rees: *In the Tent*, 1979.

According to Michael Cart and Christine Jenkins's survey of literature for young gay adults (*The Heart Has Its Reasons*), the novel was the first British example and just the eighth to be published in English anywhere. The basic plot depicts the growing bonds among four boys who get lost in the Lake District as a result of days-long impenetrable fog. The protagonist is the bookish seventeen-year-old Timothy Keegan, who everyone, including himself, is sure is gay. He has an impossible crush on the straight Aaron Brown. The other two teenagers are John Hewitt and Ramón "Ray" Suñer. Reared in the Catholic faith by a strict mother and an authoritarian father, Tim is fighting his conscience. The liberating words of William Blake fight in his mind with the strictures laid down by the priests. Tim, who has actually invited himself along on the expedition when the original fourth member falls ill, learns several things as a result of their isolation. None of the other teenagers, save one, cares about his sexuality. The one is Ray, who, to Tim's surprise, is totally closeted. While the other two sleep, they share a sleeping bag and Tim loses his virginity. He subsequently has to deal with his emotions, complicated by the fact that he has enjoyed their union even though it is sheer lust since he does not love Ray. But then he realizes, "He didn't love Aaron any more. [...] He was free!" (97). And he realizes that he is not ashamed of being who he is.

Cart and Jenkin (38) praise Rees's novel as being "the most thoughtful treatment of homosexuality produced in its time and the first to include elements of gay community." Ray has found a newspaper that has a guide to "all the pubs and places in England where gay people meet" and discovers two such places in their own hometown. He affirms that they don't have to "live in a vacuum," that it's just not possible they are "the only two nice decent homosexuals in the world" (105–06). Tim realizes that he will have to fight to be true to himself: "What he feared most was that all he had gained in the tent would be lost: the self-discoveries and the resolutions would evaporate in the cold light of routine; the friendships formed would dilute in the ordinary patterns of life" (114). And here Rees does something audacious: he introduces flashforwards into his narrative that show the reader what was gained will not be lost. The novel concludes with Tim's thought, soon after their return from the hiking trip, "I've already chosen to be what I am, which is what I always have been" (127).

Rees parallels the story of what happens to the four teenagers with a story of what arrived to four men caught in the siege of Exeter in 1646 during the Civil War. "Timothy Keegan" is assigned the task of assisting Anthony Fare. In this capacity he comes into contact with Richard Saint-Hill and the sexton Jake. The opening sentence of the novel establishes that their story is actually an elaborate fantasy being played out in Tim's mind; the war between the Parliamentarians and the Royalists is analogous somehow to the civil war being fought within himself. Many of Anthony's statements—"A man must be whatever he is. [...] Regardless of the odds" (33)—are reflections of the position that Tim is working his way towards. Young Tim allows his alter-ego the possibility of a happy ending. Exeter having fallen and Anthony killed, Tim escapes to the mountains. There he meets a farmer, John, and they begin a life together (122). From the beginning we know that Ray's family are refugees from the Spanish Civil War, a fact that has colored their lives. In a flashforward we learn that just as Tim undertakes a pilgrimage to Exeter to see what remains of the city of his fantasy, Ray makes a similar one to the Alcázar in Toledo, the site of a similar siege.

David Bartlett Rees (1936–1993) was born in Surrey. A graduate of Cambridge, he taught school, eventually becoming a lecturer at the University of Exeter. Married, he fathered two sons. He did not come out until the early 1970s. The novel *Quintin's Man*, 1976, has brief appearances of gay Cambridge students. Three later novels are also of interest to gay readers: *The Milkman's on His Way*, 1982, about a teenager receiving assurance that a gay community awaits him when he leaves home (the novel figured prominently in the 1987–88 debates about Clause 28, banning promotion of homosexuality); *Out of the Winter Gardens*, 1984, about a gay father coming out to his son; and *The Colour of His Hair*, 1989, about a couple forming and then breaking up after being ten years together. Rees died in London of AIDS-related problems.

Rees, David. *In the Tent*. London: Dobson, 1979. *Boston: Alyson, 1985.

119 Patrick White: *The Twyborn Affair*, 1979.

His biographer, David Marr (582), writes that White "worried that the label 'homosexuality' would seem to isolate men and their affections in some territory outside the ordinary experience of the human race. The devotion of Harry Roberts to the explorer Voss needs no particular name, for it is love expressed in the most admirable way White knew, through service and sacrifice. After *Voss* [1957] White began to identify a few homosexuals more clearly in his novels. Alf Dubbo looks back with gratitude to his initiation by the Rev. Timothy Calderon [in *Riders in the Chariot*, 1961]. The elegant Maurice Caldicott in *The Vivisector* [1970] is gently mocked for his furtive affections. Cecil Cutbush, the masturbating grocer at the Gash [in the same novel], is excoriated for the sin of seeing his sexuality as a badge of brotherhood." Not until his penultimate novel did White write what has been hailed as his first gay novel. But in truth, *The Twyborn Affair* seems to be more about the fluidity of gender identity than it does about sexuality.

Born Eddie Twyborn, the son of a Sydney judge for whom he seems to feel an incestuous love, the protagonist first appears as Eudoxia Vatatzes, the lover of an aging Greek living in the south of France in early 1914. Another Australian, Joanie Golson, comes across them by happenstance. She feels a mysterious compulsion to write to her old friend and lover back home, Eddie's mother, Eadie, about her encounter. Fearful about what Mrs. Golson may have discerned, Eudoxia and Angelos Vatatzes flee, and he dies. We next meet the protagonist as Lieutenant Eddie Twyborn, returning to Australia after the war. Going to work as a jackeroo on a sheep station, he has an affair with the owner's wife and impregnates her (the son dies some years after Eddie has disappeared). But he is more attracted to Don Prowse, the station manager. It turns out that the feeling is mutual, though Don must get drunk before he dares initiate what amounts to virtually a rape (284). The second time, however, he is the submissive one (296).

The protagonist emerges a third time as Eadith Trist, the madam of a London brothel owned by Lord Roderick Gravenor. The latter is in love with Eadith, but he keeps him at a distance so as to prevent Gravenor's discovery of his real sexual identity. (Eadith does have a brief sexual encounter with Gravenor's nephew, apparently blessing the lad's homosexuality.) As World War II bursts upon London, Joanie and Eadie, both now widows, appear. In a brief meeting with her son on a bench outside a church, unable to voice her thoughts, Eadie writes a note on the fly-leaf of her prayer book: "Are you my son Eddie." Eadith writes back, "No, but I am your daughter Eadith." Now able to speak, Eadie says, "I am so glad. I've always wanted a daughter" (422–23). But it is too late for the two of them; shortly thereafter they are killed in a bombing during the blitz. Earlier while with Gravenor, Eddie has faced a truth: "Yet whatever form she took, or whatever the illusion temporarily possessing her, the reality of love, which is the core of reality itself, had eluded her" (336).

Patrick Victor Martindale White (1912–1990) was born in London, but his parents relocated to Sydney before he was a year old. He was sent to London for schooling and immersed himself in the theater. He wanted to become an actor, but his father insisted he return to Australia and work on a cattle station. In 1932 he returned to England to study at Cambridge. There he had his first love affair. Moving to London to write, he came under the influence of the painter Roy de Maistre.

During the war he served with the RAF in the Mideast. It was then that he met Manoly Lascaris (1912–2003), a Greek who became his life partner. In 1973 White was awarded the Nobel Prize for literature. He published his autobiography, *Flaws in the Glass*, in 1981, speaking openly for the first time about his sexuality. He died in Sydney.

Marr, David. *Patrick White: A Life*. 1991. New York: Knopf, 1992.
White, Patrick. *The Twyborn Affair*. London: Cape, 1979. *New York: Viking, 1980.

120 Frank Moorhouse: *The Everlasting Secret Family*, 1980.

The novella *The Everlasting Secret Family: An Erotic Memoir in Six Parts* is the fourth story in the collection *The Everlasting Secret Family and Other Secrets*. The only commonality the four share is, as the title indicates, that they all deal with human secrets. This is the sole homosexual story; it is also the only one that is pornographic. Making no apology for treating pederasty as perfectly normal, the unnamed narrator recounts in explicit detail how at age thirteen he was seduced by an unnamed politician prominent in the Australian government and how he in turn, with the father's watching approval, seduces his lover's own thirteen-year-old son. He sums up: "I was joined to a line through history which went back to the first primitive tribal person who went my way, who took a virgin boy lover, and every boy who became a man and took, in due turn, a boy lover, through to Socrates. I had played a part now in the continuation of that chain. I had played my first part as a child in becoming a man's lover. I had now played my second part. I now belonged fully in that historical line. It was a way of passing on and preserving the special reality, a way of giving new life, the birth for the boy of a new reality, a joining of him to a secret family, the other family" (204). All the events in the novella are treated with the same philosophical detachment, creating a seeming link between an Australian fascination with pedophilia and the spirit of the *libertins* during the Enlightenment. In 1988 the novella became the basis for a film.

Frank Thomas Moorhouse (1938–) was born in Nowra, N.S.W. He attended the University of Queenland. He worked as a journalist before becoming a full-time creative writer. A bisexual, he was briefly married to his school girlfriend. Other of his works have gay interest, such as the two Paul Jonson stories in *The Americans, Baby*, 1972. He published his memoir, *Martini*, in 2005.

Moorhouse, Frank. *The Everlasting Secret Family, and Other Secrets*. Sydney: Angus & Robinson, 1980. **The Everlasting Secret Family*. North Ryde, N.S.W.: Angus & Robinson (Sirius), 1988. 165–213.

121 Anthony Burgess: *Earthly Powers*, 1980.

Kenneth Toomey, the protagonist of *Earthly Powers*, was clearly inspired by Somerset Maugham but is only loosely based on his life. In fact, one of the short stories that Toomey has written is a variation of Burgess's own *A Clockwork Orange* (637). And the author, in his usual fashion, plays all sorts of other games with the reader. The spirit of Joyce infuses the entire novel, as does that, to a lesser extent, of Anatole France. Toomey recounts his life from 1916 through 1971, with a brief glance at the end to the mid–1970s. At more than six hundred pages, the novel must be the longest first-person narrative in English by a gay character. It flows swiftly along, however, becoming in the process, especially for the first half, a kind of primer in gay British culture as it drops many of the names we have already encountered in this guide.

Though it is pretty common knowledge that Toomey is gay, he refuses to out himself for the greater portion of the novel. Thus, he declines to testify at the obscenity trial for *The Well of Loneliness*, defending himself by saying, "I couldn't read the damned thing. It's so badly written" (314). Thus, it is surprising when he agrees to testify for Val Wrigley in a trial for blasphemy after the publication of *The Love Songs of J. Christ*. (Here Burgess must be riffing on the 1977 trial of the poet James Kirkup for "The Love That Dares to Speak Its Name," brought about through the actions of Mary Whitehouse.) His decision is even more surprising since Wrigley has attacked him for a ruse that Toomey used to escape Nazi Germany. Then, in the most surprising twist of all, Toomey outs himself in a headline-grabbing way by averring that "homosexuals have a right to an expression of their own view of life and love. Our literature has been grievously harmed by the suppression of that right. So, God help us, has society in general. No man or woman can help being homosexual. I cannot help it myself" (530).

Indeed, throughout his narrative, we hear of the trouble he has faced as a gay man, though more on a personal than a literary level. We meet a series of his lovers. The first died, the victim of a supernatural Malaysian curse. Others proved unfaithful. At one point he justifies the May-December aspect of so many famous gay liaisons (think Isherwood, et al.): "The sexual impulse, as my coevals will know, does not die with age: it becomes merely intermittent, abating little of its pristine ferocity on the occasions of its resurgence. It needs, however, to be stimulated by youth and beauty, and this implies a certain onesidedness of passion, for what youth and beauty, except in instances of gerontophile perversion, is reciprocally stimulated by wrinkles and grey hairs? True, as I moved towards my final infirmities it was companionship I needed more than sex, but it was not, as in marriage, the companionship of one of my own generation" (487).

By chance, in 1918 Toomey becomes an intimate of the Campanati family. Raffaele is a Chicago gangster. Don Carlo is a priest. Domenico is a composer in search of a librettist. He and Toomey collaborate on an opera. Toomey's sister, Hortense, meets him, and the two marry. The union is not a happy one, but Hortense, as a Catholic, refuses to acknowledge the divorce that Domenico obtains on grounds of incompatibility. After an accident, in which her face is scarred, she moves in with an American woman, and the two share a bed. Long before then, Raffaele has been taken out by rivals. Carlo, meanwhile, keeps moving up the Catholic hierarchy, until, in a bold move into an alternate history, he becomes Pope Gregory XVII in 1958. Upon his death in 1971, a move is set afoot to canonize him. Toomey's help is requested, for he was a witness to a seeming miracle Carlo had performed in Chicago in 1925. A child was dying in the same hospital that Raffaele was also dying in. Carlo was unable to save his brother, but the child recovered after he laid his hands upon the boy. It turns out that the boy was adopted as Godfrey Manning. He has grown up to become the leader of a California cult. The same week as the pope's death, "God" (the nickname he goes by) murders all his followers with cyanide-laced wafers (a variation on the Jonestown mass murder of 1978).

Burgess's biographer Andrew Biswell stresses the religious aspect of the novel, specifically the conflict between the Pelagian heresy, which stresses free will and the perfectibility of humans without God's aid, and the Augustinian orthodoxy, which stresses original sin and the need for God's grace. But there is much, much more going on here. Secular issues are probably more important than spiritual ones, though the treatment of homosexuality in western culture necessarily intertwines the two. Toomey observes late in his account that he is writing "not merely a chronicle of loneliness but of death" (579). By the end almost everyone save the brother and the sister—Kenneth and Hortense, the gay and the lesbian—is dead. Hortense sums up: "I don't suppose any of us was really bad. We meant well, anyway" (653).

John Burgess Wilson (1917–1993) was born in Manchester. A graduate from Victoria University there, he aspired to be a composer and taught himself music. He was also a gifted linguist. He served in the army during World War II. After the war, he worked as a teacher, including stints in Malaya and Brunei. Since the Colonial Service was unwilling for him to publish fiction under his own name, he adopted his pseudonym, Anthony being his confirmation name when he joined the Catholic Church; Burgess, his mother's maiden name. Returning to England, he lived near and in London and became friends with William Burroughs. As he became successful as a novelist, he became a tax exile, living in various European countries and the United States, but he died in London. He was married twice and had a son.

Biswell raises a question about his sexuality. He points out (304), "Only Burgess's gay and lesbian characters seem to be enjoying themselves." Burgess included gay characters in many of his novels beginning with *A Vision of Battlements* (not published until 1965). Homosexuality is central to the dystopian *The Wanting Seed*, 1962, though it is told from a renegade heterosexual viewpoint. It recurs in *Honey for the Bears*, 1963, and his take on Shakespeare, *Nothing like the Sun*, 1964. The last novel published in his lifetime, *A Dead Man in Deptford*, 1993, imaginatively recreated Christopher Marlowe.

Biswell, Andrew. *The Real Life of Anthony Burgess*. London: Picador, 2005.
Burgess, Anthony. *Earthly Powers*. London: Hutchinson, 1980. New York: Simon & Schuster, 1980. *Intro. Paul Theroux. New York: Europa, 2012.

122 Michael Schmidt: *The Colonist*, 1980.

The Colonist (published as *Green Island* in the United States) is a tragedy of adolescent obsession. The unnamed narrator, a sickly child, is put under the care of a servant, Doña Constanza, at his parents' country home outside San Jacinto, Mexico. His parents are English; he attends an English school in town; later he receives his catechism from an English Anglican rector, the Reverend Purse. But Doña Constanza is the one constant in his life, and her language is really his first language. She is responsible for hiring a gardener for the grounds, the green island in the parched landscape. He brings with him his son, Chayo (the nickname for Rosario, rosary), a lad the same age as the English boy. The two develop a deep friendship, especially after the father disappears and Chayo remains to carry on his responsibilities. The narrator decides to take on the responsibility of educating the Mexican boy. Since they are transgressing the usual boundaries between classes and races, their lessons need to be carried out in secret. The narrator hatches the plan to smuggle Chayo into his bed in order to instruct him under the covers, and from there they begin to sleep innocently together. But Chayo is maturing faster than the narrator. He is sexually excited when the two boys sneak into town and spy on a prostitute servicing her client, a fact that disturbs the narrator in some ill-defined way so that for the first evening in years they do not share the bed (67). Chayo picks up on the true nature of the Reverend Purse's interest in boys: "I've seen him. The way he looks at me, the way he looks at you. I have eyes. He'd as soon have an arse as a soul" (72). And Chayo also recognizes the narrator's true nature faster than he does: "I think you like me better than a brother" (94).

Chayo comes to the realization that he must leave. In an emotional scene, he accuses the boy of using him: "So you presume on friendship. It's not friendship you want, but possession." Chayo breaks down in tears, at which point, the narrator records, "I kissed him. He put out his hand. Not, as I expected, to force me away, but to draw me to him. His body grew taut against mine. He was aroused with hatred, but with memory too. His fingernails were sharp on my back. I could see nothing—a shapeless darkness into which we poured the energy, the passion of six years—spilled out irretrievably. My skin burned, my mouth ached as we struggled, until the frenzy released us" (113–14). There remain a fiery finish and the narrator's understanding that he will never escape this experience, nor ever fully understand it. The difference between the English and the American titles is instructive. For the American reader the Edenic quality is highlighted; for the British reader the rapaciousness of the unequal relationship, along with the reciprocal violence it generates, is stressed.

Michael Norton Schmidt (1947–) was born in Mexico City. He attended Harvard and Oxford. He founded Carcanet Press, based in Manchester, dedicated to promoting poets and their works. He has been married and divorced and is the father of three children.

Schmidt, Michael. *The Colonist*. London: Muller, 1980. *Green Island*. New York: Vanguard, 1982. *Original title. London: GMP, 1993.

123 Dan Kavanagh (Julian Barnes): *Duffy*, 1980; *Fiddle City*, 1981.

Nick Duffy is the first gay protagonist of a British detective series. Having been set up by a bent cop in what appeared to be a sexual encounter with a minor and busted from the force, he now runs his own London-based security firm. He appears in four cases. In *Duffy*, he is hired by a shady importer who is being squeezed out by a rising mobster and succeeds in bringing down the cop who got him ousted. In *Fiddle City* he exposes a drug-smuggling ring coming through Heathrow Airport. In *Putting the Boot In*, 1985, his investigation of a series of threats against a football team ends up blocking a scheme to turn the stadium area into a commercial development. Only the fourth case, *Going to the Dogs*, 1987, involves a murder, that of a dog, in a send-up of cozies. It is also the gayest of the four.

Actually, Duffy is bisexual and has even worked out a sort of philosophy: "To Duffy it was like choosing between bacon and egg and bacon and tomato. Whichever you decided on you had a good time; it was what your tastebuds felt like that evening. Women were usually less likely to leave you needing a visit to the clinic. On the other hand they were a bit more expensive [...]. The other thing was that, in practical terms, men could be more relied upon if you wanted to get laid. [...] if you went to a gay club, you never left disappointed" (81–82). Sometimes he labels himself as gay, but thinks "that's where you start from, not where you end up" (191). His long-lasting romantic attachment, in fact, is with policewoman WPC Carol Lucas. Since being framed, however, though he has no problem with other women, he finds himself unable to maintain an erection with her.

The novels are uniformly well crafted examples of their genre and, if dated, no more so than all hard-boiled detective stories inevitably are. They project a lively picture of one corner of the gay world during the period in which Margaret Thatcher was prime minister. The bombing of an adult bookstore (130) elicits a sly dig against Mary Whitehouse, the rabid campaigner against social liberalism and the permissive society. One of the villains rakes up the case of Norman Scott (144), a fashion model whose allegations of an affair with Liberal leader Jeremy Thorpe brought down that politician's career. Duffy himself is fairly complex. Anal retentive, he abhors untidiness. He has a phobia against the sound that watches and clocks make. He can't abide anything that smacks of camp, but he can't resist wordplay. He dresses casually but does sport a gold stud in his left ear, until one of the crooks he comes up against rips it out. He is used to people assuming he is homosexual. The *Duffy* series vividly illustrates the fear and confusion that settled over the gay community with the identification of AIDS. In the first two novels Duffy pretty well plays the field with both men and women, Throughout *Putting the Boot In*, like so many of us were doing at the time, Duffy is constantly feeling of his lymph nodes to find out if they are swollen—after he has someone tell him where they are located.

The four novels were published under the pseudonym Dan Kanavagh (Barnes's late wife's surname was Kanavagh), complete with a fictional biography. According to Merritt Moseley (5), Barnes kept this side of his literary output so separate that he actually borrowed Ruth Rendell's cottage to write the novels in and even used a different typewriter than he would for his usual output. Julian Patrick Barnes (1946–) grew up in London and attended Oxford. He alternates between highly experimental fiction and a more conventional realistic mode.

Kavanagh, Dan. *Duffy*. London: Cape, 1980. New York: Pantheon, 1986. **The Duffy Omnibus*. Harmondsworth, Eng.: Penguin, 1991. 1–177.
―――. *Fiddle City*. London: Cape, 1981. New York: Pantheon, 1986. **The Duffy Omnibus* (see above). 179–347.
Moseley, Merritt. *Understanding Julian Barnes*. Columbia: University of South Carolina Press, 1997. Chapter 3.

124 Roger Raftery: *The Pink Triangle*, 1981. Lance Peters: *The Dirty Half Mile*, 1981.

The Pink Triangle may be labeled the first gay Australian murder mystery. The case begins with a "poofter bashing" that ends in the accidental drowning of a television news anchor, Edward Church, while he was on "the beat" (cruising in a public toilet in a park). His lover, Troy Shaw, hires a private detective to take on the case, not realizing that the agency has changed hands. The new owner, Duane Dooley, and the novel's narrator claims to be straight. That does not prevent his allowing Troy to suck him off, nor does it stop him from hightailing it to Troy's house (and ending up naked in bed with him) after he is involved in a brawl at a nightclub. And he will not give up on the case even when two of the apparent perpetrators have been dispatched by someone calling himself the Pink Triangle. Given Duane's record with women—he is in the process of getting a divorce; he mistreats his neighbor's sister and eventually rapes her—and his strange relationship with Troy, the reader has to wonder just what is going on in Duane's psyche.

He interviews a few people in the gay community whom Troy thinks may provide leads, including another man who was also thrown into the lake with Church (he could swim; Church could not). Duane suspects them all, including his own client. Troy is convinced, however, that rogue policemen on the unnamed city's vice squad are responsible. In fact, as a result of media attention, the police department conducts an internal investigation. No charges are brought, but four policemen resign. One dies in a crash in Western Australia; two are murdered, shot, but their bodies disposed of in ways to recall Church's drowning. The fourth goes into hiding. Duane fails to connect the clues. Troy actually solves the case, though Duane has the final confrontation with the killer. He is a closet case, wracked with guilt because he did not stand up against the ones who murdered Church. At novel's end, Troy is still pursuing Duane.

Church's death is clearly modeled on the notorious 1972 drowning of George Duncan, a law lecturer at the University of Adelaide.

He and another man, Roger James, were accosted by a group of men as they were cruising at a popular beat on the River Torrens. Duncan had suffered from tuberculosis and had only one lung. James did not try to identify their attackers, but three members of the police vice squad, who resigned, and an unidentified civilian were suspected of having been the perpetrators. Duncan's death spurred the immediate introduction of a bill to decriminalize consensual gay sexual relationships; it was finally passed in 1975, making South Australia the first Australian state to do so.

The Dirty Half Mile is set in 1931 in King's Cross, Sidney. A straight vice squad officer seeks revenge against a big-time brothel owner, one of whose prostitutes infected him years earlier. One of her houses caters to homosexuals. The clients are campy, many in drag. Stereotypes all, none of the gays (save perhaps for one campy policeman who appears to be a closet case) becomes a full-fledged character. Though not going as far as Duane, the sight of two men engaged in sex does provoke an unexpected response from the main character: "He wondered why he didn't feel disgusted. What they were doing was supposed to be reprehensible according to all current standards. Yet he felt guilt, not outrage. He felt like an intruder" (44). The novel has a tongue-in-cheek "Glossary Australiana" as an appendix. The entry for *poofter* is worth passing on: "You wouldn't want your sister to marry one. Your brother, maybe?" (346).

Though the Australian National Library has assigned Roger Raftery (1950–) a birth year, Michael Hurley says that the name is a pseudonym. Lance Peters (1934–2007) was born in Auckland, New Zealand, but moved to Australian at an early age. From 1973 through 1981 he was in London. A writer of plays, screenplays, and teleplays, as well as a director and producer, he died in Sydney.

Peters, Lance. *The Dirty Half Mile*. London: Granada (Mayflower), 1981.
Raftery, Roger. *The Pink Triangle*. Brisbane: University of Queensland Press, 1981.
Reeves, Tim. "Duncan, George Ian Ogilvie (1930–1972)." *Australian Dictionary of Biography*. Vol. 14. Melbourne: Melbourne University Press, 1996 (online).

125 Edward Phillips: *Sunday's Child*, 1981.

Geoffrey Chadwick, the narrator, is a middle-aged lawyer (specialty: libel litigation), a still sexually active though discreet gay, and a resident of Westmount, the wealthy and largely English-speaking enclave of Montreal. It is a little startling then when he accidentally kills a hustler he has brought home and, instead of going to the police, decides to dismember the body and dispose of it in pieces. His methodical dumping of the body parts across the city and into the St. Lawrence River provides the arc that unites the novel. As a result of his hunting out appropriate spots, he puts himself into situations wherein he is mugged, must flee the police, has his car jacked, and saves the carjacker from a fiery crash only to discover he is already dead. More important, he comes to terms with the breakup of his three-year affair with a conventionally married assistant headmaster in one of the city's private schools. He accepts a certain responsibility for his musically gifted nephew, whom he instantly realizes is gay (and understands what the young man will face with his uptight mother and her husband). He reevaluates and finally reaccepts his longstanding friendship with a queen, a throwback to the pre-liberation days. And he rescues a mother cat and her starving kittens.

What lifts the novel out of the ordinary—indeed, makes it an outstanding read—is the narrator's growing perception about what he has allowed to happen in his life, his past brought into sharp relief by his *acte non-gratuit*. He ponders the real meaning of love, friendship, guilt and confession, missed chances, the significance of being gay, the passage of time. He comes to realize an important truth: "Innocence ends when one realizes one can live, more precisely one must live, with the consequences of a deed which can never be undone" (185). The narrative voice deepens, matures as the character grows. At the beginning Geoffrey is full of quips worthy of Wilde or

Saki, two authors he obviously admires. But as a result of his grisly undertaking, though the wry comments never disappear entirely, the tone darkens. The reader closes the novel with much to think about.

Edward O. Phillips (1931–) was born in Montreal. He has degrees from McGill, Université de Montrèal (where he obtained an unused law degree), Harvard, and Boston University. He taught school in both Boston and Montreal. Phillips studied painting and embarked on a brief career as an artist before deciding his real talent was writing. *Sunday's Child* was the first in a series of six novels about Geoffrey Chadwick. It was followed by *Buried on Sunday*, 1986; *Sunday's Best*, 1990; *Working on Sunday*, 1998; and *A Voyage on Sunday*, 2004. The second novel in the series won the 1987 Arthur Ellis Award for the best work of fiction from the Crime Writers of Canada.

Phillips, Edward. *Sunday's Child*. Toronto: McClelland & Stewart, 1981. *New York: St. Martin's, 1981.

POSTSCRIPT: NOVELS AFTER 1981

On July 3, 1981, an article appeared in *The New York Times* under the headline "Rare Cancer Seen in Homosexuals." Thus the Acquired Immunity Deficiency Syndrome was first brought to the attention of the world. As the death toll for people one knew, even had had sex with, mounted, one began, like Duffy, to monitor every aspect of one's health. But it was not just medical issues that gay men across the English-speaking world had to deal with; there continued to be legal, religious, and social oppression. Matt Cook writes (*A Gay History of Britain*, 191), "Whilst the renewed visibility of gay lives and the burgeoning network of pubs, clubs and groups were hugely significant to gay men and helped to challenge antagonism towards homosexuality, British culture remained broadly hostile and grudging in its liberalism." In the U.K. Mary Whitehouse stepped up her purity campaign; under the reactionary government of Margaret Thatcher, the infamous Clause 28 was inserted into the 1988 Local Government Act forbidding the "promotion" of homosexuality. Meanwhile, in 1986 the future Pope Benedict XVI issued his "Letter to the Bishops of the Catholic Church on the Pastoral Care of Homosexual Persons," reiterating the Church's condemnation of homosexuality. Paradoxically the attacks from every corner created a greater sense of community and political solidarity in the 1980s. But then, even more paradoxically, as the Australian Dennis Altman writes (*The End of the Homosexual*, 111), "the tragedy of AIDS has, overall, contributed to the mainstreaming of gay life, which in turn has meant the decline of sexuality as a master identity."

A whole new generation of writers came to maturity shaped in the United States by the Stonewall rebellion (which assumed worldwide status as a basis for gay pride) and in the United Kingdom by the passage of the Wolfenden Report (which had an impact on all English-speaking countries). For former colonies a new sense of nationalism came into existence. While South Africa had been its own country since 1961, Canada became independent only in 1982, and Australia and New Zealand in 1986 (though all three retained the British monarchy). Whether as a result or not, Australian writers gained greater momentum, and the gay literary scenes in Canada and New Zealand shook off their sluggishness to find new vitality. For the first time anthologies devoted to gay Australian, Canadian, and New Zealand writers appeared, along with academic studies using nationalism as a base. Even as this nationalistic bent appeared, writers clearly felt a greater sense of an international brotherhood, including greater ties to gay non–English language writers. At the same time a reluctance to be labeled "a gay writer" reappeared, even as the writers themselves became more open about their sexuality.

GENERAL BIBLIOGRAPHY

Bibliographies, Guides and Encyclopedias

Aldrich, Robert, and Garry Wotherspoon, eds. *Who's Who in Contemporary Gay and Lesbian History: From World War II to the Present Day.* 2d ed. London: Routledge, 2002.

———. *Who's Who in Gay and Lesbian History: From Antiquity to World War II.* 2d ed. London: Routledge, 2002.

Bradley, Marion Zimmer. *A Complete Cumulative Checklist of Lesbian Variant and Homosexual Fiction.* 1960. Lexington, Ky.: Emereo, 2012.

Cart, Michael, and Christine A. Jenkins. *The Heart Has Its Reasons: Young Adult Literature with Gay / Lesbian / Queer Content, 1969–2004.* Lanham, Md.: Scarecrow, 2006.

Cory, Donald Webster [Edward Sagarin]. "A Check List of Literature." *The Homosexual in America: A Subjective Approach.* 2d ed. New York: Castle, 1960: 296–393.

Dynes, Wayne R., ed. *Encyclopedia of Homosexuality.* 2 vols. New York: Garland, 1990.

Garber, Eric, and Lyn Paleo. *Uranian Worlds: A Guide to Alternative Sexuality in Science Fiction, Fantasy, and Horror.* 2d ed. Boston: Hall, 1990.

Garde, Noel I. [Edgar H. Leoni]. *The Homosexual in Literature: A Chronological Bibliography circa 700 B.C.–1958.* New York: Village, 1959.

Gerstner, David A., ed. *Routledge International Encyclopedia of Queer Culture.* London: Routledge, 2006.

Gunn, Drewey Wayne. *The Gay Male Sleuth in Print and Film: A History and Annotated Bibliography.* 2d ed. Lanham, Md.: Scarecrow, 2013.

Haggerty, George E., ed. *Gay Histories and Cultures: An Encyclopedia.* New York: Garland, 2000.

Hogan, Steve, and Lee Hudson. *Completely Queer: The Gay and Lesbian Encyclopedia.* New York: Holt, 1998.

Hurley, Michael. *A Guide to Gay and Lesbian Writing in Australia.* St. Leonards, N.S.W.: Allen & Unwin, 1996.

Kirkpatrick, Robert J. *Bullies, Beaks and Flannelled Fools: An Annotated Bibliography of Boys' School Fiction, 1742–1990.* London: Privately printed, 1990.

Malinowski, Sharon, ed. *Gay & Lesbian Literature.* Detroit: St. James, 1994.

Markowitz, Judith A. *The Gay Detective Novel: Lesbian and Gay Main Characters and Themes in Mystery Fiction.* Jefferson, N.C.: McFarland, 2004.

Rayter, Scott, Donald W. McLeod, and Maureen FitzGerald. *Queer CanLit: Canadian Lesbian, Gay, Bisexual, and Transgender (LGBT) Literature in English.* Toronto: Coach House, 2008.

Slide, Anthony. *Gay and Lesbian Characters and Themes in Mystery Novels: A Critical Guide to Over 500 Works in English.* Jefferson, N.C.: McFarland, 1993.

Summers, Claude J., ed. *The Gay and Lesbian Literary Heritage: A Reader's Companion to the Writers and Their Works, from Antiquity to the Present.* New York: Holt, 1995.

Watson, Benjamin. *English Schoolboy Stories: An Annotated Bibliography of Hardcover Fiction.* Metuchen, N.J.: Scarecrow, 1992.

Young, Ian. *The Male Homosexual in Literature: A Bibliography.* 2d ed. Metuchen, N.J.: Scarecrow, 1982.

Historical and Cultural Overviews

Aldrich, Robert. *Colonialism and Homosexuality.* London: Routledge, 2003.

———. *The Seduction of the Mediterranean: Writing, Art, and Homosexual Fantasy.* London: Routledge, 1993. Chapter 4.

Brickell, Chris. *Mates & Lovers: A History of Gay New Zealand*. Auckland: Godwit, 2008.
Cook, Matt. *London and the Culture of Homosexuality, 1885–1914*. Cambridge, Eng.: Cambridge University Press 2003.
———, ed. *A Gay History of Britain: Love and Sex Between Men since the Middle Ages*. Oxford: Greenwood World, 2007. Chapters 4–6.
d'Arch Smith, Timothy. *Love in Earnest: Some Notes on the Lives and Writings of English "Uranian" Poets from 1889 to 1930*. London: Routledge & Kegan Paul, 1970.
Dickinson, Peter. *Here Is Queer: Nationalisms, Sexualities, and the Literatures of Canada*. Toronto: University of Toronto Press, 1999.
Ellis, Havelock. *Studies in the Psychology of Sex*. Vol. 2: *Sexual Inversion*. 3d ed., rev. Philadelphia: Davis, 1926. Chapter 7.
Gardiner, James. *Who's a Pretty Boy Then? One Hundred & Fifty Years of Gay Life in Pictures*. London: Serpent's Tail, 1997.
Goldie, Terry. *Pink Snow: Homotextual Possibilities in Canadian Literature*. Peterbourgh, Ont.: Broadview, 2003.
Green, Martin. *Children of the Sun: A Narrative of "Decadence" in England after 1918*. New York: Basic, 1976.
Hammond, Paul. *Love Between Men in English Literature*. New York: St. Martin's, 1996. Chapter 6.
Higgins, Patrick. *Heterosexual Dictatorship: Male Homosexuality in Postwar Britain*. London: Fourth Estate, 1996.
Houlbrook, Matt. *Queer London: Perils and Pleasures in the Sexual Metropolis, 1918–1957*. Chicago: University of Chicago Press, 2005.
Kaplan, Morris B. *Sodom on the Thames: Sex, Love, and Scandal in Wilde Times*. Ithaca, N.Y.: Cornell University Press 2005.
Kearney, Patrick J. *A History of Erotic Literature*. London: Macmillan, 1982.
King, Francis. *Yesterday Came Suddenly: An Autobiography*. London: Constable, 1993.
Nicholson, Virginia. *Among the Bohemians: Experiments in Living, 1900–1939*. 2002. New York: HarperCollins, 2003.
Tamagne, Florence. *A History of Homosexuality in Europe*. Vols. 1 & 2: *Berlin, London, Paris, 1919–1939*. Trans. not given. New York: Algora, 2006.
Taylor, D. J. *Bright Young People: The Lost Generation of London's Jazz Age*. New York: Farrar, Straus, & Giroux, 2007.
Woods, Gregory. *A History of Gay Literature: The Male Tradition*. New Haven, Conn.: Yale University Press 1998.
Wotherspoon, Garry. *"City of the Plain": History of a Gay Sub-Culture*. Sydney: Hale & Iremonger, 1991.

Further Reading

Altman, Dennis. *The End of the Homosexual*. St. Lucia: University of Queensland Press, 2013.
Aronson, Theo. *Prince Eddy and the Homosexual Underworld*. 1994. New York: Barnes & Noble, 1995.
Austen, Roger. *Playing the Game: The Homosexual Novel in America*. Indianapolis: Bobbs-Merrill, 1977.
Blond, Anthony. *Jew Made in England*. London: Timewell, 2004.
Davidson, Michael. *The World, the Flesh, and Myself*. Intro. Colin Spencer. London: GMP, 1985.
Deacon, Richard. *The Cambridge Apostles: A History of Cambridge University's Elite Intellectual Secret Society*. 1985. New York: Farrar, Straus & Giroux, 1986.
Driberg, Tom. *Ruling Passions*. New York: Stein & Day, 1977.
Egremont, Max. *Siegfried Sassoon: A Life*. New York: Farrar, Straus & Giroux, 2005.
Hillier, Bevis. *John Betjeman: The Biography*. London: Murray, 2006.
Hoare, Philip. *Serious Pleasures: The Life of Stephen Tennant*. 1990. New York: Penguin, 1991.
Kaplan, Fred. *Henry James: The Imagination of Genius*. New York: Morrow, 1992.
Lancaster, Marie-Jacqueline. *Brian Howard: Portrait of a Failure*. 2005. N.P.: Green Candy, 2007.
Levin, James. *The Gay Novel in America*. New York: Garland, 1991.
Pearson, John. *The Sitwells: A Family's Biography*. 1978 (*Façades*). New York: Harcourt Brace Jovanovich, 1979.
Rowbotham, Sheila. *Edward Carpenter: A Life of Liberty and Love*. London: Verso, 2008.
Spender, Stephen. *World within World: The Autobiography*. 1951. New York: Modern Library, 2001.
Sutherland, John. *Stephen Spender: A Literary Life*. 2004. New York: Oxford University Press, 2005.
Sutin, Lawrence. *Do What Thou Wilt: A Life of Aleister Crowley*. New York: St. Martin's, 2000.
Vargo, Marc E. *Scandal: Infamous Gay Controversies of the Twentieth Century*. New York: Harrington Park, 2003. Chapters 1, 3, 4.
Vickers, Hugo. *Cecil Beaton: A Biography*. 1985. Boston: Little, Brown, 1986.
The Wolfenden Report: Report of the Committee on Homosexual Offenses and Prostitution. Authorized American Edition, 1963. Intro. Karl Menninger. New York: Lancer, 1964.

Anthologies

Aitken, Graeme, ed. *The Penguin Book of Gay Australian Writing*. Camberwell, Vic.: Penguin, 2002.

Denisoff, Dennis, ed. *Queeries: An Anthology of Gay Male Prose*. Vancouver: Arsenal Pulp, 1993.

Dessaix, Robert, ed. *Australian Gay and Lesbian Writing: An Anthology*. Melbourne: Oxford University Press 1993.

Fone, Byrne R. S., ed. *The Columbia Anthology of Gay Literature: Readings from Western Antiquity to the Present Day*. New York: Columbia University Press 1998.

Larivière, Michel, ed. *Les Amours masculines: Anthologie de l'homosexualité dans la littérature*. Paris: Lieu Commun, 1984.

Leavitt, David, and Mark Mitchell, eds. *The New Penguin Book of Gay Short Stories*. London: Penguin, 2004.

Mitchell, Mark, and David Leavitt, eds. *Pages Passed from Hand to Hand: The Hidden Tradition of Homosexual Literature in English from 1748 to 1914*. Boston: Houghton Mifflin, 1997.

Reade, Brian, ed. *Sexual Heretics: Male Homosexuality in English Literature from 1850 to 1900: An Anthology*. London: Routledge & Kegan Paul, 1970.

Wells, Peter, and Rex Pilgrim, eds. *Best Mates: Gay Writing in Aotearoa New Zealand*. Auckland: Reed, 1997.

INDEX

Numbers refer to entries, not to pages.

Absolute Beginners (MacInnes) 47
An Acre of Grass (Stewart) 93
Adamson, Robert 108
The Adventures of Roderick Random (Smollett) Introduction
Africa, Sub-Saharan 7, 15, 19, 32, 57, 67, 68, 87, 90, 105; see also South Africa
Airscream (Bruce) 114
The Alabaster Egg (Freeman) 72
The Alexandria Quartet (Durrell) 49
Algeria 3, 14
Allatini, Rose 19
Ambassador of Loss (Scarlott) 32
Anarchists in Love (Spencer) 78
The Anarchy of Love (Spencer) 78
Anglo-Saxon Attitudes (Wilson) 50
Another Death in Venice (Hill) 104
The Apes of God (Lewis) 26
Arabian Boys (Bradbury Robinson) 99
Armed with Madness (Butts) 25
arrests, fictional 50, 60, 61, 63, 68, 74, 82, 86, 88, 92, 95, 105, 108, 115
arrests, real life 3, 14, 30, 37, 51, 52, 66, 82, 98, 115
As If by Magic (Wilson) 50
Aston, James (T. H. White) 23
At Fever Pitch (Caute) 67
At the Cross (Rose) 47
The Au Pair Boy (McCall) 94
Aubade (Martin) 59
Australia 12, 35, 47, 75, 82, 90, 93, 108, 113, 114, 119, 120, 124
Austria 19, 32, 36, 42, 55, 78, 113

Bachelor's Hall (Underwood) 32
Bailey, Paul 101
Baker, Frank Introduction
Balthazar (Durrell) 49
bar culture 28, 31, 33, 36, 49, 50, 51, 55, 59, 74, 80, 81, 90, 99, 106, 114
Bare Knees, Boy Knees (Bradbury Robinson) 99

Barnes, Julian 123
Barnes, Margaret Campbell 42
Barrie, J. M. Introduction
Batchelor, John 111
Baxter, Walter 43
Beautiful Losers (Cohen) 89
Beckford, William Introduction, 110
The Bell (Murdoch) 64
Benson, A. C. 2
Benson, E. F. 6, 17, 23, 25
Birch, Lionel 18
The Bird of Night (Hill) 103
The Birds (Baker) Introduction
bisexuality Introduction, 22, 41, 50, 55, 61, 71, 74, 78, 89, 94, 96, 106, 108, 115, 119, 123
The Black Book (Durrell) 49
blackmail 5, 11, 23, 30, 32, 37, 44, 58, 71, 114
Blood Brothers (McIntosh) 83
Bloomsbury 11, 12, 19, 25, 26, 30, 36, 110
Bloxam, John Francis 3, 4
Body Charge (Davies) 107
"Bond Strikes Camp" (Connolly) 33
The Book of Life (Kitchin) 60
Born, Edith de 55
Bowl of Roses (Moor) 88
Boy (Hanley) 26, 33
Boyd, Martin Introduction
Bradbury Robinson, C. J. 99
Breakfast with a Stranger (Kortner) 94
Breathless Hush (Batchelor) 111
Brideshead Revisited (Waugh) 28
Broderick, John 74
Brooke, Jocelyn 53
Brooke, Rupert 13, 36, 58
Brown, Richard Blake 32
Bruce, John 114
Bryher 24
Buchan, John 19
Buckland, Paul 66
Burdekin, Katharine Introduction
Burgess, Anthony (John Burgess Wilson) Introduction, 26, 121
Butler, Samuel 8
Butts, Mary 25

Caine, Hall 2
Calder Marshall, Arthur 71
camp and satire 6, 17, 20, 22, 23, 26, 28, 31, 33, 37, 41, 61, 62, 66, 80, 86, 87, 108, 112, 124
Camp Commander (Lauder) 75
Campbell, Michael 91
Canada 19, 42, 46, 79, 89, 97, 115, 116, 125
A Candle for Saint Antony (Spence) 113
Cantwell, John 58
Capitanchik, Maurice 94
Caribbean 105
Carpenter, Edward 11, 12, 19, 27, 32
Carr, Christopher (A. C. Benson) 2
Carrington, Charles 9
Caton, R. A. Introduction, 32
Cauldwell, Frank (Francis King) 54
Caute, David 67
Ceylon see Sri Lanka
The Chameleons (Broderick) 74
characters based on real persons 1, 6, 8, 11, 12, 13, 15, 22, 23, 26, 28, 29, 30, 31, 33, 38, 41, 49, 51, 54, 62, 78, 98, 102, 115, 121, 124; see also historical fiction
The Charioteer (Renault) 52
Charke, Charlotte Cibber Introduction
Chorus of Witches (Buckland) 66
Clarke, A. W. 7
Clarke, Arthur C. Introduction
Clea (Durrell) 49
Cleland, John Introduction
Cohen, Leonard 89
Collinson, Laurence 108
colonialism and post-colonialism Introduction, 45, 48, 49, 67, 68, 83, 84, 90, 105, 109, 117
The Colonist (Schmidt) 122
Combat Journal of Place d'Armes (Symons) 89
Compton-Burnett, Ivy 25, 49
Concerning the Eccentricities of Cardinal Pirelli (Firbank) 20
"Il Conde" (Conrad) 15

Connolly, Cyril 28, 33, 62, 90
Conrad, Joseph 15, 23
Constantine, Murray (Katharine Burdekin) Introduction
Conventional Weapons (Brooke) 53
Cook, Lennox 63
Cornwall 12, 17, 19, 25, 58, 79, 115
Cory, Desmond 85
Côte d'Azur 3, 33, 38, 115
Courage, James 50, 65
Coward, Noël 25, 26, 29, 34
Crazy Pavements (Nichols) 22
crime 2, 3, 15, 48, 58, 69, 70, 72, 76, 80, 85, 87, 96, 104, 105, 107, 108, 113, 114, 116, 123, 124, 125; *see also* mystery
Criminal Law Amendment of 1885 (Labouchère amendment) 1, 3, 23
A Crocodile of Choirboys (Bradbury Robinson) 99
Croft-Cooke, Rupert 51, 98
Crowley, Aleister 25, 28, 71
Cupid's Crescent (Collinson) 108
The Custard Boys (Rae) 69

The Dark Glasses (King) 54
Dark Passions Subdue (Sanderson) 46
The Dark Peninsula (Frost) 40
Dark to the Sun (Cook) 62
David, Villiers 41
David Blaize (Benson) 17
David of King's (Benson) 17
Davies, Hunter 107
Deadfall (Cory) 85
Death of Felicity Taverner (Butts) 25
decadence 1, 3, 5, 20, 22, 23, 27, 28, 90, 98, 110
Decline and Fall (Waugh) 28
The Deemster (Caine) 2
Deschamps, Marc 96
Desert Dreamers (Weston/Hamilton) 14
The Deserters (Maugham) 90
The Desire and Pursuit of the Whole (Rolfe) 26
Despised and Rejected (Fitzroy) 19
Details of Jeremy Stratton (Lindop) 56
Dickens, Charles Introduction
Dilke, Christopher 92
The Dirty Half Mile (Peters) 124
A Distant Likeness (Bailey) 101
A Domestic Animal (King) 54
Don Leon (anon.) Introduction, 32
Douglas, Norman 12, 15, 23, 24, 33
Down There on a Visit (Isherwood) 31
Doyle, Arthur Conan Introduction, 3
drag 1, 20, 24, 66, 79, 95, 99, 114, 119

Drummond, William (Arthur Calder Marshall) 71
Duffy (Kavanagh) 123
Duggan, Alfred 28, 42
Durrell, Lawrence 49
Dusty Answer (Lehmann) 25
Dyer, Charles 95

Earthly Powers (Burgess) 121
Eben, Laurence (Michael Power) 76
Egypt *see* Middle East
Ellis, Royston 88
Empress of Byzantium (Mahler) 42
End of the Corridor (Meyer) 44
Ermyntrude and Esmeralda (Strachey) 11
eroticism, pornography 1, 5, 9, 32, 36, 99, 120
espionage 33, 51, 79
The Everlasting Secret Family (Moorhouse) 120
Evil Was Abroad (Lehmann) 36
Exiles (Croft-Cooke) 98
expatriate and tourist fiction 10, 11, 13, 14, 23, 26, 33, 35, 38, 39, 49, 98, 122

A Fairly Honourable Defeat (Murdoch) 64
Family Favourites (Duggan) 42
The Feathers of Death (Raven) 68
Fell of Dark (Hill) 104
Fellow Travellers (Worsley) 102
Fiddle City (Kavanagh) 123
Fielding Gray (Raven) 68
film and television adaptations 2, 3, 11, 12, 15, 21, 25, 26, 28, 31, 34, 38, 41, 49, 50, 69, 71, 72, 85, 95, 96, 104, 120
Findley, Timothy Introduction
Firbank, Ronald 20, 28, 53, 99, 112
Fire from Heaven (Renault) 52
The Firewalkers (Cauldwell/King) 54
Firth, Anthony 79
Fisher, Stanley T. 32
Fitzroy, A. T. (Rose Allatini) 19
Flame of Freedom (Underwood) 32
The Flesh Merchants (Ellis) 88
The Flower beneath the Foot (Firbank) 20
The Fly (Chopping) 80
Fonthill (Menen) 110
Forster, E. M. 10, 11, 12, 31, 105
Fowkes, Aubrey (Richard Vere Cripps) 32
France 3, 5, 7, 9, 12, 21, 25, 27, 33, 38, 41, 49, 51, 55, 62, 74, 79, 87, 115, 119
The Frauds (Hastings) 58
Freeman, Gillian 72
Frost, Ernest 40
The Fugitives (Broderick) 74

A Game of Hide and Seek (Sargeson) 37
The Garden God (Reid) 10
Garland, Rodney (Adam de Hegedus, Peter de Polnay) 51, 87
Gaunt Island (Macpherson) 24
The Gay Deceiver (Leslie) 79
The Gay Way (Harris) 108
Generation tetralogy (Spencer) 78
George, Eliot (Gillian Freeman) 72
Gerald Brockhurst (Brooke) 53
Germany 11, 14, 31, 32, 47, 68, 79, 92, 94
Gide, André, mention of 3, 14, 15, 28, 51, 66, 99, 101
Glaskin, G. M. 82
The Glass Cage (Wilson) 58
The Go-Between (Hartley) 100
Goff, Martyn 61
Goodbye to Berlin (Isherwood) 31
gothic 3, 17, 25, 63, 77; *see also* science fiction and fantasy
Grahame, Kenneth Introduction, 28
Grant, Roderick 117
The Grass beneath the Wire (Pollock) 86
Greece and Cyprus 11, 17, 30, 31, 49, 54, 68, 78, 89
Green, G. F. 48
Green, Richard 94
The Green Carnation (Hichens) 6
Green Island (Schmidt) 122
Greene, Graham 23, 24, 44, 100
Greenidge, Terence 28, 32
Grenville-Hearne, Gundry 32
Griffin, David (Robin Maugham) 90
Guerrillas (Naipaul) 105

Hall, Radclyffe 25
Haltrecht, Montague 80
Hamilton, Gerald 14, 31, 45
A Handful of Pennies (Porter) 47
Hanford, Bruce 108
Hanley, James 26, 33, 99
The Harness Room (Harley) 100
Harris, Mark (Carl Ruhen) 108
Hartley, L. P. 28, 60, 100
Hastings, Michael 58
The Heart in Exile (Garland) 51
The Heat of the Sun (Moor) 88
Hegedus, Adam de 51
Hemlock and After (Wilson) 50
Henry and Cato (Murdoch) 64
Here's a Villain! (Mitchell) 58
Heriot, Angus 62
Hichens, Robert 3, 6, 14
The Hill (Vachell) 7, 18
Hill, Reginald 104
Hill, Susan 103
Hirsch, Charles 1, 5
historical fiction Introduction, 2, 3, 24, 32, 42, 52, 72, 90, 103, 110, 114, 118

Index to entry numbers

The History of Henry Dumont, Esq. (Charke) Introduction
Holiday (Power) 76
Homo (Deschamps) 96
Hopkinson, Tom 39
Hornung, E. W. Introduction
Hughes, Barrie 113
Hungary 51, 87, 97

Imaginary Letters (Butts) 25
Imaginary Toys (Mitchell) 73
The Imperfect Marriage (Born) 55
Imperial Earth (Clarke) Introduction
In a Free State (Naipaul) 105
In a Purely Pagan Sense (Lehmann) 36
In the Making (Green) 48
In the Tent (Rees) 118
Indecent Assault (Goff) 61
India 4, 11, 31, 32, 43, 49, 54, 68, 110
The Inheritor (Benson) 17
The Interpreters (Soyinka) 84
The Invaders (Plomer) 30
Ireland 1, 3, 14, 15, 23, 32, 33, 57, 64, 74, 91, 112; *see also* Northern Ireland
Ireland, David Introduction
Isabel the Fair (Barnes) 42
Isherwood, Christopher 11, 28, 31, 32, 38, 44, 54
Italy 8, 11, 12, 13, 15, 17, 23, 24, 26, 40, 96, 100, 104, 110

Jackarandy (Madigan) 106
Jackson, Neville (G. M. Glaskin) 82
James, Henry Introduction, 4, 10, 17
Japan 30, 47, 88
Jaspar Tristram (Clarke) 7
John Verney (Vachell) 7
Johnson, Pamela Hansford 41
Jonah and His Mother (Haltrecht) 80
Jonathan and David, allusion to 2, 11, 12, 17, 21, 59
Joseph (Capitanchik) 94
Joyce, James Introduction
The Judas Boy (Raven) 68
June in Her Spring (MacInnes) 47
Justine (Durrell) 49

Kavanagh, Dan (Julian Barnes) 123
Keneally, Thomas 114
A Killing Kindness (Hill) 104
King, Francis 45, 49, 54, 55, 60, 86, 100
Kitchin, C. H. B. 60, 100
Kortner, Peter 94

The Lady Is Waiting (Mitchell) 58
Laidlaw (McIlvanney) 104
Lake District 56, 104, 118
Lancaster, Humphrey 32

Langley, Noel 34
The Last Encounter (Maugham) 90
The Last of Mr. Norris (Isherwood) 31
The Last of the Wine (Renault) 52
The Last Resort (Johnson) 41
Lauder, Stuart 75
Laura Middleton (anon.) 5
Lawrence, D. H. 12, 23, 32
The Leather Boys (George/Freeman) 72
The Lee Shore (Macaulay) 13
Lehmann, John 11, 25, 36, 48, 62
Lehmann, Rosamond 25, 36
Leitch, Maurice 81
Leopard in the Grass (Stewart) 45
Leslie, David 75
Leslie, Peter 79
Letters from Laura and Evelyn (anon.) 1
Lewis, Wyndham 26
The Liberty Lad (Leitch) 81
Liddell, Robert 49
The Life to Come (Forster) 11
Lighted Cities (Frost) 40
The Limbo Affair (Firth) 79
Lindop, Audrey Erskine 56
The Link (Maugham) 90
Little Victims (Rumbold) 32
"Local Color" (Plomer) 30
Lofts, Norah 42
London gay life 1, 3, 6, 19, 22, 28, 30, 34, 51, 59, 61, 62, 65, 78, 80, 94, 106, 112
London Irish (Broderick) 74
The Longest Journey (Forster) 11
Look Down in Mercy (Baxter) 43
The Loom of Youth (Waugh) 18
Lord Dismiss Us (Campbell) 91
Love in a Cold Climate (Mitford) 41
Love in London (David) 41
Lovers in War (Spencer) 78
The Lute Player (Lofts) 42
Lynn, Jonathan 96

Macaulay, Rose 13
MacInnes, Colin 47, 80
Mackenzie, Compton 23, 33
Mackenzie, Seaforth 35
Macpherson, Kenneth 24
Maddy, Yulisa Amadu 109
Madigan, Leo 106
The Magnificent (Greenidge) 32
Mahler, Helen A. 42
Malouf, David Introduction
The Man on the Rock (King) 54
Mann (Isle of Man) 2
Marius the Epicurean (Pater) 2, 10
Martin, Kenneth 59
The Martini-Henry (Hughes) 113
The Mask of Apollo (Renault) 52
Maugham, Robin 90
Maugham, W. Somerset 6, 23, 29, 34, 38, 90, 96, 121
Maurice (Forster) 11, 31

"May We Borrow Your Husband?" (Greene) 44
McCall, Andrew 68, 94
McIlvanney, William 104
McIntosh, John 83
Me and the Girls (Coward) 34
A Meeting by the River (Isherwood) 31
Memoirs of a Voluptuary (anon.) 9
Memoirs of a Woman of Pleasure (Cleland) Introduction, 1
Memoirs of Arthur Hamilton (Carr/Benson) 2
The Memorial (Isherwood) 32
Menen, Aubrey 110
Mexico 12, 89, 90, 122
Meyer, Michael 44
The Middle Age of Mrs Eliot (Wilson) 50
Middle East 2, 6, 11, 17, 23, 45, 49, 62, 67, 88, 99, 119
military fiction Introduction, 7, 19, 21, 28, 40, 43, 47, 52, 67, 68, 75, 86, 90, 103, 115
Milton, Ernest 27
Miracle on San Jaime (Cantwell) 58
Mist in the Tagus (Hopkinson) 39
Mr Fortune's Maggot (Warner) 26
Mr Norris Changes Trains (Isherwood) 31
Mr Steadfast (Buchan) 19
Mitchell, James 58
Mitchell, Julian 73
Mitford, Nancy 41, 68
Monsarrat, Nicholas 79
Moor, George 88
Moorcock, Michael Introduction
Moorhouse, Frank 120
More Women than Men (Compton-Burnett) 25
Morocco 28, 50, 62, 80, 89, 90, 93, 98
Murdoch, Iris 64
Murphy, Clive 112
My Sisters' Keeper (Hartley) 100
mystery Introduction, 51, 58, 70, 71, 75, 79, 104, 107, 114, 116, 123, 124; *see also* crime
The Mystery of Edwin Drood (Dickens) Introduction

Naipaul, V. S. 105
The Name of Greene (Brooke) 53
"Nature Study" (Coward) 34
Nazism 24, 28, 31, 36, 39, 45, 69
Nelson, Michael 62
Never a Closing Door (Cantwell) 58
New Zealand 8, 37, 65, 94, 106, 108, 114, 124
Nichols, Beverley 22, 28
Nicholson, John Gambril 4, 16
Nigeria 84
No End to the Way (Jackson) 82
No Language but a Cry (Cook) 63
No Laughing Matter (Wilson) 50

No More into the Garden (Watmough) 115
No Name in the Street (Tindall) 55
No Past, No Present, No Future (Maddy) 109
Northern Ireland 10, 59, 81, 93
Nothing Doing (Campbell) 91

Odd John (Stapledon) Introduction
Orphan's Progress (Heriot) 62
Other Man's Saucer (Winter) 29
The Outer Ring (Lindop) 56

pacifism 19
"A Passion before Death" (Hanley) 26
Pater, Walter 2, 3, 10
Pearson, Bill Introduction
pederasty and ephebism 9, 16, 20, 26, 35, 47, 50, 57, 58, 60, 61, 64, 89, 90, 93, 98, 99, 100, 104, 110, 113, 120, 122
The Permanent Farewell (Polnay) 87
The Persian Boy (Renault) 52
Peter Smart's Confessions (Bailey) 101
Peters, Lance 124
Phillips, Edward 125
The Picture of Dorian Gray (Wilde) 3, 23, 33
The Pilgrimage (Broderick) 74
The Pink Triangle (Raftery) 124
The Plaster Fabric (Goff) 61
Plato's dialogues 3, 4, 8, 10, 11, 26, 32, 35, 52
The Player's Boy (Bryher) 24
Plomer, William 25, 30, 32, 103
The Pole and the Whistle (Moor) 88
Pollock, John 86
Polnay, Peter de 87
Poolreflection (Macpherson) 24
Porcsa, Michael 97
Porter, Hal 47
The Portrait of Mr W. H. (Wilde) 3
Portugal 39, 75, 106
Potter, William S. 1
Power, Michael 76
The Power of Mesmerism (anon.) 5
The Power of Sergeant Streater (Green) 48
The Pride of Summer (Broderick) 74
"The Priest and the Acolyte" (Bloxam) 3
A Proper Man (Lynn) 96
prostitution, male 1, 30, 50, 89, 94, 106, 114, 119, 124
"The Prussian Officer" (Lawrence) 12
pulps 57, 88, 99, 108
Put Out More Flags (Waugh) 28
Pyramid (Birch) 18

Quinterley, Esmond (Richard Vere Cripps) 32
Quintin's Man (Rees) 118

Radcliffe (Storey) 77
Rae, John 69
Raftery, Roger 124
Raile, Arthur Lyon 8
Raven, Simon 41, 67, 68, 94
Ravens' Brood (Benson) 17
Raymond, Ernest 31
The Razor's Edge (Maugham) 38
A Reason to Kill (Zaremba) 116
Rees, David 118
Rehearsal under the Moon (Hegedus) 51
Reid, Forrest 4, 10, 99
religion 8, 20, 26, 38, 64, 74, 75, 121
Renault, Mary 52
Rendezvous with Rama (Clarke) Introduction
The Right Thing (Porter) 47
The Ring (Chopping) 80
Ritual in the Dark (Wilson) 58
The Rock Pool (Connolly) 33
Rolfe, Frederick 16, 17, 26
romance 4, 5, 8, 10, 14, 19, 22, 32, 37, 40, 51, 52, 59, 61, 64, 65, 66, 68, 70, 74, 76, 78, 82, 88, 91, 97, 109, 115, 117
The Romance of a Choir-Boy (Nicholson) 16
The Romance of Lust (Potter) 1
Rome 12 Noon (Macpherson) 24
A Room in Chelsea Square (Nelson) 62
Room with a View (Forster) 11
Rose, Jon 47
Ross Williamson, Hugh 70
The Rotten Apple (Dilke) 92
Ruhen, Carl 108
Rumbold, Richard 32
rural England 4, 11, 12, 16, 17, 19, 25, 29, 32, 48, 50, 53, 56, 64, 66, 69, 70, 77, 88, 94, 96, 100, 104
The Rush at the End (Ellis) 88

Sado (Plomer) 30
Sandel (Stewart) 93
Sanderson, Douglas 46
Sargeson, Frank 37
A Savage Freedom (Grant) 117
The Scapegoat (Brooke) 53
Scarlott, Michael (Stanley T. Fisher) 32
Schmidt, Michael 122
school and university stories Introduction, 1, 2, 4, 7, 8, 9, 10, 13, 16, 17, 18, 21, 25, 28, 29, 32, 35, 44, 46, 48, 53, 56, 58, 68, 69, 73, 91, 92, 93, 99, 100, 109, 111, 113, 118
science fiction and fantasy Introduction, 10, 121; *see also* gothic
Scotland 19, 23, 24, 66, 93, 104, 107, 117

The Sea and the Wedding (Johnson) 41
A Secondary Character (Haltrecht) 80
sexologists 4, 11, 12, 16; *see also* Carpenter, Edward
Shadow Game (Eben/Power) 76
Shadows of Shame (Taylor) 57
Shakespeare, William, mention of 3, 7, 10, 11, 32, 58, 121
Shelley, Mary Introduction
shipboard 26, 27, 75, 90, 114
Sierra Leone 109
A Single Man (Isherwood) 31
The Sins of the Cities of the Plain (anon.) 1
A Skilled Hand (Green) 48
Smith and Jones (Monsarrat) 79
Smithers, Leonard 5
Smollett, Tobias Introduction
Snow in Harvest (Stewart) 93
So unlike the English (Langley) 34
Society Stud (Harris) 108
Sorcerer's Broth (Garland) 87
South Africa 19, 30, 33, 34, 39, 52, 58, 76, 83, 105
South Wind (Douglas) 23, 33
Southeastern Asia 15, 63, 94, 113, 117, 121
Soyinka, Wole 84
Spain and Spanish islands 20, 32, 46, 58, 80, 85, 88, 102
Spence, Eleanor 113
Spencer, Colin 78
Spender, Stephen 26, 31, 33, 40, 62, 71, 102
Sri Lanka (Ceylon) 12, 48, 50, 75, 88
stage adaptations 3, 6, 15, 20, 28, 31, 47, 95, 108
Staircase (Dyer) 95
Stapledon, Olaf Introduction
The Star Brooch (Fowkes) 32
Star Quality (Coward) 34
Stevenson, Robert Louis Introduction, 3
Stewart, Angus 93, 99
Stewart, Desmond 45
Stewart, J. I. M. 93
Stoker, Bram Introduction, 2, 3
Storey, David 77
Strachey, Lytton 11
Strange Meeting (Hill) 103
A Stranger in Eden (Stewart) 45
Street Boy, Swinging London (Green) 94
Sturgis, Howard O. 4
suicide 5, 37, 43, 46, 50, 51, 56, 58, 64, 68, 71, 74, 76, 80, 91, 93, 108
Summer Overtures (Murphy) 112
Sunday's Child (Phillips) 125
Swastika Night (Constantine/Burdekin) Introduction
Symons, Scott 89

A Tale of Pausanian Love (A.L.R./Warren) 8

Index to entry numbers

Tall, Balding, Thirty-Five (Firth) 79
Taylor, John 57
Teleny (anon.) 5
Tell England (Raymond) 21
Ten Pollitt Place (Kitchin) 60
That Summer (Sargeson) 37
theater, cinema, and television milieus 3, 24, 32, 34, 50, 66, 101, 107, 109
There's a Porpoise Close behind Us (Langley) 34
They Winter Abroad (Aston) 23
Thin Ice (Mackenzie) 23
This Sorry Scheme (Underwood) 32
The Tilted Cross (Porter) 47
Tim (Sturgis) 4
To Kiss the Crocodile (Milton) 27
The Tormented (Lindop) 56
Trespasses (Bailey) 101
The Trial of Father Dillingham (Broderick) 74
The Troubled Midnight (Garland) 51
True Yokefellow (Lancaster) 32
The Twyborn Affair (White) 119
The Tyranny of Love (Spencer) 78

Ulysses (Joyce) Introduction
Uncle Stephen (Reid) 10
Unconditional Surrender (Waugh) 28
Under the Brightness of Alien Stars (Porcsa) 97
Underwood, Reginald 32
Unreal City (Liddell) 49

The Unsuitable Englishman (Stewart) 45
Uranians 4, 8, 10, 16, 17, 23

Vachell, H. A. 7
Vainglory (Firbank) 20
Valmouth (Firbank) 20
The Vampire of Mons (Stewart) 45
Vestal Fire (Mackenzie) 23, 33
Victim (Drummond) 71
A Victim of the Aurora (Keneally) 114
The Victims of Love (Spencer) 78
Victory (Conrad) 15
Vile Bodies (Waugh) 28

Waiting for the Sky to Fall (Martin) 59
The Waking of Willie Ryan (Broderick) 74
Walpole, Horace Introduction
The Wanting Seed (Burgess) Introduction, 121
Warner, Sylvia Townsend 23, 26
Warren, Edward Perry 4, 8
Watmough, David 115
Waugh, Alec 18, 28, 29, 32
Waugh, Evelyn 18, 20, 22, 28, 29, 41, 42, 55
The Waves (Woolf) 26
The Way of All Flesh (Butler) 8
A Way of Love (Courage) 65
Welch, Denton Introduction, 53
The Well of Loneliness (Hall) 25, 53, 121
Weston, Patrick 14
What Mad Pursuit? (Coward) 34

When We Had Other Names (Tindall) 55
White, Patrick 49, 119
White, T. H. 23, 26
The White Peacock (Lawrence) 12
Whitman, Walt, mention of 3, 17, 27, 32, 66
A Wicked Pack of Cards (Ross Williamson) 70
Wilde, Oscar Introduction, 1, 3, 5, 7, 8, 20, 23, 33, 45, 62, 98
Wilson, Angus 20, 50, 58, 62, 80
Wilson, Colin 58
Winger's Landfall (Lauder) 75
Winter, Keith 29, 34
Wolfenden Report 23, 50, 51, 56, 73
Women in Love (Lawrence) 12, 93
"The Wooden Madonna" (Coward) 34
Woolf, Virginia 26
The World in the Evening (Isherwood) 31
Worsley, T. C. 102
The Wrong People (Griffin/Maugham) 90

The Young Desire It (Mackenzie) 35
Young Thomas (Bradbury Robinson) 99
The Youngest Director (Goff) 61
A Youth of Fourteen (Fowkes) 32

Zaremba, Eve 116
Zimmer's Essay (Adamson & Hanford) 108

www.ingramcontent.com/pod-product-compliance
Lightning Source LLC
Chambersburg PA
CBHW081558300426
44116CB00015B/2926